FROM
BERLIOZ
TO
BOULEZ

FROM BERLIOZ TO BOULEZ

Roger Nichols

Foreword by Jeremy Sams

KAHN & AVERILL · LONDON

Published by Kahn & Averill
2-10 Plantation Road
Amersham, Buckinghamshire, HP6 6HJ
United Kingdom

www.kahnandaverill.co.uk

First published in hardback in 2022 by Kahn & Averill
Copyright © 2022 Roger Nichols
Foreword copyright © 2022 Jeremy Sams
Index prepared by Nigel Simeone
Photo of Pierre Boulez ©
Betty Freeman/Bridgeman Images

The right of Roger Nichols to be identified as the author
of this work has been asserted by him in accordance
with the Copyright, Design, and Patents Act 1988

All rights reserved

A CIP record of this book is available from the British Library

Book design by Økvik Design
Typeset by Pindar Creative
Printed in Great Britain by TJ Books Limited, Cornwall

This book is sold subject to the condition that it shall not, by way of trade
or otherwise, be lent, resold, hired out, or otherwise circulated without the
publisher's prior consent in any form of binding or cover other than that
in which it is published and without a similar condition including
this condition being imposed on the subsequent purchaser

ISBN 978-0-9957574-7-9

For Sarah

FOREWORD

Those of us who have become intoxicated by the world of French music all seem to have our Entry Level experience, the gateway drug that hooked us in, as it were. For Roger Nichols, this was it:

> Ravel has a special place in my life because my aunt gave me a copy of his Sonatine for my 10th birthday. Why that piece, I never asked her. For years I never got beyond the middle 'Minuet', but it was the start of a lifelong love affair.

Mine was not dissimilar. Also via an aunt – in my case the Ravel *Pavane*. Equally heady and harmonically exotic (at least to this 10-year-old ear) and, most importantly, equally unlike the 19th century German fare which was the musical meat and two veg. of our listening lives. Here were harmonies that were at once intriguing and unresolved. Here, one felt, was beauty for its own sake.

I would wager that most of you who have this book in your hands will have had a similar early induction. Whether it was Debussy's Fawn, Ravel's Dawn, Saint-Saëns' *Aquarium*, Fauré's Dolly, Satie's *Gymnopédies* or Poulenc's *Mouvements Perpétuels*, there will have been something about a harmony – a colour, a scent, a frisson – that will have led you, like me, into the magic garden.

What I lacked, though, was a guide. There were experts from the previous generation (Martin Cooper, superb, if a tad dry) and various specialists (Lockspeiser on Debussy, Harding on operetta) but it was Roger Nichols who, as my explorations continued, charted my obsessions step for step. His prose, at once pellucid and peppery, elegant and witty somehow matched his subject matter. I devoured everything he wrote, from *Debussy* in the early 70's to his *Poulenc* of the 2020s, via *Ravel, Messiaen, Satie,* and his peerless *The Harlequin Years* which brilliantly pulls all the inter-war loose threads together.

Here, in this collection of articles, reviews, interviews and *belles lettres*, Nichols has created an engrossing chronicle of the century and a half or so of French music from Berlioz to Boulez. We begin with a fantastic piece on the *Symphonie fantastique* and end with a Boulez obituary. We dwell, quite rightly, on the big-hitters Debussy and Ravel who are fascinatingly unpacked – not least in a piece which connects the two by comparing their operatic masterpieces *Pelléas et Mélisande* and *L'Enfant et les sortilèges*. Both pieces shake off the influence of Massenet, both are experiments in prosody, and both concern lost adolescents who end up in forests. Satie is also well-represented – there is an indepth examination of *Parade,* as well as a radio play in which Nichols and Satie have a chat – which I'm sure would have delighted the composer.

If Debussy and Ravel are the twin stars, it is intriguing to observe the greater and lesser lights who make up the many French constellations. There are the self-taught eccentrics – Satie, Chabrier, Berlioz – one might add Poulenc. The educators, Koechlin, d'Indy, Fauré. The religious visionaries, Messiaen and Duruflé. The undervalued Lalo, Delibes and Magnard.

When one reads this wide-ranging collection various themes become visible. The cross-fertilisations of admirations, sometimes spanning the centuries. Dutilleux, we learn, is crazy about Berlioz. Messiaen's atonality owes much to Ravel's. Poulenc loved Chabrier. Fauré was endlessly loyal to Saint-Saëns. Other strands emerge. The tyranny of the Prix de Rome is such that the cast are divided between the winners – Massenet, Debussy, Berlioz, Gounod, Dutilleux – and those unfairly denied. Ravel, for instance, or as Nichols says of Lalo:

> No surprise then to find he was a member of a dining club for those composers who had not won the Prix de Rome, including Fauré, Messager, d'Indy, Duparc and, of course, Chabrier: it was called 'Le Dîner des pris de rhum' (the club for those out of their heads on rum).

Then of course, there is Germany. The fact that France was thrice invaded by her neighbour goes a long way to explaining the self-sufficient nationalism of French music. 'We're doing our thing', they're almost saying. And perhaps one might add to that history the first German invasion, that of Wagner. One which some composers – Chausson, Duparc – never quite survived, while others – Chabrier, Debussy – had to pass through in order to become themselves.

The glue, though, that binds this engaging collection together is that it is written by a British musicologist who is observing the French scene. Hence Nichols' particular fascination with how Debussy fares in England. And his talks with the key players, Messiaen, Dutilleux and Boulez. Hence, also, his ability to temper an insider's view with an outsider's overview. Roger Nichols has not only a life-time's passion and expertise, but also the rare gift of distance, which allows him to assess and contextualise so brilliantly.

This is a book to be savoured slowly like a fine wine. A work to relish and to linger over for a lifetime. It can be dipped into rewardingly but read from cover to cover it is an enthralling chronicle of a turbulent and fertile period in the history of French music, from Berlioz to Boulez.

Jeremy Sams
Rushden, 2022

PREFACE

The articles in this book date from various times over the last 40 years or so, and come from various sources. I am happy to record the following provenances and the permissions kindly given to republish:

BBC Archives (Radio 3): 23, 35, 38

BBC Music magazine: 2, 4, 5, 6, 11, 22, 23, 27, 54

Cambridge University Press: 13, 30, 34

Glyndebourne Opera House: 32

The Guardian: 52, 55

The Times Literary Supplement: 10, 53

The remaining texts were either concert notes or scripts for talks at music clubs. I have taken the opportunity throughout to bring articles up to date, so for the most part the year of their birth is no longer really relevant. But where it is, I have included it.

Inevitably, in a collection of this sort, there are repetitions. I hope you, dear reader, may take the charitable view that repetition could make the passage in question easier to remember.

I am grateful to Hugh Macdonald and Nigel Simeone for their expert advice, to Jeremy Sams for his enthusiasm, and to Sidney Buckland for her unfailing moral and literary support.

Roger Nichols

Kington, 2022

CONTENTS

Foreword by Jeremy Sams   vii
Preface by Roger Nichols   ix

1	Hector Berlioz – fantasy and fury	1
2	… and beyond …	10
3	Frédéric Chopin – a difficult genius	15
4	Charles Gounod	21
5	Edouard Lalo	25
6	Camille Saint-Saëns	30
7	Léo Delibes	35
8	Jules Massenet – a man of pleasure	40

Emmanuel Chabrier

9	Chabrier – selected letters	45
10	Heap, Heap, Hurrah! – a review	50
11	The Angel of Laughter	56
12	Gabriel Fauré – *Pelléas et Mélisande*	60

Claude Debussy

13	Debussy – the reception of his music in Britain up to 1914	69
14	Debussy as man and artist	85
15	Debussy and Degas – beyond Impressionism	90
16	Debussy, Ravel and an orchestra for the 20th century	102
17	Debussy, d'Annunzio and *Le Martyre de Saint Sébastien*	106
18	*Pelléas et Mélisande / L'Enfant et les sortilèges*	110
19	*Pelléas et Mélisande* – reviews by d'Indy, Dukas and Willy	114
20	Who was Mélisande?	130
21	*Pelléas et Mélisande* – interview with Irène Joachim	136
22	Albéric Magnard	142
23	Florent Schmitt	146
24	Erik Satie	150
25	The Trouble with Satie	154
26	*Parade* – a mix of extraordinary talents	170

27	Le Groupe des Six – 100 years on	174
28	Reynaldo Hahn	179

Maurice Ravel

29	Raveliana – new insights	183
30	Ravel and the 20th century	189
31	Ravel and the Dance	203
32	Ravel and Spain	208
33	Ravel, Dreyfus and Sex	213
34	Ravel and the critics	217
35	The Châtelet Ballet Gala of 22 April 1912	222
36	Music and Impressionism	232
37	Jean Cocteau and Igor Stravinsky	237
38	Arthur Honegger – Incantation to the fossils – a documentary	243
39	Francis Poulenc, French ballet, and the pleasure principle	259
40	Francis Poulenc – and the road to *La Voix humaine*	263
41	Maurice Duruflé	266

Olivier Messiaen

42	Messiaen and the journey to a world beyond	270
43	Messiaen – ornitheology and all that	280
44	Messiaen at 70 – an interview	284
45	Debussy and Messiaen	291
46	Ravel and Messiaen – accords and discords	295
47	Messiaen – Interview with Pierre Boulez	302
48	Messiaen – Interview with Dame Gillian Weir	308
49	Music in Paris in the 1940s	319
50	Henri Dutilleux at 75 – Conversations	327
51	Henri Dutilleux at nearly 90	346
52	Henri Dutilleux – Obituary	350
53	Pierre Boulez and André Schaeffner – a review	356
54	Thirty years of IRCAM	361
55	Adieu, Pierre Boulez – Obituary	366
Index		378

I suspect many music lovers first met Berlioz through the *Symphonie fantastique*, and maybe I did too. But the impact of this piece of red hot Berlioz was balanced by having *L'Enfance du Christ* prescribed as a set work for my degree in 1962. As a result, I've always responded with perhaps equal pleasure to the composer's more measured products as to his fiery ones. The French themselves, as recorded below, have tended to look askance at Berlioz, so I was delighted in the 1990s to find a fan in such a wise and skilful master as Henri Dutilleux, and to learn that he too was attracted to the composer's cooler aspect. Still, the *Symphonie fantastique* is always with us ...

1 FANTASY AND FURY

Hector Berlioz and the *Symphonie fantastique*

To ask 'What year did the Romantic movement begin?' makes about as much sense as asking the same question of the Renaissance. Given that historians are still arguing, nearly two centuries later, about what Romanticism actually was, we should maybe content ourselves with identifying just a few key ingredients, without bothering over the recipe as a whole.

But I think most historians would agree that any list of Romantic ingredients must include Goethe's *Faust*. Part I of the work was published in Paris in 1825 in the translation by Gérard de Nerval and among its most enthusiastic readers was Hector Berlioz. The first mention of it in his letters comes early in 1828, when the 24-year-old composer recognises that he has been born into this world 'to be battered by wind and tempest, as Goethe so finely puts it'. In fact Goethe didn't – or not in those precise words, at any rate; but there are phrases in the 'Walpurgis Night' section of Part I which are not that dissimilar.

The persona of Faust was attractive for all kinds of reasons, as was pointed out by Berlioz's biographer Jacques Barzun:

> Learned, passionate, curious, tender, courageous, bewitched and desperate, he stood for genius in all its greatness and misery ... To searchers like the young artists of the new era, it was wonderful to find a fable in which Experience and Wisdom were not shown as

already bottled and labelled by the old for the use of the obedient young, but were purchasable solely with risk and effort.

We may be tempted to think it was particularly wonderful for the young Berlioz, who had enrolled as a student at the Paris Conservatoire in the autumn of 1826 and had thereafter begun a long struggle to reconcile his passionate desire to write his own kind of music with the need he must have felt for some sort of formal tuition – otherwise he would hardly have bothered to enrol. Also he must have realized that a Conservatoire training would be helpful for career reasons.

He finished his *Huit scènes de Faust* in the last months of 1828, and on 10 April 1829 sent the published score to Goethe with a letter:

Monseigneur,

For some years *Faust* has been my constant reading. As a result of my study of this astonishing work (even though I was able to view it only through the fog of a translation) it ended by exercising on my spirit a kind of enchantment; musical ideas formed themselves in my head around your poetic ones and, although I was firmly determined never to join my feeble chords to your sublime words, little by little the seduction worked so powerfully on me, the enchantment was so violent, that the music for several scenes was composed almost without my knowledge.

Goethe, we're told, approved the tone of the letter but, not being a musician himself, passed the score on to his friend Carl Friedrich Zelter, Mendelssohn's teacher. Zelter judged the score to be a 'succession of expectorations, sneezings, croakings and vomitings; an excrescence, the residue of an abortion resulting from an act of hideous incest'.

If *Faust* was one of the elements in the maturing of Berlioz, his passion for the Irish actress Harriet Smithson can be viewed as another – the idea that it merely prolonged his emotional adolescence hardly stands up, since he married her and remained married to her, albeit unhappily, until her death in 1854.

He first saw her on 11 September 1827 as Ophelia in *Hamlet*. He later described his passion for her as being like a bolt of lightning that had struck into his heart as into a virgin forest. Two months after his first sight of her, writing to a friend somewhat feelingly about how his father was pressing him to enter for the Prix de Rome, he confessed:

> I express myself ... with some passion on the subject, but you can't imagine how little importance I attach to it. For three months I've been prey to an insurmountable affliction and I'm disillusioned with life to the utmost degree; even the success I've achieved could only momentarily alleviate the painful burden which weighs on me, and now it returns more heavily than before. I can't give you here the key to the enigma; it would take too long and in any case I don't think I could manage to form the letters to tell you about it.

We could surmise that one of the reasons Berlioz was unwilling or unable to put his feelings into words was that they could be put more readily into music. Again, I think most historians would agree that the tendency to fashion music out of literature or out of personal experiences was a hallmark of the Romantic movement; Berlioz was preparing to do both.

Not content with his *Huit scènes de Faust*, and thwarted in his attempts to get a ballet commissioned on the subject, he wrote to a friend:

> If ever I were a success, I have the undeniable feeling that I should become a colossus in music; for a long time I've had fermenting in my head a symphony describing Faust. When I let it out into the open, I want it to stun the musical world.

The chances are, that's the first reference in Berlioz's letters to the *Symphonie fantastique*; over the following year, it would detach itself from the Faust legend apart from the final 'Witches' Sabbath'. By the January of 1830, he was referring to it simply as 'an immense instrumental composition', but at the same time what had been a vague notion was now taking more tangible shape:

> I've just hatched the idea of giving a large concert at the Théâtre des Nouveautés three and a half months from now. On Ascension Day, all the theatres will be shut, so I shall have free rein for my enterprise; the Nouveautés have just engaged a body of musicians. I'll have at my disposal an excellent orchestra, conducted by a highly talented musician who is absolutely devoted to me. I shall merely have to double it in size by bringing in outsiders.
>
> As part of my plan I'm preparing a lot of new music; among other things, an immense instrumental composition of a new

kind with which I shall try to make a powerful impression on my audience.

Note the words 'large', 'immense', 'powerful'. I don't think the phrase 'small concert' was in Berlioz's vocabulary ... Partly this was because he recognised that he was not, in these early years, tempted to write music that creeps up on you unawares. Not for him the drip, drip of talent on the stone of popularity. But partly it was that the new symphony had to accommodate so much psychological material. One of the chief glories of Berlioz's music is his extraordinary use of contrast, in every conceivable domain and, although to some extent this was no doubt a deliberate ploy towards 'making a powerful impression' on his audience, it was also born of the nature of the man and the complexity of his emotional life. Here he is, for example, a month after the letter we've just read, describing the state of that emotional life and the effect it was having on his creativity:

> I have just been plunged once more into all the anguish of an interminable, inextinguishable passion, without motive, without object. She is still in London, and yet I seem to feel her all around me; all my memories are revived and come together to tear me apart; I listen to my heart beating and its pulsing shakes me like the piston of a steam engine.
>
> I was on the point of beginning my great symphony (Episode in the life of an artist), which is to describe the development of my infernal passion. It's all in my head, but I'm incapable of writing anything down ... We must wait.

Is there not some similarity here with Keats's famous sentence from the *Ode on a Grecian Urn*: 'Heard melodies are sweet, but those unheard/ Are sweeter ... '? Even so, the creative force was so strong that there was in fact not long to wait before the notes began to pour out on to the manuscript paper. The symphony, begun in the February of 1830, was finished by 16 April, the day on which he wrote a letter outlining the action of the five movements, though with the 'Scene in the Fields' and 'The Ball' the other way round from how they would appear in the final score.

This letter of 16 April is also the first time Berlioz mentions the presence of a motto theme, the sporadically repeated 'idée fixe' in which the hero of the drama finds a graceful, noble character matching the one he attributes to the object of his passion. And if, as already indicated, that object in real life was Harriet Smithson, then presumably we could call this motto theme the 'Harriet motif'? Well, yes and no. I said Berlioz's emotional life was a complex one. He'd already used a version of this motto theme in his cantata *Herminie*, which had won him second place in the Prix de Rome competition two years earlier.

If it was just a question of self-borrowing, there'd be nothing surprising in that. The reference is more complex, though. The theme goes back further still, to a setting Berlioz made in his teens of verses from Florian's *Estelle et Némorin*:

> And so for ever must I now depart
> From this fair land which my fair one doth bless,
> Oh, far from them I shall drag out my life,
> Sunk deep in tears and in regretfulness.

Just the sort of verses to appeal to the volatile temperament of an adolescent ... But beyond that, Berlioz saw in the Estelle of Florian's poem an incarnation of the real Estelle Fornier with whom he was then in love, and to whom he was to turn again in the last years of his life. We might think therefore of the motto theme as being not just an 'idée fixe' but an 'idéal fixe' - the musical image of the perfect woman that Berlioz, like Don Giovanni, was to seek in vain.

Harriet Smithson was far from perfect, as Berlioz, in that same letter of 16 April, confides. Or rather, as he'd been informed by the young and beautiful pianist Camille Moke – who helpfully passed on the gossip that Harriet had an 'understanding' with her theatrical manager, a man called Turner. Whether this was true or not, Berlioz believed her and Camille, with her smooth, dark hair and ravishing blue eyes, moved into the vacant position with a most determined promptness.

The next few months were eventful ones for Berlioz, even by his exacting standards. In May, parts of the *Symphonie fantastique* were rehearsed for the first time, but the supplementary players he'd counted on could not, after all, be available for the concert:

> I cannot have my Symphony performed with such a threadbare orchestra as the one at the Nouveautés. I enclose Friday's *Figaro* which had already advertised the concert and printed the

Symphony's programme, as it will be distributed in the hall on the day of the performance. It's caused an unbelievable stir, everyone's buying or stealing *Le Figaro* in the cafés.

We'd already had two rehearsals, very bad ones, but it would all have ended up going reasonably well after five or six more sessions. I wasn't the slightest bit mistaken in what I'd written. Everything is as I thought it would be. Only the 'March to the Scaffold' is a hundred times more terrifying than I expected.

His letters say nothing more about the symphony until August, but in the meantime he was certainly not idle. On 5 June he wrote to his father asking for permission to marry Camille; next day he eloped with her – but only as far as Vincennes, on the eastern edge of Paris. Then, on 17 July, Berlioz entered the Prix de Rome competition for the fourth time – and ten days later Paris was swept up in a revolution that removed Charles X from the French throne. Lovers of Berlioz's music may be forgiven for wondering whether the former might possibly have caused the latter; but it seems not. On 23 August, the French musical establishment unbent to the extent of awarding Berlioz the first prize for his cantata *Sardanapale*. Much as he might pour scorn on the whole business, like Debussy half a century later Berlioz was quite prepared to accept the five years of subsidised composing that came with it.

On the same day he won the prize, he announced that his 'immense concert', to include the *Symphonie fantastique*, was now scheduled for 14 November; and gave unequivocal evidence of the relative standing of the two women currently in his life:

I've just left Mme Moke's house. I part from the hand of my beloved Camille, which is why mine is trembling so and why my writing is so bad. Farewell. That wretched Smithson girl is still in Paris. I haven't seen her at all since she came back.

It could be that Berlioz's view of Harriet was even blacker than that translation suggests. He refers to her as a 'malheureuse FILLE' with the word 'FILLE' in capital letters – the inference could be either that, for all her finagling charms, she's still unmarried; or, worse, that acting is not her only profession ...

By September, the projected performance of the symphony had moved on a week to 21 November (on the way to its final destination of 5 December), and Berlioz, not for the last time, was beginning to count his financial chickens. As well as the symphony, the concert was to include the overture to *Les Francs-juges* and two choral pieces from the *Neuf Mélodies*; and, as he assured his father:

> I count on it bringing in at least a thousand francs. The Prix de Rome money doesn't start coming in until next January, and I shall find myself in financial straits between now and my concert because of the money I've spent on coats. My black coat was the only passable one I had left and I can't wear it all the time. All my pupils have gone to the country and at the moment I haven't a single one left. If you could pay me in advance your subsidy of 200 francs which I'm not due to receive until November, that would solve my difficulties.

Before the 'immense concert' that finally took place on 5 December, Berlioz had one score to settle, both with the musical establishment and with his own conscience. In his prize-winning cantata on *Sardanapalus*, he had, in a fit of diplomacy, played down the full horror of the final conflagration. But now … :

> As I had already been awarded the prize, I added a long piece of descriptive music for the burning of Sardanapalus's palace. I no longer had anything to fear from the members of the Academy and I allowed my imagination free rein. In the middle of the blazing tumult, I brought back all the musical ideas of the scene, piled up one upon the other; and then all the terrifying amalgam of sounds of misery, cries of despair, outbursts of pride which even death cannot stifle, the roaring of the flames, leading to the crumbling of the palace in which every anguished voice is silenced and the flames extinguished.

So the audience on 5 December had a full month's notice of the kind of thing to expect. With one tiny exception, it was an all-Berlioz concert, including a second performance of *Sardanapale*. To cut a long story short, it went well. But why should we cut a long story short, when Berlioz is there to tell the tale? And to his father, whose goodwill and admiration he so desperately sought. He starts off by saying he only has time to write six lines – and then goes on for another fifty or so:

> The *Symphonie fantastique* was greeted with cries and agitation. The audience wanted 'The March to the Scaffold' repeated; but as it was very late and 'The Witches' Sabbath' is a long movement, Habeneck didn't want to play the March again.
> Camille and her mother were there and were dying of fright at what Mme Moke called my 'extravagant programme'. Camille said to me last night: 'I wouldn't have thought an orchestra capable of producing such effects. Oh, how I loathe my piano now; it's so feeble and paltry!'
> Spontini and Meyerbeer clapped like madmen and when Spontini heard my 'March to the Scaffold', he shouted out: 'There's only been one man who could write a piece like that, and that was Beethoven; it's prodigious!' Liszt, the well-known pianist, more or less dragged me off to have dinner with him while he loaded me with the most energetic expressions of enthusiasm.

The composers Ferdinand Hiller and Cherubini were also there, but seem not to have joined in the back-slapping. Still, that first performance of the symphony was a milestone in Berlioz's career. It established him as a creative artist whom one could loathe but not ignore; it marked the beginning of his long friendship with Liszt; and possibly, as one of the editors of his correspondence suggests, it 'drained the abscess which had been eating away at Berlioz's morale.' It also, at least in my own view, provided an outlet for a certain amount of fury at the crassness and incompetence he found in the musical world around him: those high clarinets in the 'Witches' Sabbath' – did he have anyone particular in mind, I wonder?

More positively though, he had been right to give up the career in medicine his father had envisaged for him; he was right to embrace the literature of Romanticism as a potent source for his music – not only Goethe but, as his biographer David Cairns points out, Victor Hugo, Chateaubriand and de Quincey's *Confessions of an Opium Eater*. In short, the *Symphonie fantastique* was, and is, an astonishing compendium of the preoccupations of the crucial Romantic decade of the 1820s. And, as Cairns says, 'whether the "March to the Scaffold" and the "Witches' Sabbath" came from his imagination unaided or were drawn up from its darkest depths by de Quincey's "subtle and mighty opium" is immaterial. They remain classic visions of nightmare'.

Of all the words that have been devoted over the years to describing and analysing this extraordinary work, those of Schumann remain some of the most telling; impressive too, in that he had never heard it and had before him only Liszt's piano transcription. Throughout, he was struck by what was hallowed and conventional in the score: by the harmonic structure of the introduction, and by the harmonies themselves which he felt were distinguished 'by a kind of simplicity and even by a solidity and concision that one finds only in Beethoven'. And especially Schumann drew attention to the 'superb counterpoint' in the 'March to the Scaffold' and to the fact that in the 'Witches' Sabbath' 'what Berlioz modestly calls a fugato is written according to the rules'.

New ideas in old forms ... Like new wine in old bottles, the result can be explosive: terrifying, overwhelming, moving at lightning speed – to use a favourite Berlioz epithet, *foudroyant*'.

2 ... AND BEYOND ...

1789 ... the power of those magic numbers has never entirely faded in the memory of the French, as the *gilets jaunes* more recently demonstrated. If Napoleon's defeat at Waterloo put an end to his ambition, Louis XVIII and Charles X, the two brothers who were the figureheads of the ensuing Restoration, were not the sharpest tools in the royal box: the historian Alfred Cobban says of them respectively, 'Immensely fat and walking only with difficulty, he occupied the throne like an old idol, self-sufficient in divinely sanctioned egoism'; and '[he] had forgotten little; in intellectual goods his mind was so sparsely furnished that there was little for him to forget'. Not surprisingly, Paris in the 1820s became increasingly impatient for something better, spurred on by Charles's unshakeable belief in the divine right of kings.

One good thing Louis had done was to settle a lifetime pension on a young poet called Victor Hugo, not foreseeing the role Hugo would shortly play in fomenting dissent. He did this in particular in the long Preface he wrote to his drama *Cromwell* which became a manifesto of the new spirit, claiming among other things to be 'the voice of a solitary apprentice of nature and truth' and that 'the beautiful has only one type, the ugly has a thousand'. Readers wondering what Berlioz has to do with all this may be soothed by Hugo's observation in his Preface that 'it is the grotesque which impels the ghastly antics of witches' revels'. Berlioz certainly knew that Preface and was also among the audience for Hugo's play *Hernani* on 25 February 1830 which, blatantly mixing tragedy and comedy, lasted for 39 increasingly noisy performances, setting die-hards against young radicals. Hugo returned home one night to find a bullet hole in his window. Violence was in the air, and on 27 July Charles X left for exile. And Berlioz?

The young Hector's education, apart from two years, had come entirely from his father. He learnt the flageolet, the flute and the guitar, but Papa forbade the piano – no one knows why, but Berlioz later was grateful for 'the luck that made it necessary for me to compose silently and freely, shielding me from the tyranny of digital habits, so dangerous for thought.' Overall the great virtue of this private education, at the hands of someone he revered, was to stimulate his imagination. He read voraciously: Virgil above all, the story of Dido and Aeneas prompting his great opera some 40 years later, but also Walter Scott, Fenimore Cooper and, later on, Goethe's *Faust* and Shakespeare who, like Hugo, had the bad manners to mix high and low life, Danish princes and gravediggers. From his village near Grenoble, Hector dreamt of travelling to exotic places and being 'the voice of the solitary apprentice of nature and truth', with the accent on 'solitary'. Here was born the lonely dreamer, escaping from all that was vulgar and humdrum into a more perfect world – which is to say, a world designed by him for himself.

And here lay the deficiency of his education. As he himself later admitted, as a single boy with two younger sisters, he never had to learn the arts of negotiation and compromise (Mendelssohn had the same problems for much the same reason). His father, a conscientious and widely loved doctor, was not to be argued with. Still less was his mother, a staunch Catholic in the ancient mould. And those who know Berlioz's music will not be surprised that music would be the first and worst cause of dissension between old and young. In an attempt to please Papa, Berlioz went to Paris and began medical studies, but blood and severed limbs were too much for him. Back home, he announced that he was going to be a composer. His mother who, in his own words, thought 'I was setting foot on a path that led to disrepute in this world and damnation in the next', shrieked at him to 'go and drag yourself through the filth of Paris, dishonour your name, leave your father and mother to die of shame and misery. You are no longer my son! I curse you!' We may respond that those who dream of being solitary should be careful what they wish for ...

It could well be that, from this encounter, above all Berlioz learnt to be his own man, a lesson that brought triumph and unhappiness in about equal measure. Against his imaginings were ranged the realities of Paris music making, in which figures like Auber, Cherubini and Rossini held pride of place, and the young were expected to know theirs. Nonetheless, on 5 December 1830, some four months after the king of France had been expelled and with the Prix de Rome in Berlioz's pocket, the world first heard his *Symphonie fantastique*. A symphony, fine. But a 'fantastic symphony'? Sure, the Beethoven symphonies that were at last being played in Paris were not all easy listening, some indeed were deemed incomprehensible, but they weren't 'fantastic'. Well, this one was.

For a start, this was the first symphony ever to figure the composer as subject. He falls in love; whenever his thoughts turn to his beloved the same theme comes to mind; she haunts him at a ball and in the countryside; under the influence of opium he dreams that he has killed her and is being led to the scaffold; finally he is present among witches at his own funeral. Such revolutionary ideas clearly called for unconventional music, and Berlioz obliged. Take the theme of the beloved – since it reappears regularly throughout the symphony, it has become known as the 'idée fixe'. Since it's 32 bars long, you can, if you try hard, split it up into a regular 4x8-bar pattern. But that's not what we hear: there are ellipses and expansions, as well as two accelerandos and a rallentando, so that the whole theme radiates instability. The accompaniment too is initially grotesque, a scratchy figure on strings that doesn't start till bar 7, then stops, then starts again, then stops, like an old car in cold weather. The ball theme, though it begins traditionally, and most attractively, soon undergoes similar treatment that would fox any dancer. 'The Scene in the Fields' finds the composer reflecting on his isolation, which may soon be over. But does she really love him? 'These ideas of happiness disturbed by black presentiments form the subject' of the movement. Here Berlioz was remembering Beethoven's Pastoral Symphony, and the 'black presentiments', painted by dissonant thunder on timpani, relate to the cello and double bass passages in the Pastoral where, as Berlioz later remarked, the five rising notes on low cellos are messily matched with four on double basses: here music is giving way to sheer noise.

Noise and disruption are much in evidence in the last two movements. In 'The March to the Scaffold', complete with guillotine cutting off the head of the 'idée fixe', two chords alternating four times are enough to proclaim 'revolution': D flat major against G minor, D flat to G being 'the devil's interval'. As for 'The Witches' Sabbath' and the screeched version of the 'idée fixe' on E flat clarinet, 'ignoble, trivial and grotesque' says Berlioz, here was the *Cromwell* preface in sound. A final blow to convention came with the quotation of the *Dies Irae* plainsong, Berlioz having long abandoned religion, no doubt partly aided by his mother's intransigence. If one of the aims of revolution is to point a path to the future, then this use of the *Dies Irae* did just that, the theme being taken up by any number of composers over the next couple of centuries, including Liszt, Ysaÿe and Rachmaninov, to name but three.

The clash between Berlioz's imagination and the realities of life took many forms. With regard to the *Fantastic Symphony*, it was embodied in his real-life love for the Irish actress Harriet Smithson whom he had seen as Ophelia and Juliet in 1827 and who was the unwitting object of the Symphony. In his memoirs, a heading tells the story in brief: 'I am introduced to Miss Smithson. She is ruined. She breaks her leg. I marry her'. A careful lover would have realised that one's abilities to convey passion on stage are not necessarily the qualities required for a comfortable companion. Her acting never rose to the same heights again and Berlioz looked after her for the rest of her life. Then, of course, there was the nature of his music itself. Those parts of it that still strike us as exciting tended to strike the performers of the time as terrifying. His first opera, *Benvenuto Cellini*, is still taxing today, not least for its complex rhythms. After some early shocks, he took to conducting his music himself, and here again an unwillingness to negotiate could cause problems. With German and British orchestras he was in general happy, and Sir Colin Davis's epoch-making engagement with his music would not have surprised him. But Parisian ones were a different matter. Saint-Saëns, writing in 1899, remembered that:

> [Berlioz] in his younger days demanded, from orchestras far inferior to those of today, efforts that were positively superhuman. I have seen him take 20, 30 rehearsals for a single work, tearing his hair, wrecking batons and music stands, without getting the result he wanted. The poor orchestral players did everything they could, but the task was beyond them.

Then, as mentioned already, there was the whole contentious matter of noise. A good idea, he sometimes seemed to be saying, could only be made better by being played more loudly, though that certainly was not always the case, as in the song cycle *Nuits d'été* which was complicit in launching the *mélodie* as a purveyor of serious music. Size of musical forces of course entailed money, the lack of which was an 'idée fixe' in Berlioz's life. The massive outlays for the *Requiem* and the *Symphonie funèbre et triomphale* were paid for by the state, but otherwise the mature composer was a revolutionary in that he organized, conducted and paid for almost all the concerts he gave in Paris. As ever, this was a hit-and-miss affair: *La Damnation de Faust* was a total flop, leaving him pretty well bankrupt ('nothing in my artistic career has so grievously wounded me as this unexpected indifference'), while the gentler *L'Enfance du Christ* was a huge success. To the end of his life he regretted an A minor Symphony whose details came to him in dreams two nights running, but which he dared not write down, knowing the problems such an enterprise would entail. By the third night the music had vanished into thin air.

A final arena in which imagination and reality clashed was that of words. From 1835 Berlioz was for nearly 30 years a contributor of reviews and articles to the influential *Journal des débats*. He cursed the labour this entailed and the music that consequently he never wrote, but the money was needed and it did give him a forum for his ideas including, less helpfully, those on the music of his colleagues. He maintained, rather curiously, that those who really took umbrage at his slights were not those whose music he castigated, nor indeed ignored, but those whom he damned with faint praise. At all events he tended to shoot from the hip and, in intellectual Paris which has often been likened to a nest of snakes (or, by Berlioz, to 'a stinking bog'), this did him no favours. Few Parisians would have welcomed his view, expressed in another publication a few years earlier, that 'in the bushman as in the peasant, melodic feeling is sometimes accompanied by a very acute sense of *expression*, which, in contrast, occurs only seldom among city dwellers'. No surprise therefore that only the first of his three operas was performed by the Paris Opéra in his lifetime. *Les Troyens* finally received this accolade in 1921.

To his last days he cherished improvements to the way music was organised and played, especially in Paris. The Conservatoire should have classes in conducting and (modestly not mentioning his own *Traité d'instrumentation*) in orchestration (it did – by 1914); and singers everywhere should have classes in rhythm. His legacy has always been contested in some quarters, and we may find some wry amusement in the efforts of his successors to understand him: Fauré evincing distaste for the 'mediocre themes, baroque in form and vulgar in sonority' of the *Benvenuto Cellini* overture and being rapped over the knuckles by Saint-Saëns; Debussy finding the *Symphonie fantastique* a masterpiece but lamenting Berlioz's penchant for 'artificial flowers'; Ravel calling him 'a genius who knew everything by instinct, except what every Conservatoire student can do on the spot: write a decent bass line to a waltz'. More happily Pierre Citron, the editor of Berlioz's *Correspondance*, invites us, through reading his memoirs, to 'discern, sometimes displayed openly, sometimes more discreetly, the face and voice of an artist who was free, proud, honest, demanding: a prince'.

Although the text that follows was published to accompany Chopin recordings, it was also aimed, amicably, at a friend who, over 50 years and more, had never really 'got' the composer, feeling he was a lightweight, certainly when compared with Berlioz. I'm happy to say that, over the course of five evenings of Chopin's music, my friend was finally converted.

3 CHOPIN – A DIFFICULT GENIUS

Whether we're pianists or not, we may think we know Chopin. And if so, we're almost certainly wrong. Few composers have written music so riven with cross-currents, so multifarious in its meanings, so accurately and elegantly treading the line between tradition and revolution.

This line was perfectly observed in his requests regarding his funeral and laying-to-rest. For the latter he asked to be buried in the Père-Lachaise cemetery in Paris between Bellini and Cherubini, masters respectively of balanced melody and expressive counterpoint. For the former, which took place in the Madeleine church on 30 October 1849, he requested Mozart's *Requiem*. Nothing problematic about that, we might think. But he had died nearly a fortnight earlier, on the 17th. Liszt may be right in ascribing the delay to the desires of prominent Parisian soloists to take part in the ceremony; but undeniably Mozart's masterpiece needed female soloists and chorus, and ladies were not allowed to perform in Roman Catholic churches. The authorities finally relented (Pauline Viardot was among the soloists), but even in death, it seems, Chopin had the capacity to infuse an apparently measured, classical request with revolutionary features.

Any mention of 'revolution' in a Chopinesque context inevitably conjures up the vision of Poland and the abortive rising of 1830, which brought the composer to Paris even though he played no part in it. His position as exile has undoubtedly added to his glamour, and indeed did so in his lifetime: Parisian society was surprised to find a foreigner with manners entirely equal to its own. Although he kept in touch with Poland through other exiles from that country either living in Paris or passing through, there is no mistaking the special flavour of his Polonaises and Mazurkas – territory on to which, sensibly enough, few of his fellow composers dared follow him. If they were intended as portraits of his homeland, it has to be said that the messages were mixed. Simplicity vies with complexity, assurance with self-doubt, calmness with brutality.

The 50 or so Mazurkas may share a 3/4 time signature, but that is practically all: in matters of harmony, texture and form each one is to a large extent individual, and equally removed from anything else that was being written in Paris (or indeed Berlin or Vienna, let alone London). Even in those written before he left Poland there are surprises, scotching the idea that such things were necessarily aimed at the cosy Parisian consensus: in the F major Mazurka op. 68 no. 3, composed in 1829, he appears to write a middle section in B flat but containing E naturals – only in the penultimate bar does he let on that we've been in F major all along. As he grew older, the surprises became more elaborate and sophisticated until, in late works such as the *Polonaise-Fantaisie*, the whole notion of a polonaise underwent radical experimentation and development. This, together with the *Allegro de concert* and the F minor *Fantaisie*, was a work decried by André Gide in his *Notes sur Chopin* as being 'declamatory and not a little overwritten, leading to a facile pathos with an eye to effect'. Nor was Gide alone. Many years earlier Liszt had also expressed severe reservations over the *Polonaise-Fantaisie*, as a work 'driving the spirit to a level of irritability bordering on delirium' and as displaying 'deplorable aspects that the artist can profitably admit into his domain only with extreme circumspection'. Although Liszt later revised this opinion in the work's favour, we can still appreciate his doubts. Few piano pieces of the 19th century traverse such a wide range of disturbing, indefinable emotions.

Of a somewhat different cast is the Polonaise in F sharp minor published in 1841, in which Chopin seems to turn the mannerisms of the polonaise against itself, daring us to criticize it as boring and repetitive. Not only does he refashion our sense of time, extending the polonaise patterns so that they become almost hypnotic, but he goes further in incorporating within the polonaise framework a fully fledged mazurka. Then comes the gradual return of the polonaise – one of the most exciting, even terrifying passages in all music. For most composers this would be enough. But Chopin has a final surprise in store, as our reward for sitting through so much repeated material. After the dramatic upward chromatic scale in the left hand, suddenly the sun comes out for four bars of lyrical magic. Then the polonaise patterns return ...

At the other extreme lie Chopin's simple pieces – simple, that is, in their superficial, technical demands. A number of the Preludes and Nocturnes come into this category, and through them Chopin's reputation has often taken a serious dip. It was a mortification of the ear well recognized in late-19th century Parisian society, that after dinner on a Sunday evening the young lady (or worse, ladies) of the house would be invited, encouraged, pressed against their well-bred resistance to play for the assembled company. And it would not be Bach or Beethoven, but Chopin. Echoes of these evenings survive in Marcel Proust's masterpiece, where initially only the elderly Mme de Cambremer is a Chopin enthusiast, and has to recognize that her 'Wagnerian' daughter-in-law actually finds listening to Chopin painful. (Gide in fact makes the nice distinction between Wagner where 'each emotion is full of notes', and Chopin where 'each note is full of emotion'). Only later in the novel is Chopin rehabilitated, and that on the coat-tails of Debussy, a known Chopin enthusiast and, as the composer of *Pelléas et Mélisande*, an arbiter of taste who is beyond question. In this way Chopin becomes the preserve of the old and the young, with the middle-aged in a no-man's land of cultural uncertainty. In this way he is defined by a strange 'unseizability', in which every general statement about him has to be so variously qualified as to be meaningless.

Nowhere is this 'unseizability' so glaring as in the problems his music poses for the modern editor. One of this tribe was heard recently to declare of some ongoing edition, 'We must be scientific about this!' Unfortunately (or fortunately, depending on your point of view) Chopin took no account of science, preferring, like Debussy, to be guided by 'mon plaisir', which took the form of varying and embroidering his compositions at every turn, so that the editor is faced with an array of sources of possibly equal significance, in which 'plaisir' has had a field day. Contemporary accounts of Chopin's playing suggest that he practically always varied bars that were repeated, and his letters demonstrate beyond peradventure that he had a low boredom threshold. Sometimes this took the form of abrupt behaviour, sometimes of wry amusement, as with the Scottish ladies during his last tour whose every comment on his playing 'ends with the words: "Leik water", meaning that the music flows like water. I have never yet played to an Englishwoman without her saying: "Leik WATER!!" They all look at their hands and play wrong notes most soulfully. What a queer lot! God preserve them!'

Playing wrong notes in Chopin is clearly a crime, but beyond that the character of a true 'Chopin style' has undoubtedly generated more ink than light. Among the unarguable facts are that he never possessed the robust physique of the traditional 19th-century virtuoso. Liszt records that Chopin once explained to a fellow pianist:

> I'm not cut out for giving concerts. The public intimidate me, I feel asphyxiated by all that heavy breathing, paralysed by those curious looks, mute when confronted by those strange faces; but you, concert-giving is your destiny, because when you haven't got the audience on your side, you've got the wherewithal to knock them senseless.

Like Debussy a couple of generations later, Chopin was criticized by audiences in large concert halls for being nearly inaudible. His response was to give up such enterprises and confine himself to small gatherings of friends and admirers where the subtle nuances of his playing could be appreciated at their true value. Among Gide's many interesting *aperçus* is his comparison of Chopin's music with Baudelaire's *Les Fleurs du mal*: both works that set a benchmark for the future of their art, but through what one fellow-poet called Baudelaire's 'confessional tone'. Why go to the effort of knocking audiences senseless when you can achieve the same effect through leading them gently by the hand into another world? Here, as often, Proust was on the mark, relating, in the person of the Baron de Charlus, that 'Chopin ultimately was no more than a pretext for returning to the hypnotic, dreamlike state that you are currently neglecting.' The Baron also recalls (and here Proust was stealing shamelessly from Saint-Saëns's memoirs) that his piano teacher Stamaty had forbidden him to go to any of Chopin's concerts. Chopin could be dangerous for a young lad's musical health.

The impression that, for all Chopin's beautiful manners, his music lay somehow outside the general run is only emphasized by the apparent lack of much in the way of provenance. Bellini's *bel canto* and John Field's *Nocturnes*, of course. And from his favourite pupil Adolf Gutmann we learn that

> Chopin held that Clementi's *Gradus ad Parnassum*, Bach's keyboard fugues and Hummel's compositions were the key to pianoforte-playing, and he considered a training in these composers a fit preparation for his own works.

But Chopin's inventive use of chromaticism, for one thing, goes so far beyond anything in Clementi or Hummel that one can hardly speak of influence. Increasingly counterpoint too invaded his textures, and here Bach was undoubtedly a force, not least in the way counterpoint suddenly materializes out of nowhere, as in the fleeting passages of imitation that light up the middle section of the supremely beautiful *Nocturne* in E major op 62 no. 2: this is counterpoint not to impress, but to intensify what is already happening in the piece. The German master, though, was not current coinage in the Paris of Chopin's time. As he wrote to his friend Elsner in Warsaw in 1840, 'The public has to think itself lucky if from time to time it is allowed to hear a bit of Handel or Bach.'

But Chopin's disconnection from his time is most obvious in his music's many dangerous passages, which give Stamaty good cause for his alarm. One of Liszt's more controversial statements was that Chopin should not have confined his ideas within the forms of the concerto and the sonata, which 'violated his genius'. But where is the academic constriction in the extraordinary finale to the Sonata in B flat minor? – disliked by Mendelssohn, described by Anton Rubinstein as 'night winds sweeping over church-yard graves', and labelled nearer our own times by Alan Walker as 'futuristically athematic from beginning to end'. The whole Sonata indeed was famously regarded by Schumann as an arbitrary family consisting of four of Chopin's most unruly children. Then there is the Prelude in A minor, which the American critic James Huneker called 'almost grotesque and discordant', blaming it on Chopin's perilous state of health. Gide at first found it impossible to understand. Over the years it grew on him, until finally he could comprehend it as 'a kind of physical terror, as before a glimpse of a world hostile to love, from which human affection has been banished'. And as a final, more benign example, there is the extraordinary E flat that rings out at the end of the Prelude in F major, seen by various 19th-century editors as a misprint for F natural and amended accordingly. Gide charmingly likens it to the arrival of the Comtesse de Noailles in a salon: 'At last! Here she is!' On a more pedantic level, here in this unresolved dominant 7th, if anywhere, is the ultimate source of Impressionist piano music.

We may protest against Liszt when he writes of the 'sickly irascibility' of Chopin's final works. We may consider at least his view that the 'concentrated exasperation' Chopin felt over his poor health was disguised by his 'even humour'. But few, I think, would quarrel with his description of the slow movement of the F minor Concerto (a favourite of Chopin's) as 'tempering joy with melancholy and pain with serenity'. From the variable interplay of these elements come the many shapes and colours of this difficult yet eternally entrancing music.

The two articles that follow are accompanied, I hope not too stridently, by the sound of breaking lances – though I'm under no illusion over the long term impact of such exercises.

4 CHARLES GOUNOD

We've probably heard a few arias from his opera *Faust* ; we'll certainly know his 'Ave Maria', based on Bach's C major Prelude, and maybe a few of his songs; and if we're wind players, we may have enjoyed contributing to his delightful 1885 *Petite Symphonie* for wind nonet. But beyond that? He's a composer whose currency has devalued steeply from those late Victorian days when he sold his oratorio *Mors et Vita* to Novello's for 100,000 francs.

But already, even then, the critics were sharpening their pens. In 1893, the year of Gounod's death, George Bernard Shaw complained that most probably his eyesight had been 'damaged by protracted contemplation of the scarlet red coat and red limelight of Mephistopheles', while a few years later Ernest Newman wrote *Faust* off as 'a blend of the pantomime, the novelette, and the Christmas card'. Why the vitriol? One reason undoubtedly was that, being born in 1818, Gounod was not only of the generation of Wagner, but chose in his own compositions to ignore that composer almost entirely – a position that came increasingly under fire as Wagnerism took over hearts and minds throughout Europe. Although his personal relations with Wagner were friendly, for him Wagner was 'a passing storm: don't get carried away!' and 'not a sun without spots'; and when an English critic warned him against being influenced by the German composer, he retorted (and here we need to remember that the French 'w' is pronounced 'v') that in that case he would consult a doctor 'pour me Wag-ciner'.

Born in Paris on 17 June 1818, Charles lost his elderly father at the age of four, and his childhood was marked by his mother's considerable energy and enterprise in making a living, teaching the piano and drawing – Charles's father had been a talented artist. The boy did well at school, but music was his chief love and in 1836 he entered the Paris Conservatoire, where he was taught by Halévy and Lesueur, and in

1839 won the Prix de Rome with his cantata *Fernand*. Although Rome itself was a disappointment to the young man, who had arrived there expecting to find 'the grand, austere beauties of nature and art', he was lucky in having, as director of the Villa Médicis where the prizewinners were housed, the painter Ingres who had known his father. Ingres was also a keen music lover and on at least one occasion Madame Ingres had to separate them around midnight when they were still deep in the piano duet score of *Don Giovanni*.

It was in Rome that Gounod came into contact with the Dominican friar Jean-Baptiste Lacordaire, just then recruiting members for his Brotherhood of Saint John the Evangelist, and tension between the religious and the artistic life was to remain a force within Gounod until his death – though whether it played a part in the psychosomatic illnesses he would suffer, who can say? On leaving Rome, he spent some time in Germany and some particularly happy days with Mendelssohn, who discouraged his interest in *Faust* and recommended instead that he try his hand at symphonies: his Second Symphony was a direct response to this encouragement. Back in Paris in 1843, he was appointed organist and musical director of a church near his flat and stayed in the post until the revolution of 1848. By this time he'd composed two songs by the revolutionary poet Lamartine, five Masses and a Piano Quintet, but nothing that presaged anything like success.

Then he met the famous contralto Pauline Viardot, and his life changed. For her, he composed the opera *Sapho*, premiered at the Opéra in 1851. The last act was particularly successful and Gounod, meeting Berlioz after the performance in floods of tears, begged him to 'come and show your tears to my mother – they're the best possible review she could have!' But much greater success came with his St Cecilia Mass, given in St Eustache in 1855, in which the music's 'simplicity, grandeur and serene light rose above the musical world like the dawn', in Saint-Saëns's ecstatic response. In the 1856 honours list, Gounod was made chevalier de la Légion d'honneur. He was on his way.

But, for the time being, this way was to be operatic, not religious. In 1858 he was commissioned to set Molière's comedy *Le Médecin malgré lui*, and the result was a flop. The young Bizet wrote home to his mother, 'If you can't make a hit with music like that, then to hell and damnation with everything!' It is indeed a vivacious, enchanting score, whose continuing absence from the operatic stage is a mystery – do listen on Youtube to the astonishing 1929 recording by the 81-year-old

Lucien Fugère of 'Qu'ils sont doux', Sganarelle's hymn to the bottle. But just a few months after the work's premiere, Gounod was already at work on *Faust*. Although he called the work an 'opéra' rather than an 'opéra-comique', it contained features from both styles. The chromatic introduction, depicting Faust's unhappiness and even the disasters it sets in train, and justly described by Paul Dukas as a 'page magistrale', lay way beyond the confines of opéra-comique. On the other hand, Marguerite's anxious questioning in Act III as to Faust's identity, set to 26 quiet, repeated E naturals, as if she daren't commit herself to anything as forthright as a phrase, let alone a tune, places the work firmly in the domestic opéra-comique tradition and would be taken up by Ambroise Thomas in *Mignon* and by Debussy in *Pelléas et Mélisande*. Altogether, the predominant lyricism of the score separates it sharply from the *grandes machines* such as *Les Huguenots* and *La Juive*, which were still making good money at the Opéra. Testimony to the work's success were its spawning of parodies, like Hervé's *Le petit Faust*, and the fact that the 14-year-old Fauré played hooky from his boarding school to go and see it. He was forgiven.

Of the five operas Gounod wrote in the 1860s, only the one he wrote for the Opéra, *La Reine de Saba*, failed to make its mark, partly due to a complex, overlong libretto which meant savage cuts had to be made late in the rehearsal period. The less imposing *Philémon et Baucis*, written like its two predecessors for the Théâtre-Lyrique, and *La Colombe*, written for Baden-Baden, are still heard from time to time today, and show Gounod at his most charming and, in *Philémon*, his most witty in showing up Vulcan and Jupiter as rather less than perfect. But the two gems of this decade were *Mireille* and *Roméo et Juliette,* even if both of them had to suffer from what Hugh Macdonald has recently called the Théâtre-Lyrique director Léon Carvalho's 'wild optimism and artistic butchery', not to mention the shrill commands of his soprano wife that Mireille's part should be 'brillant, brillant'. Gounod did add the brilliant 'O légère hirondelle' for her, but was disappointed that she didn't have the stamina for the last scene, in which Mireille dies of sunstroke after crossing the plain of the Crau (Gounod himself had crossed it, in search of local colour). The work perhaps suffers in that the tenor, Vincent, doesn't have an aria until Act V, but the bull-tamer Ourrias has some very powerful music and in general Gounod is persuasive in depicting the atmosphere of rural Provence.

Roméo et Juliette has been dubbed 'the opera of four duets', which is true, as far as it goes. Here, for the last time, he tapped into the lyrical vein that had served him so well, but he also benefited from his experience, witness his satisfaction at ending each act in a different mood: I, 'brilliant'; II, 'tender, dream-like'; III, 'animated, grand'; IV, 'dramatic'; V, 'tragic'. True, he still had to write a coloratura number, 'Je veux vivre', for Mme Carvalho, but there his accommodations ended. As well as the magnificent 'Ah! Lève-toi, soleil!' for Romeo, taking its cue from Shakespeare's 'Arise, fair sun, and kill the envious moon', the four duets are meltingly beautiful and, in the words of a recent music historian, 'as close to greatness as Gounod comes as a composer'.

Beyond this point, Gounod's operatic skills deserted him, not least because he felt bound for some reason to attempt the *grandes machines* that don't really seem to have suited him. But if opera no longer loved him, surprisingly he finally found his voice in oratorio... and in Birmingham, whose Festival Committee in 1882 offered him £4,000 to conduct his *Rédemption*, and followed up with the premiere of his *Mors et Vita* in 1884, conducted by Hans Richter, no less, at which receipts came to £25,000. In this last oratorio Gounod goes beyond his previous harmonic boundaries, with surprisingly startling results. Here indeed we find 'the grand, austere beauties of nature and art' so lacking for Gounod in the Eternal City.

If one word sums up both Gounod and his music, it would be 'charm'. As a man, he exerted it widely, especially on the fair sex: the whiskered sex often interpreted it as wheedling, and a rift with Bizet did raise doubts about his *bona fides*. But he made good jokes – a soprano who performed with an unduly open mouth was dubbed 'the Aeolian carp' – and, when Lalo had a brain seizure before finishing his ballet *Namouna*, Gounod stepped in at once and met the deadline. Like him, his music is not all good. But his best is very good indeed.

My introduction to the music of Lalo has a rather circuitous history, so I'll be as brief as I can. In the 1930s my parents were both enthusiastic dancers, for whom Victor Sylvester was a form of minor deity. Although my father had learnt to play Billy Mayerl's 'Marigold' by ear, his interest in classical music was aroused only in the 1940s by fellow pilots on his RAF station in Plymouth. Among the 78s he borrowed and brought home were Eileen Joyce's recording of the Grieg Piano Concerto and one of Italian arias sung by Beniamino Gigli. These were my first tastes of classical music. Gigli has always remained my touchstone as a lyric tenor and it was years later, through his magical recording of 'Vainement, ma bien aimée' from Lalo's *Le Roi d'Ys*, that I was drawn to that splendid opera.

5 **EDOUARD LALO**

> And now, my dear friend, beer prevents me from going on with this letter; I drink, I eat, I sleep, I don't say a word, I listen with a serious expression to a mass of idiotic remarks, that's my life.

For Edouard Lalo, returning home to Lille briefly in 1852, not much had changed, it seems, since he had lit out for Paris 13 years earlier. He was also escaping the intentions of his father, an ex-soldier in Napoleon's army who wanted his son to follow in his footsteps. Whether with paternal blessings or not (accounts differ), in Paris he continued having violin lessons, first with Baillot, then with Habeneck, and in 1843 added some in composition. We know almost nothing of his life and habits at this time – maybe Papa was subsidising him, and almost certainly he was giving violin lessons, as he would for a long time, but he first rises above the parapet in that crucial year 1848, when most of Europe was either in revolution or on the brink of it.

In France, according to one historian, 'the days of June 1848 were to see a bitterer social war than ever the first Revolution knew.' Having escaped the army once, Lalo preferred to mark the occasion artistically by founding with a cousin a republican association of musicians. Its principal aim was to 'raise works of art that are worthy of that title to the rank they would of necessity occupy if public taste had not been corrupted by airs with variations and fantasies on operatic themes'. A noble aim, no doubt, and he received no fewer than 500 applications.

But tradition and what the French call the *ronron habituel,* the daily routine of life, proved too strong and in October the association folded.

Although Lalo never took any such steps again, his enmity towards the facile remained firmly in place: while composing songs and short violin pieces, in 1849 he wrote his first Piano Trio, clearly influenced by Schumann and Mendelssohn. Another push away from the facile no doubt came in February 1850 when he played in the second violins of the Philharmonic Society founded and conducted by Berlioz, probably for a performance of *La Damnation de Faust.* But the most important event of the 1850s was the formation in 1856, with Lalo on viola, of the Armingaud String Quartet, whose mission was primarily to play Mendelssohn's music for strings, still unknown in Paris. Lalo wrote a first version of his own String Quartet in the same year.

At this point it's as well to be honest about Lalo's limitations as a composer. Not that he lacked technique or imagination, let alone determination. But his output is extremely variable. Did playing the wonderful Mendelssohn quartets inspire his own? Not really. Here, as at times throughout his works, the gift of melody is in abeyance. He himself may have realised this, because he admitted that 'what makes a good tune is something no one can explain'. It makes sense, therefore, to concentrate on those works where the tunes are indeed good.

After a brief first marriage which he described as 'a washout' (the poor lady had the delicacy to pass away in 1864), the following year he married Julie Bernier, not only a fine contralto but someone who believed strongly in Lalo's composing gifts. In 1866 he began an opera *Fiesque* which occupied him for the next two years and, over possible productions, well beyond that. It's a sorry series, too long to relate here, of disappointments and broken promises, though one not unknown in the opera world. The piece was placed third in a competition, but never performed, and Lalo eventually used it as a quarry for other works. One of the finest passages is 'Fiesque's Dream' where strong tunes are allied to vivid orchestration and striking rhythms, as Fiesque imagines what it would be like to be Doge of Genoa. Lalo used part of it again in his second and final completed opera, *Le Roi d'Ys.* In the meantime the ballet he wrote for a projected Brussels performance of *Fiesque* became the *Divertissement,* including an 'Andantino' that is a miracle of delicate orchestration.

Lalo's lyrical gifts are abundantly displayed in his 32 songs, sometimes plainly Schumannesque (as in *Viens!*), sometimes in arioso style (as in

Chant breton with its oboe obbligato), but mostly in the traditions of his time and place (as in the pseudo-Spanish *La Zuecca* and the sparkling *Ballade à la lune*). An exception is the dramatic *A celle qui part*, where he seems to be trying to outdo the Duparc of *La Vague et la cloche*, premiered a decade earlier. Among his chamber works, the three Piano Trios stand out for their confidence and sweep, their wide variation in texture and, in the Third of 1879-80, their more adventurous harmonies. Quite frequently, the public of the time found Lalo's music difficult, and certainly he fought shy of anything banal or academic. Although he was in general a kind and generous person, faced with the problems of making it in the Parisian bear-pit he could be sharp about his fellow composers. He grumbled that the publisher Durand was willing to bring out any old thing if it had the name Saint-Saëns on it, wrote off Ambroise Thomas's efforts as 'musique de pion' (apprentice stuff) and – not without a hint of jealousy perhaps – taxed Massenet with being 'le chouchou des dames' (the ladies' poppet). No surprise then to find he was a member of a dining club for those composers who had *not* won the Prix de Rome, including Fauré, Messager, d'Indy, Duparc and, of course, Chabrier: it was called 'Le Dîner des pris de rhum' (the club for those out of their heads on rum). But difficult or not, Lalo was finally to achieve wide success with three works: *Symphonie espagnole*, the ballet *Namouna*, and the opera *Le Roi d'Ys*.

He never considered himself as a violin soloist, admitting to Armingaud, the leader of his quartet, 'as a composer I'm ahead of a whole host of others, but as a fiddler, I'm not worth a bean.' So he was more than happy to write works for Sarasate, the 'diableries' of whose playing he much enjoyed, and who gave the first public performance of *Symphonie espagnole* in February 1875. Lalo's original intention was simply to write a work that would allow the Spanish virtuoso to show off with some Spanish tunes. In the event, as one of his biographers says, 'this aim was singularly exceeded'. The first movement begins with Lalo being noisy, but (?pseudo-)Spanish lyricism soon intervenes together with fireworks for soloist, and the whole movement is a masterly combination of the three types of material. Unusually, the work is in five rather than three or four movements, and for many years performers left out the lovely 'Intermezzo': the 16-year-old Menuhin's wonderful 1933 recording was only the second to include it. The most Spanish movement is the last, sometimes called a *saltarello*, but in fact more of a Cuban *guajira*, with its alternating bars of 6/8 and 3/4, as in the first of Ravel's *Don Quichotte* songs. Here Lalo's violinistic expertise and mastery of orchestral nuance come into their own. But whatever the work's Spanish orientation, Lalo was as ever determined that its form should be beyond reproach: Brahms received a smart slap on the wrist for his First Piano Concerto – 'a fine orchestral work, and when the piano interrupts, it infuriates me'. The *Symphonie espagnole* expressed Lalo's basic idea, 'a violin solo soaring above the rigid form of an old-fashioned symphony'. As for the title, he chose it as being un-banal and took the trouble to run it past the pianist, conductor and polymath Hans von Bülow, who approved it and liked the fact that it was unique – a source of great pleasure for Lalo who in 1862 (before that tiresome Prussian invasion) had declared that 'Germany is my true musical homeland'.

Orchestral nuances also permeate his ballet *Namouna*, booed and whistled at on its 1882 Opéra première, but applauded later in the concert hall: Lalo made two suites from the work and said he'd put into them all the bits the Opéra audience had objected to, such as the 'Fête foraine', with its noisy outbursts and slippery harmonies. The result, in Debussy's mature opinion, was a masterpiece – a judgment according with his earlier view as a Conservatoire student, when he had made such a racket applauding and shouting 'Bravo!' that he was expelled from the Opéra box reserved for students, and they were all banned from the house for several months. Chabrier for his part claimed that 'without *Namouna*, *España* would not have existed'. But astonishingly (?shamefully) no complete recording of this wonderful work has ever been made …

It's good to be able to report that in 1888, at the age of 65 and with only four years of life left to him, Lalo finally scored an out-and-out hit with his opera *Le Roi d'Ys*. Based on the Breton legend of the submerged cathedral whose bells can still sometimes be heard ringing (another Debussyan connection), it has a strong storyline of a princess scorned and the catastrophic results of her fury. It was in connection with this work that Lalo defended his regard for noise: 'I love Wagner's excessive sonorities; I love the six pairs of drums in Berlioz's superb *Requiem*.' But there are many gentle moments too, notably the famous tenor romance 'Vainement, ma bien-aimée', based on the simplest melodic and harmonic elements, but eternally memorable. Elsewhere, notably in the choruses, Lalo obeys Wagner's suggestion that French opera composers should make more use of their own folksongs. He called it a 'simple opera' using 'very short forms', in order to 'accelerate the dramatic action in such a way as not to exhaust the attention of the spectator'. Surely it is one of the late-19th-century French operas most deserving of revival. Duparc noted that 'Lalo had the great honour of being underestimated by his contemporaries'. It should be our duty, privilege and pleasure to set the record straight.

No lances need to be broken promoting Saint-Saëns, but he remains a puzzle in that although he was technically so adept, and wrote much memorable music, one has to ask: is there 'un style Saint-Saëns'? Or did he suffer from what Debussy would later rail against as the technician's ability always to find some sort of solution to a problem, but not necessarily the most artistic one? Discuss ...

6 CAMILLE SAINT-SAËNS

The widely accepted opinion of Saint-Saëns is that, yes, he was an extremely good composer, but ... And even if the 'but' is not explicitly stated, it's often implied, giving the impression that in this beautifully crafted music there's nevertheless something missing – some inner core of passion, of what the Germans call *Schwung*. Is this true? Or is it just that we're looking for the wrong things? We may find some kind of answer if we consider the composer's relationships with his musical contemporaries: what they thought of him, and what he thought of them.

Two of his earliest supporters were Rossini and Berlioz. Saint-Saëns liked to tell of the Rossini salon evening which included a performance of the young man's delightful *Tarantelle* for flute, clarinet and piano, given, as always at that salon, anonymously. The piece's polish and wit left the assembled company quite certain it was yet another Rossini masterpiece and they duly showered him with praise – to which he replied, 'No, my friends, it's the work of this young man here.'

With Berlioz, Saint-Saëns enjoyed a long and affectionate friendship, nourished by mutual admiration. I should be forgetting my duty if at this point I didn't repeat Berlioz's well-known remark that 'he knows everything, all he lacks is inexperience'. But what exactly did he mean? To me it says that, firstly, Berlioz was slightly envious of Saint-Saëns prodigious technical skills but that, secondly, he recognized the value of sometimes making mistakes, because that way you often learnt something valuable. Did this in fact provide the impetus behind the general notion that Saint-Saëns's music was just too perfect? The younger man, for his part, was not only thunderstruck by the brilliance of Mephisto's three-chord signature in *La Damnation de Faust*, but saw through the sheer noise of Berlioz's *Requiem* to its 'poignant feeling' and 'incredible elevation of style'. As the years went by, and Saint-Saëns came to realise what a nest of snakes the Paris musical scene really was, he began to sympathize with Berlioz's often sourly negative comments on it, and at the end of Berlioz's life would play Bach to him on the piano to soothe his nerves. Probably his last article, appearing in October 1921, was on Berlioz.

One of the most interesting relationships was with Vincent d'Indy. Initially warm, it fairly soon disintegrated, and by the 1870s d'Indy was dismissing both of Saint-Saëns's early operas, *La Princesse jaune* and *Le Timbre d'argent*, as demonstrating all the tricks of the trade but totally lacking inspiration. That didn't prevent Saint-Saëns giving d'Indy generous letters of introduction to Liszt and to the publishers Breitkopf und Härtel. But the crunch came when Saint-Saëns at Bayreuth made sneering comments about *Parsifal*, after which he made matters still worse by refusing to contribute to a monument of César Franck and, in 1915, actually accusing the *pater seraphicus* of intrigue.

As for Saint-Saëns's view of Wagner, at the time it pleased practically nobody. He refused to say that Wagner's music was rubbish, or indeed that it was, of itself, dangerous. The danger came from its supporters – rather, its apostles. In his 1899 volume *Portraits et souvenirs*, in an article entitled 'L'Illusion wagnérienne', he confronted the belief that 'Wagner is not only a genius, he is a Messiah; until he arrived, Drama and Music were in their childhood and paved the way for his appearance; ... he has revealed the gospel of perfect Art to the world'. He finished by saying, 'Quite an entertaining anthology could be compiled of the errors, the nonsense and the silly sayings of all kinds that multiply themselves in Wagnerian criticism.' At a time when French Wagneromania was at its height, this was nothing less than treason.

When Saint-Saëns was not being criticized for the emptiness of his music, he was reviled for the grumpiness of his pronouncements. Not without reason, it must be said. But no doubt he would retort that he had a lot to be grumpy about, and increasingly so as music departed from the tonal world to which he always remained true: during his last years, reviewing one of Milhaud's earliest polytonal works, he wrote 'Happily, there are still mental institutions in France'. Milhaud framed the review and stuck it on his studio wall. But Saint-Saëns also had his unstuffy moments. In 1875 he went to Moscow to play and conduct some of his music and struck up a friendship with Tchaikovsky, the height of which perhaps was reached when, on the stage of the Conservatory, they danced a little ballet of their own invention, *Pygmalion and Galatea*, with the 35-year-old Tchaikovsky playing Pygmalion and the 40-year-old Saint-Saëns appearing as Galatea. The pianist was Nicolas Rubinstein. Unfortunately, there was no audience … Then, at the very end of his life, Saint-Saëns coached the young, and glamorous, pianist Jeanne-Marie Darré in his five Concertos and, after one fine performance, actually embraced her onstage. This, around 1920, was considered very bold, but no doubt being a grand-croix de la Légion d'honneur helped him get away with it.

One particular recipient of his grumpiness was Debussy. Saint-Saëns moved from complaining, as the member of a jury considering Debussy's early orchestral piece *Printemps*, that 'one does not write for orchestra in F sharp major, with six sharps', to asserting that the *Prélude à l'après-midi d'un faune* 'contains not a note of music in the true sense of the word', to telling a friend in 1902 (with his eternal lisp) that 'I'm thtaying in Parith to thay nathty thingth about *Pelléath*', to finally, in 1915, writing in a rage to Fauré after perusing the two-piano work he referred to as '*Noir et Blanc*': 'it's unbelievable, and it's imperative that the door of the Institut be closed against a man capable of such atrocities; it's on the same level as Cubist paintings.' As it turned out, the war and Debussy's death in 1918 put an end to any further animosities. Debussy, for his part, after early labours transcribing various Saint-Saëns works for piano duet to keep the wolf from the door, was surprisingly measured in his opinions. Reviewing the opera *Henry VIII*, all he could accuse the composer of was lacking 'that grandiloquence inside bad taste characteristic of the genius of Meyerbeer. [Saint-Saëns] is more of a musician than a man of the theatre.' His sharpest hit came in a review of a performance of the *Danse macabre*, of which he wrote 'M. Saint-Saëns won't hold it against me if I dare to say that there he gave promise of being a very great composer.' But perhaps his most incisive comment, and a positive one, came in a review of a virtuosic violin transcription his senior colleague had made of one of his own piano pieces, played by Ysaÿe. Noting that severer critics were likely to condemn such 'excessive virtuosity to no purpose', Debussy wrote: 'There are people who will never understand jokes; why should M. C. Saint-Saëns be forbidden to have a sense of humour?'

Why indeed? His music and his life both testify that he had a perfectly good one. After sitting in on a concerto rehearsal of Paderewski, who subscribed freely to the old habit of unsynchronised hands, Saint-Saëns asked the conductor, 'Which one are you following?' And in his music there are untold occasions when he gives in to sheer playfulness: the final 'Gavotte' of the Septet for trumpet, piano and strings (a most unusual ensemble, and not followed up, so far as I know), or the moment in his ballet *Javotte* when the severe father, until this point accompanied by equally severe fugal entries, returns from the fair 'having drink taken', at which the fugato breaks out into inebriated discords – one of the most hilarious moments in all classical music.

At other moments, this sense of humour takes on a darker tone, as in the sarcasm with which Dalila berates the stricken Samson in Act III of Saint-Saëns's opera, taking music from their earlier love duet and distorting it, thereby reminding us of the truth that love and hate can be dangerously close to one another. And at the very end of the opera, he judges to perfection the dose of almost laughable banality that can be allowed to the Philistine chorus without destroying the opera's coherence. We may well feel that people capable of such musical philistinism deserve to have heavy buildings pulled down on top of them.

Saint-Saëns complained regularly that it was *Samson et Dalila* that was staged, year after year, to the neglect of all his 11 other operas, and it's good that the distinguished scholar Hugh Macdonald has now done his best to make good this lack of interest. The trouble was, *Samson et Dalila* is such a tremendous work. How anyone, having heard even a moderate performance of it, can think Saint-Saëns's music was incapable of passion, is beyond me. To take just one passage, the Act II F minor duet between Dalila and the High Priest – this is full-blooded Verdian drama that even the great Italian maestro would surely have been proud to have written. It's not surprising that Liszt was the one to spot the work's qualities, conducting the first stage performances in 1877 in Weimar, with the Paris Opéra coming in as an also-ran in 1892.

The answer to the question in my first paragraph is surely that Saint-Saëns mined this dramatic vein only when it suited him. His favourite pupil, Gabriel Fauré, wrote in his obituary of his teacher of the 'serene regions' his music often inhabited, 'where violence and paroxysms are unknown, where gravity, wit, charm and smiling tenderness rule side by side.' In this he was echoing his teacher's own response to the world around him: 'Are smiles and graces to be ignored by all? ... Happiness is disapproved of in the music of our time ... Long live sadness! Long live boredom!' To which I respond, 'Long live keys, tunes, clarity and playfulness! Long live the music of Camille le Gentil!'

Whether they know it or not, TV viewers will almost certainly have heard a pair of sopranos warbling a 'Flower Duet', albeit given a thick, routine re-orchestration supposedly more acceptable to modern taste. Happily, the composer concerned is no longer around to suffer this - and in any case, he has other things to offer.

7 LÉO DELIBES

Although ballet retained its popularity in France throughout the 19th century, it did so on different terms at different times. Perhaps it was never again so popular as it had been under the Revolution, when numerous ballets reached their 100th Parisian performance. But in the middle of the century, only two ballets, *La Sylphide* and *Giselle*, did so, suggesting that ballet had increasingly become an ephemeral art, depending on composers and dancers who were momentarily in vogue. That this situation changed markedly in the 1870s was in no small measure due to Léo Delibes.

He was born on 21 February 1836 in St Germain du Val in the Sarthe region around Le Mans. His early upbringing combined both good and ill luck. His mother, Clémence, was the daughter of the baritone Batiste, who had joined the Opéra-Comique in 1799 and retired in 1822. Her brother Édouard, after serving in the entourage of King Charles X, became organist of St Eustache in Paris (which now looks down on the Forum des Halles) and a professor at the Conservatoire. So the young Léo, though spending his first 11 years at some distance from Parisian culture, was given a good musical grounding. His father, who was 53 when he was born and worked for the Post Office, seems not to have been especially musical; but he did take his young son along to the female director of a theatrical troupe that was touring the region, and she, having tested the boy's musical abilities, announced that he would be 'musicien et bon musicien'.

It was therefore only natural, when Léo's father died in 1847, for the remaining members of the family to go to Paris, where the boy could be sure of the best musical education under the eye of his uncle Édouard. Léo, it seems, having been brought up in the country, did not take easily to the relatively restricted life of a Paris apartment and soon acquired the reputation of being extremely rumbustious. This was why his uncle placed him in the Conservatoire class of Tariot, who was known to stand no nonsense. But Tariot soon grew to be fond of the boy, and to recognize his gifts. At his very first examination in 1849, the 13-year-old Delibes gained a second prize for solfège, and a first prize the year after. With that, though, the list more or less comes to an end. A third prize for harmony in 1854 ... but a notable lack of recompense in the noble arts of counterpoint and fugue. Also worth remarking is the fact that he never entered for the Prix de Rome: the preliminary round of this competition entailed writing a fugue, and probably his teachers thought he did not stand a chance. In the meantime he sang as a choirboy in the Madeleine church, and even as one of the children's choir in Meyerbeer's *Le Prophète* when it was staged at the Paris Opéra in 1849. After his voice broke, he became a church organist, as well as an accompanist at the Théâtre-Lyrique.

The best known of Delibes' Conservatoire teachers was Adolphe Adam, at that time in the middle of composing his series of 53 operas. Adam too had been at one time an undistinguished student, and the two got on well (indeed, Delibes was to get on well with everyone all his life – no small achievement in the narrow, jealousy-riven world of *le Paris musical*). It was to Adam that Delibes turned for advice when, in 1855, he was offered the chance of composing a one-act operetta. Should he accept or not? 'My dear boy', said Adam, 'when you get a chance like this at your age, you don't hesitate, you thank your lucky stars'. It took Delibes only a few days to deliver the music for *Deux Sous de charbon*, described as an 'asphyxie lyrique'.

He went on to write 14 more operettas in as many years, in addition to his posts in the church and opera house, before moving in 1864 from the Théâtre-Lyrique to the Opéra, as choirmaster. It was a routine kind of career, deep in the shadow of masterpieces like Gounod's *Faust* and Wagner's *Tannhäuser*, but also comprising less exciting fare. It would seem certain that, even to these, Delibes gave his detailed attention, if we are to judge by his own operettas – frothy they may have been, but the craftsman's hand is everywhere apparent, and he could well have continued along this path for many more years. That he did not was, once again, owing to his personal qualities. Emile Perrin, the director of the Opéra in 1865, had taken a liking to him and commissioned him to write the cantata *Alger* for a national holiday to celebrate the Emperor's return from Algeria. The cantata was a huge success, and the

Emperor awarded Delibes a gold medal, with his own hand fastening to his lapel a pin encrusted with diamonds.

Encouraged by this mark of favour, Perrin now asked Delibes to write the middle two acts of a ballet, *La Source*, and then in 1870 *Coppélia*, on the Hoffmann story *Der Sandmann* that would be set as an opera by Offenbach ten years later. *Coppélia* duly joined the ranks of *La Sylphide* and *Giselle*, reaching its 100th performance in 1884. With it, Delibes' reputation was made. In 1873 he produced the *opéra-comique Le Roi l'a dit*, about which the only complaint (an unusual one for opera) was that the story was too strong, leaving no real room for music. Whether as a response to the slightly cool reception of this work, Delibes wrote nothing for three years. As he said to a friend, 'No, I've nothing on the stocks at the moment, because I don't know what to do and I'm wondering what the public wants' – a curious statement from a man of nearly 40 with a string of successes behind him; but his lack of confidence was chronic, embracing not only his lack of skill in counterpoint but the question of whether or not to take on board the new techniques of Richard Wagner.

When his ballet *Sylvia* appeared at the new Opéra, the present Palais Garnier, in 1876, a number of critics thought they detected a Wagnerian influence. But this was becoming the usual stick with which to beat anything of substance, and *Sylvia* can be labelled Wagnerian only in the sense that there are no easy interludes where we can switch off our attention. Finally in his opera *Lakmé*, one of Delibes' greatest successes, given its premiere at the Opéra-Comique in 1883, the composer found a sufficiently rich vein of exoticism to carry him through without troubling himself over leitmotifs and the rest.

Delibes had been commissioned to write *Coppélia* directly after his success with *La Source*, and began it during the 1867 Paris Exhibition - while Bismarck reconnoitred the depths of Parisian decadence and an American firm called Steinway won their first gold medal as a preliminary to more peaceful conquests. The ballet's scenario was by Charles Truinet, known anagrammatically as Nuitter, the Opéra's archivist who had collaborated with Delibes on *La Source*. Although he based it on the Hoffmann story, he steered clear of the sinister atmosphere of the original and of Offenbach's opera – wisely, since Expressionist angst was no more part of Delibes' armoury than complex counterpoint.

Plans for a premiere in 1869 had to be abandoned because of the illness of the ballerina scheduled to dance Swanilda. But that summer the 15-year-old Giuseppina Bozzacchi was chosen to take over the role and the premiere was finally given at the Opéra on the rue Le Peletier on 25 May 1870, with Napoleon III and the Empress Eugénie in the imperial box.

Martin Cooper, in his classic book on French music, has written of the French ballet of that period that 'colour and movement, grace and vivacity are the qualities naturally demanded by music for this type of dancing, and these Delibes had in plenty'. In addition, he had a talent, which amounted very nearly to genius, for making his phrases danceable. This *ballabile* quality, to some extent indefinable, can nonetheless be attributed partly to his gift for producing phrases that balance each other, suggesting movement first to one side, then to another. Sometimes the pairing will consist of treble versus bass, sometimes strings versus woodwind, sometimes a held note versus a scattering of semiquavers; but in every case choreographers are given a clear starting-point for their invention. Delibes can then break this general rule when it comes to the 'Dance of the Automatons', whose continuous texture comes over as suitably mindless.

As for colour, Delibes was a marvellous orchestrator within the fairly narrow limits he set himself. Like many of his French contemporaries, he was more at home with the woodwind than with the brass, and he also had a felicitous ear for nuances of percussion. To go with his *ballabile* phrases, his harmonies tend to rest on fairly traditional, even obvious, bass lines, but every now and then he will introduce a slightly richer chord than we were expecting, before all is sorted out by the cadence.

Tchaikovsky included Delibes in a puff for contemporary French composers he sent in a letter to his patron Nadezhda von Meck. 'What pleases me', he wrote, 'is their effort to be eclectic, their sense of proportion, their readiness to break with hard-and-fast routine, while keeping within the limits of musical grace' – in all of which he compared them favourably with the German composers of the time. Diaghilev too was a Delibes fan, calling *Coppélia* 'the most beautiful ballet in existence, a pearl which has no equal in the ballet repertory', and declaring that it needed a superhuman effort to take all the colour out of it, as the Maryinsky did in 1902. A third Russian supporter was Stravinsky, who as a boy had played *Coppélia* in piano-duet form and who returned to his early love in 1927-8 in his ballet *Apollon musagète*, where the supposed influence of 17th-century France is filtered through Delibes' peculiar brand of sensual grace. And when in later life Stravinsky complained that conductors were always telling orchestras to sing, but never to dance, it is more than possible that it was Delibes and his *ballabile* phrases that he had in mind.

No lances need to be broken for Massenet, whose *Manon* and *Werther* remain firmly in the operatic repertoire. But he might have been a more complex personality than is generally thought.

8 JULES MASSENET – MAN OF PLEASURE

If you were a publisher round 1900, looking for someone to write a book called 'How to get on and upset people', then Jules Massenet would undoubtedly have been near the top of your list. Not that his literary skills were anything special: his *Souvenirs* are some of the dullest around, largely because he left out the interesting bits about the women who took up a large percentage of his time and energy. But even for Paris, which has always hidden a fierce undertow of rivalries beneath its glamorous surface, Massenet had an extraordinary capacity for causing pain. But also for getting on. The two were not unrelated.

He followed the standard 19th-century path to musical success, entering the Paris Conservatoire at the age of 10 in 1853, and leaving it at the age of 20 with the Prix de Rome. This meant being incarcerated for a month and writing an operatic scene on a given text. He couldn't afford the 20 francs for renting a piano, but to buy his meals he pawned the gold watch he'd been given at his first communion. Not the last time he would use the church and its appurtenancies for his own operatic ends ...

He spent two years in Rome, then it was back to Paris and the drudgery of giving piano lessons to make ends meet. There were, he said, only three phrases you needed when giving a lesson:

'Bonjour, Mademoiselle!'
Then, in the course of the lesson:
'A touch slower, if you would.'
And finally, when it was all over:
'My respects, I beg of you, to Madame your mother.'

Cynicism? Self-protection? Whatever you call it, it obviously did the trick. And it was this seemingly innate ability to manage the trials of life that gave ammunition to Massenet's rivals. When he won the Prix de Rome in 1863, a newspaper columnist encouraged him by saying:

> The winners of this competition no longer have to wait five or six years to have their works played. It's no longer mandatory, as it used to be until not so long ago, for them to have grey hair and to have lost several teeth before being grudgingly commissioned to write a one-act opera with just three characters and no chorus.

A nice thought, but not the truth: which was that breaking into the opera circuit for a composer was just as tough as it had always been – unless your name was Jules Massenet. As early as 1867, just a year after returning to Paris, he managed to have his one-acter *La Grand' Tante* played at the Opéra-Comique; then he progressed over the next decade, through a four-act opera with spoken dialogue, to a full scale, five-act opera, *Le Roi de Lahore*, for which the costumes alone cost 200,000 francs. It played 30 times at the Opéra in 1877, 11 times the year after, and 17 times the year after that; within five years it had been given in Turin, Budapest, Munich, London, Buenos Aires, Rio de Janeiro, St Petersburg etc ... Massenet had arrived.

But it was his next opera, *Hérodiade*, that established the pattern of his production. Of his 25 completed operas, no fewer than 11 are called by a woman's name: Hérodias, Manon, Esclarmonde, Thaïs, Manon again, Sapho, Cinderella, Grisélidis, Ariadne, Thérèse and Cleopatra. It's almost as if the women downplayed in his memoirs are having their revenge. In a newspaper article in 1901, Debussy had things to say about Massenet and the 'eternal feminine':

> Does there not exist a kind of mysterious, tyrannical destiny that explains M. Massenet's interest in finding, within music, documents to illuminate the history of the female soul? The smile of Manon in her crinoline is born again upon the lips of the modern Sapho, with the similar intention of reducing men to tears! And the knife of the Navarraise reappears as the pistol innocently delivered by Charlotte in *Werther*.
>
> Meanwhile we know to what extent this music is shaken by shudders, by outbursts, by embraces that tend towards eternity. The harmonies are like arms, the tunes like the napes of women's necks; we gaze ever more closely at these women's foreheads to try and find out at any cost what is going on behind them ...

Hence the unkind description of Massenet himself as 'la fille de Gounod' – a Gounod in petticoats. And here we touch on a further reason why people distrusted Massenet and what he stood for. The Parisians of the 1870s and 80s were still marked by the horrors of the Franco-Prussian War and the Commune, and by the apparent lack of manliness these disasters had demonstrated in the French nation. Poor old Offenbach was blamed for seducing audiences with his levity and satire from a rightful regard for order and hierarchy; Massenet, with his propensity to 'chercher la femme', and despite his stint in the National Guard during the war, was a similarly tempting target. Not only that, there's a streak of self-indulgence running through his operas that has always offended certain sections of society. And not only in his operas. For Christmas 1877, after the success of *Le Roi de Lahore*, the publisher Ricordi sent the composer a food parcel including a superb Gorgonzola cheese. Massenet wrote back:

> I kneel before it! And only after our friend Hartmann shed tears did I allow him to have a little piece. The nougat is enough to turn a hermit into a gourmet.

His fellow composers were quite outspoken about him in their letters. Bizet, for example:

> This man Massenet is so terribly devious, and I fear him like mendacity itself.

Not without reason. At a festival in 1878, Massenet, Gounod and Saint-Saëns all conducted their own works. Without telling the other two, Massenet brought in some extra brass so that the excerpts from *Le Roi de Lahore* would come off with extra éclat – never mind what that did to the balance in Gounod's and Saint-Saëns's pieces! As Edouard Lalo wrote:

> Massenet is the winner in these concerts, for which 15,000 people are all squashed together. I'm not hawking any wares on this patch, where Saint-Saëns and even Gounod have been driven from the field by Massenet – the ladies' darling.

So there's another reason ... No one ever denied the power of Massenet's charm, even while their intellect rebelled against it. Photographs show us a man of regular features with a rather gentle look in the eye – which might have been deceptive. A description published in a newspaper at the time of his 50th birthday gives us more precise details:

> Height: 5ft 7 ins. Hair: black, somewhat sparse. Moustache: black, delicate. Forehead: broad. Eyes: dark chestnut. Nose: strong. Lips: thin. Is married; has a daughter who can't stand music. Lunches simply, always the same menu: eggs, cutlets, beefsteak with potatoes; drinks Burgundy, prefers the Romanet, which helps him forget unpleasant letters. Doesn't often go out in the evening. Doesn't smoke (or not much). Ambroise Thomas and Gounod are his patron saints – not to be discussed.

What this description doesn't tell us is that Massenet was a fanatical worker, for whom a 14-hour day was nothing unusual. Saint-Saëns recalled how Massenet would refuse to see visitors, whoever they were, before he'd finished his day's labour. He also taught composition at the Paris Conservatoire from 1878 until 1896 (his classes met on Tuesdays and Fridays at half-past one). 1882 was a bumper year for his students, with three of them, including Gabriel Pierné, taking the top places in the Prix de Rome competition, so it looks as though he was an effective teacher. But it depends what you think a Conservatoire education is for. Paul Dukas, who later taught composition at the Paris Conservatoire in the 1920s and 30s, had this to say of Ernest Chausson's brief spell as a Massenet pupil:

> At the Conservatoire he realized the tawdry and fragile nature of an education that holds out, as the goal of an artist's efforts, the promise of awards, from the medal of honour to the seat in the Institut, by way of the Prix de Rome. It's true that Chausson was a man of independent means, so perhaps there was no great merit in turning his back on the material advantages these honours would bring, but the mere fact that he abandoned Massenet for the severe education that César Franck gave to his pupils, was indication enough of the high ideals behind his vocation.

But of all the rivalries to which Massenet was subject, one surpassed all others. Saint-Saëns felt (and freely expressed his feeling) that some at least of Massenet's success should have come his way, especially as regards performances of his operas. One story says it all. A journalist is said to have asked Saint-Saëns his opinion of Massenet: 'all sugar and water' was the reply. He then asked Massenet his opinion of Saint-Saëns: 'A great master, the pride of France', responded Massenet. The journalist then told Massenet what Saint-Saëns had said about him, to which Massenet replied: 'Not to worry, my friend, perhaps we're both mistaken.' One can see why the gentle look in Massenet's eye might have been deceptive.

Finally, though, to the high ideals which, if we're to believe Paul Dukas, were so signally absent from Massenet's teaching, as compared with César Franck's. Here we may well ask ourselves, 'Do we go to the opera to satisfy our high ideals?' *Parsifal*, maybe. But overall, perhaps not. Chausson was quite right to realize that Massenet's teaching was not for him – but that doesn't mean his teaching was valueless for every student, still less that Massenet's operas are to be blamed for their self-indulgence. Going to the opera could itself be deemed a self-indulgent activity; and certainly was in late 19th-century Paris, where you went not only to see, but to *be* seen. The plain truth is that Massenet was the consummate professional, giving audiences what they wanted, with just enough variety in the mix to keep the appetite fresh. The distinguished French conductor Georges Prêtre, who directed most of the Massenet operas in his time, said he was always struck by how each of these operas has its own distinctive orchestral colouring.

Debussy, as usual, put his finger on the nub of the 'Massenet problem', in the obituary tribute he wrote for the composer in the summer of 1912:

> Massenet was the most truly loved of contemporary composers. His colleagues found it hard to forgive his power to please, which is essentially a gift. Certainly this gift is not indispensable, especially in art, and it's fair to say that J S Bach, to name but one, did not 'please' in the sense we use the word when we talk about Massenet. Have we ever heard tell of young shopgirls humming the *Matthew Passion*? I think not. Whereas everyone knows they wake up in the morning singing *Manon* or *Werther*. Let's make no mistake, that's a charming kind of fame which will be a cause of secret envy to more than one of those fine purists whose hearts are warmed only by the somewhat forced respect of little coteries.

A particularly long, sharp lance is here deployed to introduce Emmanuel Chabrier, of all 19th-century French composers still, for many lovers of his music, the most unfairly neglected. His most serious crime as a composer was almost entirely to ignore pain and suffering which, according to the lights of the last century and more, are of course the proper concerns of all true artists. Instead, Chabrier relished fun and laughter, as well as love and the natural world. Surely the 21st century needs to restore the balance and embrace his music in all its life-affirming glory?

9 SELECTED LETTERS OF CHABRIER

The translations are of letters published in Joseph Desaymard, *Chabrier d'après ses lettres,* Paris, Fernand Roches, 1934. The translations and endnotes are mine.

(i) To his publisher Costallat, Wimereux, 17 July 1887:

… It's obvious that for these young masters I'm old hat, antediluvian hat, and so is Lalo, and even Franck too. I'll go further and say that in my opinion they feel Wagner to be basically threadbare. As for me, my chief preoccupation is to do what I like, with the particular aim of giving my personality free rein; my secondary one is not to be boring. *They all write the same music*; it can be signed X or Y, it doesn't matter; it comes from the same stable. It's music full of pretentions but empty of content. And then, in this field, one can easily be out of date within ten years. Bruneau and Marty[1] will be old hat in their turn; don't you worry, there are bound to be young intellectuals somewhere who are busy oldhatting them. Meanwhile, the opening F major chorus of *Oberon*[2], which I heard yesterday played more or less well by a municipal orchestra in Boulogne, is simply and straightforwardly eternal; no one's ever going to oldhat that.

All in all, it's particularly the *form* of opera librettos that's aged; ever since Meyerbeer it's the same old libretto – we're irritated, we want to find something else; on the other hand a musical conversation going on for four acts, of the sort some people are demanding today, guarantees a monotony to drive one to despair. You have three characters; each of them has his characteristic motif: get on with it, then! *With three motifs* developed symphonically you can write your work. That's what they want. Fine by me; I can do it; no doubt *the unity* of the work benefits. It's an entity. But it's also to the detriment of variety, of rhythm, of a thousand forms which can be filled out by the sublime art of music and which nowadays are happily ignored.

Berlioz, who was a Frenchman before anything else (no old hat he in his time!), what variety, colour and rhythm *he* put into *La Damnation, Roméo, l'Enfance du Christ!* They lack unity, someone will tell us! To which I say, crap! If, in order to be *one*, it is necessary to be boring, I prefer to be 2, 3, 4, 10, 20, – that is, I prefer to have ten colours on my palette and grind all the pigments up together. And for that I don't necessarily want to go everlastingly over old ground: Act I an act setting up the plot; Act II full of silly women, with vocalises for queens; Act III act with ballet and the inevitable finale which reshuffles the cards; Act IV love duet *de rigueur*, Act V the rumpus at 20 minutes to midnight, muskets crackling, Jews boiling, principal singers dying.

Under the pretext of unity (I was going to say 'uniformity') there are in Wagner, who is a stronger talent than our old friend Bruno[3], fifteen-minute stretches of music or *unalloyed recitative* in which any honest human being who has no axe to grind and is not in thrall to fetishism must find every minute as long as a century. And I'll prove it, *score in hand*, whenever you like. And no one gives a damn! They're joins, as under the old regime, to get to passages that are more interesting, though they aren't always. But I want my music to be beautiful *all the way through*, and the beautiful takes 36 forms; if one is allowed only pearl or grey or canary yellow with one's nuances, that's not good enough for me, and if you go beyond the cheap catalogue there are 300 nuances in pearl grey alone. A little red, for God's sake! Down with the niminy-piminy! Never the same shade! Variety, form, life above all and *naivety* if possible – that's the hardest. What could I possibly do to astonish the audience? That's the enemy. Yes, the audience is astonished, certainly; but that way they're only astonished once; you don't catch them second time round.

... I know *The Tempest* off by heart, and there's a lot there, but Blau[4] is right to want to develop the love interest, otherwise papa Prospero would become a bore; as for the *drama* proper, where is it? Is it really dramatic, the conspiracies of those old fogeys Alonso, Antonio, Gonzalo, Stefano, and those two scoundrels Caliban and Trinculo? How tired do we get of their wanderings all over the island?

So we'll have to sharpen up the action on that front. But that leaves (a) the Ferdinand-Miranda idyll, the first colour; (b) the whole wedding bit, sprites etc in Act 4; (c) and even a jokey section with all the drunkards. – Is that enough to make an opera? We'll see. The first scene at sea is a nuisance: it's the *Flying Dutchman* overture which, unfortunately, is not by me! That's a horror to redo. Storms and shipwrecks, grrr! After Beethoven and Wagner, re-grrr! – Let's think about it!

[1] Alfred Bruneau (1857–1934) and Georges Marty (1860–1908).
[2] The opera by Weber, premiered in 1826.
[3] Alias Bruneau ...
[4] Alfred Blau (1827–1896), the librettist of Reyer's *Sigurd* and later of Massenet's *Esclarmonde* was suggesting this opera on *The Tempest*.

(ii) To the German conductor Felix Mottl, Tours, 1 December 1887. Mottl was planning performances of Chabrier's *Gwendoline* at Karlsruhe.

... Thank you for having such a kind thought. Between now and March I'll try and learn some German words apart from *langsam, schnell, ausdruckwoll* [sic], *lebhaft* and so on.

I'll manage, I hope, to speak finally a sort of jungle German which will make everyone laugh but save me from embarrassment. I trust that in the midst of my final rehearsals I'll be able to undergo, in the theatre, a reviving bath in the shape of *The Ring* ... If it would be possible to slip in a powerful, moth-proof score called *Tristan*, that would put Chabrier in seventh heaven! Let me know as soon as you can and I'll be bursting with impatience all winter.

Obviously I love it, my poor, dear Paris – it's my duty, after all! – but here we have just two theatres, one for *La Juive*, the other for *Haydée*[1]; sadly, it's not enough and these two theatres swallow up 1,300,000 francs in subsidy! Every now and then, as a bone to gnaw, some poor devil of a composer is given two acts of a ballet to write, and again this year it's papa Thomas[2] who's done it. Ah! It's no joke! As for earning a basic living, it's impossible unless you turn to operetta where, after a decade, you can retire with a fortune. But anyone who dreams of the lyric drama, unless he has a private income, can go whistle: quite simply, he starves. One has to be made of tough stuff to go along that road.

But I have courage and, more than that, this year, thanks to you, *encouragement*. My efforts won't have been in vain since you've accepted my dear little score, which is felt to be *rebarbative* and *confused* in my dear fatherland where music is not enough loved – not enough *thought about.*

We have, together with our virtues – every nation has its own, to be sure – the great vice of gazing too complacently at our own navel and being too easily satisfied. But, if anyone has the right to declare himself satisfied, it's me, and I proclaim it loudly and thank you from the bottom of my heart.

Your very devoted and grateful, Emmanuel Chabrier

[1] The Opéra for grand operas such as Halévy's *La Juive*, the Opéra-Comique for less taxing fare such as Auber's *Haydée*
[2] *Ambroise Thomas*

(iii) To his friend the tenor Ernest van Dyck, 9 January 1889

... it's possible to produce great *comic* art and great *tragic* art; *The Mastersingers* or *Tristan*. But it's generally accepted that *great* art must be tragic. – and if *Mastersingers* didn't exist, I'd be hard put to it to cite a single COMIC work whose make-up is treated as seriously as any old grand opera. Beckmesser is as much a creation of genius as any other *grand* character in the Wagnerian repertory, and laughter is as important as tears. Laughter and tears, that's all there is; Wagner wanted to have a good laugh and he's certainly succeeded in this absolutely extraordinary work which I know from one end to the other, almost by heart, both words and music.

(iv) To his nurse Nanine, La Membrolle, 20 June 1890, on a multiple country wedding:

So on a Tuesday morning off we went to the Mass for the local weddings. The line of people snaked right through the village, with top hats dating from the reign of Louis-Philippe crammed down on the skulls of ghastly old men wearing waistcoats, and blue jackets over the top.

The brides were in white, naturally, with orange blossom which, as I write, is no doubt wilting under a glass cover on some chest of drawers between a pair of brass candlesticks. Mass was said by a priest they knew, a fat individual who looked to be no enemy to a glass of white wine. Two fine fellows stood up next to the harmonium and howled in such a way that everyone started to giggle; even the priest, who burst into fits of laughter and simply couldn't stop. In the end, they had to hold on to his head and slosh water over it, as he'd gone completely purple.

After lunch, about four in the afternoon, a charabanc turned up, on hire from Tours, and, with the happy couples and all the bridesmaids and the best men and the page boys on board, went round the houses dishing out pieces of the blessed bread. We got ours, of course, smelling of vermouth. The whole crew were all piled in together, and the carriage was crawling along on its belly. But they make a tough sort of toper round these parts, and nobody got any bones broken.

In the evening, the grand ball. But as it didn't start till 11pm, and I've never stayed up as late as that in my life, I went to bed peacefully on the dot of 9, as usual. I gather everyone had a marvellous time, which is the main thing.

(v) To his teenage son Marcel, 26 June 1890:

I know the English lady you met on the top deck of the tram. She's the Queen of England. She often travels incognita like that and, as she comes of a noble family, she has very delicate feet, which won't have escaped an observer of your metal. But the Queen of England isn't the only person who rides on the top decks of trams, so I would ask you, please, not to strike up conversations with people you don't know.

(vi) To Vincent d'Indy, [Paris] 30 March 1894; Chabrier's penultimate letter. Sadly, d'Indy found the remains of Chabrier's opera *Briséis* too sketchy for him to complete:

My dear Vincent,

Before I leave, I should very much like to have a serious, thorough talk with you about *Briséis*. The work could be completed quite easily, thanks to the musical sketches I've put to one side and which I was planning to use. I shall pass them on to you, only you. We can share the rights equally between us. From my very first work on this opera I dedicated it to Madame Chabrier.

Affectionately yours, Emmanuel Chabrier

Keep this letter. Don't lose it, please.

10 HEAP, HEAP, HURRAH!

The verve and intelligence of Chabrier and his music

A review for the TLS of the letters of Chabrier in:
Correspondance, edited by Roger Delage and Frans Durif with Thierry Bodin, 1,262pp. Paris, Klincksieck, 1994.

'Have you noticed how hermaphroditism is on the way out these days; I was saying so to the police sergeant on my walk only this morning, and naturally the sergeant agreed with me.' No, not Python or Spike or Beachcomber, but the forty-two-year-old Emmanuel Chabrier working his way obliquely and impatiently towards yet another litany on that favourite subject of the composer's lot not being a happy one.

Those who know Chabrier only as the author of *España* may be surprised to learn that he was subject to anything as elevated as unhappiness – surely the 509 bars of what he called 'merely a piece in F major' represent the ultimate in nineteenth-century musical hedonism? This is a reasonable, if unprovable claim, but the sad truth is that in many ways the explosion of *España* on the Parisian musical scene on November 4, 1883, was a highpoint that Chabrier was never to reach again, at least in that city. Explosions can be fun, but they can also upset people and give them the wrong idea about your aims in life.

Incomprehension settled around Chabrier all the more easily because he was Not One Of Us.

To begin with, he came from the Auvergne, traditionally useful in providing Parisians with cheese, cabbage and men to mend the boiler. Added to that, he never studied at the Paris Conservatoire or even at a lesser institution such as the Ecole Niedermeyer. What right had such a man to try and foist his music-dramas on the Paris Opéra, when winners of the Prix de Rome had been waiting twenty years and more for the *entrée* which was theirs by law? And as always there were the pigeon-holers – active in every society and no less so in Paris – to imply that a man capable of running up a brilliant Spanish rhapsody was, *ipso facto,* capable of no more than that.

But a third reason, not to be ignored, was that Chabrier liked to shock. Back home in Ambert he had already as a boy been classed as a *foutraud*, reacting possibly against a long line of lawyers and judges who distinguished the family name. Paris had the advantage of possessing a bourgeoisie (and indeed an *aristocratie*, though they were less predictable) who were even more delightfully shockable than their Auvergnat counterparts. For Chabrier to lament the passing of hermaphroditism was, among other things, disingenuous. He was well aware of the difference between men and women and, as hinted above, acted on this knowledge all his life. There is indeed a terrifying artistic rightness about his death from syphilis at the age of only fifty-three. But the sympathy one feels for anyone who went through his sufferings, with the false hopes, the bizarre, unpredictable symptoms, the remissions and the final paralysis the disease brings with it, can only be deepened by reading these letters, because he was so open about it all. And funny. From San Sebastián in 1882, during his Spanish trip to collect material for *España*, he wrote home to his publishers:

> The women are pretty, the men fine figures, and on the beach the señoras with lovely throats often forget to close up their costumes thoroughly; from now on I shall bring buttons with me and thread. To be of service is my passion.

Not surprisingly, sex came into his music too. His description of the *raison d'être* of the 'fête polonaise' in his opera *Le Roi malgré lui* leaves us in no doubt about the staging he would have liked, had the censor permitted, and as recently as 1994 the part dealing with peacock feathers had to be omitted as likely to cause a breach of the peace among listeners to BBC Radio 3.

But if Chabrier had only been, in Joseph Kerman's famous phrase, 'a shabby little shocker', there would be no reason to remember him. As it is, the extension of his *oeuvre* beyond *España* soon makes clear that he was far, far more than that. The letters in this volume show him to have been both a very hard worker and a very hard thinker, whose ideas often strike home as astonishingly modern. On the operatic front, for instance he had ideas about costumes:

> It's depressing to see choruses of drinkers always dressed the same, a married man always the same, with a tricoloured ribbon in his hat and a coat collar that slides up his neck etc. etc. Enough of all

that. I don't see why they can't sing in overalls, in jerseys, in evening dress, in suits.

In a letter of 1882, he ends seven consecutive paragraphs with the phrase *nous en recauserons* (we'll talk again about this), anticipating by over 40 years Satie's article 'Recoins de ma vie' with its similar recurring coda of *je reviendrai sur ce sujet* (I'll come back to this subject) – a hit against sloppily organised writers and lecturers by two artists for whom structure was of the essence. Elsewhere, Chabrier says he prefers musicians to read his opera *Gwendoline* in full score, rather than hacking through the vocal score at the piano, indicating that, even if orchestration was still something he did after sorting out the basic notes, he was already moving towards the Modernist position of regarding orchestration as integral to the piece. Eloquent testimony to this comes from André Messager, who wanted help orchestrating his opera *Isoline*, but refused to ask his friend Chabrier, saying, *Non, il en mettrait trop* (No, he'll put too much in it). On less technical fronts, further modern notes are struck by Chabrier's laments over the short attention-span of contemporary audiences and by his preference for singers 'with large eyes and large teeth'.

As for Chabrier the worker, the size of the volume under review is evidence on its own. Once he had a pen in his hand, the thoughts flowed with apparent ease and assurance. His letters were greatly prized by his friends and I don't imagine his publisher Enoch ever seriously considered obeying his request to destroy all his correspondence, on grounds that its many indiscreet remarks might one day cause embarrassment. But, like his musical language, that of his letters is a curious mixture of the outrageous and the correct. His wife and elder son both get further raps over the knuckles for committing grammatical mistakes, and it is no exaggeration to say that he regarded a missed or faultily formed subjunctive as a threat to the family name; in the same way that the clothes they wore for a holiday at their house in the Touraine had to be clean and decent, without being expensive or making any bow in the direction of fashion.

It has been the custom to call Chabrier 'un indépendant'. In our own time, the title has been given to other French composers such as Ohana and Dutilleux, but Dutilleux, certainly, regards it as a meaningless description by which the user hopes to be absolved from further thought. All artists are to some extent independent, and to some extent dependent. The interesting part comes in seeing how the two are or are not brought together into a workable synthesis. In Chabrier's case, the synthesis was at best incomplete and sporadic and at worst non-existent.

One of his closest friends made the telling remark, in a letter to a mutual acquaintance, that Chabrier's fame in the mid-1880s, such as it was, was due as much to his brilliant personality as to his music. I can only hope Chabrier never got to hear of this, because I cannot think of any observation that would have given him greater pain. One thing that tends to be forgotten is that, behind the jokes, the brilliant orchestration and the wonderful tunes, Chabrier was extremely intelligent. He knew the strength and cohesion of the Parisian musical establishment. He knew being a *foutraud* was not a sufficient condition for entry. He knew, and admitted in a letter towards the end of his life, that there were some areas of technical craft that he should have learnt when he was young and in which he would now never be adept. The only solution he saw was unremitting work (an interview reported that he got up at 4:30 am, about the time that Delibes was going to bed), allied to an unsleeping artistic conscience. Together, these would produce the masterpieces that would force the powers of dynamic conservatism to take notice of this fat, balding, middle aged Auvergnat. And perhaps, who knows, even to re-examine their own artistic criteria?

Understandably, to aid him in this quest, Chabrier liked to summon up the spirits of the past. No mention of Haydn and not many of Mozart (after *The Magic Flute* in Leipzig, '3 hrs du divin Mozart', he needed a few beers to get back to normal), but a sustaining belief in the genius of Bach, Beethoven and Wagner, the three of them being quoted together as a kind of triple icon. Interestingly, no particular work of either Bach or Beethoven is touched on in these letters: they remain iconic. Wagner, however lived through his individual operas: *Tristan*, which persuaded Chabrier he had to give up his job as a civil servant and compose full time; *Die Meistersinger*, which proved that a comedy could also be a work of genius; and most of all, *Parsifal* – 'la plus intense émotion de toute ma vie', he wrote, after seeing it at Bayreuth in 1889.

Eight years earlier, he had written, 'Wagner has killed me'. In the intervening period, he had worked hard at coming to terms with Wagner and, although there is still a debate about the extent to which his opera *Gwendoline*, in particular, is indebted to the old master, he himself felt he had won through. Two other influences had helped. First, Berlioz, whose conspicuous clashes with the powers-that-be were prophetic of Chabrier's own, lower-key encounters, and whose way with the orchestra Chabrier admired and learnt from. And second, and more surprisingly, Auber, who is mentioned twice with approval for his sensitivity to the French language: 'Auber's glory will never perish because he was always the slave of the text and *at one with the words*.' The phrase 'esclave du texte' recalls not so much Wagner as Debussy, who was to start work on *Pelléas* some 18 months after that letter.

Debussy gets a single mention in the letter of June 1889, and not a very flattering one, being lumped together with men like Chausson and Bréville who had composed 'music that's recherché and ingenious, but rather tormented, often sad, weepy, discontented, to the point that when it's sung in the salons, the singer seems either to be in league with the devil or else giving the audience the last sacraments'.

Chabrier himself prefers to produce something more cheerful, while maintaining (rightly, I suspect) that fast, jolly music is harder to bring off than evocations of 'a blubbing March, a slobbering April, a May that's biliously phlegmatic'. Further unkind words are reserved for the 'petite ordure' named *Cavalleria rusticana*, and for pretty well anything by Massenet. In 1885, he wrote to his friend the operetta composer Charles Lecocq, about Massenet's latest offering:

> The place of head of the French school is still vacant – even after [Massenet's] *Le Cid*, not to say especially after. I'm going to see that piece because of the orchestration of the ballet, which will undoubtedly be ravishing – but that's got nothing to do with the question of art.

Like Berlioz, Chabrier had more success abroad than at home. His letters from Germany are some of the most moving and heartwarming in the volume, as he comes to realise that German audiences, conductors and performers really love his music and respond to his blend of meticulousness and enthusiasm. They provide a happy contrast with the increasing evidence of his failing health, especially in the desperate letters about his two sons who never came near to reaching the ideal he had set for them. As his temper shortened, the youngest son became a *crétin ... menteur, paresseux* (cretin ... liar, sluggard), while he saw that in his own home he was regarded as *sévère, embêtant* (severe, tiresome). A similar contrast exists between the regrets we may feel over the works-that-might-have-been (a violin concerto, an opera on *The Tempest*, not to mention a 'Valse des veaux' and 'Les jeunes pintades' to go with the farmyard songs), and the fascinating details of how an opera such as *Le Roi malgré lui* was put together – and not least to marvel that such a quantity of thought should have produced such an impossible libretto. But as Chabrier said, he was always for variety over unity. Here, he and his librettists simply went too far.

Not only is there barely a single dull page in the whole of this large book, but its preparation and production have been exemplary. Frans Durif died sometime before it was finished, leaving Roger Delage with a mountain of final editing, not only of the letters themselves, but of the copious editorial notes, and of replies from friends, such as Charles Lecocq and Paul Lacôme, which often provide an invaluable context for Chabrier's highly personal view of the world. All of this Dr Delage has accomplished with an accuracy and attention to detail that demand a more extravagant epithet than the English language can command. I think 'éblouissant' would do. For that same reason, any English translator of these letters will have a hard time. But I hope and believe that resistance cannot hold out for long. In short, as Chabrier wrote, congratulating a friend on his daughter's wedding, 'Heap, heap, hurrah!'

And here's more on Chabrier ...

11 **THE ANGEL OF LAUGHTER**

Imagine you are the Princesse de Polignac in late 19th-century Paris, intent on an excellent dinner provided by your hosts. Your neighbour, a rotund gentleman of middle age, kindly passes you the asparagus — but accompanies it by saying, 'Have some of this, Madame but, I warn you, it does terrible things to your urine'. Do you exclaim in horror? Go purple in the face? Retire to a fit of the vapours on the *chaise longue*? The Princess seems to have accepted the advice, before duly inscribing it in the fund of upper-class gossip. It testifies at least that whatever was lacking in Emmanuel Chabrier — the gent in question — he had charm in abundance.

As does his music. In the words of Francis Poulenc, one of his most devoted admirers, 'Chabrier, I love him like a father! A generous father, always cheerful, with his pockets full of succulent goodies. His music consoles me through my darkest days'. And Chabrier did have need of this charm, because life would not be entirely kind to him. For a start, he was born in 1841 at Ambert in the Auvergne. As he said, 'In my part of the world there are either oafs, good at best for carrying buckets of water, or people with brains ... I made my choice'. When he was 12 the family moved to Clermont-Ferrand, and three years later to Paris, Papa clearly appreciating the talents, both musical and scholastic, of his only child, who then followed his lawyer father's footsteps. In 1863 – huzzahs all round – he became a clerk in the Home Office, where he would remain until 1880.

Here for the first time we come across the dichotomy in Chabrier's life between what the poet Apollinaire would later identify as 'order' and 'adventure'. The civil service represented order in a fairly extreme form, to which Chabrier's contributions were highly valued (his elegant, curly-wurly handwriting is still a pleasure to read). At the same time he was following up the polite little songs and piano pieces of his youth with more extravagant items such as *Bouffonnerie* (Joke) for piccolo, trombone, triangle, side drum, bass drum and cymbals, eight bars beginning the folk song 'J'ai du bon tabac' on the trombone; perhaps this was one of the pieces played to great acclaim at a meeting in 1860 of a group called the *Incompris* (The Misunderstood), of which he was a founder member? Likewise 'adventurous' were two comic operas to words by the up-and-coming poet Paul Verlaine, though no performances at the time are known. But the first work of his to make any kind of splash was another comic opera *L'Étoile*, performed to delighted audiences in 1877 and still very much alive today. We may note that the 15-year-old Debussy was thrown out of the theatre for laughing immoderately at the spoof Italian aria in praise of green Chartreuse. But after 48 performances the director closed the run. Was one of the singers ill? Or was it that, after 50 performances, Chabrier and his librettists were contracted to earn a lot more, and the director a lot less?

The 1880s began unhappily for Chabrier with serious liver problems, necessitating a visit to a spa, but more happily with one to Munich to see *Tristan and Isolde*. Two friends, Vincent d'Indy and Henri Duparc, later recalled the encounter. In the silence before the start of the opera there were sounds of sobbing. It was Chabrier. 'Are you all right?' asked his neighbour. 'Ten years of my life', replied Chabrier, 'I've been waiting to hear this A on the cellos!' Duparc remembered that 'he left us after the performance to go and shut himself up alone in his bedroom. At that time he wasn't thinking of devoting himself to music. *Tristan* revealed to him his vocation; on his return from Munich his decision was made'. Health problems also entered into this, and luckily there was a certain amount of family money to help out.

Wagner was to loom large through the last decade and a half of Chabrier's life, adding him to the list of French composers, most notably Debussy and Chausson, who struggled against the anxiety of the German master's influence. This could be interpreted as 'adventure' on the structural and harmonic fronts, but at the same time as 'order' in that it was billed as 'the music of the future' which only obstinate outliers could deny. Chabrier in any case did find a new source of 'adventure' in 1882 by taking his wife and two young sons to Spain. Letters to his publishers, complete with music examples, tell of the impact: 'The gipsies singing their malagueñas or dancing the tango, and the manzanilla that goes from hand to hand and which everybody has to drink – those eyes, those flowers in the marvellous tresses, those scarves tied round the midriffs, those feet beating out a constantly changing rhythm ... ' etc. Altogether a long way from Isolde.

The result, of course, was *España*. Although Spaniards, including Albéniz and Falla, never liked it, for many of us it has always been the ultimate Spanish work. Duparc wrote that, whereas before the Spanish visit Chabrier had orchestrated like anyone else, in *España* he had made an astonishing stride towards a unique sound, and after it all his orchestral music was invented directly in terms of its medium, not as piano music that was then orchestrated. But his battles with Wagner were no more than postponed. From 1879 to 1885 he struggled with his opera *Gwendoline*, a blood and thunder work set in 8th-century Britain and his letters of the time lament at length about what Debussy called 'the ghost of old Klingsor'. But the work contains a lot that's unWagnerian, including quite a few passages built on plainsong modes. The love duet, although it starts with a few Wagnerian chords, soon melts into suave Gallicisms, with liberal helpings of Chabrier's idiosyncratic harmonic practice. Once again, bad luck dogged a Chabrier opera: after two performances in Brussels the director went bankrupt.

Chabrier's harmonic invention is even more evident in the opening to his next opera, *Le Roi malgré lui*, of which Ravel often said to Poulenc that 'it changed the orientation of French harmony', with the overture's strings of unresolved 9th chords. This time, after three performances at the Opéra-Comique, the theatre caught fire, causing many fatalities. But Chabrier was now winning friends in Germany and here his operas had better luck – not always reciprocated by the composer as when, on a visit to Wagner's widow, he was presented with a sugary cake. 'Ugh!' said he under his breath, 'revolting', and in an unseen moment slipped it into a drawer with all the Master's shirts.

Then there is the piano music ... and the songs. Underperformed masterpieces still lie in wait for the discerning musician, such as the piano piece 'Idylle' which for Poulenc was the 'first kiss of love' that turned him into a composer; or 'Sous bois' which for Ravel was one of his greatest pieces. Among the songs, 'L'Ile heureuse' conjures up that dreamworld that Debussy was to explore later, while the four *Farmyard Songs* undoubtedly fed into Ravel's *Histoires naturelles*. Meanwhile piano duettists have the hilarious *Souvenirs of Munich: Quadrille on favourite themes from Tristan and Isolde*, and ambitious choirs can try *À la Musique*: Debussy, attending a rehearsal some time after Chabrier's death, asked for it to be repeated. 'Something wrong?' asked the conductor. 'No', said Debussy, 'it's so rarely done, I just wanted to hear it one more time'.

And then there are his letters. Sadly, no English edition exists (any millionaires reading this?). But, as the sample above may suggest, they are simply astonishing in their colour and wit.

To a musician, the title *Pelléas et Mélisande* may well immediately suggest Debussy. But he was not the first composer to be attracted by the play. Since the three following articles were written for scholarly journals, they are adorned with footnotes; I leave them as being possibly helpful towards further reading.

12 GABRIEL FAURÉ – *PELLÉAS ET MÉLISANDE*

Maeterlinck and *Pelléas* in Paris

Maurice Maeterlinck was born in Ghent in 1862 to rich, French-speaking parents. After studies at a Jesuit college, he completed his law studies at the University of Ghent in 1885. During that year, in which Victor Hugo's funeral signaled the end of an era, Maeterlinck spent a few months in Paris and was greatly influenced by the new Symbolist movement and in particular by Villiers de l'Isle Adam, whose play *Axël*, possibly to be identified as the earliest Symbolist drama, was serialized in various magazines between 1872 and 1886.

Maeterlinck's reputation was made overnight in August 1890 when the important critic Octave Mirbeau lavished praise on his first play, *La Princesse Maleine*. Thus encouraged, Maeterlinck wrote and published further plays over the next few years, the fifth of the series being *Pelléas et Mélisande*, published in 1892. All of them owe a debt to Arthurian legend and Celtic mysticism. In them:

> people with strange names, living in impossible places, where there are only woods and fountains, and towers by the sea-shore, and ancient castles, where there are no towns, and where the common crowd of the world is shut out of sight and hearing, move like quiet ghosts across the stage, mysterious to us and not less mysterious to one another.[1]

Pelléas et Mélisande was premiered at the Théâtre des Bouffes-Parisiens in a single matinée performance on 17 May 1893. Several wealthy sponsors, including Henri de Régnier, supplied funds and Tchaikovsky's friend the Princess Meshcherskaya donated the scenery. The producer was Lugné-Poe, the director of the Théâtre de l'Oeuvre, best known for his productions of Ibsen, who also played the part of Golaud. The costumes, based on portraits by Memling and the Pre-Raphaelite pictures of Walter Crane, were by Paul Vogler. The lighting was sombre, prompting Henry Fouquier, reviewing the work for *Le Figaro*, to note rather unkindly that 'the more obscure something is, the happier that makes the real Symbolists, who get irritated when people start understanding things!'[2] Among the audience, and no doubt understanding things perfectly well, were de Régnier, the painter Whistler, Debussy (who began his opera that autumn) and Mallarmé, whose review for the *National Observer* contained the observation, slightly awkward in view of later developments:

> it seems that there is enacted a superior variation on the admirable old melodrama. Almost silently and abstractly to the point that in this art, where everything becomes music in the real sense, even the addition of a single, pensive instrument such as a violin would be a pointless disservice.[3]

Mallarmé's view was no doubt reinforced by the fact that actual music in the production was confined to a setting of the short song 'Les trois soeurs aveugles', sung by Mélisande at her window at the beginning of Act III scene 2. The music was by a minor composer confusingly named Gabriel Fabre, a friend of Maeterlinck.

Pelléas in London

In March 1895 Lugné-Poe took the play, in its original French, to the Prince of Wales Theatre in London. Here it was seen by the famous English actress Mrs Patrick Campbell (born Beatrice Stella Cornwallis-West) who, contrary to Mallarmé, now envisaged a performance in English with incidental music. Word had apparently reached her that Debussy was already engaged in setting the play, and indeed he finished the first draft of his opera that August. She therefore asked him whether he would adapt his work to her intentions. But although friends such as Pierre Louÿs urged him to accept,[4] he was determined that his opera should be produced as he had written it and refused her offer. In the meantime, it would appear that she had almost certainly already commissioned, and undoubtedly read, an English translation. The author, the Oxford Classics don John William Mackail, was a fortunate find on more than one front. Not only was he the son-in-law of the painter Edward Burne-Jones, many of whose paintings in platinotype form hung on Maeterlinck's study walls, but his Classical expertise (he was a noted translator of Virgil's *Aeneid*, among many other things) showed to advantage in his version of *Pelléas*.

Two typescript copies of his unpublished text survive.[5] The earlier of the two includes the following words in Mackail's hand on the final page: 'Thus ends the play of Pelleas and Melisande, translated out of the French by John William Mackail and given by him to Beatrice Stella Campbell this fifteenth day of June 1895.' From this, written only two months after the Lugné-Poe performances, it would seem highly likely that the translation was the result of a commission from her. This copy is also accompanied by a loose sheet inscribed with a letter. Written from 27, Young Street, Kensington Square, and dated 9 Feb. 1898, it reads:

> Dearest Stella,
> My love & a thousand happinesses to you on your birthday: and I have nothing to give you but this: inside it you will find a setting forth of the scenes for Pelléas which amaze me by the fewness of their number.
> Ever your affectionate
> Jack.

It would seem that this letter refers not to his translation, but to a note (now lost) of the sets required for its first production in June 1898. The later typescript was used for the performances at the Lyceum Theatre, London in July 1911.

Pelléas and Fauré

We do not know whether Mrs Campbell tried to find another composer to replace Debussy during the period 1895–7. But the project remained very much in her mind, since she persuaded the famous actor Sir Johnston Forbes-Robertson to produce the work and to play the part of Golaud, while the young Martin Harvey agreed to play Pelléas. But she is guilty of some ingenuousness when she states in her autobiography that 'The incidental music needed was a most important element. I felt sure M. Gabriel Fauré was the composer needed.' [6] Not only had she wanted Debussy in the first place, but her meeting with Fauré and the resulting commission did not occur until March or early April 1898, a mere ten weeks or so before the premiere, again at the Prince of Wales Theatre.

During the 1890s Fauré's star was slowly rising. Even if his bid to become a professor of composition at the Conservatoire was vetoed by Ambroise Thomas in 1892, the following year he won the prix Chartier for his chamber music and the complete music of his *Requiem* was performed at the Madeleine, where he had been *maître de chapelle* since 1877. Then in 1896 he achieved a double success, being appointed organist of the Madeleine in June and in October succeeding Massenet as a professor of composition at the Conservatoire.

It is not clear on what evidence Mrs Campbell based her certainty that Fauré 'was the composer needed'. Two sets of his incidental music had been performed in Paris: for *Caligula*, a tragedy by Alexandre Dumas the elder first staged with Fauré's music at the Odéon on 6 November1888 and running for 34 performances; and for *Shylock*, an adaptation by Edmond Haraucourt of Shakespeare's *The Merchant of Venice*, staged at the Odéon on 17 December 1889 and running for 56 performances. But we do not know whether Mrs Campbell ever heard a note of these. More likely she based her choice on experiences of his chamber music and songs, which were increasingly heard in London during this decade. His First Piano Quartet and First Violin Sonata were played at the St James's Hall on 22 November 1894, and he himself took part in a Fauré Festival at the same venue in December 1896, which (on 10 December) included the Second Piano Quartet, two of the *Valses-Caprices*, and *Thème et variations*, played by Léon Delafosse, with a pendant (on 19 December) of the First Violin Sonata. The London publisher Metzler also brought out six Fauré songs in English translation in 1896 and a further dozen the following year, together with *Thème et variations,* the 6th *Barcarolle* and the *Dolly* suite.

One of the directors of the firm of Metzler was the lawyer Frederick Maddison who, with his wife Adela, became Fauré's friends and staunch supporters. Fauré was also greatly helped by Frank Schuster, from a wealthy Frankfurt banking family and a friend of Elgar's, and it was Schuster who invited Fauré to London at the end of March 1898 to meet Mrs Campbell at his house in Westminster, when she read through parts of Maeterlinck's original play to him. Her memoirs further record that:

> I stumbled through somehow, reading those parts of the play to M. Fauré which to me called most for music. Dear M. Fauré, how sympathetically he listened, and how humbly he said he would do his best!' [7]

Therefore, if she is to be believed, the choice and placing of musical numbers were hers.

Fauré returned to Paris on 7 April with an extremely busy few months ahead of him. Quite apart from his duties as organist of the Madeleine and Conservatoire professor (Ravel had joined his class that January), he had to make a tour of inspection of music schools in the Midi and compose not only two pieces (a test piece and a sight-reading piece) for the Conservatoire flute examinations in July, but now this incidental music for *Pelléas*, scheduled for performance on 21 June. From Aix-en-Provence around 25 April he wrote home to his wife:

> I'm no longer in touch with anything [that's happening in Paris]. All I know is that I'll have to get down to serious work on *Mélisande* when I'm back. I'll have barely a month and a half to write all this music. It's true, part of it's already there in this great brain of mine! [8]

Pelléas and Koechlin

Fauré's solution was to give his 'particelle' on three or four staves to his pupil Charles Koechlin to orchestrate, naturally under the composer's supervision. Koechlin had entered the Paris Conservatoire in October 1890 at the age of 22 as an 'auditeur' in the class of Antoine Taudou, graduating year by year to be a full pupil in Massenet's class in January 1894, and when Massenet resigned in 1896 he was inherited by the newly appointed Fauré. In 1898 Koechlin, now in his thirties, was beginning to make a reputation and most recently on 19 March his orchestral song *Promenade galante* had been performed at the prestigious Société nationale de musique, conducted by Edouard Colonne. Fauré may have been impressed with his talents as an orchestrator by this, or simply by his exercises in class. For his part, Koechlin had been seduced by Fauré's earlier incidental music, citing the 'Madrigal', 'Nocturne' and 'Sérénade' from *Shylock* and the choruses from *Caligula* as the 'sudden revelation of a charm that was novel, profound and pure'.[9] Their happy collaboration was concluded sometime around the end of the first week of June, when Fauré wrote to Koechlin:

Dear friend, I can't hope to pay you back for your time or for your excellent ideas! But please allow me to subscribe a little towards the cost of your rail ticket. I'm looking forward to our journey together and it is a pleasure for me, as a really *senior* composer, to offer this small contribution. Many thanks once again. Without you I'd never have made it! [10]

They travelled to London on 16 June. Koechlin returned to Paris on the 24th, but Fauré stayed on until at least the 26th, when Schuster threw a party for him at his sumptuous residence near Maidenhead called, with the typical English self-effacing humour of that time, 'The Hut', at which the guests included the famous painter John Singer Sargent, who drew two portraits of Fauré on that occasion. [11] Although Fauré is usually credited with conducting all of the nine matinee performances, the programme indicates that he did so only for the first, third and fourth afternoons. The nine performances took place on 21-24 and 27-30 June, and on 1 July. The other six performances were conducted by Landon Ronald, who had conducted at Covent Garden in 1894 and was now musical director of the Lyric Theatre.

Reactions to *Pelléas*

Unfortunately neither the set nor the costume designer is mentioned either in the programme or in the press reviews. But a letter from the poet Charles Van Lerberghe about the Berlin staging in January 1900 compared it unfavourably with that of the 1898 premiere, but was happier about

> that young man, handsome as Lord Wharton, and the wonderful Miss Campbell, both of them in costumes designed by Burne-Jones himself and surrounded by a décor of golds and liquid greens, so distant from us, immersed in legend, murmuring their sublime, childish words of love, almost without gestures, immobile, like figures in a primitive painting. [12]

Since Burne-Jones, as already mentioned, was Mackail's father-in-law, it is possible that the costumes were indeed designed by him. If so, they would probably have been his last work, since he died on 17 June, four days before the premiere.

Among the reviews, the only sour note was sounded by the critic of *The Times*, who found the music:

scarcely satisfactory, being wanting alike in charm and in dramatic power. It has, indeed, the vagueness of melodic and harmonious progression which may be held to suit best the character of the play, but its continued absence of tangible form, not to speak of its actual ugliness at any points, is such as to disturb rather than to assist the illusion of the scene. [13]

Elsewhere there was unbridled enthusiasm. In *The Athenaeum* the reviewer felt that 'The music of M. Gabriel Fauré constituted a distinct enhancement of delight' [14] and in *The Weekly Dispatch* 'The Tramp' went so far as to suggest that 'the magic of Tuesday's performance was due entirely to the amazing spirit of the acting harmonizing with the enervating atmosphere produced by M. Fauré's charming music and the *mise en scène*.' [15]

Maeterlinck was delighted with the production. He wrote to Campbell, 'In a few words, you, and the delightful, the ideal Pelléas, filled me with an emotion of beauty the most complete, the most harmonious, the sweetest that I have ever felt to this day'. [16] He seems never to have expressed an opinion about Fauré's music (not surprisingly, since he admitted to being tone-deaf) and in writing enthusiastically about the performance to Lugné-Poe he was chiefly concerned that, if the production came to Paris, it might clash with the version Albert Carré was preparing at the Opéra-Comique. From this it would seem that news of a possible production of Debussy's opera was going the rounds, even though Debussy had not as yet had any firm note of acceptance. [17] The nearest we have to Maeterlinck's views on the music may come from an interview given by his mistress Georgette Leblanc in 1910, when she referred to 'Fauré's delicate, beautiful score, with its wonderful, otherworldly atmosphere.' [18] For her, deference to the master in all artistic matters was the order of the day. Most importantly of all, Fauré was happy with his score and with the production. As he wrote from Paris to a friend in Wales, Mrs George Campbell Swinton, 'In London all is dreams and poetry: here, alas, all is work and prose.' [19]

Subsequent productions

Although Maeterlinck in his plays from around 1900 moved away from the Symbolist drama, *Pelléas et Mélisande* with Fauré's music was performed fairly often in Europe and America, at least until the First

World War. The following is a, certainly incomplete, list of performances after the initial run:

London, Lyceum Theatre, beginning 29 October 1898, five matinee performances; Campbell as Mélisande

Berlin, January 1900

London, Royalty Theatre, 28 June to 14 July 1900; Campbell as Mélisande, Harvey as Pelléas

Tour of British provinces, 1900; Campbell as Mélisande, Gerald du Maurier as Pelléas

Tour of USA, beginning 29 January 1902, Victoria Theater, New York; 12 April, Boston Theater; Campbell as Mélisande

London, Vaudeville Theatre, 1 July 1904; Campbell as Mélisande, Sarah Bernhardt as Pelléas (in French)

Tour of British provinces and Ireland, July 1905, 27 performances; Campbell as Mélisande, Bernhardt as Pelléas (in French)

St-Wandrille, Normandy, 29 August 1910; Georgette Leblanc as Mélisande, orchestra conducted by Albert Wolff

London, Lyceum Theatre, July 1911; Campbell as Mélisande, Harvey as Pelléas (Fauré's music adapted and expanded by W.H. Hudson)

Boston, Opera House, 30 January 1912; Leblanc as Mélisande, orchestra conducted by André Caplet (in French)

St-Wandrille, 22 August 1915, repeat of 1910 performance

Paris, Odéon, 10 February 1918, 14 performances; Association des concerts Monteux, conducted by Armand Ferté

Paris, Odéon, 1930; orchestra conducted by André Cadou, who composed a song for Mélisande and also inserted the 'Epithalame' and 'Nocturne' from Fauré's *Shylock* music

Paris, Odéon, January 1939, Renée Maeterlinck as Mélisande

[1] Arthur Symons, 'Annotations by the Way', *Plays, Acting and Music*, London, 1903, 77
[2] Henry Fouquier, *Le Figaro*, 18 May 1893: 'Plus c'est obscur, d'ailleurs, plus sont contents les purs symbolistes, qui se fâchent quand on comprend!'
[3] Mallarmé, 'Théâtre', *National Observer*, 1 July 1893: 'Il semble que soit jouée une variation supérieure sur l'admirable vieux mélodrame. Silencieusement presque et abstraitement au point que dans cet art, où tout devient musique dans le sens propre, la partie d'un instrument même pensif, violon, nuirait par inutilité.' (Mallarmé, *Oeuvres complètes*, ed H. Mondor and G. Jean-Aubry, Paris, Pléïade, 1945, 330)

[4] Louÿs to Debussy, 27 November 1895, Claude Debussy, *Correspondance*, ed. François Lesure and Denis Herlin, Gallimard, 2005, 1895-70

[5] (a) in the Enthoven Collection in the Theatre Museum, London, now housed in the Victoria and Albert Museum (b) in the Bibliothèque Royale de Belgique, Brussels, MS III 322

[6] *My Life and Some Letters*, London, Hutchinson, 1922, 127

[7] ibid.

[8] Gabriel Fauré, *Lettres intimes*, ed Philippe Fauré-Fremiet, Paris, La Colombe, 1951, 31-2: 'Je ne suis plus au courant de rien. Je sais seulement qu'il faudra piocher ferme pour la *Mélisande* dès mon retour. J'aurai un mois et demi à peine pour écrire toute cette musique. Il est vrai qu'il y en a une partie de faite dans ma grosse tête.'

[9] 'Souvenirs de Charles Koecklin [sic]', in *Cinquante Ans de musique française*, ed L. Rohozinski, Paris, Les Editions musicales de la Librairie de France, 1925, II, 389: 'Révélation subite d'un charme, nouveau, profond et pur.'

[10] quoted in Jean-Michel Nectoux, *Gabriel Fauré, Les Voix du clair-obscur*, Paris, Fayard, 2/2008, 213: 'Cher ami, je ne puis essayer de vous dédommager ni pour votre temps ni pour vos bonnes idées! Mais je vous demande la permission d'entrer pour une petite part dans vos frais de chemin à l'occasion de ce petit voyage qu'il me sera très agréable de faire avec vous. Faites-moi le véritable plaisir d'accepter cette très petite chose comme venant d'un *archi-aîné*! Et encore mille fois merci. Je n'aurais jamais été prêt sans vous!'

[11] These are reproduced as the cover of Emile Vuillermoz, *Gabriel Fauré*, Paris, Flammarion, 1960; and in Nectoux, op cit, plate 21

[12] Letter to Fernand Séverin of 22 January 1900, quoted in Nectoux, op cit, 214: 'ce jeune homme beau comme Lord Wharton et à cette merveilleuse Miss Campbell, vêtus tous deux par Burne-Jones lui-même, dans un décor d'or et de fondante émeraude, si loin de nous, si reculés dans la légende, et murmurant leurs sublimes et enfantines paroles d'amour, presque sans geste, presque immobiles, comme des figures de primitifs.'

[13] anon., 'Prince of Wales's Theatre,' *The Times*, 22 June 1898

[14] anon., 'Drama: The Week,' *The Athenaeum*, 25 June 1898

[15] anon. (The Tramp), '*Pelléas and Mélisande*: The Prince of Wales's,' *The Weekly Dispatch*, 26 June 1898

[16] Campbell, op. cit., 130

[17] Stadsarchief Gent B LXXII.6, quoted in Gillian Opstad, *Debussy's Mélisande, The Lives of Georgette Leblanc, Mary Garden and Maggie Teyte*, Woodbridge, The Boydell Press, 2009, 24

[18] Georges Bourdon, 'A Saint-Wandrille: Une réalisation de Pelléas et Mélisande,' *Le Figaro*, 12 August 1910

[19] Letter received by Mrs Swinton on 11 July 1898, quoted in Robert Orledge, *Gabriel Fauré*, London, Eulenburg, 1979, 17

The next nine articles all centre on Debussy, stemming from a dissertation on the composer begun in 1962 and never completed.

13 THE RECEPTION OF DEBUSSY'S MUSIC IN BRITAIN UP TO 1914

For nearly the first forty years of his life. Debussy had to make his way without support for his music from England or any other part of Great Britain. If he was worried by this, it can only be said that he kept remarkably quiet about it. We know of his interest in English literature (most notably, of course, Rossetti's 'Blessed Damozel'), but this interest doesn't seem to have extended to learning the language. As his stepdaughter Mme de Tinan told me, if he found an article in an English newspaper that he thought might be interesting, he would ask her to translate it for him. It's fair to say, I think, that he passed his eight visits to England between 1902 and 1914 in a fairly thick fog of incomprehension. More to the point, he was unable to do anything to promote his own music in the places where it mattered, and to a large extent it had to make its own way – even if, as we shall see, it had one or two champions whose names deserve to be remembered.

The first English notice of Debussy's music I have discovered comes in *The Musical Times* of 1 February 1901 – the month when Henry Wood daringly included the 'Prelude' and 'Angel's Farewell' from *The Dream of Gerontius* in one of his Queen's Hall programmes. Among the notices of foreign performances, British readers could find that 'at the Lamoureux concert, on the 6th January, two very effective orchestral *Nocturnes*, by Mr Debussey ... were much applauded novelties'. Just over a year later, *The Musical Times* had learnt to spell Debussy's name properly, but had to admit, in its issue of 1 June 1902, that 'the new lyrical drama *Pelléas et Mélisande* ... recently brought out at the Opera Comique, met with but a very qualified success'. This was the extent of Debussy's fame when he came over in 1902 with Mary Garden, and the following year when he reviewed the Covent Garden performance of *The Ring* for the journal Gil Blas.

By the December of 1903, the situation had changed very slightly. Debussy was no longer seen as an isolated phenomenon. 'M. Camille Chevillard announces his plans for the coming season of concerts ... The young French school: de Bréville, Busser, Erlanger, Debussy etc.' I'm not sure Debussy would have approved that order, but the notice ends 'also Strauss will figure on his programmes' – which might have made up for it.

In any case, the first landmark in the promulgation of Debussy's music in this country was just around the corner. In August 1895, the 26-year-old Henry Wood had directed his first season of Promenade Concerts at the Queen's Hall. From the first, he made it clear that his programmes would include a quantity of less familiar items and, in the words of *The Musical Times*,' it is gratifying to note that Jullien's British Army Quadrilles and vulgar effusions of every sort have been shelved.'[1]. So it was that on Saturday, 20 August 1904, Wood conducted the first British performance of the *Prélude à l'après-midi d'un faune* – one of two novelties of which, according to *The Musical Times*, 'neither proved very interesting'. The composer had, apparently, 'attracted much attention in Paris by his operas, notably Pelléas et Mélissande [sic], owing to the "advanced" character of the music'.[2]

Clearly *The Musical Times* critic had no pretensions himself to being advanced, a state generally regarded in English society with the deepest suspicion. And Henry Wood was wise enough to cater for the non-advanced (one would not wish to say 'retarded') who no doubt made up a large part of his audience. The programme for that concert on 20 August reads as follows:

Suite de ballet	Gluck-Mottl
Symphonic Dance in A	Grieg
'Divinités du Styx'	Gluck
'L'Après-Midi d'un Faune	Debussy
Symphony 1 organ/orchestra	Guilmant
Overture, Tannhäuser	Wagner
Funeral march of a Marionette	Gounod
'O tu, Palermo'	Verdi
Overture, Carnaval Romain	Berlioz
Largo in G	Handel
March, Pomp and Circumstance in D	Elgar

– and that was just Part I. We may well wonder whether an audience accustomed to such gargantuan offerings could possibly have appreciated *L'Après-midi* in the middle of it all; though certainly, whatever else the work was, it was not a 'vulgar effusion'. Puzzlement may have been compounded by the translation of the title in the programme book as 'The Afternoon of a Young Gazelle'.

During 1905, Britain seems on the face of it to have been Debussy-free. Of course, we have no means of knowing to what extent his songs and piano music were spreading, though I suspect it was slowly. In 1906, on 6 March, Henry Wood returned to the charge with *L'Après-midi* and again on 9 January 1907 ('Finlandia ... was succeeded by Debussy's vague Prelude ... ').[3] In saying that I have found no further notices of these performances, I should perhaps point out that *The Times* newspaper, the paper of record, did not have an arts page in these years, but still mentioned Debussy at times before 1908. Of the other traceable manifestations of interest in Debussy's work in 1906, one came in the form of the first British public performance, given in Manchester, of the 'characteristic' String Quartet by the Ladies' Quartet of Edinburgh,[4] the other in a lecture given in Newcastle-upon-Tyne by Edward Clark – later to be closely involved with the BBC and in getting them to play music by Schoenberg and his pupils. On this occasion in 1906, W. Gillies Whittaker, later Professor of Music at Glasgow, acted as what was called a 'vocalist–illustrator'.[5]

But 1907 seems to have been the year when British interest in Debussy began to grow appreciably. There were, I think, three leading factors. The first was the foundation that year of La Société des Concerts Français by one of the most effective of Debussy champions over here, T. J. Guéritte – an engineer by training who lived in Newcastle and was, as his acute accent suggests, of foreign extraction. These concerts were organised first of all in the provinces as well as in London, but, as ever, it was those in London which benefited from informed notices. The most valuable and influential of these was undoubtedly a review by Arthur Symons which appeared in *The Saturday Review* on 14 December 1907, of the last two of a series of five concerts, three given in Newcastle and two in London.

Nine composers featured in the London concerts, which boasted Ricardo Viñes as pianist and accompanist: Fauré, Chausson, d'Indy, Duparc, Debussy, Ravel, Séverac, Roussel, and Florent Schmitt. Of these composers two, writes Symons, 'stood out from the others with a definite superiority. These were Ernest Chausson, who seems to close the past, and Claude Debussy, who seems to open the future'. Symons is not so keen on Debussy's settings of Verlaine, thinking they add little if anything to the feelings evoked by the poetry. But Debussy's Quartet is a different matter, as played by the Parisian Quartet (whose cellist, Louis Feuillard, was to be the teacher of Tortelier):

> Through this playing ... I was able at last to enter into the somewhat dark and secret shadows of this wood. Here, if anywhere, is a new kind of music, not merely showy nor wilfully eccentric, like too much we heard at the two concerts, but filled with an instinctive quality of beauty, which can pass from mood to mood, surprise us, lead us astray, but end by leading us to the enchantment in the heart of what I have called the wood.

And he goes on:

> The whole point at issue is this: that here is an achievement of a new kind, which can be set somewhere in the same world of the old weightier kind, just as Villon has his place as well as Homer. You may begin by hating it, but you will surrender, while before Fauré and Ravel and the others you will find out that this genuine quality is not in them, or only here and there by accident. Fauré has a small and pretty talent, which will go the way of the stronger but not permanent talent of Saint-Saëns. Vincent d'Indy is without inspiration, Séverac scatters his fresher talent casually, Ravel does the worst possible things with a maddening energy.

Symons's finding of 'the somewhat dark and secret shadows of this wood' was surely a new note in British Debussy criticism – if you like, a Symbolist one, instead of an Impressionist or (as the English critics liked to say) an 'atmospheric' one. Debussy's music was not just vague vapouring. There were things going on in 'the dark and secret shadows' and, maybe, things you explored at your peril.

I think any reasonably musical reader of that article, noting that Symons also approved of Chausson's 'fine, simple vigour' and 'rich musical substance" might assume that Debussy's music was worth investigating further. If so, and if that reader lived in London, there was not long to wait – because the third, and perhaps the most important of the 1907 factors, was the decision by Henry Wood and Sir Edgar

Speyer, the financial manager of the Queen's Hall Orchestra, to bring Debussy over to London. Speyer, says Wood, 'wondered whether Debussy was anything of a conductor but concluded that, whether he was or not, London wanted him and London must have him'.[6] This decision had nothing to do with Symons's article, because Debussy had been visited by Wood in Paris in July 1907 and had then written on the 17th to his publisher that 'I am firmly engaged to conduct *L'Après-midi d'un faune* and *La Mer* in London on 1 February next'[7] Obviously the statement 'London wanted him' must have been prompted by a ground swell of opinion to which the two impresarios naturally lent their profit-sensitive ears.

With the turn of the year to 1908, the warmth of interest in Debussy turned into a veritable heat-wave. *The Musical Times* on 1 January, announcing that Debussy would conduct his three orchestral *Nocturnes* on 1 February, described him as 'one of the most original and fascinating composers of the day', and in the following month's issue M.D. Calvocoressi contributed an accurate and level-headed account of Debussy's career so far, stressing that his music and his theories were closely allied: that rules were anathema to the creative artist, who must 'seek discipline in freedom'.

On the very day Calvocoressi's article appeared, so did Debussy himself on the rostrum of the Queen's Hall. At this juncture, *The Times* included another notice of him. Debussy's public appearance, wrote its critic, 'of course, attracted a very large audience'[8] – the 'of course' underlining that *The Times* had long been aware of this composer's pre-eminent genius. Debussy was not thought to have thrown any new light on *L'Après-midi* (an implicit pat on the back for Henry Wood), and curiosity centred on the first British performance of *La Mer*. Here, readers were told that

> as in all his maturer works, it is obvious that he renounces melody as definitely as Alberich renounces love; whether the ultimate object of that renunciation is the same we do not know as yet. Instead of melodic subjects we have rhythmic figures, the interplay of which is extremely beautiful.

After further remarks about the importance of rhythm in this music, the writer turns to the question of form – one that exercised many of these early critics:

> For perfect enjoyment of this music there is no attitude of mind more to be recommended than the passive, unintelligent rumination of the typical amateur of the mid-Victorian era. As long as actual sleep can be avoided, the bearer can derive great pleasure from the strange sounds that enter his ears, if he will only put away all idea of definite construction or logical development ... the practical result of this music is to make the musician hungry for music that is merely logical and beautiful, and many regrets were expressed by those who were obliged to leave the long concert before the Unfinished Symphony.

Some of these points were echoed in *The Musical Times* review on 1 March. After commenting on the warmth of Debussy's welcome, and the undemonstrative nature of his conducting, the writer tries to come to grips with *La Mer*. Perhaps he'd read *The Times* review (perhaps he'd written it? – all the critics I am quoting from were anonymous). At any rate, we learn that

> such atmospheric strains, so unlike what one is accustomed to, must be listened to in a passive frame of mind, perchance in a darkened room. There can be no question as to the cleverness of the music or its poetic import; the only thing is to get one's ears educated, so to speak, in order to appreciate its strange idiom.

Today, we may have little patience with the 'darkened room' syndrome. More to the point, we may feel, was 'getting the ears educated'. But there was the major difficulty, in the case of *La Mer*, of hearing the music enough times for that education to take place. As far as I know, *La Mer* wasn't played again in Britain until after 1914, and no recording of it was made until the one by Piero Coppola in 1928. Ansermet included it in a BBC concert performance on 14 August – altogether a more generous response than the one accorded to *Jeux*, of which the same orchestra under Alexander Gibson gave the first Promenade Concert performance on 12 August 1960.

Henry Wood may have felt that his sessions preparing *La Mer*, for Debussy to take over, were strenuous enough to last him for some years – we know, incidentally, from Victor Segalen, that the strings had found the going rather less tough than the rest of the orchestra did:

> The brass, woodwind and percussion players had been at work from 10 o'clock till 1 o'clock. At first it was pitiful, despite their goodwill. It was 'La mer broken into pieces' remarked Madame Debussy; who was with me. At about 2 it was back to work, this time with the strings. This was much nearer the mark and with the right expressive nuances, in fact it wasn't far off being entirely satisfactory.[9]

Wood now turned his attention to what we may think the obvious work for an English audience, *La Damoiselle élue*. The first British performance took place in the Queen's Hall exactly four weeks after *La Mer*. *The Times* found *La Damoiselle* much more to its taste. Comparing it with other settings which had been made of the Rossetti poem, the critic felt that:

> none has caught the rarified atmosphere [again that word] of the poem as finely as the French composer whose opening phrases paint the quiet spaces of the celestial regions with exquisite insight. The themes, too, are beautiful in themselves and are combined with great skill, although the musical interest of the piece is almost entirely confined to the orchestra ... the sung notes are almost always in contradiction to those which are played.[10]

The Musical Times was similarly impressed, again taking the 'atmospheric' line in suggesting that the cantata 'breathes that atmosphere which has become associated with the French composer's method. In this instance, however, the air is less rarified than in his latest productions. Not only does the music reflect the tenderness of the poem but it makes a direct appeal to the listener by its sincerity and true beauty.'[11]

La Damoiselle continued to be performed fairly regularly in this country right up until the First World War. I think it's worth abandoning the chronological approach for a moment, to look at a notice this work received four years later, when Sir Henry Wood (as he had since become) conducted a performance in Manchester at one of the Gentlemen's Concerts (to digress still further, it was at one of these concerts the previous year – on 27 February 1911 – that Wood had given the world premiere of Ravel's orchestration of the *Pavane pour une Infante défunte*, beating the French premiere by 10 months). The performance of *La Damoiselle* on 15 January 1912 received an interesting notice in *The Musical Times*. The choral parts were sung by the Ancoats Ladies Choir, trained by Miss Say Ashworth, and *The Musical Times* reviewer felt there was

> food for much thought in this juxtaposition of Lancashire mill-girls, Dante G. Rossetti's *Blessed Damozel* and Debussy's elusive music. What was the power that enabled these comparatively untutored girls to give us the very quintessence of such subtle music? Why should they succeed where more cultured folk entirely miss their way? [12]

What a pity Debussy, almost certainly, never saw that review! But it also raises a point about what the British in general saw in *La Damoiselle*. It had been a custom in the mid-nineteenth century for music societies in London to bring down girls from Lancashire and put them up for the duration of choral festivals: the claims of North versus South over choral singing have never entirely subsided, but it was felt in many quarters that the open vowels of the North led to a fuller, purer tone (a view supported a century later by another Northern singer, Dame Janet Baker). If we listen to the characteristic British soprano sound of the early years of this century – even the trained sound of singers like Isobel Baillie or Elsie Suddaby – and compare it with the sound of their French contemporaries like Ninon Vallin or Emma Luart, it's the sound of a flute as against that of an oboe. And clearly British audiences and critics saw *La Damoiselle* as a perfect vehicle for this bright, pure, innocent, rather sexless sound – the work, if you like, enabled them to prolong the Pre-Raphaelite movement beyond its natural historical limit. No dark and secret shadows in this wood; and certainly no need for passive, unintelligent rumination.

It seems possible that Debussy's music found particular favour in the North of England. *The Musical Times* reviewer of a choral concert given by the Manchester Vocal Society on 17 December 1910 had written:

> To Mr. Alfred Higson and his Sale and District Musical Society belongs the honour of singing for the first time in Manchester the new works by Delius and Debussy produced recently at the Blackpool Festival ... both pieces were rapturously applauded by an essentially popular audience, the Debussy chanson 'Cold Winter' being doubly encored! [13]

Three weeks later, on 7 January 1911, the Blackpool Glee and Madrigal Society came to Manchester and again, 'had time permitted, both 'On Craig Dhu' and 'Cold Winter' might have been repeated – ultra-critical Manchester thus confirming the verdict of popular Manchester, as recorded here last month'.[14] On the other side of the Pennines, *L'Enfant prodigue* had already been heard in Sheffield in 1908, conducted by Henry Wood (who had encouraged and possibly commissioned Debussy to re-orchestrate his 1884 original for the occasion), and *La Damoiselle élue* at the Leeds Festival in 1910.

In 1908, the first two books in English were published about the composer: *Claude-Achille Debussy* by Louise Liebich, and *Debussy* by W. H. Daly. Daly's little book, published in Edinburgh, identifies the Strauss/Debussy dichotomy as being basic to the musical aesthetics of the time, and has things to say about Debussy's form, or lack of it. He writes:

> It has been laid to his charge that his forms and harmonies are alike vague and incoherent. There is, however, a conceivable stage in the mastery of form which may be so complete that form, in the sense of limit or restriction, disappears. Such, indeed, does the so-called 'formlessness' of Debussy reveal itself as one studies his music.[15]

This, I submit, is not bad going for 1908.

Liebich's rather longer book, published in London to coincide with Debussy's visit, also has some penetrating insights, claiming for instance that

> in the opening bars of *La Damoiselle élue*, in parts of *Pelléas and Mélisande*, in the 'Songs of Bilitis', one comes across a quiet, restrained beauty of utterance, seeming to originate from an older source than even Gregorian chant, carrying one back to early Christian hymnology, which in its turn was taken either from the Hebrew temple service or from the Greeks. [16]

She mentions that Jacques-Emile Blanche's portrait of the composer had been shown at the New Gallery in London in 1907 and, more surprisingly, begins her second chapter with the sentence 'When as a youth M. Debussy was serving with his regiment at Evreux, according to his own statement he took great delight in listening to the overtones of bugles and bells.'[17] As far as I know, this has not been followed up by later biographers; it would be interesting to discover what form Debussy's 'own statement' took, since Mrs Liebich did not meet him until around 1910. And finally she mentions *Willow-wood* as being still among his current projects, in addition to *King Lear* and *Tristan*.[18]

Then came Debussy's last two public visits to this country, in February and again in May 1909. On the first of these occasions he conducted *L'Après-midi* again, and then the complete *Nocturnes*. Neither *The Times* nor *The Musical Times* gave the concert their unqualified approval, though for slightly different reasons. The fact that Debussy made a mistake in 'Fêtes' but that the orchestra refused to stop seems to have cheered everyone up enormously. But the Sirens failed to seduce. *The Musical Times* noted that 'the voices murmur melodious passages to the syllable "Ah!"' – which incidentally solves that little problem – but felt they were too loud,[19] whereas *The Times* less kindly called it 'a persistent, wordless, wailing chant' and went on to make a rather more interesting general observation:

> ... the worst of the kind of atmospheric music that M. Debussy writes so well is that the moment realism enters the whole is destroyed; and the song of the sirens, whether well or ill sung on the present occasion, strikes so realistic a note that it is impossible to regain the poetic atmosphere which need never have been disturbed.[20]

This may remind us of the letter Debussy had written to his publisher just eleven months before, about creating 'realities, what imbeciles call "impressionism".'[21] At least, *The Times* critic was aware of the distinction.

Debussy's music received further promotion in 1909 through the continuing efforts of La Société des Concerts Français, whose London concert on 26 February consisted entirely of works by him, including the String Quartet, various piano pieces played by Viñes (including the *Estampes*, 'Poissons d'or' and *L'Isle joyeuse*) and a number of songs.[22] *The Times* by now had assumed a position of superiority where Debussy was concerned, and rather sniffily referred to the whole programme as consisting of 'very familiar works, while "Mandoline" was definitely hackneyed'.[23] *The Musical Times*, with its nose twitching at the scent of snobbery, reported that the Debussy cult is making great progress in this country ... It has reached that interesting stage when many people who are really desperately bewildered, affect to perceive beauties and wonderful meanings that have probably entirely escaped the attentions of the composer. [See note 19].

Meanwhile Herbert Hughes in *The New Age* that June could write that, even if London audiences had been slow to find out 'this most excellent society', at least they knew 'their Debussy pretty well by now (he has already entered the suburban drawing-room)'.[24]

We learn of Debussy's appearance, during one of his 1909 visits, at the 'Music Club' of London from the autobiography of Arnold Bax – in one of the best bits of musical knockabout I know:[25] Debussy was introduced by Alfred Kalisch, music critic of *The Star*,

whose French was of the school of Stratford-atte-Bow – or possibly at Oxford – it was difficult to hazard which, as he was largely inaudible. The great composer, an inordinately shy man, was planted in a chair in the exact centre of the platform facing the audience. He was clearly utterly nonplussed, and could only attempt to solve his problem by rising and making a stiff little bow whenever he recognised his own name amid Kalisch's gutteral rumblings. This part of his ordeal over, he was permitted to shamble dazedly to the rear of the hall, where he confided to Edwin Evans that he would rather write a symphony to order than go through such an experience again.

I would add just one small rider to this scene. Bax recalls that Kalisch's efforts were called upon because an address welcoming the composer was required, but that 'trouble began at once, for although Frederick Corder, who was a good French scholar, had been invited and had declared himself willing to make the address, he at the last moment failed to turn up, excusing himself on the plea of sudden sickness'.

Corder, then in his mid-fifties, was a professor at the Royal Academy of Music. lt turned out that the reason for his absence was in all probability not sudden sickness, but rather long-standing prejudice; for which we have further evidence in a letter of July 1938 from a one-time pupil of Corder's at the Academy, the composer Benjamin Dale, who remembered that Corder 'used to execrate Strauss and pooh-pooh Debussy (both of whom I secretly admired!).'[26] My French dictionary translates 'pooh-pooh' as 'ridiculiser; traiter légèrement', and I think it about sums up the difference in attitude towards the two poles of musical modernism among the older British musicians.

Among these we must number Sir Charles Villiers Stanford. He, in August 1910, proposed, for the programme of a Leeds Festival to end all Leeds Festivals, the following line-up: Strauss's *Elektra* and *Sinfonia Domestica*, Mahler's Choral Symphony, Debussy's *Pelléas et Mélisande*, a new oratorio *The Black Country* by Rutland Boughton (Part 1 'Smoke'; Part 2 'The Pit Mouth'; Part 3 'The Explosion'); ending up with a Concerto for penny whistle and tuba by A. Bax, after which all rise and sing 'God Help the Audience' ... Receipts for the Festival £1.13s.4d'.[27]

And with that less than flattering reference to Debussy's opera, we come to the main item on the agenda – and one which in Britain, as in France, set the seal on his reputation. And yet, main item though it was, there is not much to say about the opera's reception except that it was hugely enthusiastic. Already by the revival at the end of 1910 (in which Maggie Teyte sang just once as Mélisande), it was being referred to as a 'great' opera. In *The Times* review of the Covent Garden premiere in May 1909, there are really only two small quibbles: one, that 'so rarely does any part move melodically except in the treble that the ear is apt to tire of the one sort of balance which goes on through all five acts' – which could, perhaps, be laid at the door of Cleofonte Campanini's conducting; and secondly, that later in the run Yniold's scene with the ball in act IV was left out – strange, when the performer of the part, Mlle Trentini, seems to have been excellent in all respects.[28]

The Musical Times was equally warm in its praises, calling the opera 'a remarkable and impressive work, and one which, as it becomes familiar, will grow in interest'[29] – again, a reminder that one had to work in those pre-electronic days to keep up with the latest developments, and that the wiser critics were content to bide their time before settling themselves in entrenched positions. *The Monthly Musical Record* would have liked more sung tunes ('that which hitherto has been considered the most powerful factor in music-drama plays altogether too insignificant a part') but conceded that in the opera 'the drama is the chief thing, and attention is never drawn away from it ... It is a strong, wonderful work. Debussy's conception is new, but we feel that the earnest, vivid manner in which he has carried it out must and will be fully recognised.'[30] Later mentions in the same journal emphasised that supporters of the work would have to be patient: 'it is a work the merits of which can only gradually be appreciated'; 'owing to the uncommon and subordinate part played by the music in Debussy's work, it has not as yet been accepted by the public.'[31]

The view of *Pelléas* as a 'strong' work, though borne out by Maggie Teyte's memories of the Paris production in which she had taken over the role of Mélisande in 1908, was perhaps not widely shared. At all events, the perception seems increasingly to have been that the general 'insubstantiality' of Debussy's music, though perplexing, was a positive rather than a negative feature. Even the pianism of Ricardo Viñes was on one occasion criticised as 'inclined to be a trifle too strenuous'[32], while poor Hans Richter, conducting *L'Après-midi* at a Hallé concert on 22 October 1908, 'dealt with this delicate textile in a far too determinate spirit, like a square man in a round hole'.[33]

Even so, in the years immediately before the War, there's the occasional whiff of 'we've heard all this before'. In 1913, the first British performances of 'Rondes de printemps' and 'Gigues' by the Orchestre Colonne under Gabriel Pierné, moved *The Times* critic to write that

> ... they do not add very much to what we already know of Debussy, except to make one feel that he has retired more completely into a region of his own imagination where musical sounds are related in ways which differ from normal standards ... One easily admires the skill of his workmanship, but one leaves this work, at any rate, with the feeling that after all it expresses very little, much less, for instance, than Franck succeeded in expressing in his much less skilful tone poem *Le Chasseur maudit* given in this programme.[34]

This time, I am glad to think Debussy did not see that article – battling with his own technical skill was a preoccupation of those pre-War years. But the author is surely right in saying that what was difficult about the music was not so much the vocabulary as the syntax.

Criticism of the 'atmospheric' school wasn't limited to the critics, either. In March 1912, Vaughan Williams wrote to E. J. Dent: 'Have you ever heard of a composer called Eric Satie – Ravel has, apparently, discovered him – he was doing <u>all the Debussy tricks</u> [my underlining] in 1887 before D. was interested.'[35] A couple of years later, on 29 March 1914, Gustav Holst wrote to Vaughan Williams, after hearing the first performance of the *London Symphony* at the Queen's Hall two days earlier:

You have really done it this time. Not only have you reached the heights but you have taken your audience with you. Also you have proved the musical superiority of England to France. I wonder if you realised how futile and tawdry Ravel [the *Valses nobles*] sounded after your 'Epilogue'. As a consequence of last Friday I am starting an anti-Gallic League the motto of which shall be 'Poetry not Pedantry'.[36]

We can hear from parts of the *Planets* suite that Holst didn't quite succeed in expunging the French influence: in short, Debussy and Ravel bid fair to become what Wagner had been to their own generations and were likely to be taxed, as he had been, with relying on 'tricks' to get them through.

Debussy himself paid one last visit to London in July 1914, to play *Children's Corner* at a private party given by Lady Speyer. He seems to have missed the performances of *Pelléas* at Covent Garden in June. Perhaps it was just as well, since the reviewer of the *Evening News* found that 'Signor Polacco, who conducted, did not always handle the delicate music with sufficient sympathy', and especially since, according to this review, 'M. Maguenat made a picturesque Pelléas.'[37]

So, overall, even if the British lion didn't immediately greet Debussy's music by rolling over and waving its legs in the air, its roars were at the worst muted and questioning, and at best welcoming and affectionate. Certainly, a grateful nod does not go amiss in the direction of Sir Henry Wood, 'to whose broad-minded enthusiasm', as W. H. Daly wrote at the head of his book, 'British appreciation of all that is most progressive in musical art is so greatly indebted.'[38]

[1] The Musical Times (1 October 1895), 668. Quoted Percy A. Scholes, *A Mirror of Music* (London, 1947), vol. 1, p. 194
[2] The Musical Times (1 September 1904), 600
[3] The Musical Times (1 February 1907), 113
[4] The Musical Times (1 December 1906).837
[5] Scholes, *A Mirror of Music*, vol I, p. 451n
[6] Sir Henry J. Wood, *My Life of Music* (London, 1938), p. 157; repr. in Nichols, *Debussy Remembered* (London, 1992), p. 216
[7] Claude Debussy, *Correspondance*, ed. François Lesure and Denis Herlin (Paris, 2005), pp. 1014-5
[8] The Times (3 February 1908)

[9] 'Les cuivres, bois et batteries ont donc fonctionné de 10h. à 1hr. D'abord, ça a été piteux, malgré leur bonne volonté. C'était "La mer en morceaux" disait Madame Debussy que j'accompagnais ...Vers 2h., retravail, avec les cordes, cette fois beaucoup plus d'apprêt, de nuances; pas loin d'une mise au point satisfaisante.' Cited Annie Joly-Segalen, André Schaeffner, *Segalen et Debussy* (Monaco, 1961), p.91. Letter of Victor Segalen to his wife, 31 January 1908 (English trans. Nichols, *Debussy Remembered.* p. 219)

[10] The Times (2 March 1908)

[11] The Musical Times (1 April 1908), 244

[12] The Musical Times (1 February 1912), 120

[13] The Musical Times (1 January 1911), 43

[14] The Musical Times (1 February 1911), 121

[15] W. H. Daly. Debussy (Edinburgh, 1908), 11

[16] Louise Liebich, *Claude-Achille Debussy* (London, 1908), 22

[17] ibid., 14

[18] ibid., 92

[19] The Musical Times (1 April 1909), 258

[20] The Times (1 March 1909)

[21] 'J'essaie de faire « autre chose » et de créer – en quelque sorte, des réalités – ce que les imbéciles appellent « impressionnisme »'. Letter to Jacques Durand, March/April 1908, Claude Debussy, *Correspondance*, ed. François Lesure and Denis Herlin (Paris, 2005), 1080

[22] Information given in Martha J. Stonequist, *The Musical Entente Cordiale* (Ann Arbor, 1972), 169 ff

[23] The Times (27 February 1909), cited Stonequist, ibid., 202-3

[24] 24 June 1909, cited Stonequist, ibid., 185

[25] Arnold Bax, *Farewell, My Youth* (London, 1943), 58-9; repr. Nichols, *Debussy Remembered,* 222-3

[26] Letter from Benjamin Dale to Patrick Piggott, 22 July 1938. Published in Lewis Foreman, *From Parry to Britten, British Music in Letters 1900–1945* (London, 1987), 211

[27] Letter from Sir Charles Villiers Stanford to Herbert Thompson, 7 August 1910, ibid., 43

[28] The Times (22 May 1909)

[29] The Times (1 June 1909)

[30] Monthly Musical Record (1 June 1909), 136, cited Stonequist, *The Musical Entente Cordiale,* 210

[31] Monthly Musical Record (1 January 1910, 3 and 2 January 1911), 1, cited Stonequist, ibid., 211

[32] Monthly Musical Record (I April 1909), 88 cited Stonequist, ibid., 171

[33] The Musical Standard (31 October 1908), 288 cited Stonequist, ibid., 123

[34] The Times (l7 April 1913)

[35] Unpublished letter in the Dent Archive, King's College, Cambridge. I am grateful to Dr Hugh Cobbe for sending me a transcript of it

[36] Ursula Vaughan Williams and Imogen Holst (eds.), *Heirs and Rebels: letters written to each other and occasional writings on music by Ralph Vaughan Williams and Gustav Holst* (London, 1959), 43. I am grateful to Dr Alain Frogley for drawing my attention to this letter

[37] Evening News (25 June 1914)

[38] Daly, *Debussy*, 7

14 DEBUSSY AS MAN AND ARTIST

All in all, the 1860s must be reckoned as a low point in French musical life. *Tannhäuser* had been whistled off the Opéra stage in 1861 and a complete performance of Berlioz's *Les Troyens*, finished in 1858, never arrived there at all before his death in 1869. In the 1860s Offenbach was all the rage, and it's rumoured that Bismarck, visiting Paris for the 1867 Exhibition, saw in these operettas, and especially in the slights against the military in *La Grande-Duchesse de Gérolstein*, tempting signs of French decadence.

But Debussy, born in 1862, chose his time well. When he entered the Paris Conservatoire in 1872, French music was just embarking on a radical remake of itself, headed by the recently formed 'Société nationale de musique' which, under its banner 'Ars gallica', aimed to outdo German music by meeting it on the fronts where it had been supreme, namely chamber and orchestral music. Opera of course never ceased to occupy French minds, but as outlets for it came nowhere near meeting demand, a change of focus was in any case only sensible. After winning the Prix de Rome in 1884, Debussy spent two years in that city, but not happy ones – for one thing he had left a mistress in Paris. But, not for the last time, he also chafed at the institutional restraints, while realizing that his technique was still far short of what he needed: writing a vocal work about the goddess Diana, he worked in vain at creating music that would be beautiful but cold, without any hint of passion, but which would be slowly transformed by love.

Needless to say, the example of Wagner could not be far away from such an enterprise, and Debussy followed the lead of many other French composers in going to Bayreuth, seeing *Parsifal* and *Meistersinger* in 1888 and *Tristan und Isolde* the year after. The immediate results of these visits were the *Cinq Poèmes de Baudelaire*, in which Debussy's keyboard writing reached a peak of richness and complexity. In the years following, he began to find a personal way through this jungle of chromatic striving, where others such as Chabrier and Chausson laboured under what Debussy called 'the ghost of old Klingsor'.[1] One support in this quest was the Annamite theatre he saw at the

1889 Exhibition, in which, as he wrote later, 'a small, furious clarinet is in charge of emotion; a tam-tam is the organiser of terror ... and that's all!'[2] Less, he realized, could be more.

From this realization stemmed his first masterpiece. In September 1893, shortly after his 31st birthday, he complained to Chausson that 'there are things I can't yet do (write masterpieces, for example, or, among other things, be completely serious – I'm too prone to dream my life away ...)'.[3] Yet he had just finished the *Prélude à l'après-midi d'un faune*, whose dreamworld awoke modern music, in Pierre Boulez's memorable phrase. That simple opening line on the flute ... and the extraordinary bar of silence ... Music had suddenly moved out of the salon and concert hall and embraced Nature with a new sensuousness and eroticism. Debussy taxed his friend Chausson with putting too much weight on his ideas and cluttering up his textures with complicated inner parts. Instead, the task was to find a simple idea (like the opening of *L'Après-midi*) and allow it to lead on according to the composer's whims – what Debussy had shocked a straitlaced professor by calling '*mon plaisir*', as opposed to perceived duty or technical correctness.

At the same time there was a part of Debussy that wanted to be measured against accepted norms, even if he would never accept any limitations on what he might or should write. His String Quartet was a case in point. Simply by composing in this medium he was inviting comparison with Beethoven and, more recently, César Franck. While the work's cyclic construction obviously derives from the latter, the Scherzo sets the spirits dancing with almost irreverent gaiety. *Plaisir* is combined with technique, as in Degas's ballet dancers (Debussy greatly admired this painter whom he always referred to respectfully as 'Monsieur' Degas; see the following article).

By the mid-1890s it was clear to the more perceptive critics that a major talent had arrived. Debussy himself was much less sure. His motto, as delivered to a female journalist, was 'ever higher'.[4] Right up to his death in 1918 he never sat back on his laurels, and one might say that this chronic unease is one of the more fascinating aspects of his genius. From 1895 to 1902, his energies were largely spent on preparing his opera *Pelléas et Mélisande* for performance, whether in orchestrating it or – a rather more difficult task – persuading a Paris theatre to take it on. He knew that his opera flew in the face of the traditions of his time and place: no big arias, no extravert choral numbers, endless conversation. Then there was the question of what the opera 'means', something still hotly debated over a century later. As recently as 2011, Natalie Dessay, a wonderful Mélisande, admitted that the character 'is an absolute mystery. I still don't understand her – and that's how it should be'. [See interview with Irène Joachim, article 21 below]

Nowhere is Debussy's unease more evident than in his slow development of an individual style of piano writing. It was left to Ravel, 13 years his junior, to inaugurate with his *Jeux d'eau* of 1901 the style of pianism generally known as 'Impressionist' (even though neither he nor Debussy liked the term). The *Estampes* of 1903 also established the composer's interest in other cultures: Chinese in 'Pagodes', with reminiscences of the gamelan he'd heard at the 1889 Exhibition, Spanish in 'La soirée dans Grenade'. The final piece, 'Jardins sous la pluie', turns to a previous French culture, that of the Baroque harpsichordists, though it develops in ways that would have surprised them considerably. The subsequent sets of *Images* and *Préludes* pursue the same picturesque goals with an ever deeper level of invention and imagination. Popular music finds a place in 'Minstrels' and 'Général Lavine excentric' (the young Darius Milhaud was shocked by this lack of seriousness) and the whole-tone murk of the vault scene in *Pelléas* reappears in 'Voiles' as a picture of sails on the water (according to Debussy's widow, not veils).

On the orchestral front, *La Mer* took the programme symphony to new heights and depths: if the first movement shows a mastery of complex counterpoint, with as many as seven different ideas heard simultaneously at one point, the central 'Jeux de vagues' is an uninhibited display of playfulness, at the same time passionate and insubstantial. It makes clear, as does Debussy's savage review a few years later of a symphony by Théodore Dubois, that for him the great enemies were 'respect' and 'boredom' (chronically impatient, he was, by every account, an impossibly exacting teacher). In combating these enemies, humour was a prime resource. Even if, after *Pelléas* and the accolade of the Légion d'honneur, and now renting a house that he couldn't afford, Debussy left a bohemian life for a bourgeois one, a childish streak persisted, nourished by the birth of his adored daughter Chouchou in 1905. *Children's Corner*, dedicated to her 'with her father's tender apologies for what follows', pokes fun at Clementi piano exercises in 'Dr Gradus ad Parnassum' and at *Tristan und Isolde* in the middle of the 'Golliwogg's Cake Walk' (at the first perfomance, Debussy paced about nervously outside the hall in case he had caused offence ...). In every case, real life was at the heart of his music, like the water-melon seller and the whistling urchins he heard in the orchestral *Image* 'Ibéria', which explains why, as mentioned above, he had little time for the term 'Impressionism'. We know, of course, that this artistic movement was in fact based on strict scientific principles, but what bothered Debussy was the general appreciation of it as something casual and undisciplined. This view of his music has been encouraged, alas, by the fact that its firm structures are adorned with surfaces of brilliance and beauty, a perfect example of art concealing art. But a look at any of his mature scores reveals an obsession with detail, and it was not for nothing that he had spent twelve years of study at the Conservatoire.

He seems to have reached some kind of crisis around 1911: he had troubles with money and with his wife, and Stravinsky's *Petrushka* felt like serious competition. 'There are no precautions or pretentions', he wrote of this work. 'It's childish and savage. Even so, the organization is extremely delicate.' [5] This was the eternal battle, between what the poet Apollinaire called 'l'ordre' and 'l'aventure', and in the last seven years of his life Debussy continued to find new solutions to it.

For these he went back to the past. In his ballet *Jeux*, commissioned by Diaghilev for his 1913 season, he wanted to 'invent an orchestra "without feet". Not that I'm thinking of a band composed exclusively of legless cripples! No! I'm thinking of that colour which seems to be lit from behind, of which there are such wonderful examples in *Parsifal*!' [6] He wrote further of *Jeux*'s 'almost cheerful' mood and its 'quaint gestures'. [7] If Wagner's music lived on in him, it was that he took simply what he needed and eschewed the rest – notably the sheer length and the grandiloquence. The result was also Wagnerian in being 'music of the future', ignored for decades before its rediscovery by Boulez and colleagues in the 1950s.

With the outbreak of war in 1914, German music was banned from French halls and opera houses. This chimed in with what Debussy had been saying for years, that French music had been polluted by its German cousin – not just by Wagner, but from Gluck onwards. Condemned by age and incipient cancer to being an onlooker in the conflict, he directed his patriotism towards composing: not tub-thumping marches (hardly his style), but music that looked back to the grace and elegance of 17th- and 18th-century France and to what he termed 'emotion without epilepsy'. [8]

Between June and October 1915 he was granted an, almost final, period of extraordinary productivity. In the 2-piano suite *En blanc et noir* he envisaged the rampant 'Ein' feste Burg' swept aside by a delicately sunny version of the *Marseillaise,* and in the piano *Etudes* he looked both back to Chopin and Schumann and forward to Bartók and Boulez – he was rightly proud of the study in fourths which overturned the centuries-old hegemony of thirds and sixths. Finally, in the three Sonatas that were all he completed of a planned set of six, he turned on the irresistible charm that had won him friends, male and female, all through his life. Not a note in these is wasted. They also bring to mind the composing advice he gave a young friend on his deathbed: 'Distrust the exceptional!'[9]

Debussy's was a quiet revolution. The banners under which it proceeded were in themselves not startling: honesty, continual self-questioning, and a search for 'the naked flesh of emotion'.[10] He acquiesced in suffering long stretches of silence (1906 was an almost completely blank year), and believed the Muse, even in light-hearted works, should be treated with deference. As his friend Pierre Louÿs said, he never wrote a note that he did not mean. Debussy the man ended up ill, heavily in debt, and in a marriage riven with many stormy moments. But for those composers and musiclovers who have followed him, it is we who are in debt, for a body of work that is strong yet subtle, colourful yet logical, seductive yet profound. Vive Claude Debussy, 'musicien français'!

[1] 'le fantôme du vieux Klingsor'
[2] 'une petite clarinette rageuse conduit l'émotion; un Tam-Tam organise la terreur ... et c'est tout!'
[3] 'il y a des choses que je ne sais pas encore! (faire des chefs-d'œuvre par exemple ; puis être très sérieux entre autres choses, ayant le défaut de trop songer ma vie ...)'
[4] 'toujours plus haut'
[5] 'Il n'y a, ni précautions, ni prétentions. C'est enfantin et sauvage. Poutant la mise en place en est extrêmement délicate.'
[6] 'trouver un orchestre «sans pieds». Ne croyez pas que je pense à un orchestre exclusivement composé de culs-de-jatte ! Non ! je pense à cette couleur orchestrale qui semble éclairée par-derrière et dont il y a de si merveilleux effets dans *Parsifal* !'
[7] 'musique à peu près joyeuse'; 'gestes falots'
[8] 'émotion sans épilepsie'
[9] 'Méfiez-vous de l'exceptionnel!'
[10] 'la chair nue de l'émotion'

Debussy felt he had more in common with painters than with his fellow composers, and Degas was one for whom he had unbounded admiration.

15 DEBUSSY AND DEGAS – BEYOND IMPRESSIONISM

The scene is Paris; Tuesday 16 June 1896; it's still light as the guests assemble for dinner (7.30, lounge suits) in an apartment at 20 avenue Duquesne, on the Left Bank, just south of the Invalides.

The host is Henry Lerolle, a painter of no particular distinction, but even so a man at the centre of Parisian intellectual life. Some of the guests that evening remain unknown to us. But we do know three of them. The week before, Lerolle had sent an invitation to the poet and novelist Pierre Louÿs: in his letter he mentions two other guests - Edgar Degas, and Claude Debussy. Lerolle knew Degas, having bought one of his paintings of horses back in 1884, when Degas commented to a friend that Lerolle was fairly rich (therefore of interest to a painter who had considerable family responsibilities), even if the rumours were that he was governed by his wife. For Debussy, though, it was his first meeting with Degas.

Oh to have been a fly on the wall that evening! But, failing that, one can at least suggest some of the topics the two men might have engaged in, and how their views might have coincided or differed.

Edgar Degas was born in Paris in 1834, the eldest of five children of a banker, Auguste, who ran the Paris end of the family business, based in Naples, where it had been founded by Edgar's grandfather, Hilaire Degas. If Edgar's portrait of his grandfather in 1857, when the old man was 87, makes him look severe, maybe he had good reason – he'd escaped from the Paris Terror in 1793 with what he stood up in. At any rate, Edgar was very fond of him and no doubt it was from his grandfather that he inherited some of his genes of determination, not to say bloody-mindedness – of which more later.

At the age of 11 Edgar went to the Lycée Louis le Grand and appears to have been an average pupil, given to daydreaming. Two years later, his mother died. Even though he hardly ever spoke about her afterwards, we can guess the effect her death might have had on a sensitive 13-year-old. He left the Lycée at 18, began to study law, but spent most of his days in the Louvre, copying the old masters. Meanwhile he studied with various teachers, but the crucial events were two. First, his meeting in 1855 with Ingres, and then his three-year stay in Italy beginning the following year.

For the rest of his life, Degas would relate Ingres's advice to anyone who would listen: 'Draw lines, lots of lines, but never from nature; always from memory and from the engravings of the masters.' And of course in Italy there were masters on every hand. Degas returned in March 1859 to a Paris slightly bemused by the premiere that month of Gounod's *Faust*. Three years later, on 22 August, Claude-Achille Debussy was born in the Paris suburb of St-Germain-en-Laye.

No cushion of banking wealth for Claude-Achille – throughout his 55 years, money was to run through his fingers like sand. And even if his mother lived on until 1915, their early relationship was far from easy – apparently clips around the ear were a regular occurrence. Debussy, like Degas, spent time in Italy during his early twenties, though in his case funded by the Prix de Rome. And like Degas, he absorbed the old masters:

> I went to hear two masses, one by Palestrina, the other by Orlando de Lassus, in Santa Maria dell'Anima. It's certainly the right place to hear that kind of music, the only church music I regard as legitimate. That of Gounod & Co strikes me as the product of hysterical mysticism – it's like a sinister practical joke.

When, in 1911, Debussy came to write the final chorus of *Le Martyre de Saint Sébastien*, it's understandable that, in order to evoke the Roman era, he should go back to the 16th century and what he himself had heard in Rome 25 years before. But for me the most interesting thing is that, while he starts with fairly authentic Lassus, he then shades off into Debussy, neatly bypassing Gounod and his sinister practical jokes, before returning to the 16th–century fold. Debussy here seems to be treating a 16th-century style as a legitimate ingredient of contemporary music, going back in order to go forward. Here perhaps, even as early as 1896, might have been a topic to engross both Debussy and Degas: how to integrate the classics into a modern idiom? If Degas had Ingres, Debussy had 'our old harpsichordists, who held the secret of graceful profundity, of emotion without epilepsy'.

On the subject of epilepsy, might they have discussed Wagner? By the mid-1890s Wagner was a hot topic in Parisian artistic circles. After years of 'bleeding chunks' on the concert platform, and a stormy run of *Lohengrin* at the Eden-Théâtre in Paris in 1887, in 1891 the Paris Opéra had mounted the work, prompting riots in the Place and 17 stink bombs in the stalls. Degas, if not involved in the flesh, was certainly with the protesters in spirit: two years later he declared roundly, 'He's a bore! He's a bore with his Grail and his Father Parsifal. The human voice was not made to sing Greek roots.' Debussy too had Wagner problems, which he dealt with not by totally denying them (as Ravel and Satie did), but again by integrating Wagnerian elements into his own style. So on this subject they might have differed.

But where they might have agreed wholeheartedly, was that the grip of those other myths, of the Classical world of Greeks and Romans, had finally loosened. Both artists had been through this, producing in their respective media what the French call *grandes machines*. In Degas's 1861 painting, 'Semiramis founding a town', we can see from its rather stiff, artificial manner why he abandoned the genre soon afterwards ... Nice horse, though.

We may compare this painting with an extract from Debussy's earliest *grande machine*, the cantata *Le Gladiateur*, his unsuccessful entry for the Prix de Rome competition in 1883, at the point where Narbal, son of the Numidian king Jugurtha, is in a Roman prison and inveighs against his captors. But as Apollinaire put it a few years later, 'finally you are tired of that ancient world' ... Away with portentousness! The mood now was one of intimacy and a greater simplicity; and here, as we shall see, Degas and Debussy found fertile common ground.

But what of Impressionism? Despite what dictionaries and CD sleeves will tell you, neither Degas nor Debussy called himself an 'Impressionist': 'Don't talk to me about the Impressionists,' exclaimed Degas, 'they ought to be ... ' And, taking a stick from one of those present, he aimed it like a gun. And on another occasion:

> You know what I think about painters who paint out in the open – if I was the government, I'd have a brigade of police to keep a sharp eye on those people who paint landscapes from nature.

And here's Debussy in 1908, talking about his three orchestral *Images*, still in their early stages:

> I'm trying to write 'something else' – *realities*, in a manner of speaking – what imbeciles call 'impressionism', a term employed with the utmost inaccuracy, especially by art critics who use it as a label to stick on Turner, the finest creator of mystery in the whole of art!

So maybe if the Impressionists did come up for discussion at our dinner party, they didn't survive unscathed. Degas's objections to Impressionism were multiple, but two will suffice to deliver the message. First of all, the objection famously voiced by Cézanne about Monet: 'He's only an eye; but, good God, what an eye!' ('Il n'est qu'un oeil; mais, bon Dieu, quel oeil!') Degas in fact had great respect for Monet, but not so much for his less talented confreres. Ingres's advice held good. Painting on the spot meant there was no room or time for memory, reflection or imagination to do their work.

Debussy agreed. He spoke of 'the mysterious links between Nature and the imagination', and his pupil Raoul Bardac remembered:

> He was of the opinion that one should create slowly, and with minute care, the special atmosphere in which a work has to evolve; one should not rush to write things down, so as to allow complete freedom to those mysterious, inner workings of the mind which are too often stifled by impatience.

Mystery, mysterious ... The words are to be found everywhere in the speech and writings of both artists. One thinks of Voltaire's dictum: 'if you want to bore your audience, tell them everything.' Degas admitted to a friend that Emile Zola's novels were those of 'a giant working with a postal directory'.

A second objection by Degas to Impressionism was simply that 'now everybody's doing it' – and this despite his urging his colleagues 'to seek for new combinations along the path of draughtsmanship, which I consider a more fruitful field than colour. But they wouldn't listen to me, and have gone the other way.' Degas was a believer in the notion that 'more means worse'. He approved the use of a specialized vocabulary that only artists would understand – to keep out the amateurs and, not least, the art critics. When the son of his friend Rouart was considering the idea of becoming an art critic, Degas retorted, 'Is that a profession?' ... He didn't actually say 'for a gentleman', but it can't have been far off. As he said on another occasion: 'The Muses don't discuss things. They work alone ... and in the evening they dance.'

Both Degas and Debussy hated the crowd and kept it at a distance. Against the response that Degas was, after all, a prime mover of the first Impressionist Exhibition in 1874, one could come back and say, 'Precisely. Any joint venture had to be set up on his own terms'. The rows and recriminations that marked the series of those eight exhibitions would fill an article on their own, and Degas was one of the prime disturbers of the peace. He was actually heard to say on one occasion, 'the arts should be discouraged': I dare say on rational grounds that no true artist is going to be put off by any kind of discouragement, however persistent or vitriolic. Debussy, once more, was in total agreement:

> Music really ought to have been a hermetical science, enshrined in texts so hard and laborious to decipher as to discourage the herd of people who treat it as casually as a handkerchief! I'd go further and, instead of spreading music among the populace, I propose the foundation of a 'Society of Musical Esotericism'.

From the point where 'everybody's doing it' and Impressionism becomes 'the in thing', there follows the vulgar fact that it begins to make money. Now there was one subject that was emphatically *not* mentioned at our dinner party. Degas was a brilliant conversationalist, but his friend the art dealer Ambroise Vollard did remember one occasion when he was totally silenced – when the Douanier Rousseau came up to him and said: 'Well, monsieur Degas, happy with the way sales are going?' Some years later Debussy's publisher Jacques Durand organized a dinner *à trois* with Richard Strauss – who talked all through the meal about royalties. Debussy remained mute.

So don't mention money, or the claims of the crowd – and of course don't mention the Franco-Prussian War, or the Commune (in which Debussy's father had chosen the wrong side, been imprisoned for a year and been deprived of his civil rights for another four). But what about the 'realities' Debussy was to mention later in talking about his *Images*? A reasonable question, because in setting up the 1874 Exhibition, Degas had stated 'there must be a salon of realists.' But what did he mean by that?

It might seem to be contradicted by another statement of his, that 'a painting is an artificial work existing outside nature, and it requires as much cunning as the perpetration of a crime.' But the point was, the result had to *look* real – in the same way the Parthenon looks geometric, but in fact there isn't a straight line anywhere. It goes for colour too: 'painting', said Degas, 'is the art of surrounding a spot of Venetian red in such a way that it appears vermilion.'

The same point can be made through music: through Debussy's orchestral *Images*, and the violinist in the Spanish crowd scene at the start of the finale of 'Ibéria'. No real Spanish popular fiddler and his backing group would make sounds like these: but in the context of Debussy's piece they sound 'popular', 'earthy'.

The lower classes, then, had a rôle to play. And for both Degas and Debussy, that rôle was closely linked with work. Degas, in particular, was fascinated by the labour that went into the preparation of the mystery: whether it was a woman's elaborate toilet, or the arduous exercises of a young dancer. It was as if he was trying to impress on the viewer that he, Degas, had also had to undergo these physical trials, in his case through copying the old masters; in order to reach the apparently effortless glamour of the final product.

Debussy, of course, had also had his share of technical exercises – it's salutary to remember, amid all the composer's professions of being guided only by his whims, 'mon plaisir', that he studied at the Paris Conservatoire for 12 solid years, between 1872 and 1884. When in later years he looked back on his early piano practice, his evocations were tinged with an irony absent from those of Degas – probably for the good reason that, as far as we know, Degas never put his leg up on a barre. I'm sure many of us will know and love 'Dr Gradus ad Parnassum' from Debussy's *Children's Corner*, where piano practice is gradually poeticized; before Mama's voice from the kitchen brings the errant child back to his muttons (and yes, the young Debussy, like the young Degas, was a daydreamer) … And then there's the first of the Debussy *Etudes*, a five-finger exercise to which strange things happen.

… as the Bard put it, 'nothing can come from nothing'. We could even speak here of a kind of morality: whether in the form of Baudelaire's recipe that 'inspiration is the sister of daily labour', or the note Degas had made to himself in Assisi in 1858, when he found himself deeply moved by the piety of the congregation in the church of St Apollinaire: 'If I become a sufficiently committed and settled character to produce paintings as worthy as sermons – at least, if I am not to be a religious painter, may I feel the way they do.'

'Paintings as worthy as sermons' – it might seem scandalous to apply this phrase to, say, Degas's paintings of prostitutes in brothels. But it is possible to regard these along the lines of the defence put up on behalf of Flaubert's *Madame Bovary*: that they are in fact deeply moral works, in the portrait they paint of the degradation of woman and of man's part in that degradation. Even the cosiness of the relationship between the girls and the *patronne*, so wonderfully captured by Degas, can be seen as a cheap reflection of the tenderness and security denied them elsewhere – but which their male clients no doubt take as their due outside the 5 to 7pm window.

We have, then, made the journey from work, through pain, to a consideration of the darker side of human nature – a side which, if not absolutely excluded from the work of the Impressionist painters, can't be said to have been among their primary concerns. Obviously such a subject might not have been suitable for our 1896 dinner party. It's possible for one thing that the two Lerolle daughters were also present – Debussy, after all, was their piano teacher. And Mme Lerolle would certainly have been there. But that aside, we can find in the work of both Degas and Debussy, if we search, an engagement with what these days are called 'negative emotions': doubt, melancholy, regret, anger, fear.

For Debussy, these emotions were very much alive in the shaping of his opera *Pelléas et Mélisande*, of which he had completed a preliminary version in vocal score the previous August. Henri Lerolle was one of the few friends whom he had kept abreast of his progress on the work, Debussy writing to him in August 1894:

> I think of you as an elder brother whom one is fond of even when he grumbles. Pelléas and Mélisande started off by sulking and refused to come down off their tapestry, so I had to start playing around with some different ideas. Mélisande addressed me – you know that frail and gentle voice of hers: 'Leave these silly little thoughts, good only for the great musical public, and let your dreams dwell upon my hair. You know there can be no love like ours'.

Clearly, Lerolle was receptive to the idea of an opera that would be the opposite of a *grande machine*. Debussy then continued:

> I've finished the vault scene. It's full of impalpable terror and mysterious enough to make the most well-balanced listener giddy.

> The climb up from the vaults is done too, full of sunshine, but a sunshine reflecting our mother the sea.

In this scene, Prince Golaud takes his stepbrother Pelléas down to the vaults under the castle. Does Golaud harbour thoughts of murdering him? Is Golaud himself afraid of what he might do? And then they climb up into the sunshine ...

'The vault scene, full of impalpable terror' ...You don't usually hear the term 'Expressionism' used in talk about Debussy: but if that's not Expressionism, what is? And then *Im*pressionism takes over, as they climb up into the sunshine. 'Ah!' exclaims Pelléas, 'I breathe again.' And we breathe with him. So Debussy *could* be an Impressionist, when he wanted. And what better way to make a complete contrast with the *Ex*pressionist music of the vaults?

Degas too *could* do Impressionism: as his paintings of dancers show (the earlier oils, that is, rather than the late pastels). But what of the picture called 'Melancholy'? – a Degas painting you hardly ever see reproduced, although it's in the Phillips Collection in Washington, so not exactly hidden away. Generally his single portraits bear the name of the sitter. But this one is called simply 'Melancholy'. Do we not find it reproduced because of some subconscious resistance; because this is not Degas as generally perceived? To name a painting 'Melancholy' may be interpreted as taking at least one step towards Symbolism – and, given that it dates from around 1874, quite an early step.

Certainly Degas was never a Symbolist, though he was an admirer of Puvis de Chavannes. But the workings of memory, reflection and imagination – and of mystery – often mean that his pictures ask questions instead of giving answers. One of his most famous paintings, reproduced over and over again, is one he completed around the year of the dinner party: *La Coiffure*, now in the National Gallery. The art critic Douglas Cooper referred to it as 'the big red monster'; and in their joint Foreword to a 1996 catalogue, Neil MacGregor and James Wood resorted to musical terminology, calling it 'that incomparable study of dissonance in red, where every note is sharp'. Incidentally, painters may notice that of the three essential pigments used, one is red lead, and the other two are the ones already referred to as being as it were 'ghosts' of each other – Venetian red and vermilion. But there's very little in the way of ambiguity here. The application of the paint is extremely direct. It's an 'in-your-face' picture – or maybe 'off-your-face' ... For many years it belonged to Matisse.

What is Degas trying to tell us? It's one of a whole series of hair-combing pictures, but none of them uses red in quite such a provocative way. It's possible to feel the reds almost as a physical pain. Many a small boy is told, 'You mustn't pull girls' hair, dear, it hurts' – an injunction made necessary by the indisputable fact that, for some reason, girls' hair is, for small boys, eminently pullable. Obviously, in this painting mistress and maid are collaborating – there's no question of overt violence. But I feel Degas may be at least hinting that pain is a possibility, for all the care taken by both parties, and we may remember the French motto, *Pour être belle, il faut souffrir*.

More explicit, though the narrative is something we have to guess at, is a picture painted, like 'Melancholy', around 1874, and which must be one of the most terrifying artworks to come out of the late 19th century. It later acquired the title 'The Rape' (Le Viol), but almost certainly not from Degas himself. His title was simply 'Intérieur' – a frighteningly realistic view of the kind of thing that undoubtedly did go on behind those elegant Parisian facades. Here again, surely, we encroach on Expressionist territory, and we may think too of the scene from Act IV of *Pelléas et Mélisande* where Golaud violently drags Mélisande around the stage by her hair.

Inevitably, between two major artists like Debussy and Degas, there were divergences as well as agreements. The obsessive narrowing of subject matter we find with Degas in his later years – jockeys, nudes, ballet dancers – was something Debussy was never attracted to. Of course we have to remember that Degas died at 83 and Debussy at only 55, so maybe if Debussy had lived longer the same might have happened to him. As it was, he never showed any interest in the turf, any more than Degas did in the sea.

As far as we know, Degas never heard a note of Debussy's music. But in the 1890s, according to one of the composer's friends, the name Degas (or rather the more respectful 'Monsieur Degas') was continually on Debussy's lips. He revered Degas for the 'probity of his links with the past' and, in his figures, for what the friend describes as 'the sense his models bring with them of fateful destinies stretching way back in time'.

In conclusion, we may consider three more areas of agreement between the two artists. Both of them, first of all, had a horror of repeating themselves. This may seem to sit strangely with Degas's narrowing of subject matter I've just mentioned. But his aim was to find new things to say *within* the same framework of ideas, figures and gestures, and he warned that it was a mistake to cast one's net too wide and embrace subjects that one hadn't studied for a long time. One of his grumbles with the Impressionists was the tendency of some of their number to paint essentially the same picture over and over again. Debussy put it succinctly in an 1889 questionnaire, in which he cited as his motto 'Toujours plus haut' … 'Ever higher' … This aim impacted both on materials and on vocabulary. Degas, around the time of our dinner party, was experimenting with monotypes and sculpture: photography too – sessions dreaded by his friends, who had to pose for what seemed like hours while he fussed and ranted. With Debussy, some of the most fascinating extensions to his musical vocabulary come in his *Etudes* of 1915 – the study in fourths, for instance, breaking radically with the third-based harmony that had obtained in Western music for centuries. And here we touch on a further feature shared by the two artists: a move towards abstraction.

As an example we may take a pastel by Degas, painted in the early 1890s, called 'Steep Coast'. It's true, of course, that by the early 1890s Degas's eyesight problems were becoming serious. But he still knew what he was doing! And he was well aware that the lack of distinct outlines held a charm of its own. Debussy's move towards abstraction, in the three late Sonatas, was perhaps not intended as such: but rather as a return to the 'emotion without epilepsy' of the 18th-century French composers. And to sign himself 'musicien français' during the First World War was to recall the nationalist efforts of his immediate predecessors in the wake of the Franco-Prussian War.

Before concluding with the last area of shared interest between Degas and Debussy, it may perhaps be germane to touch on the likely tone of that 1896 dinner party. There might indeed have been some fairly deep philosophical and artistic discussion. But the evidence is that it was not all furrowed brows. Both artists were noted purveyors of *bons mots*. Degas said of Berthe Morisot: 'She made paintings as she would hats.' And of Cézanne, who had gone to live in seclusion outside Paris: 'He's a hermit who knows the times of all the trains'. Debussy famously called *The Rite of Spring* 'primitive with all modern conveniences', and by the time of our party he had already said of a salon hostess who would insist on singing to the assembled company: 'She makes a noise like a locomotive in distress, but her buttered scones are marvellous.' So there would have been laughs.

The final area of shared interest between our two artists was opera. Among Degas's obsessions, opera ranked high. Staying in New Orleans in 1872, he wrote home that 'the lack of opera is a real privation.' And he had an obsession within that obsession: the opera *Sigurd* by Ernest Reyer, and the soprano who sang Brunehilde at its Opéra premiere in 1885, Rose Caron, of whom he painted a portrait around 1892. *Sigurd* was performed 100 times at the Opéra over the next 6 years. Degas went to 37 of them! A photograph of her as Elsa in *Lohengrin* shows why she was nicknamed 'the Aztec'. Degas wrote a sonnet about her, praising 'Those long, noble arms, slowly in passion, slowly in human and cruel tenderness, arrows hurled from the soul of a goddess, falling to ground in this imperfect world.' The last two lines read: 'If my eyes fail, let hearing still remain,/I could divine her gestures from her voice.' He met her, and told her that her movements reminded him of the figures of Puvis de Chavannes. But she'd never heard of the painter, so he had to explain ...

Debussy too knew her, probably well. She was five years older than him, but they were fellow students at the Paris Conservatoire and in 1884 he had chosen her to sing the solo soprano part in his successful Prix de Rome cantata, *L'Enfant prodigue*. Then, nearly 20 years later, he reviewed her performance as the heroine in Gluck's *Iphigénie en Aulide*, in his open letter to the Chevalier Gluck:

> Everything in the way of interior emotion that *you* left out of the role was rediscovered by *her*. Every step she took seemed to contain music. If you could have seen, in the third act, the way she moved to seat herself near the sacred tree, before the sacrifice, you would have wept, so great was the sorrow incarnated in that simple gesture.

Debussy, we should remember, was not always so kind to sopranos.

The composer of *Sigurd*, Ernest Reyer, had this to say of her:

> Her voice is pure, harmonious, full of charm, her tuning impeccable. She is a stranger to bleating [*chevrotement* from *chèvre*, a goat], that disease of the age, to which so many singers have already succumbed. Her success grew with every performance: 'So there you are', I said to her by way of compliment, 'you're now a star. Try, even so, to remain a great artist'.

' … her voice is pure' … 'no bleating'. Happily, we can judge for ourselves this voice that charmed both Degas and Debussy, singing Degas's favourite aria from the last act of *Sigurd*, recorded in 1904 ('Des présents de Gunther', *Les Introuvables du Chant Français*, CD2, track 19, EMI 72435 85828 2). If one had to seize on one characteristic of that performance, it would be 'simplicity'. And simplicity lies at the heart of what Degas and Debussy were about. Pretty surfaces were all very well but, as Debussy wrote years later, 'How much one has to find, and then discard, in order to reach the naked flesh of emotion!'.

16 DEBUSSY, RAVEL AND AN ORCHESTRA FOR THE 20TH CENTURY

We have so much come to accept these two composers as the central pillars of 20th-century French music that we tend to forget that they both had a relationship with the French musical establishment that can most politely be described as 'fragile'.

In 1884, at the age of 21, Debussy won the Prix de Rome with his cantata *L'Enfant prodigue*, entitling him to paid residence at the Villa Médicis – an opportunity to write music free of material worries that he would never enjoy again. The news reached him as he was gazing down at the Seine from one of the Paris bridges: 'instantly my heart sank'. It wasn't only that Rome meant leaving behind a mistress. He saw at once that he was going to have to confront a political correctness in the French musical world that matched anything we find nowadays, and that the results of the confrontation were going to be all too public. And when he got to Rome, he found previous winners standing on their dignity and giving themselves airs.

In the event, two years of this was enough and he was back in Paris, scratching a living somehow, but with his principles intact, embodied in concepts such as 'liberté' and 'mon plaisir'. Meanwhile the establishment juggernaut chugged on, with respectable symphonies, imposing concertos, correct sonatas and quartets. Debussy's own String Quartet, bringing gamelan noises into the medium, was altogether too off-the-wall for his friend Ernest Chausson, imbued as he was with the 'seraphic' mindset of his idol César Franck. Then came the *Prélude à l'après-midi d'un faune* and with it an open acceptance of sex as a subject of concert performance – not that French audiences of 1894 were unenlightened on this topic: it was rather a question of knowing that your neighbour in the stalls knew that you liked this sort of thing, shorn of the Wagnerian protection of helmets and high boots.

With the *Nocturnes* and then the opera *Pelléas et Mélisande*, premiered in 1902, Debussy went further along the road from *L'Après-midi* in taking concert music out of doors to inhabit mythical landscapes, but ones that often held some small corner of terror or unease, as in the dangerous seductiveness of the sirens' song in 'Sirènes'. Not surprisingly, some elderly musical academics were wary of *Pelléas*, in case they got to like it. In which case, what price Franck or Saint-Saëns? Nowadays we can see that the dangers were at least twofold. Firstly, Debussy's syntax was new: chords that once upon a time had led inexorably to other chords now lived a free life and could lead Heaven knows where. Secondly, the orchestral colours were a curious mixture of the vivid and the opaque. The strings were no longer the uncontested masters of the field. The woodwind became virtuosos, either singly or in groups, trumpets might still rejoice in fanfares, but equally might lend their muted voice to some subtle texture; the percussion were no longer merely seasoning.

As a matter of historical record, *La Mer*, completed in 1905, owed much to what has been called the French 'message-symphony', in which composers, mostly from Franck's circle, attempted, as the American scholar Brian Hart has put it, 'to express aesthetic, philosophical, spiritual or political ideas ... '

Debussy however in *La Mer* 'freely salvages and reinterprets selected technical processes of the message-symphony but rejects its essence'. No surprise there – Debussy might take over the Lisztian/Franckian idea of themes returning at crucial points (here most notably the 'chorale' from the end of the first movement at the end of the third), but he was certainly not trying to tell us anything about how we should live life on this planet or about what we might expect hereafter. If there is any message, it is one of *'plaisir'*. He would never have had access to the letters of Chabrier, one of his heroes, and so, sadly, would never have read that composer's wonderful description of the sea as 'a theatre that gives only first performances', but it is easy to imagine him smiling in agreement.

Our familiarity with this repertoire also dulls us to what was felt by many listeners as the patchy development from one Debussy work to the next. Ravel, for instance, who as a 19-year-old still to tangle with French officialdom had been bowled over by *L'Après-midi* (and who remained an admirer to the end of his life, insisting it was the only absolutely perfect work in existence and wanting it played at his funeral), had strong reservations about *La Mer*, both about the orchestration (messy employment of the two harps) and about its formal structure. It has often been held against Ravel that formally he was not imaginative in the way Debussy was. He might have replied that there's no call for formal imagination if the old forms do the job you want them to. The *Valses nobles* of 1911 are a case in point. Their form could hardly be simpler: seven waltzes and a nostalgic epilogue, all in 3/4 time. But, the occasional cross-rhythms apart, this 'donnée' throws the interest on to the melody and harmony and, in Ravel's orchestral transcription, on to the orchestral colour. As an orchestration exercise, the *Valses nobles* are peerless, perhaps even in Ravel's own oeuvre. And here, incidentally, may lie one of the problems for Ravel's reputation. Debussy's use of the orchestra opens windows on to the future. But from Ravel it's very hard to learn anything except that you stand no chance of doing it as well as he did – not a message many composers want to hear.

In *Images* and *Jeux*, his last two great orchestral scores, Debussy continued to explore the domains of 'liberté' and 'plaisir'. What a vast distance separates these scores from the symphonies of some of his academic colleagues, designed to impress and destined to wither! With *Images* one has the impression of some sorcerer in his laboratory taking the orchestra apart and reassembling it to shine out with new colours. At the same time, as even he admitted, the feeling is (or should be) of utter spontaneity, of organisms that spring from some secret inner life, that, in his words, 'have the air of not having been written down'. As for *Jeux*, so long despised and rejected, it does finally coalesce into a waltz full of nobility and sentiment, but framed by evanescent fragments that look forward even to Webern, and certainly to Boulez.

For Ravel, dancing was an altogether more serious matter. Indeed, to judge from *La Valse*, it was an activity fraught with peril, in which physical overexcitement might tip you over the edge into some pit of nothingness. It may be not entirely frivolous to suggest that for Ravel, ever conscious of his stature of around 5' 4", dancing *à deux* was indeed something to be approached with caution – the only record of him dancing is of a solo in drag, wearing a female friend's hat. Be that as it may, and whatever the possible links with post-war trauma, in *La Valse* Ravel ventures further into the dark than in the *Valses nobles*. Where in the earlier work content and colouring are at one, here the weight and brilliance of the orchestral writing seem to be driving the music out of control, as they were to do again in *Boléro*, albeit in a quite different way. And of course, in order to go out of control, the music has to be controlled in the first place.

Debussy never wrote a piano concerto, the nearest he got being the *Fantaisie* of 1890. He was never happy with this, distrusting the

19th-century 'warhorse' element implicit in any struggle between soloist and orchestra. Ravel's two Piano Concertos show him at his furthest from Debussy. The D major Concerto relishes the warhorse element, and we might almost say it's a work Liszt could have written if he'd lived on into the jazz age, a kind of *Totentanz* with riffs. In the G major Concerto, looking back to Saint-Saëns and still further to Mozart, Ravel distanced himself from Debussy's motto *'toujours plus haut'*. 'Ever higher' is all very well, he seems to say, but the past can sometimes act as a useful launching pad.

So what do all these works have in common? None of them aspires to philosophical content, explicitly argues any kind of case or sets itself up as 'the music of the future'. For the most part their orchestral garb is brilliant, enticing, seductive (as Debussy reminds us, 'One does not catch flies with vinegar'). But there are disturbing moments too: the silent bar at the start of *L'Après-midi* (echoed in *Pelléas* but for a low drum roll) during which the orchestra seems to stand astonished at what it has just said; the roar of the sea at the opening of the finale of *La Mer*; the rhythmic insecurities of *Jeux*; the looming menace of *La Valse*; the mechanical pounding of *Boléro* and the D major Concerto. The table may be adorned with a selection of sparkling white wines; but, almost unseen, in a corner, the demon absinthe is preparing its deadly work.

17 DEBUSSY, D'ANNUNZIO AND *LE MARTYRE DE SAINT SÉBASTIEN*

In the spring of 1910, the 47-year-old Italian poet, novelist and dramatist Gabriele d'Annunzio ended his affair with the actress Eleonora Duse and, to escape the creditors into whose hands his extravagant lifestyle had committed him, fled his Tuscan villa for Paris. He arrived in time to catch the Ballets Russes season. It was not, though, the first run of *The Firebird* that took his fancy, but two ballets in which Ida Rubinstein was dancing: in the title role of Cléopatre, with music by a variety of Russian composers, and as the Sultana Zobeïda in Rimsky-Korsakov's *Schéhérazade*. His secretary later recalled that 'as soon as Ida Rubinstein appeared on the stage, he ceased to have eyes for anyone else … "Here," he exclaimed, "are the legs of Saint Sebastian for which I've been searching for years"'.

At least since 1908 d'Annunzio had been thinking of writing something on the subject of the Christian martyr, fascinated as he was by the primitive and masochistic elements in early Christianity. Legs aside, Rubinstein seemed to him to exude the appropriate air of sexual ambiguity for the part and, no less importantly, she had just decided to leave the Ballets Russes and put her own large fortune to use in commissioning roles for herself as dancer, mime and reciter. The two soon became intimate friends, and in the course of the autumn of 1910 commissions to write music for the enterprise were offered unavailingly to Roger-Ducasse and Henri Février. D'Annunzio's thoughts then turned to Debussy, while keeping Florent Schmitt standing by in case Debussy were to refuse. In the end d'Annunzio wrote on 25 November to Debussy, on tour in Vienna, and was delighted to receive a reply stating that 'the thought of working with you fills me with feverish anticipation.' Never one to pass up an opportunity, d'Annunzio proceeded to exert his epistolary charm on the composer's wife. On 9 December Debussy signed a contract.

The general feeling has been that between composer and poet there was an essential mismatch. Reynaldo Hahn, reviewing the premiere in May 1911, wrote of a 'flagrant disparity' between the composer's 'native reserve' and the poet's 'flamboyant eloquence and luminous delirium'. But this was to take a narrow view of Debussy's gifts: the outer movements of *La Mer*, Golaud's music in *Pelléas et Mélisande*, the prelude 'Ce qu'a vu le vent d'ouest', all demonstrate Debussy's ability to evoke power and awe. It's true that in 1910 he was, as usual, short of money and could not be expected to take a casual view of the offer of 20,000 francs, 8,000 of them due on signature of contract. But any idea that for him work on *Le Martyre* was forced labour is strongly denied by the evidence. His friend and publisher Jacques Durand remembered some years later how he was 'enthused by the subject of *Saint Sébastien* ... he wrote this wonderful work in a spirit of exaltation. The mystical subject accorded with his particular inner aesthetic.' More than that, d'Annunzio quickly became a friend of the family. Debussy's five-year-old daughter Chouchou called him 'the old wizard with the little yellow beard', and a month after the premiere Debussy himself signed off a letter to him with 'Votre affectueusement dévoué', not an appellation with which he favoured all and sundry.

One area of mismatch might have been d'Annunzio's attraction to war and bloodshed (whether inflicted by arrows or not), but the list of their shared tendencies and interests is surprisingly long. Both were fascinated by religious trappings, while remaining stubbornly irreligious; both lavished on *objets d'art* money that was really needed for the housekeeping; both were enthusiasts for Japanese art, the pre-Raphaelites, the Symbolists, Huysman's novel *A rebours*, the music of Liszt ... and, relevantly or not, both had wives who attempted suicide. Certainly too, Debussy was in tune with d'Annunzio's claim for his novels that they should combine 'the precision of science with the seductions of the dream'.

A further link was 'anxiety', or 'inquiétude' as the French more poetically call it. D'Annunzio was chronically discontented with a life that never quite seemed to match his aspirations, including his failure to be anything like a decent composer. Debussy for his part distrusted what he called his 'mandarin' technique that allowed him to find a solution to every technical problem – but was it the right, artistic one? He was admitting to his publisher only a matter of months before starting on *Le Martyre* that 'I'm in a period of anxiety – rather like someone waiting for a train in a waiting room with no sunshine. I have simultaneously the desire to go off just anywhere and also the fear of departure!' This sense of unease was shared by other French composers of the time. Late in 1914, Vincent d'Indy could consider this war 'extremely beneficial since it has forced from the depths of our hearts our old French qualities of clarity, logic, integrity, and uprightness ... and I believe that artistic progress will take the road of simplicity and beauty instead of seeking the small and rare as in recent years'. Likewise in 1916 Albert Roussel, writing home to his wife from the front, expressed surprise after looking again at the score of his opera-ballet *Padmâvati*, written just before the war, to find that it betrayed no 'morbid or deliquescent influences'. It's worth mentioning that both d'Annunzio and Debussy sought inspiration from a time other than the present, the poet in the *Matthew Passion*, the composer in the *Missa Papae Marcelli*, a copy of which he asked Durand to send him. When theatened by morbid deliquescence, fortify yourself with Bach and Palestrina ...

At this stage the work was to include three dances for Rubinstein, four symphonic movements and two choruses – a 'Madrigal' for five voices (eventually a passage for four voices in Act I – or the 'First Mansion') and 'Widows' Lamentations' in Act V. Although the final version was to be considerably different, with additional vocal items in Acts II and III and the loss of a 'Dance of the planets' in Act II, Debussy decided at once on his orchestral forces, including 'three harps and a celesta (large model)'. A major problem however was that at the time of signing the contract Debussy had not seen a word of d'Annunzio's text – the only time in his life he put himself in this dangerous position. But there can be no doubt that, once engaged, he involved himself with the work totally, being intrigued by the possibilities of doing things differently: for example, 'the stupid habit of positioning the choirs as if they were taking a bath – men on one side, women on the other. That'll have to go.'

The text of Act III, which the poet thought 'musically the most important', was the first to reach Debussy on 11 January 1911, the last sections arriving on 2 March. As Robert Orledge has suggested, March and April were probably the two months 'when most of the score was composed, the interlude before the paradise scene and the "lamentations" at the end of the third act coming last of all.' Rehearsals for a premiere at the Châtelet towards the end of May had to begin before the orchestral parts were all ready (Debussy had engaged André Caplet to orchestrate almost all of Acts II – IV, reserving most of the first and last for himself), but despite the rush, these early rehearsals were promising, to the point that Debussy, in the words of one of the chorus masters, 'could no longer retain his habitual attitude of sarcastic benevolence and, quite simply, wept'. In August indeed, he would look back on these days wistfully to Caplet as 'those when we were in charge' – that's to say, before the choreographer Fokine and the designer Bakst started to interfere! Perhaps Debussy should have anticipated that a cast of 150, with 350 players and a wardrobe of 500 costumes to be organized, might have an impact on his vision for the work.

But the most serious impediment to its success was the ban imposed, a few days before the premiere on 22 May, by the Archbishop of Paris, who declared it offensive to the Christian conscience and forbade all Roman Catholics to attend on pain of excommunication. At the same time the Vatican placed all d'Annunzio's writings on the Index of forbidden books. In this, Rubinstein's bare legs again played their part (even Marcel Proust was excited by them), as certainly did the fact that in Act IV she mimed the Passion of Christ. Some Catholics may have been glad of the excuse to cancel their boxes, given the high prices demanded. But the theatre for the premiere was nonetheless fairly full. For every society lady who found the whole five-hour experience, not to mention Rubinstein's French diction, incomprehensible, there were those who, like the composer Alfred Bruneau, were struck by the work's 'new-found power', as well as its 'hieratic, fantastical orchestral passages, both religious and voluptuous.' As for Debussy's fans, the 'Debussystes' and 'Pelléastres', they were, as many listeners were to be over the ensuing century, 'troubled and divided'.

In a newspaper article in February 1911, Debussy had admitted 'wishing to sing of my inner landscape with the naïve candour of childhood.' If the work began out of financial need, it ended as something much more, tapping into some private corner of the composer's psyche rarely explored elsewhere in his œuvre. Hence his snappishness when, after fierce altercations with Bakst over the designs for the final act, the painter asked sarcastically: 'So, Monsieur, you've been to Paradise?' 'Yes,' retorted Debussy, 'but I never talk about it with strangers.'

18 *PELLÉAS ET MÉLISANDE / L'ENFANT ET LES SORTILÈGES*

Up until recent decades, opera in Paris followed twin tracks of very different provenance and purpose. The Opéra, deriving from court entertainments and given an apparently unassailable lustre by Lully, writing for Louis XIV, promoted the *grandes machines*, a phrase probably dating from those early years when stage spectacles – floods, tempests, volcanic eruptions – were a crucial ingredient of the evening's fun. The plots, not exactly noted for their simplicity, dealt with kings and gods, and the acting tended towards a 'stand-and-deliver' style. Against all this, the Opéra-Comique was the home, not necessarily of comedy, though this was not outlawed, but rather of real life as lived by lesser mortals, with the accent on naturalness and believability. Other organizations did appear from time to time, notably the Théâtre Lyrique in the mid-19th century, but basically the Opéra/Opéra-Comique dichotomy held firm.

Claude Debussy's operatic experiences in the 1890s exemplify this split with some clarity. First he tried his hand at a *grande machine* on the story of El Cid, but soon realized that, as he put it, 'I was winning victories over myself'. Then, in May 1893, he saw Maeterlinck's play *Pelléas et Mélisande*, and the grand gestures were definitively abandoned. But what to put in their place? The story most definitely does not concern the lower bourgeoisie who made up the majority of the Opéra-Comique audience: there's a king, various princes and princesses, and a castle. On the other hand, royal trappings are barely in evidence even if, as Virgil Thomson put it, the family 'seem to be running some sort of kingdom'. The one moment of regal majesty, when Golaud identifies himself as 'the grandson of Arkel, king of Allemonde', albeit underlined by Debussy with rich horns and bassoons, lasts a mere couple of bars. Instead of ceremonial, we are witnesses to a searing family tragedy that owes much to the plays of Henrik Ibsen, which were being staged in Paris as Debussy was beginning work on his score. In one of his letters, the composer mentions 'la beauté du théâtre d'Ibsen' and over the last 70 years or so the opera has increasingly been absorbed into 'the theatre of cruelty'.

The overwhelming sentiment of the work, and one it shares with *L'Enfant et les sortilèges*, is that of being lost – lost both physically and psychologically. This feeling is superbly evoked in the orchestral introduction. We start with two bars of modality, calling up olden times and far-away places; then, abruptly, what will soon be recognized as Golaud's motif over the deeply unsettling harmonies of the whole-tone scale; then, most potently of all, a bar of near-silence (just a faint rumble on timpani) in which the tentative beginnings of syntax are negated – after which, we start over again, shortly to find Golaud lost in the forest. The feeling of being 'perdu' is imprinted indelibly in our hearts. So also at the start of *L'Enfant*, the two oboes wander aimlessly around for what seems an age before the child gives voice to his boredom and repressed rage. He too is 'lost', in the sense of being without purpose. Further evidence of his 'lostness' comes in the two chords accompanying the key word 'Maman!', set to Ravel's favourite descending fourth. In the course of the opera, the second of the two chords is never given a solid bass note, as the Child continues to search for the love that can only return with (his) repentance and (his mother's) forgiveness. Only on the very last chord of the opera does Ravel seal the pact with that missing bass note, just as the return of the wandering oboes is finally anchored with beneficent G major string harmonies.

The 'stand-and deliver' method of singing referred to above, while tolerable (apparently) in operas that depended on spectacle, big tunes and solid orchestrations, was clearly inappropriate to this new kind of 'inward' theatre, and we can sympathize with Debussy when, at a rehearsal, he enjoined the cast 'forget you are singers!' ('oubliez que vous êtes chanteurs!'). Even if this did not go down well initially, step by step the singers got the message and, contrary to what Saint-Saëns once claimed was the case in all opera, they realized that Debussy's orchestration allowed the words to be heard. Not that this was entirely new. The great French conductor Georges Prêtre has emphasized the subtlety and efficacy of Massenet's word setting, and that composer's influence can be heard in both these operas: in *Pelléas*, at the opening of the Act IV love duet, 'On dirait que ta voix … ', which is where Debussy began work, and in *L'Enfant* in the boy's solo 'Toi, le coeur de la rose', which Ravel admitted took as its model Manon's aria 'Adieu, notre petite table'.

We know that Ravel attended many of the 14 performances of the initial run of *Pelléas* in the early summer of 1902 (not all, as has been sometimes claimed, since he had the small matter of a Prix de Rome cantata to write in the middle of the run), and Debussy's way with the French language had a lasting effect on him. Vincent d'Indy, in a perspicacious review of the premiere (see following article), suggested links with Monteverdi's word setting, though one wonders what Monteverdi Debussy knew. At all events, Debussy's practice took its lead from the inflections of the spoken language, and a few years later Ravel took this idea and ran with it in his song cycle *Histoires naturelles*, to the extent of sometimes ignoring the mute 'e' at the ends of words that, according to all the rules, had to be enunciated separately when sung. In the ensuing furore (a modern tabloid headline might read 'Young Composer Punches Face of Establishment'), no one pointed out that, from time to time and for artistic reasons, Debussy had done the same in *Pelléas*. In the first scene, Mélisande admits she has run away ('je me suis enfuie') with the final 'e' of 'enfuie' in place. Golaud picks up on the phrase, but now 'enfui(e)' is shorn of its final 'e'. Why? Because this is the first, tiny hint of that impatience and uncertain temper which will so radically determine the course of events. It might have caused Ravel some wry amusement to note that, by the time of *L'Enfant*'s premiere in 1926, possibly as a result of the democratisation of society that a World War brings, the sense of social outrage had died off, so he was able, like Debussy, to vary this technique in accordance with the dramatic situation. Whereas, in the Child's opening outburst of fury, he is made to exclaim 'je n'aim(e) personn(e)', with vigorous enunciation of the 'm' and 'nn', in his lyrical duet with the Princess and the following 'Toi, le cœur', every mute 'e' is in place.

Inevitably, two such ground-breaking works have had their detractors. Some way through a performance of *Pelléas*, Richard Strauss muttered to his companion, Romain Rolland, 'Is it all like this?' and complained that it lacked what he called *Schwung* (verve, zest, what we might term 'zip'). Then, during the 1930s, the opera fell out of fashion, to the extent that the English musicologist Edward J. Dent could write in 1940 that 'the strain of listening to this rather long opera ... never knowing what the harmonies of the music are, never knowing what the characters are really supposed to be thinking and doing ... is to some people unbearable.' As for *L'Enfant*, Ravel knew that his use of multiple numbers, as in an American musical, would cause upset in some quarters, but perhaps even he was surprised that at no single performance in his lifetime was he allowed, in Paris anyway, to hear the 'Cats' Duet' without audience participation.

Whether either of these two operas bears a message continues to excite opinions. That of *Pelléas* would seem, from the verbal text alone, to be bleak. The last words of the opera, 'Now it's the turn of the poor baby girl', suggest, in the word 'pauvre', that maybe Mélisande's character will find an echo in her daughter: and, given that (Virgil Thomson again) 'a lonely girl with a floating libido and no malice toward anyone can cause lots of trouble in a well-organized family', you will be lost in the forest at your peril. But does Debussy's final major triad offer hope? The message of *L'Enfant* is altogether more comforting. We know that forgiveness was in Ravel's mind at the time of writing the opera, since he made clear that his visit to Vienna in 1920 was intended to help heal the wounds of the war. Maybe also the opera was meant to beg his late mother's forgiveness for abandoning her in 1916 for the front and, possibly, thereby hastening her death in January 1917? One can only speculate. But happily we have now gone well beyond worrying about mute 'e's, the lack of *Schwung*, the obscure motives and the all-too-realistic cats, and can abandon ourselves to the enjoyment of two supreme masterpieces.

The original French of the three reviews translated below, together with the endnotes, can be found in '*Pelléas et Mélisande* cent ans après : études et documents', ed. Jean-Christophe Branger, Sylvie Douche and Denis Herlin, Lyon, Symétrie, 2012. In fact I had studied the texts some years earlier in the Bibliothèque nationale de France when preparing my contributions for the Cambridge Opera Handbook of the work (CUP, 1989).

19 *PELLÉAS ET MÉLISANDE*
Reviews by Vincent d'Indy, Paul Dukas and Willy

19a. Vincent d'Indy: review of Pelléas, 'A propos de *Pelléas et Mélisande*. Essai psychologique du critique d'art', *L'Occident,* I/7 (June 1902), p. 374–381

A very beautiful work has just made its appearance. Naturally, the art critics, with a few exceptions, have entirely failed to understand it.

I wouldn't want anyone to attach an intention of irony or blame to what I've just written, given that the art critic is, in my opinion and simply by virtue of his job, far more to be pitied than blamed.

In fact I don't believe there is any profession in the world, apart from that of a banker or politician, which is sadder and more useless than that of critic ...; useless because I can't think of any artistic product of real value, from *Armide* to *Carmen* and *Tannhäuser,* that has ever been destroyed by the disapproval of writers or journalists, any more than their enthusiasm has succeeded in bringing life and longevity to works of little value; and sad because a critic's job consists in judging a work without knowing it and pronouncing it sublime or detestable from a single glance, a superficial reading, just one hearing.

That however is the situation of the poor art critic, and the necessary haste in making a judgment that aims to be definitive, while it cannot be anything other than a very arguable personal opinion, must excuse the lack of seriousness with which this judgment is usually pronounced.

It is, I repeat, perfectly natural that the professional critic should not be able to appreciate the beauty of a work conceived in an artistic form that he has never before encountered, because *the article to be written –* and written promptly – puts him inevitably in the following situation:

– He arrives at the theatre (since we're talking here about dramatic art) with a very clear idea in advance of what he *wants* to hear.

In the case of music, one such critic will have come to hear *opera*, and what opera? Not that of the old Italian school, or of Rameau or Gluck (these are works he knows only from vague ideas taken out of Larousse's dictionary) but the opera that enchanted him as a young man, the opera of the Jewish school [1] that flourished through the greater part of the last century. For another, his anticipated type will be the Wagnerian music drama, in which he is allowed to show his erudition by making casual and meaningless mention of the word 'leitmotiv'. For a third, it will be that comfortable compromise between these previous two that has reigned for 20 years or so in French opera houses. A fourth, finally, cannot conceive of any opera that does not contain the kind of people you bump into in the street, wearing modern dress – he resolutely supports that superficial *verismo* that comes to us from Italy ... and which can hardly be termed a godsend for him!

The professional critic, with his horror of the *tabula rasa*, will dispense his praise of a work only to the extent that it conforms as closely as possible to the type he has made his own, and that's why every development of a new kind in art will find more detractors among journalists than partisans.

And furthermore, will these partisans themselves be sincere in their appreciation? There's room for doubt.

For musicians, even those well instructed in their art, *understanding* a work is always a rather difficult business, and I admit sincerely, and humbly, that I can never remember having fully taken on board a work of any quality in a single, or even two hearings ...

So what is the critic's first duty? Understanding; understanding at all costs and understanding immediately, because printing deadlines don't admit of delay. So all the critic's faculties are hypnotically concentrated on this word: understanding.

And when he happens to find himself faced with a work of profound and powerful significance, he does not understand, he *cannot* understand, that is without casting doubt on his innate intelligence.

And then what does this state of mind lead to?

A sophism:

What I don't understand is bad,

Now, I don't understand this work,

Therefore, this work is bad.

This is the most common, the most widespread mode of reasoning, because it's simple, it satisfies the natural vanity of the man whom his newspaper raises to the lofty position of judge and, what's more, it's easy to put into practice. Other critics, being more humble and therefore far less numerous, will think to themselves:

Whatever I don't understand must be sublime.

Now, I don't understand this work,

Therefore, this work must be sublime.

And they dash off an enthusiastic article, but coldly enthusiastic, without really understanding what their praise is based on.

In both cases, a naïve contemporary of Guillaume de Champeaux would have cried out: 'Nego majorem! ... ' [2], but we are no longer in the 12th century and after the successive 'affairs' of recent years, sophism is not likely to amaze anybody.

That is the reason why the Parisian critics have produced so many opinions ... shall we say 'bizarre' opinions about Claude Debussy's *Pelléas et Mélisande*. The critics have been nonplussed. And we have to admit, with good reason.

No two-part arias (andante and allegro), no duets, trios or grand finale with chorus and military music, for the Jewish opera fans; no purely symphonic treatment of the orchestra, no leitmotifs after the Wagnerian fashion which might allow Bayreuth regulars to find their way through the darkness of a first hearing; nothing of the art – maybe not 'bastard', but anyway 'of mixed blood' – which the Paris Opéra regularly serves up for us every year under the banner 'the height of novelty'; not a glimpse of a jacket, a workman's blouse or a Paris street, those mandatory accessories of the modern soul, according to the rite of Italian *verismo*.

Nothing, in short, that could find a place in one of the catalogues prescribed in advance by those catalogue-making art critics, but, on the contrary, a musical discourse 'closer to *pronunciation* than to pure declamation', in Saint Augustine's phrase about the singing in the church of Milan; characters acting in a dream, if you like, but acting in a human way; scenes, or rather tableaux, connected by a poetic link and not by the logic of the action; an individual instrumentation but one that is constantly and deliberately muted, having no resemblance to the fairground noise currently called 'dramatic orchestration', in which the violins sometimes have rests, the trumpets practically never; harmonic combinations that are strange, unusual even if explicable, but designed to call down avenging fire from all the conservatoires – this, I say, is the *exterior* aspect of Debussy's new work.

It is at this superficial aspect that the art critics have aimed their judgments, since they have neither the time, nor maybe the ability, to judge a work *in depth*.

Some of them, the shrewd ones – not sure how the future will turn out – haven't been able to find epithets extreme enough to express their enthusiasm, even though they can't find reasons for it: 'Gluck and Wagner? ... Do you mind! They're nothing next to Debussy!' – and I imagine the composer of *Pelléas* with a certain smile at the corners of his mouth. Others, more numerous, needless to say, have condemned *Pelléas* using all the so-called witty clichés that had already been used against the same Gluck and Wagner ... who haven't suffered thereby, and I see the smile now expanding into hearty laughter ...

So, apart from two or three who know what they're talking about, all the critics have been mistaken in their responses to this new work, for the simple reason that they insisted on incorporating it into one of the types that were familiar, established and duly labelled.

But the method required was really very simple: it was merely a question of showing goodwill and to proceed by finding in *Pelléas et Mélisande* not what you had gone to look for in it, but what the composer had intended to put there.

Pelléas is, quite obviously, neither an opera nor a lyrical drama in the ordinary sense of the term, nor a piece of *verismo* nor a Wagnerian music drama, it is both less and more: less, because the music, *by itself*, for the most part plays only a secondary role, like the illumination in Middle Age manuscripts or the painting on statues of the same period; more, because unlike what happens in modern opera and even in lyrical drama, here it is the text that is the main element – the text whose conception in sound is wonderfully adapted to the inflexions of language and which is bathed in variously coloured musical waves that sharpen the outlines, reveal the hidden meanings and magnify the expressivity, meanwhile always allowing the word to come through the fluid envelope that surrounds it.

The comparison I made above with past centuries was not accidental because if Claude Debussy's work is, as we've seen, essentially different from lyrical drama and opera, it seems to me like a reworking in an extremely modern style of what was written at the beginning of the 17th century by the Florentine academies.

There is in fact, even if the composer probably never had it in mind, a close resemblance between his way of setting the text and the *stile rappresentativo* of Caccini, Gagliano and Monteverdi; I will even say (and in my view it is no small praise) that it is with the admirable creator of *Orfeo*, *Ariana* and *L'Incoronazione di Poppea* that the composer of *Pelléas* seems to me to have the closest rapport.

There is the same system of expressive recitation illumined by the surrounding harmony, to the extent that you could apply to Debussy the maxim Monteverdi voiced on the subject of Marenzio: 'l'orazione padrona dell'harmonia e non serva' (the word is the master of the harmony, not the slave). There is the same preoccupation with colouring sentiments through a general atmosphere in the instrumentation rather than through detail. The same audacities too in the harmonic writing, and I don't think I'm exaggerating when I say that Monteverdi's audacities would today strike art critics and makers of treatises – if they knew them – as even more outrageous than those of the composer of the *Nocturnes* and the *Damoiselle élue*.

I certainly wouldn't want anyone to be misled about the force of the above observation and suppose – which would be utterly ridiculous – that I am claiming Claude Debussy as an imitator of Claudio Monteverdi, and that I am trying to make a comparison between the former's poetical, discreet instrumentation and the latter's four trombones, two organs, viols and double harps. Even so, while one must keep things in proportion, I thought the analogy between these two exceptionally aristocratic styles was worth pointing out, and certainly without wishing to diminish Debussy's merits as an innovator.

If I may be allowed to pick some flowers out of the bouquets offered by the critics, the analogy will become more striking still – if you would kindly read the brief quotations that follow:

'All these contrary movements', writes one critic, 'these lavish false relations, these piled up dissonances, these denied consonances, all these dust clouds of clashing sounds, whether subtle or not, surrounding dust clouds of ideas or of inexpressive declamation, all of this cannot disguise the futility of the aesthetic concept.' [3]

... 'And the orchestra', says another, 'creates dissonances with the voice whose resolution and technical address testify to a surprising level of invention, but the ear does not know what to make of it and cannot avoid irritation and boredom.' [4]

A third writes: 'You hear a mixture of sounds, a harmonic rumbling unbearable to the ears. One person sings fast, another slowly; one goes right up to the highest treble, the other sinks down to the bass ... How can anyone hope to make sense of such a hullabaloo!'

That last quotation, which seems to be a copy of the previous two, is not however taken from the columns of *Le Figaro*, but dates from 1608 and was written by Artusi about an opera by Monteverdi. In criticism, there's nothing new under the sun!

Be that as it may, whatever the genre to which you wish or don't wish to assign *Pelléas et Mélisande*, what is the result of hearing it for any ear not burdened with prejudice? ... the sensation of a very beautiful work of art that you cannot understand straight away, – as I've explained, this is the case with most professional critics and also a fair number of composers, – but which nevertheless awakens in the soul that vibration, that appreciation of beauty so familiar to those whose enthusiasm for art is not atrophied, and also the desire to hear it again, which is a sure indication of a work's value.

And I defy anyone who possesses a scintilla of artistic feeling to resist the enchantment of the scene on the terrace, the charm of the first duet by the well, the captivating seduction of the poetic dialogue during which Pelléas, all unaware of the nature of what he's doing, ties the shining locks of his beloved to the branches.

And I defy anyone with a soul open to pity for human suffering to remain unmoved hearing the admirable scene in which Golaud orders Mélisande to go and look for the ring she has lost, not to gasp with Pelléas as he climbs up from the dank dungeons towards the daylight, the music too becoming ever more luminous, not to be profoundly shaken by the sad love duet in the fourth act which one feels so strongly must end in a terrible catastrophe (the terror at the appearance of the assassin's shadow!), and profoundly moved by the long agony – maybe a touch too long for me – of poor Mélisande.

So what is the cause of this emotion which listeners of goodwill find it impossible to deny? In the play itself? ... yes, of course, but the play *on its own* could not produce an impression of such a special kind. In the music ..., which presents none of the harshness or obscurities of which some uncomprehending critics have accused it (Debussy is, perhaps, the one of our modern composers who *modulates* the least)? ... yes, of course, but the music *on its own* could not produce the complex emotion I'm talking of.

Could it not be that quite simply the composer has felt and expressed in *human* fashion feelings and suffering that are ultimately *human*, despite the outward aspect of mystery and dreaming that the characters present?

Two years ago on this same stage of the Opéra-Comique another drama was staged, written with equal sincerity, and whose emotional impact was no less. But I don't think any two works are more diametrically opposed as both poetic source and musical realization than *Louise* and *Pelléas*. Might there not be a useful lesson to draw from this fact, namely that *technique* is of small importance in art provided that the artist, blessed with a creative gift, feels and expresses human passions sincerely?

But it is only *technique* that critics generally latch on to, it is only *technique* that most of the professionals have dealt with in their articles, it is only *technique* that the sub-Debussys and sub-Charpentiers will try and imitate, swarming as they are already in the schools of music, without seeming to understand that *a work of beauty* can appear in any shape or form, provided it is honestly, sincerely and humanly considered, suffered and expressed.

Believing it to be such a work, I offer fraternal acclaim to Claude Debussy's noble drama, *Pelléas et Mélisande*.

[1] Here d'Indy is referring to Meyerbeer and Halévy
[2] Guillaume de Champeaux (1070–1121) was a theologian and philosopher. 'Nego majorem' indicates 'I regard the premise of the argument as false.'
[3] Louis de Fourcaud, 'Musique', *Le Gaulois*, 1 May 1902
[4] Théodore Ferneuil [Fernand Samazeuilh], 'Pelléas et Mélisande de M. Claude Debussy à l'Opéra-Comique', *Revue philomatique de Bordeaux et du Sud-Ouest*, 5e année, no 8 (August 1902), pp. 337-350

19b. Paul Dukas: review of *Pelléas*, 'Chronique musicale', *La Chronique des arts et de la curiosité*, no 19, 10 May 1902, p.148–150; reprinted in Paul Dukas, *Ecrits sur la musique*, Paris, Société d'éditions françaises et internationales, 1948, p. 571-6

Something very unusual has just happened to M. Albert Carré, the director of the Opéra-Comique: he has put on a masterpiece. Not a classical or recognized masterpiece, one of those famous works about which critics and public have made up their minds in advance, and about whose production the greatest oaf in the land would think himself dishonoured not to be trembling with enthusiasm. No. We're not talking about a revival of Gluck or Beethoven. Nor about the performance of an unpublished drama – if there are any – by Richard Wagner, nor about any generally acknowledged scores. The masterpiece in question, even if it's the work of men whom many artists admire, was totally unfamiliar to both critics and public before its appearance. Neither M. Maeterlinck nor M. Debussy was, I think, particularly well known. I have no idea whether they are more so now and whether the future reserves unmitigated glory for them. But it has to be said that neither the poet nor the composer has done anything to deserve it. It is unpardonable to be unaware, after all this time, that success in Paris is decided almost exclusively by routine, snobbery and self-advertisement. It smacks of extraordinary presumption to believe that one can dispense with these prime engines of triumph. And when you present an art of some individuality, you owe it to your reputation, not to mention the intelligence of your contemporaries, to warn everyone in advance. Without this, people rightly blame the 'new' work for forcing them to compromise themselves; because it's really going too far to claim that spectators should form an opinion on their own. Nothing grates on their stupidity so much as appealing to their taste, judgment and sensibility. That much was clear from the dress rehearsal of *Pelléas et Mélisande*.

The truth of the matter is that the poetic conception and musical realization of this opera are too far removed from what the public is used to accepting as the modern formula of music drama for anyone to laugh unduly at their surprise, even if they had been forewarned. Maeterlinck's text itself must seem like an insoluble enigma to the host of people who are more familiar with Jules Barbier than with Shakespeare[1]. The work's episodic structure, deliberate naiveties, often strange symbolism and the primitive roughness of some scenes, in contrast with the fluid delicacy of some others, all that may well surprise and disturb many in the audience. When you add to this the fact that M. Debussy's music presents practically no analogies with tradition, nor with those scores recently produced under the influence of Wagner, you can understand that those who claim to be the arbiters of theatrical opinion have shown themselves vexed at so much intransigence all at once. You can understand, if not excuse, why being shaken out of the comfortable positions they had already assumed, and deprived of reliance on the usual reference points, they thought it more elegant to refuse any attempt at understanding. By concentrating on the opera's more wayward moments, they cleverly avoided the problem of commenting on its splendour and novelty. It's an old story which will end like its predecessors: in a few years' time, everyone will want to have been the first to procalim the work's beauty; the critics, suffering like audiences from faulty memories, will be leading the chorus. And comforted by the spectacle of their own greatness of soul, they will feel all the more energetic, next time round, in repeating this diverting joke.

I feel that one crucial element, which has been rather overlooked, is the particular nature of the collaboration between M. Maeterlinck and M. Debussy. It's absolutely not a question here of a libretto and a score, but of the musical transformation of a play that was conceived independently of any possible musical setting. Through its poetry, through the touching humanity of its characters, through the expressive power of every aspect of this dreamworld against which we see, as silhouettes of innocence, goodness, violence or passion, human beings whom tragedy has taken unawares, the literary drama touches continually on those regions of feeling in which the expression of words tends to lose itself in that of sound. It is musical thanks to the mysterious atmosphere that envelops even those scenes that are the most decisive and straightforward. It is musical too thanks to the harmonious richness of its language and its dialogues with their uncertain meanings, whose echoes only the orchestra is able to prolong and reflect. The play's structure, however, did not necessarily demand music. Its discourse does not call for orchestral treatment. Because its musicality is innate, its poetic integrity would not in any way have been affected. Perhaps it would even have been better suited to music that was incidental and married to spoken words as melodrama, rather than sung throughout[2]. But it is precisely in this respect that the novelty, originality and boldness of the composer's undertaking consists. In taking over M. Maeterlinck's original text, M. Debussy was not borrowing from the poet a canvas of the kind composers normally choose to decorate. Nor did he intend to superimpose on this text a score that had its own life and some kind of professional interest; nor even to write music for those moments where the poetry seems especially to demand it, while leaving others in the shadow of a *recitativo* that was more or less *secco*. Such different approaches would not have corresponded entirely with his aim: which was to provide a complete musical expression of the play, exactly tailored to the musicality of the words and, setting aside any thoughts of self-serving adaptation, simply to realize the music of this spoken song.

That, I think, is what M. Debussy wanted to do. He has, in my opinion, succeeded absolutely and magnificently in surrounding M. Maeterlinck's play with the atmosphere it required. He has succeeded in this without any part of his intention being sidetracked by his musical originality or by the abundance of his talent – something that for anyone else might here have been a cause of difficulty. The novelty of the result became a source of astonishment for the most highly educated of judges; many of them thought they should give the poet his due by claiming that there wasn't any music, whereas, on the contrary, there is nothing except music; but music that is so naturally incorporated into the action, that rises so naturally from the situation, the setting and the language, music that is so close to the music heard beneath the words, that in the total impression produced by this sort of sonorous transfusion it becomes impossible to dissociate it from the text into which it is bound; to the point that, in the last resort, it can even seem like the unconscious work of the poet, just as the poem does of the composer.

It is my task in this article to speak about the music on its own terms, which can only be done by abandoning the perfectly unified image it offers with the words and considering it in its details. Examined in this way, it is reduced to phrases that are either brilliant or imbued with a touch of darkness and, if this sort of game appeals, to taking them apart and analysing what gives them their colouring. But if you look at a stained glass window in the dark, what's left except dead tints and strips of lead?

It's this kind of approach to the score of *Pelléas et Mélisande* that has led certain people to feel justified in declaring that there was no rhythm, no melody, no harmony; others found no trace of thematic development nor even any themes that were musically intelligible; several of them, finally, nothing but a pleasant, monotonous orchestral murmuring that rumbled on to no purpose. This was to assume that the music, divorced from the drama from which it grew and not split into separate scenes, could and should find its equilibrium within itself; and that the rhythm, the melody and the harmony were self-sufficient entities, independent of the individuality of the creative artist and not the most intimate expression of his characteristic creation; that thematic development was for ever linked to the form Richard Wagner gave it to conform with the necessities of his particular genius!

The truth is that if we abandon this tiresome habit of judging by comparison, which reduces most critics to vacuity and paralyses all spontaneous reaction, we shall realize very quickly that M. Debussy's music is, on the contrary, very melodic, very rhythmical, and based on a conception of harmony that is as new as it is audacious. The only thing is that this melody, this rhythm, this harmony are not those that imitation of the masters has turned into public property. They are his own, especially the harmony, over which there have been complaints about the continual violation of rules, whereas it is no more than a remarkable extension of principles. The same applies to the economy of the thematic development, which operates not merely from a musical point of view but one that is profoundly psychological and entirely novel. The same goes too for the logic of the orchestral commentary, admirable in its compositional consistency. All that is his own, entirely his own, and it is piquant to find him reproached for it, after the complaints about his colleagues' opposite faults, which finally turned into excellent qualities.

As space is limited, I shall not say more about the music of *Pelléas et Mélisande*. For one thing, it doesn't lend itself to such treatment and in this case general remarks are preferable to expert dissections. In order to appreciate the beauty of the composer's work fully and easily, it is enough to look at it not from the viewpoint of shadows, technicalities and strips of lead, but from that of the light which the words shed upon it. It is from this that everything moves and has its being, that every phrase of the work shows up distinctly against a shared background of emotion and humanity, that every bar marks its correspondence with the scene it underlines, from the darkest to the most brilliant, and with the feelings it wishes to convey, from the tenderest and most passionate to the most terrible and most mysterious.

Pelléas et Mélisande is not only a fine work, it is also a marvellous spectacle. M. Carré has blessed the work of MM. Maeterlinck and Debussy with the advantages of a most intelligent and sensitive production, giving proof of a determination for which he deserves our warmest thanks. The scenery of M. Jusseaume and M. Ronsin must count among their most beautiful creations. The interpretation is in no way inferior to the production. Mlle Garden is the most poetic and touching Mélisande, M. Dufranne the most tragic Golaud, M. Vieuille the most moving Arkel one could wish for. Mlle Gerville-Réache's vocal abilities are fully demonstrated in the role of Geneviève, as are

M. Périer's dramatic ones in that of Pelléas. As for M. Messager, who conducts the orchestra, his task is the most important and the best fulfilled. He conducts the performance with a care, an accuracy and a passion that the composer himself has recognized in affectionately dedicating the score to him.

[1] Jules Barbier contributed librettos for Gounod's *Faust* and Offenbach's *Tales of Hoffmann* among many others, often in collaboration with Michel Carré

[2] It would seem from this remark that Dukas was unaware of Fauré's treatment of the play on these lines, premiered at the Prince of Wales's Theatre in London on 21 June 1898

19c. Henry Gauthier-Villars (Willy): review of *Pelléas*; 'Les Premières', *L'Echo de Paris*, 1 May 1902

The heroine, married to an unattractive lord whom she doesn't love, finds herself drawn to another, younger and more handsome, who happens to be her husband's brother. The husband, innocently alerted to his unhappy situation by his own son, in his jealousy exacts a bloody revenge.

This story I'm relating is not that of [Francis Marion] Crawford's adaptation of Dante's *Francesca da Rimini*, made more powerful still by Marcel Schwob's splendid translation,[1] but of *Pelléas et Mélisande*, an entirely human drama in Maeterlinck's early manner, one that out-and-out realists could have treated as something brutal, but which here becomes a drama of overwhelming charm, thanks to the indefinable atmosphere that envelops it ... Mélisande, 'a poor little mysterious being, as mysterious as the world itself', a vast forest, an old, gloomy castle, and there we are carried far back into the past, a past without history, beyond the reach of Time.

You leave the house, your head still buzzing with the vacuities of daily life, burdened by (unimportant) feminine betrayals, annoyed by (cruel) attacks on friendship, you cross the busy, banally modernist boulevard, and you enter a theatre a-twitter with all the prattle of a first night ('At the dress rehearsal, some fuddy-duddies began to whistle[2], but I, my dear, I'm all for the new in art and I clapped all the time, even during the orchestral interludes'). And then silence falls, the lights go down, a plaintive melody breathes out like the stammering of some precocious, all-too-aware child, and we fall under the spell of the enchanted forest where men get lost. Who is this blonde Mélisande, weeping by a well? Who is this rough hunter, a good man, but one who initially terrifies the unknown girl? We don't know. And the continuing music leads us on towards the gloomy castle ...

As for analysing works like this, I wouldn't know how. The very special suggestiveness that it breathes can perhaps be best explained by a comparison.

Ancient Byzantine frescoes are clumsily inserted between heavy Roman pillars; it's a naïve, recherché image; even so, our educated experts are careful not to laugh at them and we turn away from them with regret, interested as we are to understand the soul of the past which emanates from the discreet silence of the lines. Bit by bit this simple décor seems to come alive, as our captivated eyes unwittingly give it presence; the statue, artlessly formed by inexpert hands, detaches itself, apparently to walk slowly through the ancient atmosphere of its dream, which has become ours. So it is with Mélisande, frail, exquisitely blonde, whose melancholy profile is merely the visible soul of a forgotten ideal.

M. Claude-Achille Debussy is not just any old composer; his works are few in number, but each one excites equally passionate enthusiasms and denigrations, equally irritating for anyone trying to reach some dispassionate judgment. Whether he writes his marvellous *Chansons de Bilitis*, or the *Proses lyriques* (so unfortunately saddled with feeble texts), or the *Après-midi d'un Faune*, a landscape of delightfully accessible 'mallarmism', you can hear frenzied admirers trumpeting his fame, ineptly, and block-headed detractors refusing him any kind of merit. Let us pass on, keeping an equal distance between devotees and detractors and their matching absurdities.

There are people, who don't admit the fact today, who once upon a time whistled at *Namouna*[3]. Others at *Tannhäuser*. At the dress rehearsal, some people whistled at *Pelléas et Mélisande*. At the first night, despite some sensible cuts, they laughed. Why?

To begin with, Maeterlinck's text may have shocked them by certain deliberate awkwardnesses. When Golaud, thinking himself betrayed, grabs Mélisande by the hair, pulls her left and right, forward and backward, bangs her head on the ground and then leaves, saying 'I don't attach any importance to that', you can understand why people should be astonished. And then, there's the fact, is there not, that a deceived husband can never be other than ridiculous. Whether it's Othello or Golaud, as soon as a husband enters whose intimate trust has been abused, the whole audience, thanks to an attitude that is incorrigibly

French, feels the need to burst out laughing, even if up to a third of them are cuckolds themselves. What can one do?

But crucially, the hitherto unknown art of *Pelléas* has outraged the unintelligent. M. Debussy's plan and shaping have totally escaped the public's understanding; if it is inexcusable to have protested, it is excusable not to have understood.

Any number of innovations may have contributed to their bewilderment: first of all, the deliberate use of psalm-like declamation, written almost exclusively in the middle and lower registers. Then the almost total absence of any songlike phrase, designed to infuriate the lovers of Wagner's immense flowerings; in *Pelléas*, melodic outlines do not really exist (at any rate, never in the voices) and the music's effects are produced only by sonorities and harmonies, – sonorities that are wonderfully expressive, but collections of harmonies that are unorthodox and the personal property of the composer who, far from avoiding them, goes energetically in search of fourths and fifths, with the latter especially common in the chains of parallel ninths, a prodigal source of falses relations and dissonances.

My God, yes! Dissonances! I don't subscribe to the thinking of M. Théodore Dubois[4], recently mentioned in high places, nor to his technical rules, but even so, without according Reber's *Traité d'harmonie* more importance than it deserves[5], I admit that certain clashes in *Pelléas*, especially when they occur between the voice and the orchestra (when, as a result, they are not softened by timbres), – well there it is, this is probably me turning into a reactionary, and it *is* my turn, – I confess that these clashes I've just mentioned, well yes, they rather get my goat!

The young Debussystes among you, being apostles of unresolved appoggiaturas, will object that it took years and years before anyone dared use sevenths unprepared. It's true. You will remind me of how the Parnassians backed away in horror from the irregular extensions of 'free verse'. I don't deny it. And probably I'm wrong, like those painters wedded to their dull blacks and greys when they rose up against the sparkling colours of the Impressionists. All right, I take it all back!

And yes, 'Impressionist' is indeed the label that suits M. Debussy, with the proviso that it carries no pejorative intent. The composer who has found those wonderful sounds to underline the flight of Mélisande's doves, the entrancing ambiguity of the keys of F sharp and C sharp major in the duet scene between Golaud and his wife, the outburst of youthful passion at the words 'On dirait que ta voix a passé sur la mer ... ' (trumpet, solo cello and strings), and finally the harmonies that decorate the bed in which this 'little life' fades away, with the caresse of a ray from the setting sun, like a scent whose perfume one cannot identify, this composer is more than an Impressionist; he is, just like Maeterlinck, a poet.

Among his other original qualities, M. Debussy possesses that of not imitating Wagner; he recalls the looming god of Bayreuth only once, but on that occasion does so accurately. It happens in the interlude linking the first two scenes (not included in the Fromont edition)[6], where you seem to be hearing the entry of the knights in *Parsifal* – the same rhythm, almost identical harmonies, and the trumpet in a high register[7]. – Another composer, brought to mind more readily by Debussy, is the strange and too little known Mussorgsky, whose influence is undeniably present in the letter read by the queen (in which Mlle Gerville-Réache was perfect); the declamation and the poignantly correct prosody evoke, through their attention to precise notation of the words, the astonishing inventions of the *Nursery Songs*. But the unexpected modulations (from F major to F sharp major, for instance), our native composer did not borrow these from anyone.

His original, personal orchestration too belongs to him alone ... with so little polyphony! No one could accuse him of overloading it: the violins are sometimes silent for nearly forty bars at a time (between ourselves, I would prefer it if the muted trumpets observed the same reserve); and in the third act you cannot help loving the sudden silence from the orchestra that leaves the voices of the two lovers whispering their confessions with no one else to hear them.

I should like to mention, to the experts in particular – and beyond that, to everybody – the very opening with its delightfully archaic colouring, its whole-tone scales and chords of the ninth (unprepared, naturally); the orchestral babbling that accompanies the dialogue between the two women with its flutes and divided strings; the semiquaver patterns in the harps that join with the enchanting woodwind harmonies in the scene from the second act between Pelléas and Mélisande; the extraordinary rustle of modulating chromatic chords as he sings with his hands buried in her golden, fairy hair; the tragic notes of bassoons, horns and double basses grumbling away in the vaults; and the escape from them, in an astonishing blaze of sunlight from exultant harps, trumpets and glockenspiel, telling us of Pelléas's joyful relief.

Mlle Garden is infinitely touching; MM. Vieuille (Arkel) and Dufranne (Golaud) perform marvels; M. Jean Périer seems to me a Pelléas more dexterous than poetic; little Blondin [Yniold] is entirely charming. The designer Jusseaume is some form of deity. Messager remains Messager, thanks be to God!

[1] Crawford's play *Francesca da Rimini*, in Schwob's translation, was produced in Paris in 1902 by Crawford's friend Sarah Bernhardt

[2] French house keys of the time were hollow and so could be used as whistles for demonstrating disapproval

[3] Edouard Lalo's ballet *Namouna* was premiered at the Paris Opéra on 6 March 1882. On that occasion the wildness of the 19-year-old Debussy's applause led to the banning of Conservatoire students for some months from their designated box

[4] Dubois had been Director of the Paris Conservatoire since 1896

[5] Reber's *Traité d'harmonie* of 1862 went through numerous editions

[6] The vocal score published by Fromont on 10 May 1902 did not include any of the orchestral interludes

[7] In fact, two trumpets

20 WHO WAS MÉLISANDE?

If we look back at the history of the French over the last couple of hundred years, I think we have to say 'a hard time they had of it'. A bloody revolution in 1789, defeat at Waterloo, two more revolutions (if rather less bloody) in 1830 and 1848, a *coup d'état* in 1851, defeat by the Prussians in 1870 followed by a welter of self-inflicted blood during the Commune. Add to that the near-military-takeover by General Boulanger in 1889 and anarchist bombings in Paris during the early 1890s, and we're really rather a long way from Renoir and his placid, delectable surfaces.

It's tempting to compare this tormented history with the relative stability of Britain during those same years. True, we also removed a king's head; but nearly a hundred and fifty years earlier. And by 1689 we'd settled on a good old British compromise. After which nothing on the French scale happened to our civilian population until the First World War.

The hundred years from 'the' Revolution of 1789 had, then, been for the French a time of questioning the right to hold power. Not that there was any real hope of the monarchy being restored: one historian has written of 'that contempt for the facts which was the hallmark of the French royalists' and their dreamworld had little to do with the realities of French politics. But once you've shaken up the beehive, as the French did in 1789, and indeed killed the queen, then who knows where the workers will go? Or who they may sting? Shakespeare, as usual, put his finger on the nub, in the dialogue between Kent and King Lear. 'You have that in your countenance,' says Kent, 'which I would fain call master.' 'What's that?' asks Lear. 'Authority'. But where should authority be found?

'Nowhere', replied anarchists like Ravachol. And in July 1892 he paid the price, singing revolutionary songs on his way to the guillotine. So it was into no very settled society, one decidedly not 'at ease with itself', that a single performance of Maeterlinck's play *Pelléas et Mélisande* insinuated itself less than a year later; with Debussy in the audience.

Had he read the play beforehand? Had he already decided to set it as an opera? We don't know for sure – testimonies differ. In any case I don't think it matters much. Far more important was the way in which *Pelléas* the play met his own specific requirements. These were so detailed and peculiar that, as he admitted some years later, 'after several attempts I had almost given up the idea' – that is, of writing for the theatre at all. And when he lighted upon *Pelléas*, well-meaning friends were quite sure the result was going to be a disaster.

The distance between Debussy's vision and the current realities of French opera can best be judged, I think, by direct comparison. Take the opening of Messager's *La Basoche*, premiered at the Opéra-Comique in 1890 – a story of 16th-century royal folk. Well, you may say, royalty demands a certain amount of pomp and circumstance; it'd be fairer to choose a more intimate drama – Massenet's version, for example, of Goethe's *The Sorrows of Werther*, given its French premiere, again at the Opéra-Comique, in January 1893, just 4 months before Debussy saw Maeterlinck's play.

'We've just had a *Werther* by Massenet,' wrote Debussy a few weeks later, 'displaying an extraordinary talent for satisfying all that is poetically empty and lyrically cheap in the dilettante mind! Everything in it contributes to providing mediocrity, and it's all part, too, of this appalling habit of taking something which is perfectly good in itself and then committing treason against its spirit with light, easy sentimentality: Faust eviscerated by Gounod, or Hamlet more honoured in the breach than the observance by Monsieur Ambroise Thomas.'

The opening bars of Debussy's opera *Pelléas et Mélisande*; a story that is both royal and intimate, turns aside from the 'poetically empty', the 'lyrically cheap'; it even dares, apparently, to run out of steam after a mere 6 bars and starts repeating itself – ... by which time any audience more interested in unwrapping its boiled sweets has already missed the boat.

In 1940, the Cambridge Professor of Music, Edward J. Dent, as already quoted, wrote that 'the strain of listening to this rather long opera, almost all in subdued tones, never knowing what the harmonies of the music are, never knowing what the characters are really supposed to be thinking and doing, is to some people unbearable'. He went on to make clear that he wasn't one of such people (nor was Vaughan Williams, who adored the work) but even so this general reaction makes sense in the light of what Debussy admitted he would be looking for – almost four years before he saw *Pelléas* in the theatre: 'a playwright who only hints at things. Two dreams in combination, that's the ideal. No set place or time. No big scene'. He also hoped for ingredients he would not in fact find in *Pelléas*, like a short libretto and characters who didn't discuss things – though the question of what does or does not constitute a discussion lies close to the heart of the opera.

If *Pelléas* differs in its initial approach from *La Basoche* or *Werther* - saying not 'now hear this!' but rather letting us overhear something private and secret – it also differs markedly from the run of 19th-century operas involving royalty (quite a large number). I've already taken the liberty of putting into your mind the suggestion that royalty begets pomp and circumstance. It seems to us quite natural that after the Royal Hunt and Storm in Berlioz's *The Trojans*, Dido and Aeneas should be fêted with dances to celebrate the victory over the Numidians. In Verdi's *Don Carlos*, the spectacle of King Philip presiding over the burning of heretics in the piazza contrasts abruptly and brutally with the following scene as, alone in his study, he reflects miserably that his queen never loved him; but the power of this contrast lies, surely, in its dramatic truth. Twentieth-century newspapers, if they have taught us nothing else, have shown us that 'the royals' are nonetheless people with feelings like our own, even if *noblesse* often obliges them, as in King Philip's case, to wear the mask of duty. But in *Pelléas*, there are no public demonstrations of any kind. So why make the family a royal one? Surely the tale would work just as well if Golaud were a woodcutter or a stockbroker?

I suggest Maeterlinck may have had at least two reasons. The first, perhaps, was to arouse our expectations in order, then, to overturn them. Look at the symbolic objects that come into the story: a well, a ring, a crown, a forest, a castle, a tower, a dungeon, the sea – and a young girl with long fair hair. Put together, they form almost a parody of traditional fairytale ingredients. But the one item that's missing is crucial: magic. There is no love potion, as in *Tristan*. Nor, as in 17th- or 18th-century opera, does some god providentially descend in the last act to sort things out. To this extent, the fairytale element is a deliberate blind on Maeterlinck's part: and as the drama proceeds, he injects various elements of realism so that we cease to expect any kind of magic – instead, we sense ever more strongly that the characters are out on their own, left to struggle through as best they may.

One of these elements of realism is the kind of dialogue both Pelléas and Golaud engage in with Mélisande. In the very first scene, Golaud assumes the role of questioner. Where has she come from? Who gave her the crown? And so on. Sometimes she gives a straight answer. But not always. 'You look very young', he says, 'how old are you?' Altogether too personal and specific. And like a character in Pinter or Beckett (or, if you prefer, like an MP in difficulties) she answers a quite different question.

Maeterlinck actually makes a joke at this point, which works only in the original French. Golaud asks: 'Quel âge avez-vous?' And Mélisande answers: 'Je commence à avoir ... ' What will it be? Vingt ans? Dix-sept ans? Quinze ans, and surely there'll be trouble with the censors. But no. 'Je commence à avoir ... froid.' Needless to say, Debussy picks up on the joke: to begin with, she echoes Golaud's notes – then, on the word 'froid', he gives her a note of her own.

There's no labouring the point – Golaud comes straight in with yet another question. Indeed, one of the unsettling things about this kind of dialogue – one can hardly call it 'discussion' – is that Golaud, and later Pelléas, accept her evasiveness, instead of repeating the question. But maybe that's simply their noble upbringing: if she doesn't want to answer, it is impolite to press.

And this brings us to what I feel may be Maeterlinck's second reason for setting his play in a royal household: simply that Golaud, Pelléas, Arkel, Geneviève and Yniold are of royal blood; Mélisande, so far as we know, is not. Fairytale convention would have us suppose that she might be a distant princess, a 'princesse lointaine'. But the nearest she has come to being royal, to our knowledge and to Golaud's, is that she has been abandoned by some man who, for whatever reason, gave her a crown. For the purposes of the opera, she is an outsider in every sense. Well may Arkel grumpily comment that Golaud might have done better to follow his advice and marry the Princess Ursula, which 'would have put an end to a long war and a history of inveterate hatred'. He doesn't say so, but presumably the qualities of the Princess Ursula would also have been posted on the royal grapevine and the kingdom of Allemonde would have had some idea of what it was getting.

The dangers of simply following one's instinct in matters like this are, you might think, amply demonstrated by what follows. But Maeterlinck was not in any sense publishing a royalist tract. In one of the passages Debussy cut from Arkel's often lengthy pronouncements, the old king admits: 'I am very old, and yet I have never been able, even for a moment, to view myself clearly. How can you expect me to judge the actions of others?'

Commendable humility, we may say. But if the king is not going to exercise his authority in the matter of dynastic marriages, when is he going to? We learn from Golaud at the beginning of Act IV that the famine in Allemonde continues: 'They've found another peasant starved to death, down by the sea. Anyone would think they're all determined to die before our very eyes'. Debussy captures marvellously Golaud's peevish tone. Whether because Arkel has vetoed his plan for effective action, or because he doesn't think it's his responsibility, or simply because he doesn't know what to do, Maeterlinck's text does not make clear: but Debussy seems to go for the last option, setting the end of his phrase to whole-tone harmonies which, throughout the opera, can indicate vagueness and indecision as well as menace. So, presumably, the peasants will go on dying until the weather changes.

Neither Maeterlinck nor Debussy is actually giving us any recipe as to how authority can best be constituted. Their attitude is nearer to Arkel's: 'how do you expect me to judge the actions of others?' But for an unstable, uneasy society like the Paris of the 1890s *Pelléas et Mélisande* told important truths about what can happen when authority breaks down, when the king is 'blind' to what is happening around him, and when emotions are allowed to get the better of common sense – the two main emotions in question here being love, and anger leading to violence.

Love, of course, has always been a mainstay of opera, and even if Debussy's treatment of it has many wonderful features, I wouldn't say it was revolutionary – or not beyond being less noisy than in most other operas. But I do think his treatment of anger and violence is extraordinary; and, rightly performed, terrifying. I should point out that the view of Debussy as the lazy voluptuary is only half the picture. His stepdaughter, Dolly de Tinan, assured me that he had a violent temper and that as a teenager she would hide in her bedroom while the storm blew itself out.

Golaud's first outburst of anger, when he sees that his ring is missing from Mélisande's finger, is in some ways the most terrifying of all, because it marks the beginning of the catastrophe. In some cases the horror comes straight from Maeterlinck, as in Golaud's insistence that she goes and looks for it in the cave by the sea, sarcastically echoing her fearful 'Now? Immediately? In the darkness?' In some cases it comes from additions by Debussy, as in the orchestra's mocking laughter when Golaud tells her to take Pelléas with her and that he won't object: 'I know Pelléas better than you'; or as in the spine-chilling chord that ends Golaud's cry 'I shall not sleep until I have the ring'.

Maeterlinck and Debussy were not only commentators on society, they became prophets. The composer finished his first draft of *Pelléas* in the August of 1895. By the time of its first production in 1902 France was riven by conflicting loyalties. Was the Jewish army officer Alfred Dreyfus a spy, passing military secrets to Germany? Or was he the innocent victim of an Establishment setup? There were riots, condemnations, forgeries, suicides, fear of anarchy. Lifelong friendships were broken, families irrevocably split. The opera audience at the premiere of *Pelléas*, like the rest of France, was in no doubt about the power of the outsider to divide and subvert.

Among the many recordings of *Pelléas et Mélisande*, a unique place is occupied by the one made by HMV in April and May 1941, in which Roger Désormière conducted a cast including Irène Joachim as Mélisande, Jacques Jansen as Pelléas and Henri Etcheverry as Golaud, all of whom had performed in the Opéra-Comique run of the opera the previous year. For me, 24 June 1985 was the very special day on which Mme Joachim talked to me about the opera and wrote in my copy of the orchestral score, 'Thinking of our discussion about the profundity and striking "subtlety" of the opera's silences, the former Mélisande that I am is very happy to have made your acquaintance.' Our mutual friend Madeleine Milhaud, the composer's widow, later said to me with one of her naughty grins, 'Dear Irène, I never see her without her talking about *Pelléas*!' I was pleased to respond that, in my case, her memories had been very much to the point ... Mary Garden sang Mélisande in the original production of 1902.

21 *PELLÉAS ET MÉLISANDE* – INTERVIEW WITH IRÈNE JOACHIM

Paris 24 June 1985

Translated from the French original

RN: (after tape recorder finally agrees to cooperate): Enfin, nous y sommes!

IJ: C'est ici. Nous y sommes! [*Pelléas*, Act II sc 3] It's extraordinary, with *Pelléas* you can always find a phrase to fit any situation.

RN: And Debussy quotes the work all the time in his letters.

IJ: Indeed he does. Well now, as we're talking about *Pelléas* and the Opéra Comique and the various productions of the work, I may say I began to study it as soon as I left the Conservatoire with my singing prizes, and worked on it with the famous Georges Viseur, the *chef du chant* at the first performance. I had a contract for the role with Jacques Rouché and it was my official debut. Rouché was a marvellous director, adored by everybody, and very rich, and he spent millions on organizing the electricity at the Opéra immediately after the First World War.

RN: Lighting is a very important part of *Pelléas*, would you agree?

IJ: Certainly. We're talking here about the Opéra Comique where it didn't work very well, especially for certain scenes. We were very surprised when we took the opera to Covent Garden in 1949 with the same cast for the main roles as in 1942, and with quite extraordinary scenery by Valentine Hugo that caused quite a scandal. This had been badly lit at the Opéra Comique in 1947. Now we saw the opera with what I would call 'cold' lighting, with faded blues, whites and greys: there was a certain influence of William Blake which was tremendous and which came from the lighting.

For the 50th anniversary in 1952 at the Opéra Comique, – Désormière was ill by then, so the conductor was Albert Wolff – we were delighted to have a recreation of the layout and décor of the première, with the simplicity created by Jusseaume: it was so easy to find one's way round those sets. Because it has to be said that there are rules to be observed over this, and even the cleverest people get things wrong, if they don't understand what it is to move around a stage, what with various problems including timing, as well as being dragged around the stage. So in general if the tower is in the centre, it's very difficult, because Pelléas is standing at the foot of it and once he begins to play with Mélisande's hair, he can no longer see the conductor. That's why it's always better to have the tower slightly to one side. The same applies to the well: if it's in the centre, as in the production by Cocteau, it's extremely difficult for Pelléas to manage. As I say, there are rules one has to follow in this opera which are very hard to go against.

RN: Then there is the whole question of the work's symbolism ...

IJ: I think it's crucial to keep things as simple as possible because, once you get into that world, you never get out. To become too philosophical about the opera, in my view, to some extent undermines its strength. There's no need to underline things. The opera works very well on its own and if you go down that road you find yourself, philosophically speaking, in a very Germanic world, and I think perhaps that this is not Debussy's simple solution. It's unsettling.

RN: We should say something about Mary Garden ...

IJ: Mary Garden for a time lived in my mother's house. That's why, when she heard that I was working on Mélisande, the connection was made and she took me right through Albert Carré's production of the première. But if I'd followed her instructions in every detail, it wouldn't have worked because things have to evolve – when I was young, I was very close to various film makers including Jean Renoir, and that had an influence. But Mary Garden's thought processes were unforgettable, the way she felt things, I shall never forget them.

RN: Talking about things evolving, do you think Mélisande's character changes during the course of the opera?

IJ: I think she evolves because she is subject to the constraints of her time. I reached my deepest understanding of Mélisande's thoughts and reactions from reading the remarkable diary of Paul Dukas, because of the language he uses to describe Ariane in his opera *Ariane et Barbe-bleue*. He writes of Ariane who wants to set the other wives free, but who realizes that they are 'frozen' to such an extent that, in the last act, when the peasants deliver Bluebeard, bound and bleeding, to the castle and she says 'I'm leaving. Are you coming with me?', they don't move. For me there is a link, even if Dukas's music was written after *Pelléas*. There is only one person. It could have been a subconscious gesture on Maeterlinck's part, it's possible.

In the first scene of *Pelléas*, with 'Ne me touchez pas, ou je me jette à l'eau', what is she frightened of? It's Bluebeard. And suddenly she says, 'Your hair is grey … and your beard too.' Then there's the phrase 'C'est la couronne qu'il m'a donnée. Elle est tombée en pleurant', the second part of which is rather comical in French, but which the chords in the orchestra turn into something extraordinary. She wants to get rid of everything, to liberate herself. She doesn't want to get married, but she's caught in a trap because it's cold, she's alone and she needs to feel safe. Mary Garden and I were in complete agreement that she had already been married once before, and in her words 'In the gardens it is dark, and what forests all round the palace!' we can tell that she once again fears she may be a prisoner as she was in Bluebeard's dungeon – it's plausible. I don't know whether you agree, but it's something that has always helped me create the character.

And then suddenly Pelléas arrives. And Mary Garden said to me, 'You look at him. You devour him with your eyes, but he must not see you. For you, though, it's love at first sight.' You can hear Mélisande's disarray as she says, 'Look, my arms are full of flowers'. Jacques Jansen and I agreed on the way to play this ending to the scene. He takes her arm and then he says, 'It could be I'm leaving tomorrow'. After a brief pause, she looks at him – 'Oh, why are you leaving?' He turns his head and she turns her eyes away — because, in the final scene at the well in Act IV he says, 'And I have not yet met her gaze'. So all the producers who haven't applied this remark back to the end of Act II — it's wrecked!

As for Mélisande's evolution, you can talk of destiny or whatever you like, but everything in the opera can take on an extraordinary importance. I gave so many performances with Henri Etcheverry as Golaud, and I can tell you that in every performance there were things that were new. This is something I tell young singers: 'You can find something in the smallest reaction that gives rise to a different thought.'

But to return to your question about whether Mélisande evolves, yes, because at the moment of that terrible scene 'Absalon! Absalon!' she understands what has been said in a different way, going back to her first meeting with Golaud. In the crucial scene — though Mary Garden said to me that all the scenes were crucial! — at Mélisande's bedside in Act V she remembers everything that has been said, including her own words in Act II: 'One never sees the sky here. I saw it for the first time this morning.' And there is no duplicity in her behaviour. She's a creature of instinct. She's like a child, she really believes she has seen a certain thing. If something was glistening in the well, she might see it of course.

RN: May I read you an extract from Inghelbrecht's book *Comment on ne doit pas interpréter 'Carmen', 'Faust', Pelléas*? 'After Golaud's question "What is that glistening down in the water?" a reflex of feminine, childish curiosity makes her exclaim almost cheerfully "Where?" and at once her "Ah!" plunges us back once more into her melancholy.'

IJ: And that is perhaps a memory of Bluebeard.

RN: One thing that interests me is that she says to Pelléas, 'I never lie. I lie only to your brother.'

IJ: It's absolutely marvellous. It's because she's afraid, afraid of Golaud. She dissimulates. She doesn't dare to tell the truth — children are like that sometimes, they dissimulate. I remember my son when he was around four or five doing that. An excess of imagination, if you like. I didn't have time one Christmas Eve, what with my teaching at the Conservatoire, to buy him any toys, and he said to his godfather, 'No, Father Christmas isn't coming tonight because he's hurt his leg.' And his godfather said, 'But if you say that and he does come, then what?'

And my son said, 'You don't understand, it didn't happen to the real Father Christmas but to the fake one.' Mélisande has an instinct of self-preservation and she feels like a little bird caught in a trap. For me, none of the phrases of hers that are generally felt to be ambiguous are in fact so. I was told, when I started studying the role, 'She is sly, she is this, she is that.' Not at all.

RN: So how do you account for the exchange with Golaud in the first scene, when he asks her, 'How old are you?' and she replies, 'I'm starting to feel cold'?

IJ: For me, that's highly significant. Some people who don't understand the situation think it's coquetry on her part, not wanting to say how old she is. But it's because 'This is the age when I must die'. Her coldness looks forward to the last act when she says, 'It's cold and there are no more leaves'.

I strongly disagree with certain designers and producers who have the regrettable tendency to treat Mélisande as a feminine object [la femme-objet]. I find that intolerable. It's here that I find relevant the problem of liberty raised by Paul Dukas – the liberty of the woman who is the equal of the man – because we are here in a story of the Middle Ages. And it's against the constraints of the time that she's defending herself, that she's floundering around. She revolts, as Carmen does. Golaud has no understanding of this, none at all, nor does Pelléas, he's too young.

RN: How do you interpret the last line of the opera: 'Now it's the turn of the poor little one'?

IJ: There you have the link with *Wozzeck*. In the midst of sorrow and pain there is always this glimmer of hope, in Berg as well as in Debussy. Life has to go on despite all the terrible events.

RN: I know you sang Mélisande in many different opera houses. What are your memories of those occasions?

IJ: Before going to London in 1949 we took the opera to Venice. There were no proper sets or costumes, as it was so soon after the war! For Mélisande's long hair we had to make do with attaching blue scarves to mine; all our friends came from Paris and said it didn't matter in the slightest. It was there we heard the most extraordinary remark, one difficult to understand for a Parisian public that has fixed ideas about Impressionism and so on. One morning we all went to see the glassmakers of Torcello and Murano, and they were music-lovers and had boxes at the opera, as the Conservatoire students do in Paris. Of course they didn't understand a word of what we sang, but they brought us coloured glass bowls as presents and one said to us, 'Really, Debussy is your Puccini.' Désormière, naturally, was thrilled.

If Berlioz and Massenet, and indeed Debussy, had their awkward sides, they were nothing compared to the prickly hedgehog that was Magnard. This, of course, has not helped his music, but he certainly doesn't deserve the almost total oblivion into which he has fallen. Herewith another lance – short this time, but still sharpish.

22 ALBÉRIC MAGNARD

If your immediate reaction on seeing this title was 'Albéric who?', you may be forgiven. The fault, if fault it be, can be attributed to no one more reasonably than to the composer himself. On the lines of the rebuke aimed by the Soviet authorities at Prokofiev, that 'he trod on the throat of his own song', one may say that Magnard trod on the toes of his own career, and did so with a truly remarkable persistence and ingenuity. Most composers demonstrate some affinity at least between their own characters and those of their music, but in Magnard's case the link is unusually clear: the message runs 'music is a vocation: there is no room for compromise.' So it was in his life.

One doesn't need to be a trained psychologist to trace such determination to his early years. Although born, on 9 June 1865, into an apparently settled middle-class family, his world was turned upside down in April 1869 when his mother, in a fit of depression, jumped out of an upper window and died a few days later. His father, Francis, was on his way up to being eventually editor of the prestigious journal *Le Figaro*, but was himself given to taking a gloomy view of the human race and, like many a modern tabloid journalist, was becoming feared for his ability to prick bubbles and nose out scandals. His watchword was 'truth', 'la vérité', the personification of which was to figure years later in Albéric's opera *Guercoeur*.

The young boy found solace in reading, in nature and in his piano lessons with Charles de Savignac, a pupil of Halévy. But like so many fathers in musical history, Francis insisted his son had a conventional education and should then train as a lawyer. The only sign of anything unusual in Albéric was his enjoyment of his mandatory military service, in which he rose to the rank of sub-lieutenant. But, as for many French musicians of his time, Wagner was waiting round the corner: *Parsifal* and *Tristan* at Bayreuth in 1886 could not be gainsaid, and that autumn, to papa's fury, Magnard joined Théodore Dubois's Conservatoire class as an 'auditeur'. From here he moved on to Massenet, *Die Meistersinger*, and finally Vincent d'Indy, who from 1888 was to remain his guiding star. Many years later Varèse was to stigmatise d'Indy's teaching as 'bigoted', but Magnard found in him the assurance he needed, and also an emphasis on fugal writing that was to bear vigorous fruit.

If d'Indy was proving a useful counterweight to papa, the latter could not be ignored. For one thing, now editor of *Le Figaro*, he was commissioning his son to write articles on music, among them three on the complete performance of Berlioz's *Les Troyens* in Karlsruhe under Felix Mottl – a treat Paris audiences didn't enjoy until 1921 and then in a condensed form. Albéric also had warm words for the Chanteurs de Saint Gervais and their promotion of Renaissance polyphony, and an article on Rameau in March 1894, pointing out the shameful fact that there was no reliable edition of the composer's music, found an immediate response from the publishers Durand. Meanwhile, Magnard was composing: an orchestral suite 'in the ancient style', some songs, an opera *Yolande* (all of two performances in Brussels), and two symphonies in which one can still hear the wheels going round, rather creakily in spots, as well as a set of piano pieces inspired by his walks with Julia Bartet, whom he was to marry in 1896: in the last piece, 'Rambouillet', the fanfares are a reminder of those that accompanied the switching off of the lights in the park of the castle, after which the courting couple are left haplessly (and syncopatedly) searching for an exit.

Although Magnard was determined to follow his own musical path, he was not deaf to the world around him and in 1894 tapped into the rise of interest in wind instruments, sparked off by Paul Taffanel's founding in 1878 of the Société de chambre pour instruments à vent. Magnard's Quintet for flute, oboe, clarinet, bassoon and piano already displays some of the composer's characteristic gestures: a fugue in the development of the first movement, a modal, folky tune for the oboe in the third, and in the finale a plethora of dotted rhythms, duly soothed by a more flowing second idea (the piece is, incidentally, one of Jean-Efflam Bavouzet's favourites!). This was his last score before the defining event on 18 November 1894 of his father's death.

It had certainly been a difficult relationship, but now Magnard, to his surprise, felt bereft. An answer was also supplied to the question of how far Papa's influence had eased Albéric's way in the musical world – the very possibility of which the son had always resented. The answer of the musical world was a decisive 'yes' and took the form, not of antagonism but, more woundingly, of outright rejection and abandon. Between 1895 and 1902 Magnard's music was played just twice in public concerts, and for the 1900 International Exhibition was totally ignored. One can perhaps forgive the sidelining of the *Chant funèbre*, written in memory of his father, and of the Overture in A, both of which are possibly overlong for their material. But the splendid Third Symphony, completed in 1896, benefits from his declared intention 'to clean up my style and technique'. Here he rations the counterpoint which had tended to clutter up textures, and now ideas flow far more easily from one to another. At the same time we are aware of his creed that 'to create works that last, one has to be in advance of one's time', even if there must always be one dominating key round which the others are disposed.

By 1899 he realized that musical oblivion called for a radical response. Taking a leaf out of Berlioz's book, on 14 May he conducted an orchestral concert entirely of his own music, including the Third Symphony. It was an undoubted success, with the symphony being especially praised, even if the cost equalled the annual budget of a modest bourgeois family. But then the cloud of oblivion engulfed him once more … At least he was consoled by a happy marriage (Julia felt his rejections far more keenly than he did) and by a warm relationship with the musical powers in Brussels, most notably with the violinist Ysaÿe. While Albert Carré, the director of the Opéra-Comique, was rejecting his opera *Guercoeur* as being too static (true, but it contains some magnificent music), Ysaÿe gave the first performance of Magnard's Violin Sonata, one of his best works. But the date, at the Salle Pleyel in Paris, was 2 May 1902 – just two days after the premiere of *Pelléas et Mélisande*. Result: oblivion once more. And worse still, Ysaÿe, in a huff at the cool reception, would never play it again.

In 1898 Magnard had been one of the first to congratulate Emile Zola on publishing his incendiary letter to the President, 'J'accuse', proclaiming Dreyfus's innocence. Four years later, and true to his passion for 'la vérité', Magnard composed his *Hymne à la Justice*, whose structure follows that of André Chénier's poem of the same title: the violent, dramatic first section depicts the struggles of the oppressed, the second, calm and majestic, glorifies Justice (it was the first orchestral work played in public in Paris at the Liberation in 1944). The work ends with a Franckian chorale and with just a hint of *Tristan and Isolde* in the final plagal cadence. But in general Wagnerian influence is surprisingly scarce. Magnard has a highly individual way of moving from one key to another, often at high speed, but without the slithering chromatics which bedevilled so many of his French contemporaries. If tradition weighed too heavily on him in his String Quartet, there's more light and air in the Piano Trio he finished in 1905, with a few delicate Fauréan touches to the harmony.

More and more, though, Magnard retreated from the world, moving in 1904 to a village, Baron, north of Paris, where he repelled all friendly advances from the locals. He also abandoned publishers, producing his own scores from 1902 onwards, but omitting basic actions such as making sure scores were available for performances. Increasingly, too, he refers in his letters to his works as *mes ordures*. Well might Chausson's wife say that 'Magnard could be a good friend if only he weren't so disagreeable.' On which front, his behaviour over the rehearsals for his opera *Bérénice* at the Opéra-Comique in December 1911 takes the proverbial biscuit: not liking the soprano lead offered him, he engaged another soprano without consulting anybody, all the time accusing the director's wife of trying to sabotage the whole enterprise! Sadly, the opera, which Magnard regarded as his best work, has never been recorded commercially, though there may be a tape somewhere in the vaults of French Radio.

If Magnard was famous for anything, it was for the manner of his death. When the Germans arrived in the first days of September 1914, he sent his wife and two daughters away to safety and, with his stepson, René, remained in his *manoir* to await the invaders. René was returning there just as the Germans arrived, and they promptly tied him to a tree. It seems that Magnard, crouching behind the bathroom shutters with his gun, may have thought they were about to shoot René. At all events, he opened fire, killing one German and wounding another. They responded by setting fire to the *manoir*. Magnard perished in the blaze, together with some of his manuscripts. D'Indy's response to the news was laconic: 'c'était bien lui'. Or as we might say, 'Typical!'

Happily, what does survive from his last years is the magnificent Fourth Symphony, premiered in April 1914. Alternately lyrical and playful, sombre and radiant, it marks the high point of his skill both as structuralist and orchestrator. Together with the Third Symphony, *Guercoeur* and the Violin Sonata, it really ought, on his 150th birthday, to supply the primary material for a re-evaluation of this remarkable composer – saving him, if you like, from himself.

Magnard was not the only prickly hedgehog on the Paris music scene ...

23 **FLORENT SCHMITT**

It's 29 May 1913 and, in the Théâtre des Champs-Élysées in Paris, the premiere of Stravinsky's *The Rite of Spring* is producing one of those splendid *scandales* in which the city specializes. In the midst of the uproar, with the aristos in their boxes shouting, hooting and blowing on their hollow door keys, a stentorian voice breaks through: '*Taisez-vous, garces du seizième*!' ('Shut your gobs, you posh sluts!') It is the voice of the composer Florent Schmitt – and not the first or last time it will be heard sowing discord and aggravation. Of course, this sort of behaviour is not recommended if one wants to make friends and influence people, and in Schmitt's case it has undoubtedly gone some way to marginalising him in the field of French culture. So if his name is unknown to you, no shame is attached.

It all started quite normally. Florent was born on 28 September 1870 in Blâmont in the Vosges, near the border with Germany that would be agreed the following year after the Prussian siege. His father, a haberdasher, was also an amateur organist and both parents encouraged Florent's interest in music, although the boy's independent spirit was already demonstrated in his complaint that 'organists are people who always play in 4/4' (signs of things to come). Music he wrote between the ages of 14 and 17, already showing his love for complex textures, was enough to gain him a place in the Nancy Conservatoire. In 1889 his piano teacher recommended him to Théodore Dubois, the director of the Paris Conservatoire and in September of that year he moved to the capital. Even if Dubois was unhappy with Florent's addiction to chromaticism, Massenet recognised his '*nature exceptionnelle*'.

Massenet resigned in 1896 to be replaced soon afterwards by Fauré, and it was under the latter's tutelage that in 1900, in his last chance as a 30-year-old, Schmitt won the Prix de Rome with his cantata *Sémiramis* (his typically vivid response being 'if I hadn't hit the bull's eye this year, I'd have had to jump in the lake!'). So off to Rome he went. Arriving at the Villa Médicis on 30 December on the stroke of midnight, he had to climb over the fence into the garden. Similar physical activity then marked his four years there, during which he actually spent most of his time travelling round Europe, the Near East and North Africa, imbibing 'exotic' music that was soon to mark his own. The other major influence was César Franck, and in particular his Piano Quintet which, said Schmitt, 'contains more ideas and emotions than the complete works of five members of the Institut, including Saint-Saëns'. In Schmitt's own Quintet, begun but not finished in Rome, the double-dotted rhythms proclaim their allegiance.

His last two years in Rome produced his first two works now in the repertoire. The symphonic study *Le Palais hanté* of 1904, on the poem by Edgar Allan Poe, depicts the mysterious, fear-ridden atmosphere of the 'evil things, in robes of sorrow' that assail the king's palace. Spooky tritones on bass clarinet begin the piece, after which unease is, as often with Schmitt, painted by a series of crescendos and diminuendos. His friend Ravel wrote to him after the first performance to say how much he'd enjoyed it, while admitting 'that our tendencies are not exactly the same'. This is certainly true of Schmitt's last work from Rome, a tumultuous, triumphal setting of Psalm 47. He extended the original text to about three times its length through internal repetitions, most notably of the opening invocation 'O clap your hands, ye people', in which the hard, percussive sound of 'frappez' is dominant. Altogether it's a very exciting work, much recorded, whose reception in 1905 by the French Academy the contrarian Schmitt no doubt savoured: 'violent methods, a horror of the simple and natural, noisy orchestra, almost impossible choral parts, these are the features one notes in this work full of talent, but whose tendencies the Academy is unable to approve'.

Schmitt died in 1958 at the age of 87, his last work, a four-part Mass, bearing the opus number 138. Not surprisingly, the standard of this vast output is variable. The Academy's verdict was one often echoed over the years, French critics quick to sense Schmitt's tenuous relationship with the hallowed national virtues of lightness, clarity, elegance and wit: sarcastic remarks are rife on the lines of 'he never uses one note where five will do'. In some ways, he reminds one of Berlioz and, like him, Schmitt made enemies through his many articles and reviews in which he wrote without fear or favour. That loud voice could also deliver stinging remarks at lesser volume. In 1932 the Paris Opéra, putting on Milhaud's opera *Maximilien*, found itself saddled with one of the most resounding flops ever (it lasted seven performances). After the premiere, friends gathered in a café where, Poulenc recalls, 'we said nothing about the music'. That, if difficult for Milhaud, was after a fashion polite. Not so Schmitt. Meeting Milhaud in a corridor during the half-time interval, he asked the composer 'Are you staying?' Half a century later, when Schmitt's name came up in the presence of Milhaud's widow, she was heard to mutter 'Stupid man!'

Some bright spark had had the idea a decade earlier of offering Schmitt the directorship of the Lyon conservatoire, which he duly exercised between 1921 and 1924. But he was unwilling, or unable, to temper the wind to the shorn lambs in his charge and, after too many young ladies had been found in floods of tears, their efforts sharply dismissed as rubbish, he resigned in 1924 to general relief. A final example of the awkward Schmitt – and one that still reads badly today – was his closeness to collaborators during the Occupation, even though he later claimed he'd been too intent on his work to be really interested in politics. With the arrival of peace, the forces of the *épuration*, the settling of scores, nonetheless condemned him to a year in which he was forbidden to perform himself, to have his music played, or to write for any music journal.

Given this vast output, it's only sensible to describe just a few of his best works. Schmitt was an excellent pianist and Alfred Cortot had good things to say about his music for the instrument, admiring its 'magnificent combination of enthusiasm and disrespect, of sensitivity and brusqueness'. But, as someone not really in tune with modern music, his real love is for the first volume of *Musiques intimes* op 16, published in 1900 but containing pieces written throughout the 1890s (vol 2 from 1904 is more complex and harder to play…). Here Schmitt is not trying to impress, just taking Fauréan patterns and giving them a slightly new twist. Also from 1904 are the wonderful Three Rhapsodies for two pianos op 53, in fact waltzes, dedicated to three of his 'gods', Chabrier, Chopin and Johann Strauss; though the modulations in the third one might have choked the dedicatee on his Sachertorte. In 1905 Schmitt got married and his sense of humour surfaced again in the nickname given to their son Jean – 'Raton' or 'Little Rat', despite which father and son remained very close.

The light-hearted Schmitt does reappear occasionally in his music, as in the delightful *Suite en rocaille* of 1934 for flute, harp and strings (*Rockery Suite* – or possibly *Rubble Suite*?) which puts Baroque clichés through the mincer. But he's heard at his finest and most impressive in three orchestral scores written from 1907 onwards: *La Tragédie de Salomé*, *Antoine et Cléopâtre* and *Salammbô*.

Originally, in 1907, *La Tragédie de Salomé* was a long ballet score. Either in that form or the shorter version for larger orchestra he made in 1909, it was danced by Loïe Fuller, Tamara Karsavina, Natasha Trouhanova and Ida Rubinstein and remained in the Opéra repertoire until the 1950s. This is Schmitt in exotic vein, with sparkling orchestration, trills and middle-Eastern melodies, often with a long initial note flowering into melismas of shorter ones. The work ends with two dances for Salomé, a 'lascivious dance' before she seizes the severed head of John the Baptist and hurls it into the sea, followed by a 'dance of fear', in 5/4, as the palace is engulfed in flames. As in much of Schmitt's orchestral music, he does wonders with repeated short phrases, varied simply through changes of key and orchestral colour.

Rubinstein was also the moving spirit behind the ballet *Antoine et Cléopâtre* put on at the Opéra in 1920. It suffered from being too long – Cleopatra didn't die till 2am – and from her spoken dialogue with Antony being inaudible, but the music is dramatic in the extreme, ranging from the magical Impressionism of the 'Night in the Queen's palace' to the wild energy of 'The Battle of Actium': here the chaos of warfare, leading to Antony's defeat by the emperor-to-be Augustus, is depicted in Schmitt's favourite smorgasbord of metres, successively 3/8, 9/8, 6/8, 3/4, 3/2, 4/2, 5/2. Finally, Schmitt's exotic interest was assuaged in 1925 by writing music for the film *Salammbô*, inspired by Flaubert's 1862 novel about the Carthaginian princess. Again, Impressionism and modernist barbarism rub shoulders, and Schmitt's reduction of the two-hour score to three orchestral suites has rightly been praised as 'a worthy match for Flaubert's impassioned prose'.

Some poor pianist, engaged on disentangling Schmitt's counterpoint, might well have to cope with that voice from the back of the hall shouting 'It's a C SHARP!' Yes, life around Schmitt was never dull. And his music, likewise – now mercifully free of the composer's *fortissimo* exhortations.

One of the best things about Satie is that so much of his piano music is easy to play. But very, very hard to play well. This is but one of the paradoxes explored in the next two articles: the first prosaic; the second, if not exactly poetic, at least dramatic, in the form of a programme of conversations mixing quotations with inventions.

24 ERIK SATIE

Erik Satie was born in Honfleur (Calvados) on 17 May 1866, the eldest child of Alfred and Jane Satie. She was Scottish and later Satie's friends would often refer to his Northern origins as contributing to his individual world view, one reporting that 'Erik came to us from the north in a leather bark manned by a crew of trolls.' More prosaically, the family moved to Paris in 1870 and then, on his mother's death in 1872, Erik was sent back to Honfleur to live with his paternal grandparents. In 1874 he began music lessons with Vinot, a pupil of Niedermeyer. On the death of his grandmother in 1878 he rejoined his father in Paris and the following year entered a preparatory piano class at the Conservatoire. Also in 1879 his father remarried and set up as a music publisher. Erik and his stepmother had a difficult relationship.

Whether as a result of this disturbed childhood or not, his seven years at the Conservatoire were, to say the least, chequered: reports record him as 'gifted but indolent', 'the laziest student in the Conservatoire' and 'worthless. Three months just to learn the exam piece'. But he was already composing and the *Ogives* and *Trois mélodies* date from 1886, when he left the institution, without prizes, for a brief period of military service. Around this time he became interested in mysticism and the Middle Ages, spending hours reading in the Bibliothèque Nationale. The third of the *Mélodies*, 'Sylvie', and the *Ogives* already show, in dispensing with barlines, Satie's penchant for floating rhythms and harmonies, in which traditional tonal functions are greatly weakened.

The *Trois Sarabandes* of 1887 and the *Trois Gymnopédies* of 1888 continue this exploration of a new tonal space, in which pseudo-archaic chords and modal harmonies combine with melodies that seem to derive simultaneously from church and from music hall. For the next ten years he found a home in the capital's flourishing café society, playing the piano at the Chat noir and then at the Auberge du Clou, where in 1891 he met Debussy. Piano pieces continued to flow from his pen, with increasingly strange titles, including *Gnossiennes* (whose relationship with Knossos is at best doubtful), *Sonneries de la Rose + Croix* (he had been appointed 'chapelmaster' of the Rosicrucians in 1891), *Messe des pauvres* and *Pièces froides*. In 1892, 1894 and 1896 he presented himself as a candidate for vacant seats in the Académie des Beaux-Arts – unsuccessfully – but a small move towards wider acknowledgment came with the successful first performance in 1897 at the Salle Erard of Debussy's orchestration of *Gymnopédies* 1 and 3.

One day in October 1898 Satie pushed a wooden handcart containing his worldly goods out of Paris to the southern suburb of Arcueil-Cachan, to a house called 'The Four Chimneys' and into a single room over a dingy café that would be his home for the rest of his life. From here he would walk the six miles to and then back from the city, with stops for cognac and calvados along the way. This was the period of 'The Velvet Gentleman', referring to his wardrobe, which consisted of a dozen identical velvet (or corduroy) suits. He earned a meagre living playing the piano in Montmartre cabarets and wrote songs still sung today, such as *Tendrement, Je te veux* and *La Diva de l'Empire,* as well as putting together from his cabaret material the delightful piano duet suite *Trois Morceaux en forme de poire* – a sly dig at his friend Debussy who had complained of a lack of form in his music.

But sly digs apart, Satie was aware that as a composer he was not achieving any real success and had been made aware by friends and others that he lacked technical proficiency. He therefore took the brave decision to go back to school, and in 1905, as he approached his 40th birthday, enrolled at the Schola Cantorum, the teaching institution founded by Vincent d'Indy to uphold the traditions of his own teacher César Franck. After studying with d'Indy and Roussel for three years, he graduated with first-class honours in 1908. But still he preferred to express himself in small piano pieces with challenging titles, such as the *Aperçus désagréables* of 1908–12.

His final emergence from obscurity can be dated precisely to 16 January 1911, when Ravel performed the prelude to Act I of *Le Fils des étoiles,* the second *Sarabande* and the third *Gymnopédie* at a concert of the newly formed Société musicale indépendante. For a short period the two composers became close friends, with Satie greeting *Ma Mère l'Oye* as a masterpiece and Ravel saying how much he owed to Satie (on which Satie's comment to his brother was a typical 'It's all the same to me.') Later that year the *Sarabandes, Trois Morceaux en forme de poire* and *En Habit de cheval* were published by the major firm Rouart-Lerolle and Satie could be said to have 'arrived'. Spurred on by recognition, he now began to publish piano pieces in abundance, still with titles designed to perplex, such as *Préludes flasques (pour un chien)*, Flabby preludes for a dog, and *Embryons desséchés*, Desiccated embryos, and still with parallel performance instructions, such as 'Like a nightingale with toothache' and 'The moon has had a row with the neighbours'. He also began to publish articles in newspapers and journals. His 'Mémoires d'un amnésique' started to appear in 1912, in which, among other fantasies, he denied being a composer, having been included 'from the beginning of my career among the phonometrographers. My works are pure phonometrics.'

As his friendship with Ravel began to cool, he made the acquaintance of artists who were to be important to him during his final years, including Stravinsky and Diaghilev whom he met in 1912 and 1914. In that year he also composed the 21 tiny pieces that make up the *Sports et divertissements*. As the Satie scholar Robert Orledge writes, 'Whilst Marcel Duchamp or Picabia introduced words into their paintings, only Satie employed a simultaneous counterpoint of poetry, music and drawing within a single composition. This, together with their Japanese concision and immaculate calligraphy, is what makes *Sports et divertissements* such a remarkable achievement'. The drawings by Charles Martin depict various sports and entertainments (hunting, golf, sledging, fireworks) and in many cases the score is a graphic representation of the activity in question. There are also quotations from popular sources, like *Frère Jacques* and the *Marseillaise*, as well as little poems by Satie. The collection is prefaced by an 'Unappetizing Chorale', dedicated by him 'to those who do not like me', and marked to be played 'hypocritically' and in a 'severe and grumpy manner'.

In 1915 he met Jean Cocteau and there were plans for a collaboration on *A Midsummer Night's Dream*, of which only *Cinq grimaces* survive, published posthumously in 1929. But also Cocteau was inspired by hearing Satie and Ricardo Viñes playing the *Morceaux en forme de poire* to sketch out ideas for a ballet, including a Chinaman, an American girl and an acrobat. Picasso was then brought in on the project and the result was the ballet *Parade*, premiered by the Ballets russes in May 1917. Apollinaire was asked to write a programme note, in which he coined the term 'sur-réaliste'. Against the expostulation of one woman in the audience that 'If I'd known it was going to be so silly, I'd have brought the children' must be set the element of failure and non-consummation of ideas deliberately evoked by both scenario and music. In the words of Richard Axsom, 'a thin scrim of anxiety rests over the ballet from the beginning. *Parade* was tragic-comedy of the highest order ... '

Altogether un-serious was the *Sonatine bureaucratique* Satie wrote immediately after the premiere of *Parade*. Here Clementi's C major Sonatina op 36/1 is turned and twisted into a variety of hilariously distorted shapes, accompanied by Satie's ever-inventive commentaries, and all this a couple of years before Stravinsky in *Pulcinella* applied the same musical treatment to Pergolesi and others. In 1919 five elegantly lyrical *Nocturnes* and in 1920 a *Premier Menuet*, never followed up, marked Satie's farewell to the piano. Instead he devoted his last years to the 'symphonic drama' *Socrate* and to two ballets, *Mercure* and *Relâche*.

Socrate, for female voice and small orchestra, was heard in a few society salons before its public premiere in 1920. Reactions varied from deep disappointment (Ravel found it 'poor in invention, in everything') to praise for its 'clarity, directness and simplicity', with Stravinsky partaking of both views: he found the orchestration clumsy, the metrical regularity boring, but the music for Socrates's death 'touching and dignifying in a unique manner'. Satie may have derived some satisfaction from knowing that one of the charges against Socrates was corruption of the young, since not a few elderly critics regarded his patronage of Les Six in a similar light. The resolutely neutral, unhysterical tone of *Mercure* and *Relâche* caused similar head-scratching, before his death from alcoholic poisoning on 1 July 1925.

Over 90 years later, his music still divides audiences. As his admirer John Cage wrote in 1958:

> To be interested in Satie one must be disinterested to begin with, accept that a sound is a sound and a man is a man, give up illusions about ideas of order, expressions of sentiment, and all the rest of our inherited aesthetic claptrap.

Not everyone is willing to do this. But for those with ears to hear, Satie's message, uninflated by bombast, unencrusted with meretricious ticklings of the senses, still retains its clarity, directness and simplicity.

The following documentary, produced by Edward Blakeman, was broadcast on BBC Radio 3 on 25 February 1994, with Clive Swift taking the rôle of Satie. Other contributors were, on BBC archive tape, the composer John Cage and Satie's friends Darius and Madeleine Milhaud, Jean Hugo and Jacques Guérin; and recorded for this programme, Satie scholars Patrick Gowers and Robert Orledge, the critic and historian Paul Griffiths, the pianist Peter Lawson and my wife Sarah, a dyslexia specialist. The contributions from Georges Auric, René Chalupt and Francis Poulenc are taken from their writings.

25 THE TROUBLE WITH SATIE

A door opens

Roger Nichols: Good morning, maître!

Erik Satie: Good morning, my very dear sir! This is most kind.

RN: I'm very glad you can be with us. Please make yourself comfortable.

ES: Thank you. But I'm rather concerned, I seem to have mislaid my umbrella. I know I had it when I left the hotel. Oh well, let's get on. Mind you, I don't know I can be much help with this ... documentary, you call it?

RN: I was wondering whether you'd start us off with a little biography?

ES: The origins of the Saties, you mean? Well, I don't imagine they were ever part of the nobility; nor even of the Papacy; but good, humble serfs, which used to be an honour and a pleasure (for their overlord, that is). Yes. As to what they did during the Hundred Years' War, I can't say. Nor do I have any information as to their attitude and the part they played in the Thirty Years' War – one of our loveliest wars. Yes.

For myself, I was born in Honfleur on 17 May 1866. I left the town when I was 12 and came to Paris. After a fairly short adolescence, I became a tolerable young man, no more than that. And it was at that moment that I began to think and write in music. A thoroughly bad idea! I lost no time in making use of an originality that was original, unpleasant, irrelevant, anti-French, anti-Nature, and so on ... Music has done me more harm than good. It's led me to quarrel with any number of people of quality, very honourable, highly distinguished, extremely respectable people.

Courtroom ambience

Critic: The trouble with Satie is, he's got no technique.

Paul Griffiths: I think the big problem with Satie is knowing what his intentions were ... and knowing how relevant those intentions are to what he produced. If one judged the music by the usual criteria by which you judge other composers of the time – and I suppose by 'other composers of the time' one means Debussy – then technically it's maladroit: the orchestration is poor, the development of ideas is almost non-existent. Now, is it deliberately poor? Or is it poor inadvertently?

We're used to thinking we can establish intention. We're used to thinking that if a composer does something, and we detect him doing something, then that's because he's meaning to do something. Now with Satie, he may do something, and we may detect him to be doing something, but he may not have meant it at all – it may just be a mistake. It does create problems.

Patrick Gowers: If you compare Satie's music with, say, the first movement of Ravel's *Mother Goose* suite, which is also extremely restrained and beautifully poised, at the same time Ravel's other works, and indeed later movements in the *Mother Goose* suite, show you that Ravel could jolly well turn it on if he wanted to, but nothing in Satie shows that because, actually, I don't think he could. If people admired him, they admired him as a pure poet and not as a technician. And for that reason the 'trouble' with Satie is very interesting. I think you can learn something about how normal people appreciate normal music normally from this rather special, exaggerated case.

I think the *Gymnopédies* were written the way they were because that was one of the few recipes Satie had in his cookbook at the time – he was about 21, a little more than that, when he wrote them – and composing is rather like cooking: there are certain things you know how to do; and there were just a few things he knew how to do, and that was one of them.

Peter Lawson: Just looking at the score, yes, you couldn't find anything simpler – the kind of pieces any Grade 5 pianist should be able to have a go at. But just to cope with the repetitive element and yet build something musically sensible out of those repeated shapes, I think is very difficult to do.

Robert Orledge: So many of these things that Satie is claimed to have been unable to do, he in fact could do but chose not to. There's this terrific element of renunciation in Satie: he deliberately took things out of his repertoire because it wouldn't make what he saw as the right, or the new, chic impression in public. He was very conscious of his image right from the start. He could manage perfectly well to write conventional 19th-century chromatic harmony. You can see that in his *Le Médecin malgré lui* in 1923, when he was writing pastiche Gounod with all the naturalness in the world – it caused him no problem whatever. He could do quite lavish orchestral effects when he chose. In 1916 he orchestrated a piece by Albert Verley, who was a pupil of his, and that's got harp arpeggiated passages, timpani rolls supporting underneath, lush divisi strings in six parts – Satie knew all about it, he just chose not to use it.

He had a different view of the orchestra, and I think a lot of it sprang from his work with cabaret orchestras around the turn of the century, when he had a very small number of players available. I think that concept of being extremely economical stuck with him. He drew up his own list of safe ranges for instruments: even on the violins, the range is more or less that of Handel and Mozart. And he was concerned that things should work with as little rehearsal as possible – perhaps he was a realist and knew what the Paris scene was like. The other thing he didn't like was unnecessary doubling. He didn't like Beethoven's orchestration and disapproved of Schumann's. He set out to show them how he thought it should be done, with immense clarity and no notes doubled at the same pitch.

Patrick Gowers: Some people think that Satie orchestrated his music tremendously well. He orchestrated it in a very characteristic way, but I think, for instance, that his orchestration of the first movement of *Socrate* goes against the character of the music. Satie was a composer, not an arranger, in my view.

And then Debussy has been tremendously criticised for his orchestration of the *Gymnopédies* because people say that he added a sort of Impressionist mist to Satie's pure, wonderful, crystalline lines, and muddied the whole thing up and completely misunderstood what Satie was about. Unfortunately, if you look at Satie's notebooks, you see that Satie himself attempted an orchestration of the *Gymnopédies*, and other works of the time, which went further than Debussy in the direction of muddying them up with harp runs and all that sort of thing, so I don't think that argument stands up.

ES: So they've been ferreting around in my notebooks, have they? And I suppose they've been looking at my drawings too?

Sarah Nichols: He thought all the time in at least 3D and in time as well, so certainly in 4. And although we don't have any evidence that he had the classic difficulties of writing and spelling that occur in most dyslexic people, we do know that he found writing extremely laborious. We know it took him 20 minutes to write the address on an envelope. He has several, five or six, different, beautiful, calligraphic hands, but he doesn't have an easy, fluent, everyday hand, such as you and I have. The dyslexic, typically (and we're talking about a very high-order dyslexic here), doesn't really feel happy with developmental types of thought. He sees his ideas whole, as an entity ...

ES: Before I write a work, I like to walk round it three times, accompanied by myself.

Sarah Nichols: ... and so he is not happy moving slowly along a line of linear development. He sees one idea and then, instantly, transformationally, another. Many high-order dyslexic people have this. It's at least interesting that he found Hans Christian Andersen his favourite writer, and that he was so interested by *Through the Looking Glass* and patently saw Dodgson as a kindred spirit. Both these writers are now generally recognised to have been dyslexic. We don't know how rapidly he could read text, but we do know that his sightreading of music was regarded as 'feeble' by examiners at the Conservatoire in 1882 and again in 1886. Most dyslexic people have extreme difficulty in reading music.

ES: I wrote a song about the Mad Hatter, you know. The words were by a young friend of mine called René Chalupt. I dedicated a piece to him.

René Chalupt: He dedicated a piece to me called 'His legs' – did he know I was crazy about dancing? He used to set out from Paris for his home in the suburb called Arcueil at the most God-forsaken hours of the night. When I expressed surprise, because it meant crossing deserted and decidedly unappealing areas of the city, he said, 'There's no problem. If I spot some evil-looking type, I just lie down in the gutter and pretend to be drunk.'

Critic: The thing about Satie is, he's totally undiscriminating, intellectually impoverished, and just plain boring.

ES: That sounds like three things to me! But then, I rather *like* things in threes.

Critic: ... lack of discriminating invention and incapacity for clear and continuous thinking set Satie fumbling for some sort of originality, until he hit upon the idea of letting his poverty-stricken creations face the world under high-sounding names.

RN: Did he make sketches?

Robert Orledge: Thousands. Sometimes as many as 25 versions for a two-bar passage. An apparently simple piece to us like the *Trois Enfantines* for teaching young players to play the piano, probably as much work went into that as into a big work like *Socrate*.

RN: In general, are the sketches more complicated than the final version?

Robert Orledge: Very often, yes. And he was always taking wrong turnings in the sketches. He accumulates the elements that were going to be part of what he could see as the final composition, could hear in his head, but wasn't quite able to write down. He would gradually weed out the ones he didn't like so much, till he got a version he was satisfied with. Part of it was making a striking impression when he started a piece, and he worked very hard to make the first bars have an impact. You see that in *La Belle excentrique* especially.

Patrick Gowers: Cocteau said that after a period of complex over-refinement, which is what he thought the Impressionists were, the only answer is to strip all that away and have a period of simplicity. And then he said that he's not talking about basic, primitive simplicity, but about a very refined sort of simplicity that distils the richness that's been acquired through the previous thing. That sounds marvellous. But if you've actually got a piece of music in front of you, and you ask 'Does this simplicity distil the richness of what's gone before?', it's awfully hard to say ...

Madeleine Milhaud: He was a man of absolute honesty towards his own art. Nobody could have any influence on Satie, he knew exactly what he wanted.

ES: I recognize that voice! Madeleine Milhaud! 'La gentille petite dame !'

Madeleine Milhaud: He kept on working, even if he was criticised, without bothering about all the critics or the audience. It doesn't mean he couldn't be hurt – he was extremely 'vulnérable'.

Jean Hugo: His funeral took place on 6 July 1925 ...

ES: So you're killing me off already?

Jean Hugo: ... The humble country church, the cemetery which looked like nothing in particular, the pine coffin placed almost at ground level in the shallow grave – everything was in keeping with the poverty of the maître of Arcueil, with the simplicity of his music and with the humility of his death.

Jacques Guérin: Satie was very punctual, in his rendez-vous as well as in his works. He was a kind of maniac of honesty, of strictness. He would not speak very much because he was very shy. His appearance was often jokey, with jokes of a very poor kind. But we used to laugh as though it was very clever – we had a kind of pity for that timidity. During a meal he wouldn't say anything, and at the end of the meal, when someone offered him some kind of sweet, he would just say, 'No, I want an apple, but an apple in the air, not an apple in the earth – 'une pomme de terre'. And he would cut it up very slowly and say, 'An apple is necessary to have good health.'

ES: Don't I recognise that voice also?

RN: Jacques Guérin.

ES: The dear boy! How many more of my friends do you have?

RN: Only one ... and we're keeping him as a surprise.

ES: Very well. On we go!

Paul Griffiths: How Satie lived is not, I think, expressed in the way of his music. You could say that his lack of skill does express it – thst his refusal of the standard road led him into the kind of existence that he had to live. And if his aim was to rid the music of as much trace of himself as possible, then he's in fact asking us *not* to take into account the way he lived his life.

ES: Goodness me, how clever! That gentleman sounds to me like a critic!

RN: You're right.

ES: Hmmm! You know, there are three sorts of critic: those who are important, those who are less important, and those who are not important at all. The last two sorts don't exist. All critics are important.

But you were going to explain that I was boring? Or at least somebody was ...

Patrick Gowers: If you take a small musical fragment and repeat it, as he tended to do, until the ear gets bored with the repeat, you can then go on and do something else which is relatively contrasted, because you've built up the anticipation of a contrast, and then you do that for two bars, and then you build up something else. So Satie's pieces, which had a little of this, then a bit of that and then a bit of the other, those things themselves were, paradoxically, dull enough that the succession of them works as a form.

John Cage: When I arranged in New York the 18 hour 40 minute performance of Satie's *Vexations*, the piece which was repeated 840 times, my closest friends, who ordinarily would come to any concert that I would arrange, failed to turn up. Why? Because they had read in the newspaper that this thing was going to happen, and they felt they could understand it without having to attend. I in fact, when I arranged the concert, did it as a responsible action to a composer whose work had never been performed, and I thought, 'It'll just be this thing just going over and over.' Not at all. The *Vexations* of Satie I would be willing to equate, in terms of experience, with any religious work of any culture – any of the Bach Passions. Now I noticed that my feelings were not different from the other people involved in the performance (we were some 12 pianists). I remember Philip Carter, another composer, coming down after the tenth time he'd played, for twenty minutes, looking absolutely transformed. He said, 'It's fantastic, this work.'

ES: And who was that?

RN: John Cage. He was a composer. He died some years ago.

ES: What a pity! We could do with more like him. But boredom is a strange thing, you know. The public venerates boredom. For them, boredom is mysterious and profound. Against boredom, the listener is defenceless: boredom overwhelms him. Why is it easier to bore people than to entertain them?

Critic: The trouble with Satie is all those silly words he writes over the top of his piano music.

Madeleine Milhaud: It's very difficult to explain why there are many jokes in his music that are sometimes the complete opposite of what the music expresses. He said that it was a confidence between the person who was playing and himself. I don't know if it is was from a sort of *pudeur* that he hides what he expresses musically. It's possible.

Robert Orledge: They were meant for the performer only. They were never meant, I think, for mass communication, though Satie might have approved of them going up on a cinema screen. If you put them up as subtitles, you wouldn't incur Satie's wrath from beyond the grave by doing that.

Patrick Gowers: The theory was that he put on some of this humorous side as a sort of defensive mechanism, because if people say, 'This is stupid and is absolutely nothing at all', he could turn round and say, 'Well, that's what it's meant to be – come on, it's just a joke!'

Francis Poulenc: So many composers think of the piano as a makeshift instrument which can cope with anything. But Satie in his meticulous way knew exactly what suited it. The novel directness of his writing, a bold reaction against the other-worldly atmosphere of Debussy and Ravel, shows up as an influence as late as 1944, in Stravinsky's Sonata for two pianos. I don't mind the delightfully crazy titles which upset the public and, I'm sorry to say, most pianists. I don't think the music would profit by having less bizarre titles; far from it, the allusive nature of certain quotations would thereby become completely unintelligible.

Patrick Gowers: I think they're quite interesting for another reason, and that is that though those things were not meant to be read out, the relationship between those comments and the music adds something to the music. Just as, in what many people would regard as Satie's greatest piece, *Socrate*, I think it's no accident that people were very moved by that, and even though that is very, very still – and you get lines like 'Shortly afterwards he made a convulsive movement' and it's set to music which is just like a plainsong recitation – in his particular case, this great discrepancy between this very restrained and held-back thing and the appalling things that were going on in the words is one of the elements that made it very moving for some people. When you've got music which isn't aimed straight at the bull's eye, but is aimed off a bit, it's like hearing stereo rather than mono: two different things are coming at you and they interact.

Darius Milhaud: Satie told me one day, 'I chose the parts in Plato related to Socrates and to his death because I always thought it was such an unjust story.'

ES: Darius Milhaud – that was your surprise! Dear Darius! You know, I was very disappointed with the moral attitudes of Poulenc and Auric. Lack of courage and character is one of the things I find most repellent. But Milhaud was always *magnifique*.

Darius Milhaud: Sometimes I think of the last words of his *Socrates*, which say, 'This is the way such a noble and right man lived,' and I think that those last words of the Plato figure of Socrates can be applied to Erik Satie.

Critic: We were supposed to be talking about the silly titles. But all right, if you want to talk about *Socrate* … Are we really intended to take the work seriously?

Paul Griffiths: I would like to think that *Socrate* is a wonderful work – there's a lot about it that very strongly appeals to me. But, certainly when I hear it in the orchestral version, I can't but be worried at almost every minute about what I'm supposed to be hearing – whether the way it goes against the grain of the instruments is deliberate or not. It seems to me undecidable.

Patrick Gowers: When the people at the time were praising Satie for his restraint, one of the things they were very keen to avoid was musical rhetoric, which was partly a nationalistic thing – they wanted to get back to what they thought was a very clear, lucid type of French music, as opposed to German music and all the rhetoric that went with that.

Critic: If only he had not allowed himself to be hailed as a prophet by a small group of youths who only wished to make use of him. But he preferred to listen to the voices of malicious flatterers; and thus one sees him, like an old actor who, because he has once played the part of Napoleon and been applauded by provincials, imagines himself to be really the great captain; but who, looking in a mirror, sees only an old man abandoned in the melancholy twilight of a deserted café.

Darius Milhaud: Satie was like someone who brings luck. We loved him as an old friend because he always gave credit to youth, and he was with us against the older ones.

Jacques Guérin: He liked the young because they were like the assistants who used to be with Socrates.

Madeleine Milhaud: He liked to be with young people – he had perhaps hope that they wouldn't become as the old ones were!

ES: There is no school of Satie. Satie-ism could never exist. I would have fought it all the way. There must be no slavery in art. I was continually being forced to trip up my followers with each new work. It's the only way for an artist to avoid becoming the head of a school – a pundit.

Critic: ... which brings me very nicely to my next point: the trouble with Satie is he's so unreliable, unpredictable – there's no *centre* to his output. It makes life so hard for everybody.

ES: Hard for critics like him, he means. I think I'll just pop out for moment or two, if I may. I wish you luck with Monsieur Critic. You know, a critic's brain is like a huge department store. You can find anything there: orthopaedic implements, beds, travelling rugs, smoking accessories, gloves, umbrellas, hats, sports equipment, perfume ...

Exit Satie

Critic: I'm waiting. The charge is 'Unpredictability'.

Patrick Gowers: Satie's styles changed roughly once every ten years. From about 1885 to 1895 he was writing his Rose-Croix music, from 1895 to 1905 he was writing mainly café-concert, Montmartre cabaret type of music (and his most famous piece of that era, the *Trois Morceaux en forme de poire*, is in fact practically all just a compilation of pieces he'd actually written for cabarets he'd been pianist in), then from about 1905 to 1915 he wrote piano pieces with all those comments and stuff like that, and then for the last ten years of his life he wrote things like

Parade and *Socrate* and *Relâche*, his stage works, and slightly different piano things like the *Nocturnes*.

Robert Orledge: You couldn't draw up a series of ground rules for composition, other than those that Satie drew up himself about the melody governing everything, and the harmonic potential of what went on beneath being infinite, and that the harmony was supposed to be a reflection of the melody, which was the basic idea behind the piece. But beyond that, the way in which it's a reflection varies so much from piece to piece that it becomes very unpredictable. Satie was very anxious that, although it was essentially a self-renewing style like Fauré's was, within fairly narrow means, there are no two pieces that are in any way identical. If a piece became too similar to another one, he wouldn't let it go out.

Peter Lawson: I think the interesting things about the later pieces, the *Nocturnes* and so on, is the harmonic elusiveness, the twists and turns in the harmony which create problems for the player in the same way they do with late Fauré. As I find with late Fauré, with some of the pieces, it's very difficult to make them work musically.

Madeleine Milhaud: I think everything was natural with Satie. I don't think anything was calculated – strangely enough, because his handwriting *is* calculated. And then he would keep copies of letters that just said, 'I shall come tomorrow at 4 o'clock.' Darius was much younger than Satie, but sometimes he behaved as if he was much older. He would take care of Satie and try and find him money: he would arrange for him to sell some of his manuscripts to an American, and ask the American to send three separate cheques, because if he sent just one, Satie would spend all the money straight away. He behaved really as if he was his godfather, more than being his much younger friend.

Jacques Guérin: He said he was a communist – that's the reason why he would live in Arcueil. But, the year before he died, I remember one day he had lunch with my mother, which he often did, and he said, 'I'm not a communist any more. They are all very bad people, jealous and envious. I hate them.' You know, everybody can change their mind, even later on!

Georges Auric: I remember Satie and Cocteau at a dinner party. Right from the start of the meal, Cocteau began to improvise one of his brilliant monologues – and ventured to speak at rather too great a length about music. Satie suddenly went white with anger, got up and went over to Cocteau's chair. We were terrified, seeing him with his pince-nez, and his serviette in his hand, looming over Cocteau, carrying his plate. Cocteau had stopped talking or even moving, and was preparing to receive a plateful of dinner over his head.

Satie lifted his arms as though to brain him, then delivered a single word: 'Imbecile!' His face suddenly took on an appearance of extraordinary cruelty, while Cocteau's was rigid with terror. We were all petrified and waited for the worst. But Satie almost immediately moved away, and slowly and calmly went back to his place. He gave us a relaxed, happy smile, and said, in amazingly tranquil tones, 'Ah! That's better, we can breathe again.'

Sarah Nichols: The moods of dyslexic people swing very quickly. Educational psychologists label them as indulging in 'inappropriate behaviour' – they suddenly have a terrible row with their best friend and never speak to him again. And yet their friends love them. There's something immensely sensitive about them, they're very, very *sympa*.

Madeleine Milhaud: Why wasn't he on speaking terms with his brother, for instance? When Conrad Satie lost his wife, Satie went to the funeral and after the funeral he said to his brother, 'Let's go and have a drink!' And the poor man, who had just buried his wife, didn't feel like it. Satie said, 'Well, I'm coming to Paris just for you. If you don't want to have a drink with me … ' And he never saw him any more. And so, when he was in hospital and we were trying to find somebody, a member of the family, because we felt that this man was going to die, we asked, 'Do you have somebody of your family that you would like to see?' 'Oh no, absolutely not. My sister's in Argentina; and my brother, certainly not, after what he did.'

Darius Milhaud: After his death we had to go into his room, where nobody had ever been. It was absolutely devastating, because there was nothing there – just a poor bed, a broken piano, a chair, a table, in a house of really poor, poor people. It is difficult even to imagine how this man, with his complete lack of comfort, could come out every day elegantly dressed up, extremely clean, and always so perfectly like a gentleman.

Madeleine Milhaud: You couldn't win. I don't think, if you began to reason, that you could be absolutely sure you were right, because Satie had a way of reasoning which was utterly different. Why should he ask for a present of handkerchieves when he had nearly 100 at the laundry? Why? You can find explanations, but I'm not sure that you can reason.

RN: I admit, I have trouble with the logic, the syntax of some of the piano pieces: 'Les quatre-coins', for instance, from *Sports et divertissements* ...

Peter Lawson: I look at the mice, I look at the cat, I think of a game between them, I guess, pouncing, crawling, hunting, stretching out, and try and relate those to the music. He seems to me to be the sort of composer who could write music to a TV commercial: just pick a mood, sell something in say, 20 seconds, which is the average time it takes to play each of the pieces in *Sports et divertissements*. That's a considerable skill – and from a performer's point of view it's also a considerable problem, because there's no scope for musical introductions or large development sections to get your teeth into. It has to be 'bang', straight into the music from the word go.

Robert Orledge: His pieces went together like a sort of cellular jigsaw, and I think it sprang from the early years when Satie perhaps didn't have really very much technique, but he wanted to make a new language out of very, very little. I think probably the music of his parents had something to do with that. There's a piece called *Souvenirs d'Honfleur* by his father Alfred which has, as its material, two 16-bar sections, and he makes 150 bars out of it by repetition.

Certainly the pieces never arrived in the order that we know them, except when Satie was extremely rushed for time, right at the end of his life: he wrote *Relâche* more or less straight through. But when he was writing pieces to no time scale, they emerged in little cells, and there are some quite extreme examples. The *Prélude en tapisserie* is probably the best one, in which he began somewhere around bar 70 and ended up at bar 3. He had to devise two different numbering systems in different coloured pencil because the whole process got so complicated, he couldn't remember where all the bits went. But the way the cells join together, that's the bit you really can't explain.

Paul Griffiths: I can't think of any composer before Satie where this problem arises: where you can't say clearly, 'This is amateurish; and this is good.' Satie creates that problem.

Re-enter Satie

ES: Vivent les amateurs!

RN: Ah, maître!

ES: Strange laws you have over here – the bars were all shut ... Anyway, where have you got to?

RN: We were just saying, in effect, that you've called into question the whole business of professionalism.

Critic: Huh! Let's call a spade a spade, shall we? The trouble with Satie is nothing less than contempt for tradition and disrespect for his elders.

Sarah Nichols: They very often seem to themselves odd. It's characteristic that they feel they are born into the wrong period or into the wrong place – that they're born ahead of their time, or behind their time.

ES: I *was* born very young into a time that was very old.

Sarah Nichols: They're very often deeply frustrated because the whole of our civilisation, or at least this Western civilisation, is built on the written word. Because you know you have a huge talent, that you are highly intelligent and you're being constrained by these people who may be stupider than you are, but they are 'in charge', you become very anti-authoritarian.

Critic: Erik Satie. A pretty unimpressive student. Signed, Ambroise Thomas.

ES: Ambroise Thomas! I'll confine myself to recording a few vague impressions. No point mentioning his extraordinary word-setting: 'Je- - - e suis Titania.' Where on earth can I have left that umbrella? Due to his advanced age, Ambroise Thomas was the automatic choice to represent the musical greatness of France. Nobody protested. Nobody cared a hoot, in fact. Just as well it was a cheap umbrella. The position he occupied in the official musical world ... (yawns) ...

Robert Orledge: Virgil Thomson says that Satie's one of these people you need to know nothing about the history of music to understand. This isn't in fact the case, and he knew his 19th-century music extremely well. In the *Embryons desséchés*, bits of his past come back in, including a snippet based on the 'Orangutang Song' from an operetta called *La Mascotte* by Edmond Audran , which was the Paris hit of 1881.

ES: I don't like jokes, or anything resembling them. What does a joke prove? Jokes rarely derive from the gracious entrails of Beauty; more likely you find them leaping out of the smelly armpits of Malice.

Jacques Guérin: Satie used to make allusions to the private life of Cocteau, and say, 'Cocteau is not an *homme*, he is an *hommelette*!'

Critic: One simple question, Monsieur Satie. What are you ?

ES: Everyone will tell you I'm not a musician. It's true. From the beginning of my career, I've been classed as a phonometrographer. My works are pure phonometrics. It's scientific thought which predominates.

Peter Lawson: I don't know why more pianists don't play Satie. Perhaps one's training is geared up to the main Classical repertoire and the Romantic warhorses, and things in miniature of the sort that Satie provides are looked down on, sneered at by all sorts of musicians. A great shame!

Darius Milhaud: It has been for me one of the very great things of my life to have the friendship of a man of the stature of Satie. He was a man who never made any concessions.

Madeleine Milhaud: He never gave up. And even if he suddenly hated somebody, he didn't give that up either!

Robert Orledge: In places, I think he would have liked to use a thicker style, perhaps, but felt he must be consistent to his principles, and I think he was to some extent imprisoned by his own philosophy.

Paul Griffiths: We don't know what the intention is. That may be the intention. But if so, I wish, like Cage, he'd said it a bit more obviously, and then we could all relax a bit more with the music, maybe. But I think Satie is worth all the trouble simply because he creates the trouble. Anything that is that troubling is worth thinking about, simply for that reason.

Madeleine Milhaud: I think Satie's life is a mystery, and will always be so.

Patrick Gowers: Some people, then as now, absolutely loved his music and some people thought it was completely empty. So, then as now, one thinks of critics judging the music; but, then as now, the music in fact judges the critics.

ES: Alas, poor critics, what a life! Is that it then?

RN: Only that we've found an umbrella ...

ES: Allons, enfants de la BBC! Will the bars be open yet ? Do please explain the opening hours ... etc.

Exeunt Omnes

26 *PARADE* – A MIX OF EXTRAORDINARY TALENTS

'How on earth,' groaned Charles de Gaulle, 'can one govern a country that produces 246 kinds of cheese?' For those seduced by the placid, pastoral paintings of the Impressionists into thinking of the French as naturally cosy or subservient, his complaint comes as a healthy dose of realism about a nation ever eager to prick the balloon of pomposity or fume against the outrage of condescension. Napoleon clearly shared the views of the later general in making his Code as detailed and draconian as he did.

French musical life provides any number of examples of the critical spirit at work. In the 19th century Berlioz's whole life can be seen as one long battle against a conformist Establishment, while Debussy's revolutionary music, if mostly less noisy than Berlioz's, is none the less powerful for that, and to some degree nourished by his antipathy to Gluck and Wagner. On the operatic front – always pre-eminent in France – peace was maintained by a careful distinction between the three genres of *opéra*, *opéra-comique* and *opérette*, each with its own location and rules, while below them the vulgar elements of the *café concert* likewise went their own way. As for ballet, until 1909 it continued to be defined by ballerinas in tutus in works such as Delibes' *Sylvia* and *Coppélia*. The change in attitude, when it came, was both general, in the application of what we might call 'the democratic imperative', and specific, in the arrival of Diaghilev and the Ballets russes.

When France became a republic in the aftermath of the 1871 Commune, the education authorities issued instructions as to how French should be pronounced, complete with illustrations of the necessary mouth-shapes. How ineffective this was can still be heard by comparing the accents of Paris and Grenoble, but at least it showed an intention that the French should 'all be in it together'. In music, this democratic spirit showed up in 1902 in Debussy's *Pelléas et Mélisande*, where the composer insisted the cast 'forget you are singers' and pronounce the text without distortions, and more insistently in 1907 in Ravel's song cycle *Histoires naturelles*, where his text setting went as far along the democratic route as omitting the mute 'e's at the ends of words. Cue scandal: for many listeners, the old rules of 'posh' word setting remained sacrosanct.

The impact of the Ballets russes needs no emphasising here. Nijinsky and his astonishing leaps turned ballet on its head, ending the long primacy of the ballerina. But equally important was the fact that Diaghilev, with his low boredom threshold, was always on the lookout for something new, and the first step towards *Parade* was taken in 1912 with just two words that he spoke to Jean Cocteau: 'Etonne-moi!' (Astonish me!). Cocteau admitted later that it was only with the production of *The Rite of Spring* in 1913 that he understood what astonishment really meant ...

Cocteau had already provided the scenario in 1912 for the ballet *Le Dieu bleu*, which flopped, so he had ground to make up. His first idea was a ballet called *David* in which acrobats would perform before the king; he approached Stravinsky for the score but, after initial signs of interest, the composer walked away. Cocteau's second idea was *A Midsummer Night's Dream*, with music by Satie, Ravel and Varèse among others, but the outbreak of war and Varèse's departure for America put an end to that. His third idea was *Parade*. Satie again came on board and, to Cocteau's intense delight, Picasso too to provide set and costumes for his first stage work.

The theme of the ballet is essentially 'failure'. A 'parade' was a show put on outside the performing venue to entice the audience inside – Seurat painted a well-known picture of such a scene. In Cocteau's scenario, despite all efforts, the public remain uninterested in the spectacle proper – and that's the whole storyline. Not, we may think, particularly gripping. But this would be to ignore the details. Cocteau realized there was no way he could astonish Diaghilev by trying to outdo *Le Sacre*. Instead, he turned his back on ancient Russia and wild primitivism in favour of real, contemporary Parisian life in the form of the circus performers he had been entranced by as a child. Here his interests met those of Picasso who, in his early years in Paris after 1901, had spent time with such people, famously painting a family of six *saltimbanques* in 1905. As representatives of outsiders, *les marginaux*, they clearly embodied the democratic spirit. Were the talents of acrobats and conjurors any less than those of ballet dancers? Did they train less assiduously? In any case, as a historical fact, the *pliés* and *entrechats* of classical ballet actually derived from the movements of acrobats.

It was hardly to be expected that three such individual talents as Cocteau, Picasso and Satie would work together in perfect harmony. Cocteau, ever on the watch for slights to his authority, introduced Satie to Picasso and then, when these two instantly recognized each other's stature and became inseparable, suspected them of plotting behind his back...which they were. The central panel of Cocteau's three-part scenario is itself triple (did he know of Satie's attachment to the number 3?), consisting of three dances for a Chinese conjuror, a Little American Girl, and a group of Acrobats. All three took their inspiration from acts currently running in Paris: the Chinese conjuror from one such dubbed Chung Ling Soo (real name William Ellsworth Robinson) with the dancer Massine painted and costumed to look like his real-life model; the Girl from a combination of the American cinema stars Pearl White and Mary Pickford; the Acrobats from those of the Médrano Circus in Montmartre. The central dance, essentially the core of the ballet, took its lead from America as found on the silver screen, so Cocteau wanted relevant transatlantic noises: sirens, a typewriter, revolver shots. Satie did not, no doubt thinking his music for the dance was quite American enough (which it was – see below). Poor Cocteau! Diaghilev and Picasso weighed in on Satie's side and at the première on 18 May 1917 there were no noises off, though they did feature in later runs from 1919.

Reports of that premiere vary considerably. Cocteau's claim that immediately after it a lady advanced on him furiously brandishing a hatpin has to be set against less excited versions; certainly it was no scandal on the scale of *The Rite*. But Picasso's gently Cubist set and costumes, including ten-foot-high wood-and-cardboard boxes enclosing the French and American managers who introduced the show and at the end tried their best to avert its failure, certainly made their mark, as did his serenely, sadly beautiful drop curtain, which shortly afterwards became the trademark of the Ballets russes programmes, demonstrating to the Parisian public the extent to which the organization had moved with the times. For those likely to be puzzled by *Parade*, the poet Guillaume Apollinaire had written an article, reprinted in the programme, in which he coined the word 'sur-réalisme', meaning 'a kind of super-realism'. Here again we join the democratic thrust of what Apollinaire called 'l'esprit nouveau'. This 'new spirit' was bright, witty, anti-elitist. In 1913 Apollinaire had published his first volume of poetry, *Alcools*, and in the opening poem takes an irreverent look not only at religion, pointing out that the ascended Christ 'is the holder of the world altitude record', but at the whole Greek and Roman world. 'À la fin tu es las de ce monde ancien', he writes: 'when it comes to it, you're fed up with that ancient world'. And certainly *Parade* is quite some way from Aeschylus and Sophocles.

As to Satie's contribution, it's a miracle of surface simplicity above strangely powerful depths. It is, even more than the set, costumes and action, close to 'surrealism' as it was to develop: one idea is suddenly abandoned for another without apparent reason, leaving us to ponder on any possible links. The orchestration is sparse, with a minimum of doubling (no warm held chords on horns to bind things comfortably together), but the ideas themselves are utterly individual and stick in the mind. As for the American angle, the 'Steamboat Rag' (at the very centre of the ballet) builds on Irving Berlin's *That Mysterious Rag* - and I use the word 'build' advisedly because, while adhering closely to Berlin's textures and harmonies, Satie improves his tune out of all recognition. Berlin never asked for copyright payment. Perhaps he preferred to leave the improvement unrecognized?

Not all Satie's colleagues were impressed by the ballet. It seems that Debussy's lack of enthusiasm lay behind the cooling of the two men's friendship in the last months of Debussy's life, while Ravel, taken by Cocteau to one of the rehearsals, said he could not understand the mechanism of music that was 'not bathed in any sonorous fluid'. But over the last hundred years the work's influence is everywhere: the whip, the lion's roar and the microtonal siren in Varèse's *Amériques*, the sirens and percussion in Antheil's *Ballet mécanique*, Honegger's *Pacific 231*, Mossolov's *Iron Foundry,* up to the 'happenings' of the later 20th century with their vacuum cleaners and china smashing – all go back in some degree to the democratic, inclusive tone of *Parade* as Cocteau imagined it, and to those two magic words from 1912: 'Étonne-moi!'.

27 LE GROUPE DES SIX – 100 YEARS ON

To make sense of the collection of young composers who in January 1920 were given the above label (often shortened to Les Six), we have to go a little way back in time. In the late 19th century, French composers were facing the Wagner problem. Letters of the time from composers such as Chabrier, Chausson and Debussy groan under complaints of how the German's musical vocabulary, what Debussy called 'the ghost of old Klingsor', dominated their efforts, try as they might. But ignoring him, while not easy, could be done, as shown with considerable success by two younger composers, Maurice Ravel and Erik Satie.

The compositional path Ravel marked out for himself led, as we know, to masterpiece after masterpiece. But the pre-war group of *Jeunes Ravélites* never amounted to much, largely because, as Alexander Goehr has said, Ravel was 'a bit too clever to be of much influence, because you've got to be too good at it to actually do it'. Satie, though, was a different matter. It's hardly a cause of dispute these days that Satie was not a great musical technician: but also that this misses the point – his contribution to 20th-century music lies elsewhere, in cleansing the sonorous palate of his time from the over-choice morsels left over from the 19th-century banquet. He also had a soft spot for the young, and towards the end of the First World War became a kind of guru to a group of budding composers whom, in March 1918, he christened the Nouveaux Jeunes: Darius Milhaud, Arthur Honegger, Germaine Tailleferre, Louis Durey ... and himself, with later additions in the shape of Georges Auric and Francis Poulenc. Then, in November, Satie resigned from the group (still no one knows for sure why), and his place was taken by the upwardly mobile Jean Cocteau.

Although not a trained musician, Cocteau was deeply attracted by the possibilities of collaborating in musical enterprises. Given the cold shoulder by Stravinsky, he saw this young group bereft (he thought) of intellectual leadership, and between March and August 1919 used his column in the journal *Paris-Midi* to create a public for it. Also laid under contribution was Cocteau's 74-page pamphlet *Le Coq et l'Arlequin*, published in the spring of 1918 and taking its cue from Satie's ballet *Parade*, staged by the Ballets Russes in May 1917, which had brought a gale of fresh air into the ballet scene. A sample of quips from *Le Coq* gives a good idea of where the Nouveaux Jeunes were now heading: 'knowing how far to go too far', 'a composer always has too many notes on his keyboard', 'build me music I can live in like a house', 'all music to be listened to head-in-hands is suspect'. Audacity, economy, down-to-earthness, lightheartedness, these were the new watchwords.

The first use of the name Les Six came in the collaborative composition of the *Album des Six* for piano in the second half of 1919. There followed an article 'Young French Composers' by Roussel in an English magazine that October, before the crucial one in the mainstream music journal *Comoedia* by Henri Collet, 'Les Cinq Russes, Les Six Français et Erik Satie' on 16 January 1920. A follow-up article by Collet a week later used the short title 'Les Six'.

At this point two misconceptions need to be laid to rest. Firstly, that the group was in some sense ordained by fate. But Madeleine Milhaud, the composer's cousin and later wife, felt that Roland-Manuel could easily have turned it into 'Les Sept', as he subscribed in some degree to the same Coctelian aesthetic. But then he started taking lessons from Ravel so, for this purpose, became *persona non grata*. The second misconception is that among the group's members all was sweetness and light. Poulenc later explained that 'we never had an aesthetic in common and our works were always different from each other. With us likes and dislikes were always at odds. So, Honegger never liked the music of Satie, and [Florent] Schmitt, whom he admired, was a *bête noire* for Milhaud and me'. Likewise Honegger's oratorio *King David*, which in 1921 made a huge hit with the public, was written off by Milhaud as 'full of clichés and fugal exercises from the classroom, thematic developments, chorales and reach-me-down formulae'. At the same time, Poulenc and Auric were taxed with thinking only of immediate success, to the point that the splash made by *King David* was making them both ill.

Before looking at the music of Les Six in a little more detail, it may be useful to consider the social milieu they were working in. The France of the early 20s saw a questioning, in a number of uncomfortable ways, of the old assumptions of what it was to be French. Some of this questioning, not surprisingly, arose directly from the war. The heavy loss of life among the soldiery (1,400,000 killed, including 300,000 in the first five months) led in some quarters to a refusal to subscribe to the ancient notion of 'la gloire'. Ideas about tradition and a stable hierarchy had to struggle against memories of a war that had seen too many instances of gross disobedience toward an officer class no longer commanding automatic respect. The world of art could not expect to remain untouched by this cataclysm. The poet Guillaume Apollinaire, who died in 1918 from a combination of Spanish flu and war wounds to his head, put it succinctly: *À la fin tu es las de ce monde ancien* –'when it comes to it, you've had enough of that ancient world'.

While 'that ancient world' could be identified as that of the Greeks and Romans, it could as easily refer to that pre-1914, with its head-in-hands obeisance before 'high art' and its catalogue of composers who were expected to wait their turn and perhaps become rich and famous in their fifties or sixties, if they were lucky. No longer. The future now belonged to the young, with all its insouciance, energy and bravado. We may well say how fortunate Les Six were to be waiting in the wings of this life-enhancing change of heart. France's morale was low: what it needed, above all, was being cheered up.

As explained above, the six didn't wait for Collet's 1920 articles to respond to what Apollinaire defined as 'l'esprit nouveau'. One of the first was Francis Poulenc, with his *Rapsodie nègre*, premiered in December 1917. Today, of course, this would be accused of 'cultural appropriation', even though Poulenc had not the faintest idea of what black music sounded like. Instead, he filled the piece with 'forbidden' consecutive 5ths and a 'primitive' text ('Kati moko, mosi bolou/Ratakou sira, polama!') made up and published by two pranksters. Looking for a teacher at the age of 18, he brought his score to a 54-year-old Conservatoire professor, Paul Vidal, who slung him out on his ear. Satie was sympathetic: 'Never mix "schools": it leads to an explosion – quite understandably, in fact'. Poulenc followed this with a Sonata for two clarinets in which they gurgle delightfully, and a Sonata for piano duet which starts with the prima player's left hand *below* that of the seconda player, enforcing a certain intimacy. A new spirit indeed.

Honegger meanwhile, in his 1918 short orchestral work *Le Chant de Nigamon*, used three authentic American Indian tunes. The work rivals *Rapsodie nègre* in deliberate brutality but far surpasses it in contrapuntal interest. We find similar complexity in most of his *Le*

Dit des Jeux du Monde, but also any number of lyrical tunes. The second movement, for percussion alone, takes its cue from Milhaud's use of choir plus unpitched percussion in his opera *Les Choéphores* of 1915-16 - both passages speak of the charm of exotic cultures that was to mark Milhaud's music over the next few years. Between February 1917 and early 1919 he was in Rio de Janeiro as secretary to the playwright and diplomat Paul Claudel and was much struck by the music, and the jungle, he found round him. These influences fed into the ballets *L'Homme et son désir* and *Le Boeuf sur le toit* of 1918 and 1919 and the *Saudades do Brasil* for piano of 1920. *Le Boeuf* is built round a simple, catchy tune Milhaud picked up in Rio and he enjoys himself presenting it in every one of the 12 major keys. The *Saudades* proclaim the Cocteau message of simplicity, their hummable melodies enlivened by South American rhythms and spiced with wrong notes – but not too many to cause alarm. The final exotic influence on Milhaud was jazz. His first taste of it came from black musicians in London, but in 1922 he and a friend heard it in its native Harlem: 'the snobs and aesthetes had not yet discovered Harlem: we were the only whites there. The music I heard there, absolutely different from what I knew, was a real revelation for me'. Under this impact he wrote what many consider his masterpiece, the ballet *La Création du monde*, premiered in 1923. If the magical, bittersweet world of the opening saxophone solo can't exactly be classed as cheering-up music, the toe-tapping, blue-note fugue and its subsequent development certainly can; the ending, with the saxophone whispering a C sharp against a D major chord on strings, is pure genius.

The three composers mentioned above were the core of Les Six. Auric had his time in the sun through the three ballets commissioned from him in the 1920s by Diaghilev. Thereafter, following the critical mauling of his 1932 Piano Sonata, he concentrated on film music, making a fortune out of his contribution to the 1952 film *Moulin Rouge*, starring Zsa-Zsa Gabor. Tailleferre's adherence to the ideals of the group was short-lived and, apart from a brief experiment with serialism, her music adhered very much to the graceful, charming tradition the group claimed to suppplant. Durey's allegiance was even briefer, since he parted company with his colleagues as early as 1921 over their joint venture *Les Mariés de la Tour Eiffel* and the rude comments they were currently making about Ravel, his friend and mentor.

This ballet, premiered by the *Ballets suédois* in June 1921, is the collaborative summit of Durey's five colleagues and their nose-thumbing at the musical establishment (audience cries of 'Give us our money back!'). Fairground tunes, sparkling orchestration, crazy plot by Cocteau (a lion jumps out of a camera and eats a general), pastiche (the funeral march is based on the waltz from Gounod's *Faust*), it has it all. 'Of the many artistic conspiracies I've been involved in,' said Cocteau years later, 'this is the only one that hasn't aged. Why? Because we made no concessions.'

28 REYNALDO HAHN

Sometime around 1907 the Duchess of Manchester gave a soirée in London in honour of the King and Queen. The music chosen for the occasion was *Le Bal de Béatrice d'Este* for wind band by the 33-year-old French composer Reynaldo Hahn and conducted by him. The Queen was enchanted and, after a pause for refreshments, asked for an encore. The King went off to play bridge, but returned shortly after. A courtier wondered whether, perhaps, some Offenbach? And so Reynaldo sang to his own accompaniment aria after aria by Offenbach, taking the King back to those happy, carefree days when, as Prince of Wales, he had so often escaped to Paris to be entertained by *les petites femmes*. If the Queen preferred *Le Bal*, Reynaldo thought that might have been simply because she was seriously deaf, and quite a few of the tunes were on the trumpet.

Was he then a French aristocrat? Indeed not. He was born in Caracas in Venezuela in 1874 (not 1875, as often stated) from a Jewish German father and a Roman Catholic Spanish/Basque mother. His father had not only built up a thriving commercial empire, helpfully in view of his 10 surviving children, but was a close friend of the head of state, Guzman Blanco. It was not surprising then that in 1878, when Blanco fell out of favour and emigrated to Paris, Carlos Hahn followed. The young Reynaldo was the Benjamin of the family and later admitted that he had been rather spoilt by his elder sisters. But the charm that distinguished him throughout his life was no doubt already in evidence, as was his talent for music. In 1885 he entered the preparatory class of the Conservatoire and joined a boys' choir – his first taste of singing, which was to be the bedrock of his life.

When he entered the Conservatoire proper, among his fellow pupils was Maurice Ravel, though they never became friends, possibly because their Basque mothers came from different social classes, Reynaldo's the upper bourgeoisie, Maurice's quite a few layers below. But the Conservatoire teaching suited Reynaldo down to the ground, not least that of Massenet, who did much to launch Reynaldo's career and remained a friend until his death in 1912. In 1892, we even find the 18-year-old Reynaldo being entrusted with reading the proofs of *Werther*!

Two facts indicate the breadth of his early tastes. Like many of his fellow musicians, he was enthralled by Wagner, and especially by *Die Meistersinger*. But at the same time he was one of a group (perhaps 'gang' is a better word) of students, including the 24-year-old Erik Satie, called *Les Vieilles Poules* (the old hens) to which both of them contributed musical farces. Neither of these interests, though, accords with Hahn's first success as a composer, the song *Si mes Vers avaient des ailes*, published in 1889. Even if Massenet's influence is umistakable, here, at the age of only 15, Hahn gave notice of the invaluable contribution he was to make to the repertoire of the French *mélodie*.

In a letter of 1892 he delivers a tirade against vulgarity, *chose insupportable* and certainly he lived up to his words. Complicit in this was his meeting in 1894 with Marcel Proust, the two becoming lovers for the next two years, after which they remained close friends until Proust's death in 1922. Not that they always agreed with each other – early on, when Hahn admitted liking the music of Mendelssohn and Saint-Saëns, Proust merely laughed, and they never agreed about Debussy, whose music Proust adored, while Hahn found his more extreme inventions downright dangerous. Both men patronised the Paris salons, and Hahn suffered from his reputation as a 'salon composer', with its undertone of scorn. Even though the salons were in fact hives of artistic activity, where you might meet anyone from the Prime Minister or the Director of the Opéra, to Monet or Zola, the implied criticism doubted that anything written for such an audience could be really serious. Hahn's continuing fidelity to Massenet's musical language didn't help, but one hopes that today, with a longer perspective, we can listen to his music shorn of the idea that music must necessarily 'progress'.

Hahn's musical output is extensive, and any brief resumé must confine itself to the high points of his life and works. *Le Bal de Béatrice d'Este*, referred to above, was Hahn's delightful reworking of 16th-century ideas in a deliberately aristocratic style, hence Queen Alexandra's enthusiasm. A parallel stylistic reworking is his piano *Sonatine* of 1907, which begins like Mozart, then introduces some Scarlattian acrobatics, finally in the last movement inserting some Wagnerian harmonies (and from *Tristan* rather than *Die Meistersinger*). Among his chamber works, the Violin Sonata of 1926 and the Piano

Quintet of 1922 stand out. The first movement of the Violin Sonata is interesting in that there's really only one theme, varied by changes in harmony and texture. The sparkling central scherzo is a prequel of John Adams's *Short Ride in a Fast Machine*, inspired by the hectic car journeys Hahn was having to make between gigs in Paris, Cannes and Deauville. The Quintet clearly looks back to that by César Franck in its dotted rhythms and downward-sliding chromatic harmonies. This is Hahn at his most powerful and, given that the world is not overendowed with piano quintets, needs to be heard far more often.

Hahn's contributions to musical theatre are split into serious and light operas. Hahn's most successful serious operas were *Mozart* of 1925, including some quotations from the master, and *Le Marchand de Venise* of 1935, based on Shakespeare's play; in Shylock's terrifying aria 'Je le haïs' Hahn proves once again that he was no milksop. Of his 12 light operas, by far the most successful was *Ciboulette*, first staged in 1923, and then around the world, giving rise to talk of 'the rebirth of operetta'. The sparky heroine of the title, which means 'little spring onion', makes fun of middle-class girls with posh names like Julie, Gertrude, Camille and Charlotte (sung with langourous disdain): then, thrown off, 'moi, j'm'appelle Ciboulette' in a phrase once heard, never forgotten.

But Hahn would not have been dismayed in the slightest that his reputation today rests firmly on his 100 or so songs. His attitude to singing is summed up in one of his many talks on the subject:

> A person who's been asked to sing introduces himself in the most natural way. Then suddenly, you hear a voice and wonder where it's coming from; you don't recognize the voice that's just spoken. Instinctively, you look under the furniture ...

True singing is merely an extension of speaking.

In 1891, before he met Proust, he was much smitten with the great beauty Cléo de Mérode, if only from a distance, and dedicated to her a setting of Verlaine's poem 'Green', already set by Debussy. Hahn entitled it 'Offrande' and in his two recordings, as almost always to his own accompaniment, with the voice playing rhythmic tricks around a rigorously regular piano part, one is struck by the apparently strange stresses on some syllables ('*souf*frez que ma *fa*tigue'), but which work wonderfully. Hahn was very fond, like Fauré, of descending scales, and here a C major scale sets the last two lines, giving the sense of their repose. We note too that on the score the song is carefully dated '1891, in the spring': Fauré made his setting of the poem that summer and autumn! A more melancholy tone is sounded in the 1892 setting of another Verlaine poem, 'Le ciel est pardessus le toit', written when the poet was in prison, having shot at his lover Rimbaud. The atmosphere is at first consoling in the regularly pulsing pairs of crotchets, all at a *piano* dynamic or lower. Then, like a hammer blow, comes the *forte* question, 'What have you done with your youth?' The rhythm becomes restless, the regular crotchets only returning with a repeat (not in the poem) of the opening line – but now the blue sky speaks, not of comfort, but of Nature distant and uncaring. To have written both these songs before he was 20 tells of Hahn's extraordinary talent. For a jollier song we may turn to 'Fêtes galantes' on yet another Verlaine poem, again set to music by both Debussy and Fauré (was this deliberate rivalry on Reynaldo's part? The first few notes and rhythms of the vocal line unmistakably copy Debussy ...).

Any thoughts that Hahn was merely a self-regarding dandy can be dismissed by looking at his behaviour in World War I. At his own insistence and now in his 40s, he fought in the trenches. He got on well with his men, encouraging them to sing popular songs, and his efforts were rewarded by his being appointed chevalier de la Légion d'honneur and awarded the croix de guerre.

Hahn's activities during the 20s and 30s remained the same, as composer, singer, conductor, administrator, scholar, lecturer and teacher. In 1940 the Nazis began by cancelling performances of his music but, on receipt of documents of his baptism, first communion and confirmation as a Catholic, pronounced him as being of 'diluted Jewishness', and left him alone. But their oppressive presence in Paris distressed him and he moved down to Toulon. Returning to Paris after the Liberation, he was duly honoured by being appointed Director of the Opéra; but soon after, it was apparent that he was not his old clearheaded, energetic self. He had a brain tumour, and died on 28 January 1947.

Let us hope that the 75th anniversary in 2022 of the death of this remarkable man and musician will spark more performances and recordings.

29 RAVELIANA – NEW INSIGHTS

Ravel is now fully accepted as one of the most important and popular composers of the last 150 years, but this doesn't mean he's always easy to place, either as a man or as an artist. Ravel the man was at once shy and reclusive, though fully aware of his own gifts and willing to be aggressive in his music's defence. Some people found him cold and offhand; others profoundly treasured his friendship. Possibly the most intriguing mystery concerns his sexuality: all we really know is that he never married and that he was not gay. As for Ravel the artist, while giving interviewers intelligent answers about his music, he preferred to let it speak for itself.

Much is already known about his life, his friendships and the composition of some of his works of genius. But scholarship continues and fascinating new material has been published in *Maurice Ravel: L'Intégrale*, ed. Manuel Cornejo, Paris, Le Passeur, 2018, 1771pp. We are grateful to Dr Cornejo for making these insights available.

Ravel the Teacher

Like most composers, Ravel did not only compose. In 1906 the 31-year-old was giving lessons to private pupils in a Paris flat. One of them, Frances Wilson-Huard, an American, commented in 1969 that obviously 'teaching bored him, but one has to live!' The lessons, in harmony, counterpoint and composition, to a group of four, took place 'every Sunday morning in Thérèse Chaigneau's drawing room', as at the time Ravel was living with his parents. She remembers him (always the dandy) as 'very small, sporting a long black beard and a purple suit'. He in turn, remarked to a friend, 'Miss Wilson? She's too tall, she terrifies me!'

In his socks, Ravel is variously measured at 5'3" and 5'5". The beard was shortlived.

Miss Wilson remembers how 'he began to initiate us into the mysteries of music. He would go to the piano and give us examples from Wagner or Berlioz'. To anyone familiar with Ravel's views on these composers, his choices seem astonishing, devoted as he was to the French tradition.

Ravel on the Franco-Spanish Entente

But all things Spanish were part of Ravel's life blood too, as his mother hailed from Ciboure, on the Spanish border. The notion of a 'national school' of music may seem odd to us now, but for Ravel it was crucially important. He wrote an article to accompany a Franco-Spanish concert held on 29 October 1913 in the Théâtre des Champs-Elysées under the patronage of King Alfonso XIII of Spain. He declared that

> Until the end of the 19th century there was no really national school of music in Spain. It was Russia, whose musical history offers many analogies with that of Iberia, which revealed her treasure to her.

He claims that Glinka's 'picturesque and evocative symphonic poem Summer Night in Madrid of 1845' marks 'the beginning of this renaissance'. He sees the 'multi-faceted music of Albéniz' as that of a 'precursor', despite

> having needless complications and some heavy patches and clumsinesses ... from time to time. But the inspiration – always national – is so exciting, so varied, prolific and profound that it obliterates all the faults and errors.

Ravel's deep love of the Spanish landscape and of Spain's Catholic and Moorish heritage is clear; for him:

> Albeniz's themes have the uneven curves of the Iberian mountains, his harmonies are rich and complex like the Jesuit altars of Castile, and his rhythms are diverse and intertwined like fleeting, supple arabesques.

Ravel and Stravinsky

Ravel's friendships, like most friendships, waxed and waned, influenced by musical judgments as well as social ones.
For a few years after joint work on Mussorgsky's *Khovanshchina* for Diaghilev in 1913, he and Stravinsky were close friends. But Ravel was

not thereafter an uncritical admirer: he liked *Les Noces* and *Symphony of Psalms* but rather spoilt his enthusiasm for the latter by calling it '*a successful* Oedipus Rex'. He actively disliked *Mavra* and the Concerto for piano and wind. Until now, no other specific reason has been given for their drifting apart after 1923. But now we find him in 1929, after the first performance of Stravinsky's Capriccio for piano and orchestra with the composer at the piano, claiming that 'Stravinsky can permit himself what I cannot authorise for myself, because he is less of a musician than I am.' If you gulp at this, no wonder. One possibility comes to mind. The conductor Ernest Ansermet remembered a conversation between Ravel, Stravinsky and himself over whether it was permissible in a chord to place the major 3rd above the minor 3rd instead of below it, as usual. Ravel maintained the traditional arrangement was the only right one. But Stravinsky insisted, of the major-over-minor, 'If I will it, I can do it,' – as indeed he does in the opening fanfare of *Symphonies of wind instruments*, where the clarinets' high B natural clashes with the trumpets' B flat two octaves below. At any rate, if Ravel truly believed what he said, then the cooling of relations is hardly a surprise.

Ravel on his piano music

Pianists may be grateful for these detailed extracts about his piano pieces.

The sources are a pair of master classes (cours d'interprétation) he gave at the École normale de musique in Paris on 12 and 15 June 1925, described in *Le Monde musical* the following July. (They were followed by a third class on 19 June dealing with some of his chamber music and songs.) He wasn't a great one for talking in public, like Poulenc or Reynaldo Hahn, and these were the only such classes he ever gave. The pianists were members of the public, or invited students.

The first programme included *Pavane pour une Infante défunte*, *Jeux d'eau* and *Gaspard de la nuit*. Of the *Pavane*, Ravel insisted, as is recorded elsewhere, on not dramatising the piece, stressing that it was:

> not the funeral lament for an Infanta who has just died, but the evocation of a pavane that such a princess might have danced, painted in the past by Velázquez, at the Spanish court.

This has to be taken in conjunction with his well-known remark, prompted by an over-relaxed performance, to the effect that 'it's not the pavane that's defunct, but the princess'. The result should be of 'a serious character, slightly melancholy, but remaining that of a slow dance'. Notes taken by members of the audience tell us further that the piece 'was inspired by a Velázquez portrait of a young girl in the Louvre. Do not imagine that it's a pavane for a corpse'.

Over details, he asked that 'all the arpeggios (end of bar 7 and elsewhere) should be very rapid, like harp glissandos'; also that the final chord should be *'piano subito'*, which agrees with his own piano roll recording, but not with his orchestral version or many piano editions. In bars 47 and 48 the pairs of phrased chords from quaver to crotchet should be played with diminuendos, as in bars 57 and 58.

Over *Jeux d'eau*, in bar 25, 'manage the crescendo from *piano* [in fact *pianissimo*] to *fortissimo* without adding nuances' – which I imagine means making it smooth and continuous, without bumps. In bar 48, 'hold over the ff trilled chords [with pedal] until the beginning of bar 49'. Bar 77, 'the B [sharp] is held, lift the pedal after the chord. Emphasise the B in the left hand. Lots of élan on the final arpeggio'. Bar 78, '*pianissimo*, lifting the hands very high'.

If he did make detailed observations about *Gaspard*, they are not recorded. In general, the work 'is a kind of pastiche that must be played, at least for the first piece [Ondine], with the feeling of Liszt or Chopin' [another note says 'Chopin or Schumann']. For 'Le Gibet', 'a rendition that is uniform, implacable, by its very simplicity'.

The second programme included the *Valses nobles et sentimentales, Miroirs*, the *Sonatine* and *Le Tombeau de Couperin*. Here again, his recorded remarks are all general. Of the *Valses* he said:

> Their general conception is on the lines of Schubert's waltzes, some to be played nobly, others with feeling, with the two characters alternating. Avoid excessive rubatos or rallentandos, to preserve their true attractiveness as idealised waltzes, but ones that never cease to evoke dancing.

His comments on *Miroirs* and the *Sonatine* were judged as impossible to understand without hearing them played, but those on *Le Tombeau* do deserve noting:

> Don't pay too much attention to the title. Only the 'Forlane' was inspired by the style of Couperin, duly interpreted. The

work is rather in the style of Scarlatti, apart from the 'Rigaudon' and 'Menuet' which are closer to the French school of the late 18th century.

The Housekeeper's Tale

Early in 1921, Ravel moved into the little house called Le Belvédère in the hamlet of Montfort l'Amaury, some 45 miles south west of Paris, the first and last house he ever bought. After one disastrous housekeeper, later that year he struck lucky with Marie Reveleau, and in 1946 she gave an interview about him, including this extract:

> I remained in M. Ravel's service for 14 years [in fact 16], and I mourned him deeply. One doesn't look after a man like my master for so long without feeling a great sadness. He was a character! All of a piece, very touchy and not a great talker. As I'm always saying: my master was a true 'aristo'. He found trivial chat unbearable. And he was as modest as a young girl. Once I happened to catch him as he was getting out of bed in his pyjamas. What a ticking off he gave me! There was nothing he detested more than lies and slander. If I came back from the shops with one or two good stories in my bag, he would categorically refuse to listen to them, saying 'To the devil with you and your nasty gossip!' A fine Frenchman, incapable of pettiness. He never asked to see the accounts. Anyone but me would have had fun stealing from him.

From around 1933 Ravel had trouble with both memory and speech. Mme Reveleau commented:

> That his final illness darkened his mood goes without saying, but he wasn't so much 'out of it' as was thought. He suffered mostly from his difficulty in talking. When I saw him looking well and said so, he would counter with 'It's not how I look that concerns me, it's ... it's ... ' and he would take his head in both hands, rub his jaw extremely hard, and then return to his silence.

His friends decided at the end of 1937 that a brain operation to restore him to something more like his old self was worth the risk. But sadly he did not survive it and died on 28 December. As to his legacy, his friend and pupil Manuel Rosenthal takes up the story. The evening after Ravel's death, he was conducting a concert performance of *L'Enfant et les sortilèges*:

> As I was leaving the stage, a double-bass player said to me on my way past, 'I understand why you are weeping for your maître, but take comfort in this: he, at least, is not leaving any rubbish behind.'

Ravel has a special place in my life because my aunt gave me a copy of his *Sonatine* for my 10th birthday. Why that piece, I never asked her. For years I never got beyond the middle 'Minuet', but it was the start of a lifelong love affair.

30 RAVEL AND THE 20TH CENTURY

No sane commentator has ever doubted Ravel's talent. He was a wonderful technician, a superb orchestrator, a consummate stylist… BUT…

The sense of disappointment is as often an undertow as a fully fledged current. Jim Samson, for instance, sums up Ravel's harmonic practice by saying that 'ultimately…the more astringent harmonies in his music are an extension and enrichment of a traditional type of tonal thinking rather than a reshaping of tonality along new, radical lines.'[1] Professor Samson might reasonably argue that this is a neutral, non-value judgment; but in the context of a book entitled *Music in Transition* it is, I submit, easier to read it as a criticism than as a eulogy. There is surely more than a little truth in Michael Russ's contention with regard to the two Piano Concertos that 'musicology is wary of declaring as "canonic" works which set out to entertain rather than those which confront the audience with what it might find unpalatable as a necessary part of discovery and self-expression'. It is, in essence, the ways in which Ravel is thought to fall short of the canonic, the 'but' of my first paragraph, that I want to examine, for what they tell us not only about Ravel but also about the twentieth century and the demands it has made of its 'serious' composers.

First of all, his structures (or at least, what are perceived to be such). Sir George Benjamin, a Ravel lover, nonetheless confesses that

> the aspect of Ravel that I'm more foreign to is the conservatism of his structures. They work perfectly for his music, but he is a bit unadventurous in his structures. It's all so clear-cut and all so classical on the surface that the type of experimentation with phrase-structure and long-term structural exploration you find in German music, in the Second Viennese school, and even up to a point in Debussy, is absent there; it is quite compartmentalised,

and in a way he's a miniaturist. The structures do have a certain similarity and indeed cleanness about them.

Now that may be on purpose, because with the harmonies being as subtle as they are, if the form became more subtle and complex, there'd be overload perhaps, which he would have hated. But I love it in German music when you get the feeling of structures bursting out of their bounds and going into territory you could never imagine from the beginning of the piece – you find that in Beethoven, and in Brahms and Wagner also, but you don't find that in Ravel. He remains basically within his borders once he's set them up; to do otherwise would probably be contrary to his character, but I find that problematic. [2]

This feeling, that Ravel could have been more adventurous if he chose, is widespread, as is the feeling that on the occasions he did choose to be adventurous, it was in the wrong directions. Debussy was one of the first to take this line, complaining to Louis Laloy:

> I agree with you Ravel is extraordinarily gifted, but what annoys me is the attitude he adopts of being a 'conjuror', or rather a Fakir casting spells and making flowers burst out of chairs. [3]

Elsewhere in his letters, Debussy speaks of his own 'personal alchemy' and we may feel that in the context the distinction between an alchemist and a conjuror is rather a fine one. Perhaps one of the things that upset the notoriously secretive Debussy was that Ravel tends to make plain what his technical and emotional intentions are (linked, maybe, with the setting up of borders that Benjamin alludes to). At the same time, like a conjuror, he cultivates surprise within this closely defined environment.

If we are looking for a source for this emphasis on surprise, we can find it in Baudelaire's definition of the dandy. In his view, the dandy is 'devoted above all to individuality' and embraces 'utter simplicity which is, in fact, the best way of marking oneself out'. He feels 'the burning need to create an originality, *contained within the outer limits of convention*' (my italics). He is motivated by 'the pleasure of causing astonishment and the profound satisfaction of never being astonished'. All dandies 'partake of the same character of opposition and revolt' and experience 'this need to combat ... and destroy triviality'. In short, they pursue 'the project of founding a new kind of aristocracy'. [4] and [35].

A mixture of aristocratic attitudes with aggression, and even a balance between the two, certainly helps to explain some of Ravel's music – and in the case of *Boléro*, the distaste of many may be attributable to what they hear as its too wholehearted embrace of aggression and an abandonment of the 'aristocratic' lineaments of the *Pavane pour une Infante défunte*, the *Sonatine* or *Le Tombeau de Couperin*.

There can, at all events, be no doubt over Ravel's determination to be different: witness his willingness to claim of some technical innovation 'et puis, vous savez, on n'avait jamais fait ça'[5] and his complaint that 'with every new endeavour, the critics throw your previous characteristics back in your face'[6] *(la critique vous oppose vos qualités précédentes)*. To that extent, and with suitable caution, one may disagree with Roland-Manuel when he writes that 'as a pure craftsman Ravel was utterly different from those aesthetes who, to use Nietzsche's charming expression, always fear "that they will be understood without too much difficulty"'; though he is surely right in claiming that Ravel is not one of those 'who are eager of their own accord to give their art a significance which lies far beyond its actual range'.[7]

It is relevant to quote the only mention of Ravel in Proust's *A la Recherche du temps perdu*. At the end of 'Le Temps retrouvé' a young man, hearing the Kreutzer Sonata, mistakenly 'thought it was a piece by Ravel which someone had described to him as being as beautiful as Palestrina, but difficult to understand'.[8] Given Proust's sensitivity to artistic opinion in all its manifestations, we may presume that this blend of beauty with difficulty was the received judgment on Ravel's music in the salons at the end of the First World War and just after. I can't help thinking Ravel must have been pleased when he read it, possibly taking the reference to Palestrina as a tribute to his teacher Gedalge.

Another disconcerting factor for some, including Pierre Boulez, has been the perceived split between Ravel's pre-War and post-War music, with *Le Tombeau de Couperin* acting as a slightly awkward bridge over the divide:

> For me what is important is works like *Shéhérazade*, *Miroirs*, *Gaspard de la nuit* or *Ma mère l'Oye*, where he has no restriction, with a certain spontaneity. After the war, the second period is, for me, much less attractive, although very attractive from outside. He tends to be too much self-restricted, he doesn't want to go out of himself. After the Trio you don't find the same deep feeling as before, but

more a kind of stylistic game, which is absolutely extraordinary. Only in the second song of *Don Quichotte à Dulcinée* does he go back to something very genuine.

Boulez and Benjamin agree about Ravel's self-restrictions and both Benjamin and Alexander Goehr make the point that, whatever feeling there may or may not be in the post-War works, a piece like *Boléro* has been crucial for the minimalists. Goehr goes further in going back:

> I think *Valses nobles et sentimentales* (which I have written imitations of several times) is a model – you can learn from Ravel something that was very unfashionable in the '50s and '60s, but could well be important: which is how you deal with something which is outwardly familiar, such as a waltz, which has a lot of 'givens' in it – and it's not just got to be 3-in-a-bar, it's got to have a certain bass pattern – and you fill in the middle in a very original way.
>
> For instance, minimalist composers, stuck as they are – because once the initial impact of minimalism has been made, what does a composer such as Glass do? – I would have thought Ravel would have been an extremely valuable model for them, because where the outward is given, you go for the subtlety in the middle.

After this exposition of some of the problems the twentieth century has had with Ravel, perhaps it is time for some development in the shape of a more formally organised synopsis of the influences, acknowledged and unacknowledged, positive and negative, which Ravel has exerted.

Edward Lockspeiser observed that Ravel's transcriptions and orchestrations of Debussy's music provided 'ample proof of [his] sincere devotion to Debussy. On the other hand, the name of Ravel is not once mentioned by Debussy without a note of sarcasm, irony or concern, certainly never with any sort of unreserved admiration'. [9] One explanation for this could be that, where Ravel could accept the fact of Debussy's influence on him and put his natural aggression on hold for the most part (always excepting his defence of the primacy of the 'Habanera' in the harmonic stakes and of *Jeux d'eau* in the 'Impressionist' piano ones), Debussy was perhaps as anxious for a time about Ravel's influence on him as he continued to be about Stravinsky's, even if this anxiety was nowhere so openly expressed. The coincidence of the two men's Mallarmé settings was unfortunate, but already by then Ravel had given signs in *Valses nobles* that he was pursuing ends far from Debussy's and it is hard to see that for the six years or so that remained of Debussy's composing life he was indebted to Ravel's music in any way: the quotation from 'Le Gibet' in the fourth of the *Epigraphes antiques* I take as the exception which proves the rule.

The extent of Stravinsky's indebtedness to Ravel is equally disputable. Among the printed sources, Eric Walter White notes a couple of possible instances: in Stravinsky's setting of Verlaine's 'Un grand sommeil noir' of 1910 (Ravel's 1895 setting was not published until 1953) 'an occasional chord of the 13th reminds one of Ravel' and in *Jeu de cartes* of 1936 'the waltz in the third deal sounds like a light-hearted skit on Ravel's *La Valse*'[10], while Stephen Walsh detects some Ravel influence in Act I of *The Nightingale*.[11] Many commentators have also noted the plagiarism of the end of *Rapsodie espagnole* in the final flourish of the 'Danse infernale' in *L'Oiseau de feu*. But altogether it's a fairly meagre haul. And in the last instance it is tempting to regard Stravinsky's borrowing as somewhat crudely simplistic – for one thing, where his up-down-up pattern is consistent in all instruments, Ravel slightly overlaps the three components, presenting the final C major chord as a welcome solution to threatened chaos.

To these examples, however, George Benjamin makes one challenging addition:

> I don't think *The Rite of Spring* would have been *The Rite of Spring* harmonically if Stravinsky hadn't been friends with Ravel, because (and Messiaen told me this) in the '20s and '30s people thought that Ravel was the more modern of the two because his music was more dissonant. The degree of sensitivity in Ravel's polytonal, polyharmonic world is fabulous; and you find that in *Miroirs* and *Gaspard*. Who else was doing that around then? Not Debussy. And where does Stravinsky get the harmonic language of, say, the beginning of Part 2 of *The Rite of Spring*? That's from 'Le Gibet', I think, among other things.

In calling this view 'challenging' I am thinking especially of Richard Taruskin's warning re the 'Petrushka chord': that 'by understanding the origins of Stravinsky's triadic-symmetrical octatonicism in Rimsky-Korsakov's work and teaching, one can distinguish his "Petrushka chord" from the ones in Ravel's *Jeux d'eau* (1901), for example, or in Strauss's *Elektra* (1908), which have very different historical backgrounds and different functional explanations, but which an analyst unarmed with historical perspective might be tempted to adduce as precedents for Stravinsky's usage'.[12] It could be that Taruskin would not adduce 'Le Gibet' as a precedent for the above passage of *The Rite*; the fact remains that Benjamin, as a practising composer and conductor, hears it that way.

It seems unlikely that Stravinsky's use of jazz owed anything to Ravel – apart from anything else, he got there first. Ravel's latecoming in this sphere was also implicitly commented on by Milhaud who in 1927, the very year of the first performance by Enescu and Ravel of the latter's mature Violin Sonata with its central 'Blues', stated firmly that

> the influence of jazz has already passed like a cleansing storm after which you find a clearer sky and more settled weather. Little by little a reviving classicism is replacing the exhausted gasps of syncopation. Our young composers are embarking on paths marked out for them by the new orientations of Stravinsky on the one hand and of Erik Satie on the other.[13]

No mention of Ravel… Milhaud admitted he was allergic to Ravel's music and increasingly this had come to be true of Milhaud's mentor Satie. In 1911 Satie dismissed Ravel as a 'highly talented Prix de Rome winner, a flashier version of Debussy'[14] and eight years later declined to write an article on Ravel for Jean-Aubry, saying that it 'might not be very much to your taste. The fault lies entirely with the deplorable and outmoded aesthetic professed by our friend. It would be difficult for me to water down what my thinking dictates. I love Ravel deeply but his art leaves me cold, alas!'[15]

Against Satie's complaint about Ravel being 'outmoded' we have to set Messiaen's claim that in the 20s and 30s people thought that Ravel was more modern than Stravinsky! The only answer seems to be that Satie and the young Messiaen moved in different circles, but it certainly serves as a warning that Ravel's standing was not an acknowledged constant across the whole spectrum of Parisian musical life.

In the case of Honegger and Poulenc, Ravel's influence has to be described as patchy. Honegger's 'Hommage à Ravel', written in 1915 and subsequently published as the second of *Trois pièces* for piano, pays lip service to the older composer in its use of modality and of Ravel's characteristic major 9th over a minor triad, but its stiff gait is most unravelian. Thereafter, in the opinion of Harry Halbreich, there are echoes of *Ma Mère l'Oye* at the end of Honegger's First String Quartet (1917) and in the powerful 'De profundis' in his Third Symphony (1945-6), and the Finale of his Sonatina for violin and cello (1932) is close in spirit to that of Ravel's earlier essay in the medium. But by and large the two men's composing worlds were far apart, as can be judged from a denigratory remark Honegger made in 1950: 'Ravel is a little like Utrillo, who used to paint pictures from postcards.' [16]

Poulenc too was ambivalent about Ravel's music. After *L'Enfant et les sortilèges* had won him back into the fold of Ravel admirers, he went on to wax ecstatic about both the Piano Concertos, his epithet 'sublime' for the Concerto for the Left Hand being underlined 13 times. [17] But elsewhere we find accusations that Ravel's music is cold, [18] that his orchestral technique is inappropriately applied, [19] and that 'neither the blues of the Violin Sonata nor the foxtrot in *L'Enfant et les sortilèges* will add anything much to Ravel's fame.' [20] His ambivalence shows itself most markedly over *L'Heure espagnole*, a work that has in general provided a focus for discussion of the technique/emotion dichotomy in Ravel's music. In 1943 he found *Mavra* 'more démodé than *L'Heure espagnole*' (the word 'even' is implied), but a year later, when working on *Les Mamelles de Tirésias*, he could admit

> I've read the orchestral score of Ravel's *L'Heure espagnole* with unparalleled care, and with the piano reduction in the other hand. What a miraculous masterpiece! But what a truly dangerous example (like all masterpieces)! When you lack Ravel's spellbinding precision (as, alas, I do), you have to set your music on sturdy feet. [21]

The apportioning of technique/emotion in that passage is hard to disentangle…We can find a similar ambivalence in Messiaen who, like Poulenc, was no jazz fiend:

> I've never believed in jazz and I've always thought that the poetic and refined figure of Maurice Ravel was spoiled in his last years by this jazz influence, which really had nothing to do with his personal inclinations. [22]

I find it particularly interesting that, in the original French, the adjective translated as 'refined' should be 'racée', meaning 'thoroughbred, true to one's race or stock': the implication being clearly that not only was

Ravel's attachment to jazz bad taste, it was actually unpatriotic. As Roy Howat has pointed out[23], Ravel's Frenchness was achieved rather than inborn. But it was nonetheless how he was perceived by all but the closest of his friends who came to recognize a typically Basque stubbornness, even cussedness in him.

Messiaen's view, like Boulez's, was coloured by his preference for the same works: *Miroirs*, *Gaspard*, *Ma Mère l'Oye*, *Daphnis*. But occasionally, as George Benjamin recalls, one could find cracks in the facade:

> Messiaen was rather iffy about quite a lot of Ravel. He would play *Ma Mère l'Oye* on the piano and he would be in tears; *Gaspard* too. But he would try and find a flaw in Ravel – maybe that's part of the question of growing away from something you're very fond of. In *L'Heure espagnole*, you could hear him consciously finding flaws. I can't imagine him saying very nice things about *Le Tombeau de Couperin*, but one day he was in a very good mood and came into the class singing the opening of the 'Rigaudon' – and he kept on going too!

One Ravel work Messiaen certainly did like was *Valses nobles et sentimentales*, since he played them at the 1937 concert that also contained the first complete performance of his *Poèmes pour Mi*.

Messiaen, like all composers, tended to find in other composers' music what he needed to find: *Daphnis* was a treasure trove of irrational Hindu and Greek rhythms; 'Laideronnette' fed into the *Trois petites Liturgies* where, in Boulez's view, the 'side order' (the gamelan sonorities) was more interesting than the 'main order', and this in turn fed into *Le Marteau sans maître*; the coda to 'Oiseaux tristes' was metamorphosed into the opening of the 'Amen du jugement' in *Visions de l'Amen*.

But perhaps the most fascinating idea Ravel's music sparked off in Messiaen came from 'Le Gibet', in the passage from bars 121 to 154 where a short value (a semiquaver) is followed by a longer value of decreasing duration: the proportions are 1:59, 1:47, 1:37, 1:21.[24] Bearing in mind that *Gaspard* was one of Messiaen's earliest possessions - he was given it between the ages of seven and ten, before the score of *Pelléas* – we may ask whether this was the breeding ground of the 'personnages rythmiques' which he was later to apply in his analysis of *The Rite of Spring* and in the composition of the *Turangalîla Symphony*, among other works. Over and above that, *Gaspard* remains a clear influence on Messiaen's piano writing, as a link between *Islamey* and *Vingt regards*.

Henri Dutilleux, born between Messiaen and Boulez and beginning his studies at the Paris Conservatoire in the 1930s, found Ravelism entrenched as 'the' official style and experienced considerable difficulty escaping from it. Certainly some of his earlier works which he later preferred not to think about too much, such as the Flute Sonatina and the piano suite *Au Gré des ondes*, bear marks of Ravelian influence in their elegant modality. While yielding to no one in his admiration of Ravel's technique, Dutilleux may have been obliquely criticising his post-War stylistic games when he stated that 'an artist has a very small number of things that he has to say very firmly, and they are always the same things.'[25] On the other hand, one could equally maintain that one of the miracles of Ravel's output is that, whatever the problem being solved, the authorial voice remains constant.

Boulez had little to say about Ravel over the years and admitted that in his view

> for the twentieth century, of course he's not as important a figure as Debussy, for instance, although the comparison is maybe wrong - but Debussy was more inventive, from a certain point of view, trying to get completely out of earlier formal frames, more inventive also in the rhythmical aspect. But I think that without Ravel the profile of French music would be completely different; and that's something of patrimonial interest, certainly, and without him the patrimony would be much poorer.

For me, almost the most interesting point there is Boulez's admission that we should not be comparing Ravel with Debussy, and yet we do. Boulez admits Ravel's importance for the French composers who came after him, but at the same time denigrates him because it is not the kind of importance (of language, form and rhythm) which Boulez particularly values. In saying that Ravel is 'not as important' to the twentieth century as Debussy, Boulez is also implying 'or to the twenty-first century and beyond', an implication I shall challenge below.

The Second Viennese School seem either to have ignored Ravel's presence, as in the case of Schoenberg, or as in Webern's, to have taken a narrow view of his achievement – Eduard Steuermann remembered that 'Webern once did the Mallarmé songs; he adored them, especially the last, which is very close to Schoenberg.'[26] On the other hand, Joan Peyser quotes Webern asking of a Ravel orchestral piece, 'Why does he use so many instruments?'[27], which perhaps tells us more about Webern than about Ravel.

Ravel's influence on English music is probably a good deal greater, but even here it is hard to adduce specific evidence. Much is owed to Sir Henry Wood who introduced Ravel's music to Britain with commendable promptness: *Introduction and Allegro* in 1907, *Rapsodie espagnole* in 1909, *Pavane pour une infante défunte* in Manchester in 1911 (the world premiere of the orchestral version, beating the French one by ten months) and *Valses nobles* in 1913.

Among composers, Vaughan Williams benefited from his lessons with Ravel but, apart from the shortlived French fever he himself spoke of, the direct influence of the French master is disputable, being largely confined perhaps to ideas of orchestral spacing, especially in the string writing, and in the use of models, Alain Frogley claiming that Vaughan Williams 'firmly believed in the value of modelling as a compositional training technique.'[28] Fiona Clampin suggests that Ravel's String Quartet possibly acted as a model for Herbert Howells's Third Quartet, *In Gloucestershire*, as his Sonatine may have done for John Ireland's Sonatina.

Among a slightly younger generation, Arthur Bliss 'at fifteen years of age (1906) ... was immediately captivated by the French masters', including the 'cool, elegant music of Ravel – no beetling brows and gloomy looks here, but a keen and slightly quizzical look at the world.'[29] Lennox Berkeley in his turn studied with Ravel in Paris during the late 1920s and the same 'cool elegance' distinguishes much of his music, though not all. Ravel was an early influence on Britten too. By the time he was thirteen or fourteen Britten had heard the String Quartet and been excited by it[30] and the summer holidays of 1930 were 'largely spent studying Ravel's *Miroirs*'.[31] The astonishingly assured orchestral sounds of the *Quatre Chansons françaises* also indicate a close study of Ravel's scores.

And yet in 1947 Percy Scholes could write that although 'some few pianoforte and orchestral pieces have become well known...there is not much evidence in *The Musical Times* of any really wide public acceptance of the composer.'[32] That there was however acceptance by an elite is confirmed by Norman Demuth who, writing in 1952 as a Professor of Composition at the Royal Academy of Music in London, opined that 'those who deal with young students find that when these begin to branch away from their traditional basic technique, it is Ravel who appears to give the direction.' [33]

In summing up the situation at present, it is important to distinguish between the example of Ravel's music itself and that of his approach to composition. Alexander Goehr makes the point, echoed, if less challengingly, by Henri Dutilleux, that Ravel 'is a bit too clever to be of much influence, because you've got to be too good at it to actually do it, and people nowadays aren't characterised by their high technical abilities in this direction'.

Where influences are to be recognised, it is more in the tone and the technique than in any of Ravel's musical styles or masks, which remain too personal. Julian Anderson confesses to 'tearing Ravel's scores apart to find out how it's done;' John Casken muses on Ravel's 'astonishing ear for the potent magic that steers individual notes from chord to chord, for a unique orchestral resonance ... How is it possible that it all seems so effortless?'

Enter Baudelaire's dandy ...

For Michael Berkeley it is

> hard to think of a greater model in terms of orchestration. But of course it goes much deeper than that, since the extraordinary feel and flair for scoring is always put to the service of the musical idea ... I feel that my own orchestration is profoundly influenced by the French school and in particular by an axis that is formed quite clearly in my mind by Debussy, Ravel, Stravinsky and Bartók with, strangely enough, Webern too. For I see a very strong aspirational link between the economy of Webern's little jewels and Ravel's somewhat more sumptuous but no less economical settings.

I have been intrigued that so many of those who have responded to my questions about Ravel have, *au fond*, been plagued by doubt and ambivalence. Robin Holloway expresses something of these quandaries:

> Maurice Ravel stands for a model of technical perfection. When younger I saw this only in terms of finish, neatness, impeccability, orchestration – something almost fetishistic, but deficient in visible/audible technical prowess à la Bach – fugue, canon,

ritornello etc – or à la Beethoven – motivic rigour, organic growth, symphonic argument or architecture. Ravel's perfection isn't measurable in terms of mastery of things that of their nature require mastery to be shewn. It's more simple, yet more elusive; it can't be defined ... the mastery is of spontaneity in capturing with precision the personal predilections of a remarkably individual appetite – garlic and onions – what Virgil Thomson calls 'the discipline of spontaneity – the toughest discipline there is'.

So what happened to the *petit maître* who, we were advised in the 1960s (I speak as a student during that era), had nothing new to say to us, whose prettily voluptuous music could safely be left to tickle the ears of the bourgeoisie?

I submit that that 'surface' Ravel was never the 'real' Ravel. I can only applaud the common sense and humility of Peter Kaminsky's remark, in his discussion of the links between Ravel's song texts and his compositional strategies, to the effect that 'if the connection remains obscured, then the fault lies with the analysis rather than the song.' [34]. Ravel, it turns out, is a far more baffling, problematic and 'deep' composer than he has so far been given credit for. Added to this is the enigma of his orchestration. In many of the eulogies directed at this aspect of Ravel's craft, it is impossible to miss a sense of embarrassment, of guilt almost, that a practising composer should be singling out the sublimely sensuous instead of more 'important' things like form or motivic coherence or octatonic scales. In Julian Anderson's words:

> Ravel disturbs with his curious mixes, with his experiments couched in traditional forms. He is unpigeonholable. What to do with him? Like Ligeti, he is having serious fun – both are enjoying themselves at an aristocratically high level.

And so we return, yet again, to Baudelaire's dandy who flourishes, so Baudelaire tells us, especially in transitional epochs when democracy is not yet all powerful and aristocracy only partially tottering and debased. [35]

While we must all make up our own minds as to how Ravel's music and the social order are likely to interact during the twenty-first century, the present fact, crudely put, is that the length of listings in the CD catalogues seems to lie somewhere between those of Gershwin and Stravinsky. But continuing analysis suggests that we have barely begun really to understand how Ravel's music works. Will the twenty-first century be long enough for us to find out?

[1] Jim Samson, *Music in Transition* (London: Dent, 1977), 50
[2] I am grateful to Sir George Benjamin, Pierre Boulez, Henri Dutilleux and Alexander Goehr for giving me their views on Ravel in the course of interviews in November 1998; and to Julian Anderson, Michael Berkeley, John Casken and Robin Holloway for doing so by telephone, letter and e-mail during January and February 1999
[3] Letter to Laloy of 8 March 1907, *Debussy Letters*, ed. François Lesure and Roger Nichols (London: Faber, 1987), 178
[4] Charles Baudelaire, 'Le dandy', *L'art romantique* (Paris: Calmann-Lévy, 1924), 92-4
[5] Quoted by Calvocoressi in Nichols, *Ravel Remembered*, 181
[6] Letter to an unknown woman of 16 February 1907; Arbie Orenstein, *A Ravel Reader*, 86
[7] Roland-Manuel, Maurice Ravel, tr. Cynthia Jolly (London: Dobson, 1947, R/1972), 136
[8] Marcel Proust, *A la recherche du temps perdu*, III, ed. Pierre Clarac and André Ferré (Paris: Pléiade, 1954), 1025-6
[9] Edward Lockspeiser, *Debussy: His Life and Mind*, II (London: Cassell, 1965), 40
[10] Eric Walter White, *Stravinsky: The Composer and his Works* (London: Faber, 1966, 2/1979), 193 and 396
[11] Stephen Walsh, *The Music of Stravinsky* (Oxford: Clarendon Press, 1993), 19
[12] Richard Taruskin, 'Chez Pétrouchka: Harmony and Tonality *chez* Stravinsky', *Music at the Turn of Century*, ed. Joseph Kerman (Berkeley: University of California Press, 1990), 74
[13] Darius Milhaud, 'La musique française depuis la guerre', *Etudes* (Paris: Editions Claude Aveline, 1927), 71-92: 74
[14] Erik Satie, *Ecrits*, ed. Ornella Volta (Paris: Editions Champ Libre, 1977), 244
[15] Ornella Volta, *Satie Seen Through His Letters*, tr. Michael Bullock (London, New York: Marion Boyars, 1989), 89; these last two quotations given in Robert Orledge, *Satie the Composer* (Cambridge: Cambridge University Press, 1990), 251
[16] Harry Halbreich, *Honegger*, tr. Roger Nichols (Portland: Amadeus Press, 1999), 255, 270, 321, 599
[17] Letters of 12 January 1932 and 23 January 1933 to Nora Auric; Francis Poulenc, *Correspondance 1910–1963*, ed. Myriam Chimènes (Paris: Fayard, 1994), 361, 382
[18] Letters of 10 June 1919, 25 August 1928 and 8 November 1943 to Georges Jean-Aubry, Henri Sauguet and Roland-Manuel respectively; ibid. 292, 547
[19] Letters of 10 June 1919 and 7 May 1921 to Georges Jean-Aubry and Paul Collaer respectively; ibid. 93, 125
[20] Francis Poulenc, 'Mes maîtres et mes amis', talk given on 7 March 1935, pub. *Conferencia*, 15 October 1935, 524: *Francis Poulenc, Articles and Interviews*, ed. Nicolas Southon, tr. Roger Nichols (Farnham: Ashgate, 2014), 99; *Correspondance*, 704

[21] Letter of 24 June 1944 to Pierre Bernac; ibid. 553-4; *Selected Correspondence*, tr. and ed. Sidney Buckland (London: Gollancz, 1991), 135
[22] Olivier Messiaen, *Music and Color: Conversations with Claude Samuel*, tr. E. Thomas Glasow (Portland: Amadeus Press, 1994), 195
[23] 'Ravel and the piano', *The Cambridge Companion to Ravel*, ed. Deborah Mawer (Cambridge, 2000), 71
[24] Olivier Messiaen, *Traité de rythme, de couleur, et d'ornithologie*, I (Paris: Leduc, 1994), 129; Alexander Goehr, *Finding the Key*, ed. Derrick Puffett (London: Faber, 1998), 52
[25] Pierrette Mari, *Henri Dutilleux* (Paris: Zurfluh, 1988), 91
[26] Hans Moldenhauer, *Anton von Webern* (London: Gollancz, 1978), 236
[27] Joan Peyser, *Boulez, Composer, Conductor, Enigma* (London: Cassell, 1977), 50
[28] quoted in Fiona Clampin, *Englishness Revisited: The Influence of Debussy and Ravel on English Music 1900-1930* (unpublished MA in Musicology, University of Exeter, 1997), 65. I am grateful to Ms Clampin for sending me the relevant portion of her dissertation
[29] Arthur Bliss, *As I Remember* (London: Faber, 1970), 21
[30] Humphrey Carpenter, *Benjamin Britten* (London: Faber, 1992), 15
[31] ibid., 32
[32] Percy Scholes, *The Mirror of Music,* I (London: Novello/Oxford University Press, 1947), 451
[33] Norman Demuth, *Musical Trends in the 20th Century* (London: Rockliff, 1952), 54
[34] 'Vocal music and the lures of exoticism and irony', *The Cambridge Companion to Ravel*, ed. Deborah Mawer (Cambridge, 2000), 163
[35] Charles Baudelaire. 'Le dandy', 92-94: 'épris avant tout de distinction'; 'la simplicité absolue, qui est, en effet, la meilleure manière de se distinguer'; 'le besoin ardent de se faire une originalité, contenu dans les limites extérieures des convenances'; 'le plaisir d'étonner et la satisfaction orgeuilleuse de ne jamais être étonné'; 'participent du même caractère d'opposition et de révolte'; 'ce besoin ... de combattre et de détruire la trivialité'; 'le projet de fonder une espèce nouvelle d'aristocratie' [4]

31 RAVEL AND THE DANCE

A few months before the Second World War, Olivier Messiaen launched into a diatribe against the lazy composers who were, he felt, so characteristic of his century: and among them he numbered as 'lazy the craftsmen of sub-Fauré and sub-Ravel, lazy the pseudo-Couperin maniacs, the manufacturers of rigaudons and pavanes'. Messiaen was in no way inveighing against Fauré and Ravel themselves, nor against their rigaudons and pavanes, but he surely had a point in believing that by 1939 composers should have moved on to other things. At the same time, the fact that he needed to say what he did shows what a powerful hold Ancient Dance Syndrome had established over the French musical imagination.

We could trace the syndrome's attractions for Ravel simply along the tradition that linked him through his teacher Fauré to his teacher Saint-Saëns. In the matter of pavanes, for instance, Saint-Saëns introduced them into his operas *Etienne Marcel* and *Proserpine* in 1877 and 1886, and included two in the ballet sequence for his opera *Ascanio* in 1888 – the year in which Fauré's well-known *Pavane* was heard for the first time. That Ravel was a devoted pupil of Fauré and an admirer of Saint-Saëns is not in doubt. But he shared with them, whether through training or innate disposition, a distrust of Wagner, of the grand gesture, of the dramatic surprise. For similar reasons Fauré was once rude about Berlioz. And it is easy to sense a similarity of approach between this Saint-Saëns/Fauré/Ravel axis and Stravinsky's later complaint, made à propos a recording of a Bruno Walter rehearsal, that the players were constantly being enjoined to make the music sing but never to make it dance.

We know that Ravel learnt Spanish songs at his mother's knee and their rhythms stayed with him to the end of his life. It was indeed in a Spanish dance, a 'Habanera' for two pianos, that the authentic Ravelian voice was heard for the first time in 1895, when the composer was 20. Interestingly, the French tradition embodied in the *Menuet antique* of the same year produces less original results – but of this more anon. It is only natural for a young composer to build on his earliest success, and the scrunchy harmonies of the 'Habanera' were to be a key ingredient of Ravel's later harmonic practice. But notoriety came first through the French tradition and the *Pavane pour une Infante défunte* he wrote in 1899.

The success of this piece (whose influence, as we have seen, was instrumental in reducing Messiaen to near-apoplexy forty years later) must, I think, be traced not merely to Ravel's qualities as a composer but to the meaning that these old French dances held for him. It's fair to say that politically Ravel was a divided soul. He counted himself as a Socialist but he was also a socialite. The most natural and unaffected of men, he nonetheless hankered after an age in which France had been powerful, stable, and above all, orderly. Pre-revolutionary France of the late 18th century was his ideal, with the period of Louis XIV a close runner-up. Pavanes, minuets and the rest therefore carried with them the weight of a whole era of civilisation when, supposedly, people knew their place and remained there. How apt that a reviewer of the first performance of the G major Piano Concerto in 1932 should have commented that each note knew where it came from and where it was going!

The courtly French dance was, then, a means by which Ravel and others could keep music, and society, 'on the rails', at a time when anarchy, corruption and Emile Zola were threatening the body and the soul of France. But against this plea for order, Ravel's love of Spanish dances suggests a taste for wildness and excess – the dichotomy labelled by Apollinaire a few years later as 'l'ordre' against 'l'aventure'. The "Alborada del gracioso" from the piano suite *Miroirs* of 1905 is a portrait of a mercurial, Figaro-like character, and Ravel uses Spanish musical idiom to create vivid textural and harmonic contrasts, as against the relatively narrow harmonic range suitable to the French dances. At the same time, the Spanish dances never degenerate into disorder - something that had no place in Ravel's scheme of things.

Apart from one wholly unimportant composition, *La Parade*, probably designed to accompany dancing at some private function around 1896, Ravel seems not to have thought about writing a ballet until some ten years later, when he first considered composing an orchestral work called *Wien* which was to be an apotheosis of the Viennese waltz. After the war this was to turn into *La Valse*, but in the meantime three other dance projects intervened. The ballet *Adélaïde, ou le langage des fleurs* for which he orchestrated his piano suite *Valses nobles et sentimentales* merely confirmed, as did the ballet on *Ma mère l'Oye*, what has already been implied: that Ravel's music, like Stravinsky's, tended towards the danceable. *Daphnis and Chloé*, on the other hand, took Ravel's relationship with the dance several stages further.

It was agreed between Ravel and the choreographer Fokine that *Daphnis* would be an integrated whole. Mention of such a thing in the early 20th century naturally suggests the influence of Wagner but, if we are to believe Fokine's own description, the idea of a ballet as a developing entity had more to do with the prestige such a work might bring to its creators and interpreters. For Ravel, too, *amour propre* had a part to play. Now in his mid-thirties, he had a one-act comic opera in his portfolio (*L'Heure espagnole*), but had yet to shake off the tag of being a miniaturist. And more than likely Debussy's quip about his being no more than a conjuror who could make flowers burst out of chairs had been passed on by some kind acquaintance.

If, with hindsight, we look at the two operas Ravel did write, there is no denying that the styles of wordsetting he employed were highly idiosyncratic and particular to individual situations and characters. Could it be that he was uncomfortable with the vocal tradition of Gounod and Massenet? If so, then dance offered him the obvious vehicle with which to breach the closely guarded defences of the serious French stage, and Fokine's conception, on this front at least, married closely with his own.

The scale of *Daphnis* is sufficiently indicated by Ravel's description of it as a 'symphonie chorégraphique'. There could be no question here of relying on tastefully scored minuets and pavanes, and it was not the least part of Ravel's genius that at the first attempt he was able to control such a long span of music, while responding with wonderful accuracy to the drama and humour of the story within the confines of a perceptibly 'classical' atmosphere. Among the most powerful strokes is the choral link between the two sections of the ballet, in which the balletic element is deliberately withdrawn. This temporary 'unearthing' of the work could only succeed in a medium where the rhythm of physical contact with the stage had been established as the norm. Throughout, the ballet is irradiated by the tension between the formal inclinations of classical legend (or at least the formal expectations it arouses) and the tendency of Ravel's chromatic harmonies and rich orchestration to break the formal bonds. This tension can be summarised as one between the horizontal (dance rhythms) and the vertical (chords and sensuous moments). To wax more philosophical still, one could assess the culmination and resolution of this tension in the final 'danse générale' as representing the absorption of the lonely Romantic artist (Daphnis/Ravel) into the social fabric: Daphnis wins Chloé, Ravel wins acceptance.

Not a great deal needs to be said about the ballet made on four movements from the piano suite *Le Tombeau de Couperin*. Like *Adélaïde*, this capitalised on the danceable element in Ravel's music, although it marked one of the last real successes of Ancient Dance Syndrome, in the French musical theatre at any rate. More interesting is the question of why Ravel now, after more than a dozen years, found it possible to bring *Wien/La Valse* to completion. No doubt the money promised by Diaghilev's commission was a help. But was *La Valse* a comment on contemporary society? The composer strenuously denied it. What he always insisted on was that the waltz itself was the subject. It was the waltz that induced the work's terminal frenzy, and if we like to take the waltz as a symbol of collective hysteria, that is up to us. The most one can say is that, for Alfred de Musset in the early nineteenth century, the movement from the minuet to the waltz symbolised that from monarchy to republic. For Ravel, *La Valse* marks the end of the courtly French dance and the spread of Spanish fire into other areas of endeavour.

As is well known, Diaghilev refused *La Valse* because, being about dancing rather than telling a story, it was too abstract for his taste. There is some reason to think that Ravel, like Mendelssohn before him, valued wordless music for its ability to go deeper than words. We can find evidence for this in the heart-stoppingly beautiful ballet sequence he put into the second half of his opera *L'Enfant et les sortilèges*, where 'abstract' dance, allowing the audience respite from the brilliant but demanding word-play, not only continues but deepens the profound message of the opera. In this sense the sequence is the inverse counterpart of the choral link in *Daphnis*.

Although *Tzigane* is more about fiddle-playing than dancing, it stands as a kind of warning (if that's the right word) that *Boléro* is just round the corner. *Boléro* has been widely reviled. It was, it's true, a very late substitute for the orchestration of movements from Albéniz's *Iberia* which Ravel was unable to make for copyright reasons, and the composer himself was astonished at its runaway success. But it combines at least three elements which were central to his music: Spain, virtuosity, and the dichotomy between 'l'ordre' and 'l'aventure'.

The feeling of order soon imposes itself: this rhythm is set to go on for some time. And of course the physical actions of the dancers reinforce this. The feeling of danger arises from the question, 'How is Ravel going to get out of this one effectively?' The answer (and possibly one of Ravel's most brilliant strokes of genius) is through the sudden modulation from C to E, after which we cling passionately to the return of C 'for fear of finding something worse'. The effect of the modulation is perhaps analogous to that of a dancer's difficult 'lift', which we know has at some stage to lead to a complementary release.

Boléro was Ravel's farewell to the ballet. But there are the usual danceable elements in the works that followed, especially in the Piano Concerto for the Left Hand and in the two outer *Don Quichotte* songs. Since few composers of the last 150 years have been as resourceful as Ravel in treating the dance, it is natural to look for reasons. Obviously such things must remain tentative, but my own feeling is that, first of all, dance was congruent with Ravel's wish to emphasise tradition and to suppress the ego. It is true to say, I think, that whereas solo singers have often played the most appalling tricks on their music, dancers have by and large, if only through necessity, been more respectful: as Ravel said, 'Performers are slaves'. Secondly, because dancing operates through conventions and is to a large degree abstract, it perhaps allowed Ravel to remain at a comfortable distance from reality. I feel that this composer, who was in his own words 'artificial by nature', must have relished the artificality of ballet that tends to remove it from the embrace of raw, overheated, ill-considered emotion.

This article was written for the 2015 Glyndebourne staging of Ravel's two operas, directed by Laurent Pelly. This followed shortly after Pelly's production at Covent Garden of Donizetti's *La Fille du régiment* in which the girl of the title had most effectively combined singing with ironing, so in *L'Heure espagnole* the opportunity to have Concepcion follow suit was too good to miss – a touch of *fantaisie* which, I'm sure, Ravel would have loved.

32 RAVEL AND SPAIN

It's tempting to begin with *Boléro*, by far Ravel's best-known piece of Spanish inspiration. But here one should be cautious. Certainly he described the themes as 'impersonal – folk tunes of the usual Spanish-Arabian kind', but even this is problematic: why 'tunes' in the plural? And why 'usual Spanish-Arabian' when, despite Spain's long history under Muslim rule, many of her characteristic tunes show no Arabian influence whatever? Then there's the fact that various Spanish musicians declared it wasn't a bolero. Ravel retorted that this was irrelevant: far more important to him was that it was 'an experiment in a very special and limited direction', that is as a continual crescendo using only one set of melodic material. So can the Spanish element, while certainly present, be regarded as not the primary factor? Or was Ravel fooling himself, and us?

Less ambiguous are the two outer songs of the triptych *Don Quichotte à Dulcinée*, Ravel's last work. The final drinking song, with its dissonant scrunches on the piano and pseudo-Arabian melismas in the voice, gives a vivid picture of a less-than-sober Don Quixote, down to his ultimate collapse, described in the final downward bass chromatic scale. But the most interesting fact of all emerges from the recollections of the Breton baritone Yvon le Marc'hadour, who was at a rehearsal in the composer's presence of the orchestral version of these songs, sung by Martial Singher under the Spanish conductor Pedro de Freitas-Branco. After the first song, the conductor turned to Ravel and said, 'I suppose you realize you've written a *guajira*?' Although the *guajira* is in fact a Colombian dance, Ravel had assumed it was Spanish, and he proceeded to dance around the studio chanting 'J'ai écrit un *guajira*! J'ai écrit un *guajira*!' As the format of the dance is simply one bar of 6/8 (two groups of three) followed by one of 3/4 (three groups of two), we might be surprised at such a reaction from an eminent composer in his late fifties. But this would be to underestimate the place of Spain and the 'exotic', both in French history and in Ravel's own. We need to go back in time ...

The French love of the exotic goes back at least as far as the Baroque era. Rameau's opera-ballet *Les Indes galantes* of 1735 contained action in Turkey, Peru and Illinois, but instead of authentic music the spectators were treated to a spectacular volcanic eruption. With the 19th century some semblance of authenticity began to make itself felt, and here the Spanish strain took the lead, possibly helped by the immigration of Spaniards fleeing the First Carlist War of 1833-39. Operas on Spanish themes included Boieldieu's *Le Bouquet de l'Infante* (1847), Adam's *Le Toréador* (1849), Ferdinand Poise's *Le Roi Don Pèdre* (1857) and Massenet's *Don César de Bazan* (1872). The way was thus paved for *Carmen*, Lalo's *Symphonie espagnole* written for the Spanish violinist Sarasate and, not least, Chabrier's *España*.

The question of why the exotic, and Spain in particular, should excite such interest among French artists takes us back again to the 18th century and to the writings of Jean-Jacques Rousseau. His most famous remark, 'Mankind is born to be free but everywhere is in chains', was aimed particularly at French civilisation which, he felt, was a burden on the human soul, a denial of the rights of the 'noble savage'. All that 'civilised' behaviour, with its 'je vous prie, Monsieur' and 'votre serviteur, Madame', was no more than a thin carapace covering the welter of passions to which the human animal is subject. Not without reason, some historians claim that Rousseau's writings helped bring on the 1789 Revolution. The traditional virtues of French culture – moderation, clarity, grace – had a hard time countering the aftershocks of that revolution over the coming century, and it's at least feasible that Spanish culture, replete with colour, energy and wildness (not to mention, in the case of *Carmen*, sex and a proto-feminist embrace of freedom), offered a less bloody outlet for those artists feeling smothered by the carapace. We find plentiful evidence for this in the enthusiastic letters Chabrier sent from Spain in the autumn of 1882, when he was collecting material for *España*, and in the judgment of his friend Henri Duparc, that before then Chabrier's orchestration was like anyone else's; afterwards, it sounded like Chabrier.

Carmen and *España* together provided a storehouse of Spanish tropes that later composers plundered freely. Here three must suffice. The smallest is a little triplet ornament that falls back on a longer note ('tid-de-ly pom'). Like many of these Spanish tropes, it's a delaying tactic, almost a tease: we know the long note is coming and relish the delay. The second trope is a taste for repeated notes. Probably this derives from guitar strumming, but again it's a delaying tactic, often emphasised by the fact that the repeated note is a discord against the accompaniment. The third trope is merely an extension of this: the rule of implacable rhythms that, as in *flamenco*, continue beyond our reasonable expectations – 'reasonable', that is, according to the norms of civilisation. Here we come back to *Boléro*, and are forced to question Ravel's statement that the work is no more than the working-out of a particular structure. Surely this is an expression of Rousseau's 'freedom from chains', freedom from Teutonic development and respectability? And, not to put too fine a point on it, a prolonged orchestral orgasm, as the film *10* suggested? Further freedoms are called to mind in Richard Langham Smith's observation re Spain that 'common to many writers is the portrayal of a country locked in a time-warp behind "civilised" Europe; a place of atrocities caused by the untamed passions of its people, rife with smugglers and brigands'.

This then was the picture Ravel inherited when he was born in 1875, just four days after the premiere of *Carmen* at the Opéra-Comique. But he inherited far more than that. His father, Joseph, had met Marie Delouart (possibly herself descended from pirates) in the Gardens of Aranjuez just outside Madrid while he was chief engineer for the railway line from Madrid north to Irun. She was a Basque, born in Ciboure, over the river from St-Jean-de-Luz, but Ravel heard Basque melodies only later in life. As a small boy, it was the Spanish *boleros*, *sevillanos* and *habaneras* that his mother sang to him as he sat on her knee. It seems likely too, given Marie's initial ignorance of French, a language she never wholly mastered, that much of the conversation in Ravel's early childhood was conducted in Spanish, which Joseph must have learnt for his job. For Ravel therefore, Spain was an emotional home, which might explain that outburst of dancing half a century later.

In November 1888, a year or so before entering the Paris Conservatoire, Ravel met a Spanish boy of his own age, Ricardo Viñes, who was to give first performances of a number of Ravel's piano works. Together, in 1898, they played the first of Ravel's Spanish pieces, a *Habanera* for two pianos written in 1895, with a heading taken from Baudelaire: 'Au pays parfumé que le soleil caresse' (In the scented country caressed by the sun). Ravel's playing indication 'In muted colours and a lazy rhythm' shows another side of Spanish music, the idleness of *mañana*, during which the locals may be imagined taking their ease after a bout of virtuosic clapping and stamping . The *habanera* rhythm, a group of three followed by a group of two over a dotted figure in the bass, runs through the whole piece, mostly on repeated C sharps (in 41 of the 64 bars) which, from the start, the harmony tries to dislodge with D naturals and B sharps, producing the semitonal scrunches that survive in the *Don Quichotte* song mentioned above. The story goes that Debussy was present at the 1898 performance and he asked to take a copy of the score home with him. When his 'La Soirée dans Grenade' appeared in 1903, also sporting repeated C sharps and *habanera* rhythms, Ravel was incensed and thought of bringing an action, but was apparently advised by friends that a charge of 'he stole my C sharps' was unlikely to carry much weight in court.

Ravel waited ten years before turning to Spain again in the fourth of his *Miroirs* for piano, entitled 'Alborada del gracioso'. 'Alborada' presents no problems, being the Spanish for 'aubade', or 'morning song', usually sung by a lover under the window of his inamorata urging her to wake up. But 'gracioso' is more difficult to translate. Ravel likened a *gracioso* to Beaumarchais's Figaro, while agreeing that Figaro is 'more philosophical, less well-meaning than his Spanish ancestor'. The piece requires extreme virtuosity, another Spanish trait that appealed to Ravel, not least in the fast repeated notes, even more taxing on heavier modern pianos. The outer sections are in the form of an Andalusian *seguidilla*, enclosing a slow central *copla*.

But Ravel's truly Spanish years, by his own account, were 1907 and 1908. A *Vocalise-Etude en forme de Habanera* for voice and piano does what the title says. The *Rapsodie espagnole*, originally for two pianos then orchestrated, explores the extremes of languor and energy, and the orchestral version of the final 'Feria' almost destroys itself through sheer volume and brilliance, prompting Ravel's teacher Fauré to complain of 'new-fangled procedures, so-called'. For the third movement, Ravel orchestrated his old 'Habanera': the score bears the date 1895, to prove who got there first. But from April to October 1907 his main efforts were directed to completing the vocal score of his first completed opera, *L'Heure espagnole*.

Franc-Nohain's similarly titled play had been a great success in 1904 and Ravel's changes and cuts in the text do not affect the message in any way. He wrote it for his father, and possibly the Spanish atmosphere was to act as a reminder of those happy days when Joseph was courting Marie in the Gardens of Aranjuez. But, as with *Carmen*, the risqué storyline caused trouble at the Opéra-Comique where, traditionally, well-brought-up girls went in search of a husband. Sadly, the delays meant that Joseph died before the premiere, though Ravel may well have played him the score on the piano.

The opera is a compendium of the Spanish tropes already mentioned. If the opening 'clock symphony' is non-Spanish, that's because Ravel took it from his abandoned opera *Olympia* based on Hoffmann's story of Dr Coppelius. But from the entry of the muleteer Ramiro, Spain, and particularly Concepcion, are in command. Fauré again delivered a brief barb against Ravel: that never had a text offered such opportunities for writing wrong notes – of which Ravel took full advantage. But he admitted his pupil's extraordinary ability to colour the conversations orchestrally and to make the orchestral writing funny in itself. As for the vocal writing, Ravel had, with the opera already in mind, deliberately tried out a natural, demotic style of delivery in the song cycle *Histoires naturelles*, premiered in January 1907. Once again the old battle between naturalism and civilisation reared its head, with the bourgeosie harrumphing furiously over Ravel's sporadic suppression of the final mute 'e's which tradition dictated should always be sounded in sung texts. Ravel follows the same pattern in the opera: in Ramiro's third speech, the words 'office' and 'fixe' are designated as ending on their last consonant. The bourgeoisie may have disapproved, but the process helps the words carry to the back of the theatre.

In 1944 Poulenc, hard at work orchestrating *Les Mamelles de Tirésias*, wrote to Pierre Bernac of *L'Heure espagnole*:

> What a miraculous masterpiece, but what a treacherous example (like all masterpieces). When one doesn't have Ravel's magical precision – which is, sadly, the case with me – one has to plant one's music on robust feet.

Magical it certainly is, and even Reynaldo Hahn's insult, delivered in the course of a sour review of the premiere, can be read as an unintended accolade, when he describes the orchestra's contribution as 'a kind of transcendent jujitsu'.

33 RAVEL, DREYFUS AND SEX

There seems to be fairly common agreement about the four things that interest us humans most: politics, religion, money and sex. Not that everyone by any means feels strongly about all four. In the case of Maurice Ravel, religion was irrelevant (he was so unclear about his own motives, he said, that those of an unseen being were totally beyond him), and he seems to have had little or no interest in money – the only thing you might possibly call a financial scandal was the huge sum brought in by the royalties on *Boléro*, about which the composer might well have agreed with you. Which leaves politics and sex ...

All his life, Ravel was a political Leftie. This attitude can be traced, if you like, to his maternal ancestry among the fisherwomen of the Basque port of Ciboure, the *kaskarotes* who, in earlier times, had been thought to carry the plague. His friends remarked on his extraordinary ability to talk in exactly the same way with children and with princes, to the delight of both parties, and it could well be that the resounding success of his American tour in 1928 owed something to his appreciation of that country's democratic spirit.

In France the great political scandal of the early 20th century was, of course, the Dreyfus Case, and not surprisingly people have wanted for years to know where Ravel stood in the *affaire*. On the surface, a pro-Dreyfus stance would seem probable. But let's look at the three bits of evidence. The first two consist of an exchange of letters in November 1906 between Ravel and his fellow musician D-E Inghelbrecht – later conductor of the French National Orchestra, but in 1906 a member of the group of young artists known as the Apaches to which Ravel also belonged. In his letter of 8 November, Ravel writes:

> There are places where, necessarily, we can no longer see each other, but there are others where we shall be obliged to meet. So it would be useful, I think, if you're not worried by anything that might stand in the way, to regularise our reciprocal behaviour through straightforward explanations.

Two days later, Inghelbrecht replies:

> I should, on your behalf, regret the abandonment of group solidarity which you seem almost to insist on by leaving the neutral territory adopted by almost every one of our mutual friends. [1]

Although it is certainly possible to relate this to the Dreyfus Affair (the second 'almost' can be explained by the virulent anti-Dreyfus attitude of Ravel's friend and fellow Apache, the pianist Ricardo Viñes) the name 'Dreyfus' is not mentioned in the correspondence and some quite different explanation is always possible. But, again, a firmly, even outspokenly, Dreyfusard Ravel would fit the scenario.

The third piece of evidence comes from Viñes, who in his diary entry for 31 May 1899 writes, 'I went to invite Ravel for a meal. Then, I had dinner with Mme Morillot Deschamps: all dreyfusards.' The punctuation here is tantalisingly unclear. 'Tous dreyfusards' ... does that apply just to the guests at Mme MD's table? Or does it include Ravel? There the evidence, such as it is, ends.

Which leaves sex. Here again, the evidence relating to Ravel is far less decisive than many people would like, and rumours abound. One, vouchsafed to me recently by the wife of a high-ranking clergyman, relates how, as a young man, Ravel had gone with student friends to consult a fortune teller. Much to the woman's surprise, time and again she dealt the cards and turned up the queen of spades (The Black Lady). This apparently caused great hilarity among the company, who knew that 'a black woman was Ravel's special friend'. Since there is no mention of a black female friend anywhere in the Ravel literature, we can only surmise (if, of course, the story is true) that she was a prostitute. But it is tempting to find here a link with the song 'Aoua!', the second of the *Chansons madécasses*, where the cry of pain on behalf of the betrayed Madagascan natives seems wrenched from Ravel's innermost being.

On the question of ladies of the night, Inghelbrecht again appears in the picture since, half a century later, it was he who told Ravel's biographer H. H. Stuckenschmidt that 'Ravel had occasional encounters with prostitutes'. [2] Stuckenschmidt does not say whether he believes this or not – and wisely, because he may well have picked up that the difficult relations between Inghelbrecht and Ravel only deteriorated with time. More telling, I think, is the memoir by Vaughan

Williams, who went to Paris to study with Ravel in 1907-08, of being taken out to lunch with Ravel by his publisher Jacques Durand, who at the end of the meal said, 'Now we go see some jolly tarts, ha?' VW's later response was that these were 'guaranteed not to tempt any young man to lose his virtue', but sadly says nothing of Ravel. [3] In my view, though, Durand, who knew Ravel well, would hardly have made the offer if he hadn't expected him to accept.

As to relationships with ladies of the day, again the evidence is inconclusive. Friends believed that at one point he had proposed marriage to his friend, the violinist Hélène Jourdan-Morhange, who replied along the lines of 'Oh Maurice, do try not to be silly!' Of the marriage of his friends Maurice and Nelly Delage, he said 'They're a real pair! (ça, c'est un ménage) If I was married, it would have to be like that. Only I could never stand it.' [4] Elsewhere he wrote of composers not being normal human beings, unfitted for any such close encounter. [5] Recently, the French scholar David Lamaze has made an interesting case for Ravel having a longstanding, unrequited passion for Misia Sert, the high-powered Parisian networker, finding her forename encoded in the composer's music, but I think it's fair to say the jury's still out on this one. [6]

Then there are the rumours of his homosexuality. The only evidence I know for this comes from Benjamin Ivry to whom the American composer David Diamond confided that, when he was in Paris as a 13-year-old boy, Ravel, on their second meeting, kissed him on both cheeks and neck. [7] We must all decide for ourselves how much weight to place on this unique and unsupported assertion. But even if true, does this constitute proof of anything other than avuncular affection, at the most?

For me, the most decisive evidence of Ravel's sexuality comes from a letter for long unknown in the Ravel literature, written on 11 July 1895 when he was 20 – indeed it is the earliest letter of his that we possess. [8] He has been to an optician to buy a lorgnette for a female friend, but has forgotten to ask her the strength of lenses she needs:

> and I felt completely stupid (no change there) when the distinguished optician asked me what they should be ... I lay at your feet, as the saying goes, my most respectful homage (but inside, I'm thinking something entirely different ...).

How Ravelian this sounds – the outer skin masking the true feeling within; here he is, preparing for a whole lifetime of covering up his sexuality since, like his musical sketches, it is no one else's business. Strange as it may seem to the Facebookers and Twitterers, in 1895 such *pudeur* was not so very extraordinary. Let's respect it. Perhaps those who still routinely dismiss the whole business by saying 'Ravel was probably gay' may be prompted to think again.

[1] Correspondence of November 2006 in Morgan Library and Museum, New York. French text published in Manuel Cornejo, *Maurice Ravel: L'Intégrale*, Paris, Le Passeur, 2018, 149-150

[2] H.H. Stuckenschmidt, *Maurice Ravel: Variations on his Life and Work*, London, Calder and Boyars, 1969, 105

[3] Ursula Vaughan Williams, *RVW: A biography of Ralph Vaughan Williams*, London, Oxford University Press, 1964, 81

[4] Hélène Jourdan-Morhange, *Ravel et nous*, Geneva, Éditions du Milieu du Monde, 1945, 23

[5] Letter to Hélène Casella of 19 January 1919, in Arbie Orenstein (ed.), *A Ravel Reader*, New York, Columbia University Press, 1990, 185

[6] David Lamaze, *Le Coeur de l'horloge*, www.lulu.com., ID 5104505

[7] Benjamin Ivry, *Maurice Ravel : a Life*, New York, Welcome Rain Publishers, 2000, 151

[8] Letter offered for sale by Lecloux at Maison Drouot, Paris, 14-15 December 1972. French text published in Manuel Cornejo, op. cit., 65

34 RAVEL AND THE CRITICS

Like most composers, Ravel had his staunch defenders and his virulent opponents as well as one or two critics (in many ways the most interesting) who tried to take each of his works on its merits.

Of his defenders, the eldest was Willy (Henry Gauthier-Villars, 1859-1931) who, despite his love of Wagner, had also been one of the few early champions of Debussy's *L'Après-midi*. If he was caustic over the early overture *Shéhérazade*, this was no more than Ravel came to be himself, and his willingness to praise the 'orchestre de rêve' of *Daphnis*[1] may have been due in part to his pleasure in seeing fulfilled his prophecy of 1899 that Ravel might 'become something if not someone in about ten years, if he works hard'.[2]

Ravel's remaining supporters were men nearer his own age. Charles Koechlin (1867-1950) had been a fellow student at the Conservatoire and, as a brilliant teacher of musical technique, naturally recognised Ravel's abilities in this area and regarded him as one of France's leading composers.[3] Of *L'Heure espagnole*, Koechlin claimed that it was the work of a Japanese sculptor in ivory 'with the impeccable sureness of his accurate line and his ironic, intimate view of objects'.[4] Another friend, M.D. Calvocoressi (1877-1944), one of the Apaches and the dedicatee of 'Alborada del gracioso', became the chief music critic of *Comoedia illustré*. Even though he liked to think of himself as unusually objective, his unwavering support of Ravel prompted Debussy to dub him a 'valet de chambre'.[5]

Other defenders of Ravel included Louis Vuillemin (1879-1929), Emile Vuillermoz (1878-1960) and Henry Prunières (1886-1942). Vuillermoz, a fellow pupil of Fauré, wrote for a number of journals including *La Revue musicale* and *Le Temps* and was quick to emphasise the particularity of Ravel's music, especially of his word-setting in *Histoires naturelles* and *L'Heure espagnole*, while regretting the choice of subject in the latter by a composer 'for whom some of us nourish loftier ambitions'.[6] Prunières, as editor of *La Revue musicale*, was in a good position to maintain Ravel's reputation after the war, as in his enthusiastic review of the Monte-Carlo premiere of *L'Enfant et les sortilèges* in which he welcomed Ravel's unaggressive use of bitonality, the 'suavité céleste' of the final fugue, and the mixture of speaking and singing that leads up to it (what Ravel calls 'la déclamation plaintive, souple, presque sans timbre') which he reckoned would 'open up new horizons for opera'. [7]

Any list of Ravel's detractors must begin with Pierre Lalo (1866-1943), the son of the composer Édouard and from 1898 chief music critic of *Le Temps*. Beginning with the overture *Shéhérazade*, which moved him to hope 'that M. Ravel will not eschew unity and will turn his thoughts more often to Beethoven', [8] he conducted what can only be called a campaign of denigration. He condemned Ravel as a blind follower of Debussy [9], as a devotee of over-complication [10], as a purveyor of 'an affectation, a mannerism, an awkward and aggressive pretentiousness' [11] and as an incarnation of 'insensibility' [12] – the 'bagatelles sonores' of *L'Heure espagnole* evoking for him *The Ring* 'seen through a microscope'. Not that these fulminations had any effect, it seems. As Roland-Manuel noted in 1927, 'the corpses which Pierre Lalo has slaughtered are doing quite well'. The composer simply wrote Lalo off as 'a dilettante with good connections'. [13]

No other French critic pursued Ravel with the same determination. But the composer could usually be certain of unfavourable comment from Gaston Carraud (1869-1920) in *La Liberté* : the orchestral version of 'Une barque sur l'océan' was 'a confusing kaleidoscope' [14] (Ravel's permanent withdrawal of this version suggests that he agreed) and 'the langourous rhythms' of the 'Habanera' were just so much childishness (*enfantillages*). [15] Nor could Carraud find any rhythmic or melodic originality in *Daphnis*, whose instrumentation tended to obliterate 'the demarcation line hitherto set up by us, timid souls that we are, between sound and noise'. [16] Altogether more comprehensible was the mismatch between Reynaldo Hahn (1875-1947) and Ravel's more virtuosic productions. Where Ravel inclined in the direction of Mozart, Hahn, another devotee of the older master, could follow without much trouble. But *L'Heure espagnole* left him aghast, striking him as 'a kind of transcendent jujitsu' in which the performers tried to rectify the mistakes in this 'learnedly cacophonic symphony' by missing out beats. [17]

Between these two extremes of general acceptance and refusal, two critics in particular preserved a more thoughtful, flexible approach.

Jean Marnold (pseudonym of Jean Morland, 1859-1935) was both polemical and erudite: he was the French translator of both Nietzsche's *The Origins of Tragedy* and the libretto of Strauss's *Feuersnot*. After falling in love with the String Quartet and the *Miroirs* (whose impact on him he likened to that of Schumann's *Kreisleriana*),[18] in 1905 he took up the cudgels for Ravel over the Prix de Rome affair. But his enthusiasm foundered over *Histoires naturelles* and *Valses nobles*: Renard's poetry was in the style of 'a constipated Alphonse Allais' [19], while for him the complicated harmonies of the *Valses* were disproportionate to the essence of the exercise.[20] Only with the Piano Trio did he find himself once more in accord with the composer who, 'on a larger scale, belongs to the authentic line descended from our gentle, profound Couperin'.[21]

As Christian Goubault says, 'Jean Marnold's ideas are almost identical with those of Louis Laloy – apart from their opinions of Ravel...' [22] Laloy (1874-1943) founded *Le Mercure musical* with Marnold in 1905 and was a powerful force in French music for many years, writing the first French biography of Debussy (who thought of him as having been 'long ago almost the only person to understand *Pelléas*') and from 1914 holding the post of general secretary at the Opéra. Unlike Marnold, he found the early Ravel 'uncertain, diffuse and often languishing' [23] and it was precisely *Histoires naturelles* that turned him into a supporter. In his important article on the work,[24] Laloy explored a number of points that were soon to become clichés of Ravel criticism. Whereas, for him, the returns of the opening phrase of the Quartet were somewhat artificial and some passages in *Miroirs*, for all their 'couleur rare', suffered from a 'surcharge ornementale', in *Histoires* he found all the qualities that had been lacking until then: 'clear construction and close linkage of all the sections, the sobriety of a continuously and exactly expressive style and, at the root of all that, unfailing inspiration and emotion'.[25] He recognised that Ravel always remained an observer, not only of nature but of his own reactions, that he was 'disposed to be entertained by what moved him'; from where it was a short journey to words such as 'ironie' and 'esprit'. But, as Laloy admitted, this article pleased neither the d'Indy faction, who regarded him as a traitor, nor those who, like Vuillermoz, nourished loftier ambitions for Ravel than that of 'farceur'.

After the First World War and the death of Debussy, Ravel's reputation in France was reasonably secure. Cocteau, Satie and Les Six all had their reservations about him, as did Henri Sauguet, noting that

Tzigane had been a 'huge success, naturally, with the ladies in pince-nez and the gentlemen behind large stomachs' and suggesting that 'Ravel does not like the music of today. He must like it as little as we like what he's now producing'. [26] From time to time there were also diatribes against what was perceived as Ravel's *petitesse*. Two days after a London concert of Ravel's music, including the first British performance of *Tzigane*, the critic of *The Times* wrote:

> To hear a whole programme of Ravel's works is like watching some midget or pygmy doing clever, but very small, things within a limited scope. Moreover, the almost reptilian cold-bloodedness, which one suspects of having been consciously cultivated, of most of M. Ravel's music is almost repulsive when heard in bulk; even its beauties are like the markings on snakes and lizards.[27]

But by then, as Roland-Manuel said, Ravel's corpse was doing quite well. As for Ravel's own view of the trade of music criticism, he realised that composers had their own furrows to plow and could not be expected to be without bias. But he still found himself being astonished that the job should so rarely be put in the hands of practising composers, given that a review, 'even when it is perspicacious, is of less importance than a piece of music, however mediocre'. [28] His attitude is neatly resumed in his defence of Debussy's orchestral *Images* against the critics: namely 'M. Gaston Carraud, to whom we owe three songs and a short symphonic poem, M. Camille Mauclair, who has become known entirely through his literary and art criticism, and M. Pierre Lalo, who has composed nothing at all ...' [29]

[1] Cited in Christian Goubault, *La Critique musicale dans la presse française de 1870 à 1914* (Geneva/Paris: Slatkine, 1984), 405. I am indebted to this excellent book for a number of the quotations used in this article

[2] Henry Gauthier-Villars, *Garçon, l'audition!* (Paris: Simonis Empis, 1901), cited in Orenstein, *Ravel*, 24; review of 29 May 1899

[3] *Chronique des arts et de la curiosité*, 7 May 1910, 148, and 3 June 1911, 172

[4] ibid.

[5] Letter to Louis Laloy of 22 February 1907, in 'Correspondance de C. Debussy et de L. Laloy', *Revue de musicologie*, numéro spécial, 1962, ed. François Lesure, 24

[6] *La Revue musicale*, numéro spécial, 'La critique contemporaine', 1 April 1925, 99; review of 15 June 1911

[7] id. 108

[8] id. 91; review in *Le Temps*, 13 June 1899

[9] review of the *String Quartet, Le Temps,* 19 April 1904
[10] review of *Histoires naturelles, Le Temps,*? January 1907
[11] review of *Rapsodie espagnole, Le Temps,* 24 March 1908
[12] review of *L'heure espagnole, Le Temps,* 28 May 1911
[13] "Maurice Ravel and Recent French Music", *Les Nouvelles littéraires,* 2 April 1927; Orenstein, 445
[14] *La Liberté,* 5 February 1907
[15] quoted in the *Revue musicale de Lyon,* 26 March 1911, 751
[16] quoted in *Guide du concert,* 22 April 1911, 359. This notice was of the concert performance of the first suite from the ballet given on 2 April by the Colonne Orchestra, conducted by Gabriel Pierné
[17] quoted in SIM, 15 June 1911, 74
[18] Goubault, op. cit., 119
[19] *Mercure de France,* 16 January 1908
[20] id. 1 May 1912, 188
[21] *Le Cas Wagner* (Paris: Legouix, 1920), 72; article of November 1915
[22] op. cit., 116
[23] Goubault, op. cit., 113
[24] SIM, 15 March 1907; reprinted in Laloy, *La Musique retrouvée* (Paris: Plon, 1928), 163-5
[25] id., 164
[26] Letter to Francis Poulenc of 16 October 1924, Poulenc, *Correspondance, 1910-1963,* ed. Myriam Chimènes (Paris: Fayard, 1994), 241
[27] *The Times,* 28 April 1924
[28] SIM, 15 February 1912, 62-3
[29] 'Regarding Claude Debussy's Images', *Les Cahiers d'aujourd'hui,* February 1913, Orenstein, 366-8

Ravel also makes contributions to the two following articles. The first was a talk in 1982 for BBC Radio 3. The producer was Piers Burton-Page.

35 THE CHÂTELET BALLET GALA OF 22 APRIL 1912 AND ITS MUSICAL ENVIRONS

If you wander along the right bank of the Seine, going upstream from the Tuileries, past the Louvre and the Pont Neuf, you end up at the Place du Châtelet and, on your left, the Théâtre du Châtelet. Nowadays it has large plate-glass doors and inside, too, much renovation has gone on in recent years, but the solid exterior remains as it was when built on this prime site in 1862.

The architect, Gabriel Davioud, intended it to be something special. By the 1860s the French love of spectacle had reached all-time heights and the resources of the Châtelet ensured that this love should be catered for. It holds 2,500 spectators, the stage is 24 metres wide and 35 metres deep, and there is a vast area of flies above it and of storage and machinery spaces beneath, so the Parisian public could be given its fill of battles, bullfights, earthquakes, fires, floods, train crashes and even, with the advent of the 20th century, aerial ones. But little in the way of art came to the theatre until the impresario Gabriel Astruc put on Richard Strauss's opera *Salome* there in 1907, with Emmy Destinn in the title rôle. Two years later Astruc acted as Diaghilev's 'man in Paris' for the first season of the Ballets Russes – at the Châtelet – and with the productions of *The Firebird* in 1910 and *Petrushka* the following year the theatre became a Mecca for Parisian musical society.

The Stravinsky ballets were the most exciting things to hit Paris since Debussy's *Pelléas et Mélisande* in 1902 and they caused as much controversy. Nobody could deny their artistic splendour and integrity. But why couldn't the French do something like this? The answer was that French ballet was in a pretty sorry state, having degenerated into little more than a display of female legs, and even the male rôles were often played by women *en travesti*. However, in the very year of *Petrushka*'s production an unprecedented step was taken at the Paris Opéra – a non-French ballet master was appointed: Ivan Clustine, who'd been ballet master of the Bolshoi. Clustine declared that he wanted to abolish the use of *travesti* and encourage male dancers, and that he also wanted to abolish the tutu, giving rise to press speculation: 'Clustine v the tutu; the tutu v Clustine. Who will win?' It was he who took control of the Ballet Gala given at the Châtelet Theatre on 22 April 1912, with not a tutu in sight.

After leaving the Bolshoi, Clustine had gone to Monte Carlo and there had worked with Natalia Trouhanova, a Russian ballerina in her early twenties who had already danced at the Paris Opéra but had, it seems, found the atmosphere too stifling and fuddy-duddy. The problem was, Trouhanova was an intellectual. She not only read widely but had ideas of what the art of ballet might become with a bit of imagination. Clustine's appointment to the Paris Opéra encouraged her. She could not expect a lone foreigner to change Parisian habits overnight, but at least there might be the opportunity for an occasional experiment. And even though she did briefly team up with Diaghilev, she was too much of an individualist to last long in that tyrant's entourage.

In May 1911 she put on two 'concerts de danse' at the Châtelet. The music was a ragbag of bits of opera, *Peer Gynt*, Chopin, Fauré, three Renaissance dances and, finally, Rimsky-Korsakov's *Capriccio espagnol*. Pierre Monteux conducted but, according to the press, even he couldn't make a satisfying programme out of such a heterogeneous collection. One work, though, obviously made an impact – on Trouhanova, if on nobody else: d'Indy's symphonic variations *Istar*. From this work grew her programme for April 1912. With the French feeling sore, even if impressed, about the Russian takeover of their balletic life, why not offer them an evening entirely of French ballets?

The impresario for the venture was Jacques Rouché, one of the most enterprising theatre directors of his time. In 1912 he was in charge of the Théâtre des Arts and in January had put on the premiere of the ballet version of Ravel's *Ma Mère l'Oye;* and it's fair to assume that this, together with the Châtelet gala, did not exactly hinder his subsequent appointment as director of the Opéra, where he remained from 1914 to 1944. He had travelled all over Europe, studying stage machinery and lighting techniques and, with a personal fortune from soap and perfume at his disposal, he was not one to skimp.

The evening was to consist of four ballets, with Trouhanova dancing the title rôle in each: d'Indy's *Istar*, Florent Schmitt's *La Tragédie de Salomé*, Paul Dukas's *La Péri*, and lastly Ravel's *Valses nobles et sentimentales* set to a scenario of the composer's own devising and given the new title of *Adélaïde ou le langage des fleurs*. Each ballet was to be conducted by its composer and, the advance publicity promised, each composer had written a specially commissioned fanfare to introduce his work. Something of a mystery surrounds these fanfares: one critic claimed to have heard then all at the first performance, but other evidence suggests that only two were in fact played: Dukas's for *La Péri* which survives in its original state (although his biographers assure us it was written *after* the premiere), and Schmitt's for *La Tragédie de Salomé*, which he re-used in 1920 under the title 'Camp de Pompée' in his incidental music to *Antoine et Cléopâtre*.

D'Indy's *Istar*, which began the evening, was the oldest of the four works, dating from 1896. Shortly after finishing it, d'Indy wrote to a friend:

> I'm not displeased with it; only, this pleasure will remain a purely personal one, shared with a few friends, because I don't imagine for a moment the ordinary musical public will understand the unusual way in which it's put together ... Mind you, I don't think it will be too much of a bore to listen to; but no one's going to find its secret, especially as it's just called *Istar*, without any further explanation. But writing it was huge fun.

The story is taken from a poem by an Assyrian poet called Izdubar (some years earlier d'Indy had been bowled over by the Assyrian scuplture in the British Museum – the 5th-century Athenian stuff was dull by comparison). The legend is similar to that of Orpheus. Istar, the goddess of war and love, goes down to the underworld to bring her young lover, the Son of Life, back from Irkalla, the land of the dead. On her journey she has to pass through the seven gates in the seven walls round the kingdom of Ereshkigal, the goddess of Irkalla, and at each gate she must remove a jewel or a piece of clothing. The seven guardians divest her in turn of her tiara, her ear-rings, her necklace, her breastplate, her belt, her ankle rings, and finally the veil that covers her body. Then 'Istar, the daughter of Sin, entered into the land that changes not, she received the Waters of Life and presented them again. Thus, before the eyes of all, she delivered the Son of Life, her young lover.'

This story gave d'Indy the opportunity to reverse the usual variation process. Where variations usually get more complicated, or at least further from the tune as the piece proceeds, here d'Indy leads us gradually on a journey of clarification until the veil is removed and the theme of Istar is heard in octaves on the whole orchestra. For some reason, he thought the final section too 'Italianate'. Certainly it's one of his most exciting and convincing endings. One 'secret' of the work is obviously the reversal of standard variation procedure, but another may be that there is not just one theme, but two, and he runs them in parallel, just as Haydn sometimes does. As to the *mise en scène*, the newspaper reports are not explicit, indeed are positively veiled, as to whether the scenario was followed to its natural conclusion. The indications are that Mlle Trouhanova did remove the stated items: one report says that she ended up 'unencumbered even by a veil', but given the times in which this performance was given we must probably assume that the Châtelet audience was offered no more than a full dorsal view.

When the curtain fell on this performance, Trouhanova then set about reclothing herself in a long, white, flowing robe for Florent Schmitt's *La Tragédie de Salomé*. Schmitt had studied at the Paris Conservatoire with Massenet and Fauré, but his temperament was very different from theirs in that he had a taste for the grand and the dramatic, and the Salome story brought out the best in him. He wrote his version first of all for quite a small orchestra, to fit the resources of Rouché's Théâtre des Arts, and it had been danced there in 1907 by Loïe Fuller, the famous 'exponent of veils'. Schmitt then reorchestrated it for a concert performance in 1911 and this larger version was the one to be given by Trouhanova. It was thus a premiere of a kind, and one followed up in later performances by Karsavina, for Diaghilev in 1913, and then by Ida Rubinstein in 1919.

Schmitt owed Trouhanova's interest in his score to the machinations of Paul Dukas. In these days when operas and even concerts have to be set up two or three years in advance, it's interesting to find Dukas writing to Schmitt as late as November 1911, a mere five months before the performances, saying:

> I've played *La Tragédie de Salomé* to Mlle Trouhanova. It's got some splendid things in it; I'll talk to you later about them. It would be marvellous if she would agree to put on the whole ballet with *first-class* scenery. I'm doing my best to persuade her.

Typical as this may seem of Dukas's disinterested kindness, he was also a man who knew his own mind and he not only recognised in *La Tragédie de Salomé* the tough musical fibre mentioned above, but no doubt also saw what an excellent foil it would be to his own ballet *La Péri*.

Schmitt's work is based on a long poem by Robert d'Humières. The Prelude depicts the terrace of Herod's palace overlooking the Dead Sea. The sun is setting. Torches are brought on and by their light Herodias plunges her hands into a chest overflowing with jewels. Salome appears, adorns herself with some of the jewels and begins the 'Danse des perles'. When she leaves, strange lights appear over the sea and echoes are heard of the songs of Sodom and Gomorrha. Herod sits in terror, unable to move, and out of this manacing atmosphere comes Salome once more, to dance her 'Danse lascive', lit only by flashes of lightning. Herod pursues her but, as he seizes her veil, John the Baptist appears and surrounds her with his cloak. John is duly sent to execution and his head returns on a platter. Salome grabs it, dances with it, and eventually throws it into the sea which turns blood-red. The head now multiplies and heads appear from every part of the stage, gazing at her. She dances ever more furiously while a storm begins to rise. The work ends with her 'Danse de la terreur', as the mountains spit flames, the Dead Sea overflows, the palace tumbles to destruction – and the Châtelet's backstage crew are kept unusually busy.

Schmitt dedicated the work to Stravinsky, who wrote: 'I must confess to you that your ballet has given me more pleasure than any work has for a long time.' This view might relate to the 5/4 + 9/8 rhythms of the 'Danse de la terreur', in which it is not impossible to hear a pre-echo of *The Rite of Spring*, the 'Danse sacrale' of which dates from the November of 1912. It's only fitting that when *The Rite* was given that famous first performance in May 1913, Schmitt should have been in the van of the fisticuffs.

But in the spring of 1912, even without *Le Sacre*, the Parisian musical public had plenty to occupy them. Schumann lovers could compare Emil Sauer's playing of the *Fantasie* on 29 February with Cortot's of *Carnaval* next day. Mischa Elman, Mark Hambourg and Casals could also be heard and, for organ devotees, on 12 March Marcel Dupré gave the first performance of Louis Vierne's Third Symphony in the Salle Gaveau. Meanwhile Alfredo Casella was inaugurating a series of popular concerts at the Trocadéro on Thursday evenings, with the cheapest seats at 50 centimes: 'popular' meant Bach and Wagner, with the inevitable César Franck Symphony and Saint-Saëns's Third (the Trocadéro had a nice loud organ as well as an overwhelming resonance), though Casella did show some imagination in also programming Mahler's Fourth Symphony.

Authenticity also made a showing. On 17 April the Salle Gaveau hosted an ensemble led by Arnold Dolmetsch in music by Byrd, Bull, Morley, Purcell and anon, while on the 30th at the Opéra-Comique Reynaldo Hahn, conducting *Don Giovanni,* not only had three real orchestras on stage for the ballroom scene, but actually restored the cheerful finale to Act II which had not been seen on a Paris stage for more than a century; during which the opera had ended with Don Giovanni's descent into the flames and the satisfaction of bourgeois morality.

Perhaps the richest feast of all was spread over five Tuesdays from 27 February to 26 March at the Salle Erard. Each of the five concerts began with a *Concert en trio* by Rameau (Casella played the harpsichord) and then moved on to contemporary French music: Debussy accompanied Maggie Teyte in his own songs, Ravel accompanied Jane Bathori in his (in different concerts, that is: by this time the two composers were no longer on speaking terms), Fauré accompanied his *Poème d'un jour,* Edouard Risler played *Children's Corner,* Ricardo Viñes played music by Saint-Saëns.

Rehearsals meanwhile were in progress all over Europe for the *Grand concours musical de Paris* to be held at the end of May, for which 497 choirs had entered, including 129 from abroad, of which 66 were from Britain. The North Country choirs were known to Paris audiences by repute only, but every now and then a French critic would actually venture up to the fastnesses of Leeds or Huddersfield and bring back further fuel for the flame of interest: Fauré himself had been thrilled by the 'expressive suppleness' of the 400-strong Leeds Choral Society when he conducted them in his *La Naissance de Vénus* in October 1898. One such bold critic noted that of the 66 choirs, 14 were composed entirely of women and that the British suffragette movement had furnished a musical victim in March, when a Miss Ethel Smyth was sentenced to two months' hard labour in Holloway for 'breaking all the windows of the Colonial Office'. The French correspondent further noted that, while incarcerated, Miss Smyth had composed a hymn to female liberty, which in French came out as 'Chantez, chantez, criez d'allégresse' – perhaps rather too French to give a true idea of the dauntless Ethel in full cry.

Two days after the ballet gala, the Opéra mounted Massenet's last offering, *Roma*. Massenet's biographer Louis Schneider, called it 'the purest invention of a master at the apogee of his glory'. Be that as it may, the production had its problems. The Musicians' Union in Paris, though of recent birth, showed its teeth when the management insisted that all the chorus men be clean shaven, to conform with Roman practice. Said the Union: 'Beards are not a negotiable item.' So the beards stayed, and the incorrectly hirsute Roman army came on stage, dragging with it a contingent of correctly hirsute Carthaginian captives.

The newspapers, as usual, relayed news from the provinces, more (one feels) out of duty than real interest, but occasional items were well worth noting. In Toulouse, for example, *Tosca* was already accumulating legends: not the bouncing diva this time, but a soprano of a certain age and weight who simply refused to jump off the battlements. History does not relate what, if anything, the stage hands had prepared for her landing, but apparently the audience, enraged at her continuing presence, roared and screamed every bit as loudly as she did. Afterwards she claimed that such gymnastics were suitable only for light sopranos.

Back in Paris, Diaghilev was far too intelligent not to realize the French patriotic sensitivity to his Russian invasion and had been doing his best to persuade the major French composers of the time to write for him. Ravel and Fokine had been working on *Daphnis et Chloé* since 1909, but they differed fundamentally in their views of Ancient Greece, Ravel got a composing block over the finale, and Diaghilev had to wait until the summer of 1912 to produce the work. Debussy got as far as finishing the scenario for a ballet called *Masques et bergamasques* but no further – his one ballet for Diaghilev, *Jeux*, didn't reach the stage until 1913. But in 1911 Diaghilev thought he'd succeeded in his quest: Paul Dukas was to write a ballet called *La Péri*, Trouhanova was engaged to dance the title rôle, and Bakst was to design the décor and costumes – Trouhanova in his Péri costume is one of the most frequently seen reproductions of his work. But she never wore it on stage. According to Diaghilev, Bakst let him down and in June 1911, a matter of days before the premiere, Dukas withdrew the score, claiming time was too short to do it justice.

It's hard to place the blame amid the welter of recriminations that broke out with Russian fervour. There were rumours that Trouhanova, who at the time was Dukas's mistress, persuaded him to let her have the ballet for her own use, leaving Diaghilev in the lurch. Certainly we might be led to some such conclusion on seeing Dukas's own copy of the programme for the 1912 gala, in which Trouhanova wrote 'à Paul Dukas, mon dieu pour toujours.' At all events, *La Péri* was the basis of Trouhanova's 'concert de danse', and the public were no doubt all the keener to see it, knowing at least something of its contentious history, and with their enthusiasm further sharpened by Diaghilev, who wrote to the press emphasising that Trouhanova's enterprise was nothing whatever to do with him ...

Dukas based his 'poème dansé' (a title borrowed by Debussy a year later for *Jeux*) on an old Persian legend. Iskender (the Persian version of Alexander, with possible links to Alexander the Great) is seeking the Flower of Immortality and finds it at the ends of the earth in the hands of a sleeping Peri, a fairy vowed to the service of Ormuzd, the God of Light. Oskender steals the Flower from the Peri, who wakes up and is terrified. But Iskender is fascinated by her beauty and in his hands the Flower grows red with desire. The Peri dances, their faces touch and Iskender gives her back the Flower which, in her hands, turns white and gold. She and the Flower slowly disappear into a shaft of brilliant light and Iskender, feeling the darkness encircle him, knows that his end is near.

Since the stories of both *La Péri* and *La Tragédie de Salomé* require dancing, the critics naturally felt obliged to pass judgment on Trouhanova's skill in this direction. Not everyone by any means was impressed. One critic claimed:

> This year Mlle Trouhanova has given up dancing. She undulates, she leaps, she throws her beautiful arms this way and that, she comes and goes gracefully, she acts with expression ...

The influence of Isadora Duncan was blamed. Isadora, indeed, could be read in the music magazine *SIM* on 15 March, saying that dancing was the only art that still lagged behind the times:

> People think they like dancing because of the spectacle of the ballet; which is rather like a man saying he's susceptible to female charm, when all he likes is the make-up!

She went on to claim that

> the great composers are the only ones who write danceable music, because it conforms to the natural movements of the body.

All this was very much, it seems, in line with Trouhanova's own beliefs. There is also the point to be made – at the risk of sounding ungallant – that she was in no sense a small lady. She had a most expressive face and beautiful arms and wrists, but early, pre-Clustine photographs of her in a tutu show that, above the knee, she was a very large lady indeed. The long, flowing robes she wore for the gala were therefore a nice mixture of the personal and the artistic. In any case, a year after the gala she was already thinking about giving up dancing and becoming an actress. Expense, a lack of composer and a lack of general interest, all, she said, made her life as a dancer in Paris impossible. Dukas gave her the sole rights to *La Péri* for five years, but in 1917 she wrote to him, renouncing all claims in the ballet:

> I do it not without pain, because *La Péri* was the joy of my joys; but I place love of beauty above personal considerations. I shall never forget, and hope one day to be La Péri once again.

She never was. By 1917 she had married a Russian colonel and then involved herself with the Russian Revolution. She was the French translator of Stalin's speech at the 16th Congress of the Communist Party in 1930 and in 1935, at the age of 50, was back in Paris giving a talk on 'The reflection of the new human condition in Soviet literature.' She died in Moscow in 1956.

The 1912 gala ended with Ravel's *Adélaïde ou le langage des fleurs*. On 9 May the previous year his piano work *Valses nobles et sentimentales* had been played for the first time, at a concert where the names of the composers were withheld, allowing the audience to guess the composer. Or at least try. The *Valses*, variously attributed to Ravel, Satie and Kodály, were not particularly well received. So when Ravel was approached to complete the quartet of composers for the gala, he thought of the *Valses* and the chance to give them a hearing in another form.

It was an extraordinarily busy time for him. Not only had he been closely involved with the preparations for the premiere of the ballet version of *Ma Mère l'Oye* on 28 January, but *Daphnis et Chloé* was scheduled for June and trouble was already brewing, with Diaghilev seeming to have lost interest and to be transferring his attention to Nijinsky's version of *Prélude à l'après-midi d'un faune*. Ravel now had to orchestrate the *Valses* (which he did in a fortnight in early March) and then prepare himself to conduct it in public, a task he had last performed in 1899 – and he was not a born conductor. The *Valses* contain a number of passages where groups of three on some instruments are set against groups of two in others; when asked how he conducted these, he said: 'Oh, I just go round and round' – which may well have been horribly near the truth.

As late as March, the ballet was going to be called *Paméla ou les deux roses*, but maybe the one finally chosen was meant as a link back to *La Péri*. The story Ravel concocted, set in the Paris of 1825, is hardly worth telling in detail. A courtesan (Trouhanova in a dress with flounces at ankle level) has two rival suitors, Lorédan and the duke. Love, hope, rejection and so on are symbolised by exchanges of flowers between the parties. In the epilogue Adélaïde offers the duke a branch of acacia (platonic love) and to Lorédan a corn poppy (forgetfulness). But when Lorédan threatens to commit suicide, she offers him a red rose and falls into his arms.

For this final ballet Trouhanova approached more nearly the classical steps she'd been trained in. As for Ravel's score, it seems classical to us now. But not at the time. The anonymous reviewer for the *SIM* had punctiliously been playing the piano version to himself in preparation for the ballet, but in his February article he had to confess

> that the *Valses nobles et sentimentales* inevitably make us think of certain kinds of exotic fruit: when you taste them for the first time they set your teeth on edge. You try again out of curiosity, then out of pleasure and end up preferring them to anything else. But at the moment we're still at the point of not being quite sure.

More surprisingly, the critic Pierre Lalo, who normally took every opportunity to say harsh things about Ravel, praised the whole evening as:

> a spectacle that was the most tasteful, the most beautiful, the most harmonious and fulfilling that we have ever seen ... Mlle Trouhanova gave us a synthesis of the art of our time.

So much has been written about Impressionism in music that I offer the following article with some misgivings. Certainly it does not pretend to be the last word on this slippery subject.

36 MUSICAL IMPRESSIONISM – SCIENCE OR SPLASHING AROUND?

The first problem in thinking about Impressionism, whether in art or music, is where to begin? In art, do we begin with Vermeer, who was one of the first to work on the principle that when our eyes focus on an object, the surroundings are blurred? Or, coming nearer to our present concerns, with Constable and Turner who by the 1830s were being admired by French painters such as those of the Barbizon school? As for musical Impressionism, we could go back at least to the dark trombones that signal the underworld in 17th-century opera; or, moving on some two hundred years, to 'The Ride of the Valkyries'. Clearly our field of reference needs to be circumscribed more narrowly: in general parlance, Impressionism as a movement, rather than as a local accident, may be said to date from the middle of the 19th century and to be placed in France, and especially in Paris.

Berlioz could do Impressionism as well as anybody (think of Héro and Ursule praising the beauty of the night at the end of Act I of *Béatrice et Bénédict*, or of Hylas, the young sailor, singing up on his mast in *Les Troyens*), but it was only one of the many gifts of this extraordinary genius. The colours of an opera such as *Carmen* come rather under the heading of Exoticism, as do Ravel's *Alborada del gracioso* and songs such as Delibes's 'La belle fille de Cadix', and if we accept that the artists we regard as 'Impressionist' were not only French but painted predominantly French scenes and people, then it makes sense to look away from the exotic and at what French composers were doing likewise.

The distinguished Debussy biographer Edward Lockspeiser reckoned that the first French Impressionist composer was Chabrier. If *España* clearly comes under the exotic label, prime candidates among his works as early examples of the new French style must be the delightful piano pieces *Impromptu,* and 'Sous bois' from his 1881 collection *Dix Pièces pittoresques,* with its murky ostinato in the bass conjuring up the depths of a forest – Ravel adored this piece and maybe it fed many years later into the low rumbling that begins the Piano Concerto for the Left Hand. From the same collection comes 'Mélancolie' which Ravel said reminded him of Manet's *Olympia,* staring out at us from the canvas with what could be anything from acceptance to boredom to outright depression. But here already we broach a problem that concerned both painters and composers.

For what it's worth, we do know of the specific moments when the term Impressionism was first used in both arts. In painting it was Monet's *Impression: Sunrise* of 1872, shown in the First Impressionist Exhibition of 1874, which provoked the use of the term Impressionist as an insult. In music it was the verdict of the jury on Debussy's symphonic suite *Printemps* 13 years later, in which they warned the 24-year-old composer 'to be on guard against that vague impressionism which is one of the most dangerous enemies of truth in works of art'. But, looking back, we can see that the term had already become slippery. The painters preferred to call themselves 'naturalistes' or 'réalistes', since they aimed to paint exactly what they saw, unimpeded by memory or by intellectual knowledge of what 'must' be in front of them. Their argument would have been, on lines already mentioned, that what you actually see is not nearly as cut and dried as tradition would have you believe. We don't know of Debussy's reaction to the above slur (probably either a disdainful silence or something unprintable), but we do know of his intentions in the work: 'to express the slow, laborious birth of beings and things in nature, then the mounting efflorescence, and finally a burst of joy at being reborn, as it were, to a new life'. But already 'naturalism' or 'realism' is being invaded by the so-called 'pathetic fallacy', in attributing the emotion of joy to 'beings and things in nature'. This is the problem mentioned above.

The clash, between what may be distinguished loosely as Impressionism and Symbolism, runs through the whole corpus of art under consideration. It helps, I think, to abandon chronology at this point, and turn to a remark made by Debussy around the end of March 1908. Putting the finishing touches to the orchestral *Images,* he writes to his publisher Jacques Durand:

> I'm trying to write 'something else' – *realities*, in a manner of speaking – what imbeciles call 'impressionism', a term employed with the utmost inaccuracy, especially by art critics who use it as a label to stick on Turner, the finest creator of mystery in the whole of art.

While appearing to conform to the Impressionists' view of themselves as realists, Debussy at the same time seems to deny them the quality of mystery. We may think of Cézanne's famous comment: 'Monet, he's nothing but an eye. But, good God, what an eye!' (considerably less flattering with the observations the other way round...). Emile Zola too reprimanded the Impressionists for dealing in idylls, ignoring the foul, animal existence of many of Paris's poor.

Whatever the rights and wrongs of this, musical Impressionism made a huge impact in 1894 in the shape of Debussy's *Prélude à l'après-midi d'un faune*. When, 18 years later, Nijinsky scandalously choreographed it to end with the Faun pleasuring himself with one of the nymphs' veils, he was doing no more than externalising the latent sexual heat of Debussy's score. But even in 1894 this work crucially altered the traditional balance between tunes and accompaniment; and in so doing might be said to have copied the painters who were no longer interested in portraying narratives from the bible and classical authors (= tunes), but instead in the unchanging beauties of nature and the ways these could be translated on to a canvas. No less extraordinary than the sexual charge of *L'Après-midi* is the simplicity of Debussy's means. At one end of the work, a solo flute conjures up a whole world in fewer than four bars; at the other, it is closed off by just three high notes on an antique cymbal.

The next boost to musical Impressionism came in the following decade, largely in the form of two objects: water and bells. Understandably the painters couldn't do much with bells, but water was a substance whose possibilities entranced them – not least, as a recent exhibition in San Francisco has shown, because many of them came from families with marine connections. Ravel too had a maternal line that included fishermen, and possibly pirates, not that his piano piece *Jeux d'eau* of 1901 was exactly wild, though it did take Lisztian textures in new directions. It purports to represent one of the fountains at Versailles, by employing fast-moving figurations largely in the upper reaches of the instrument, and ones that, as many pianists will surely agree, 'feel' different from anything that's gone before, and take some getting used to. He followed this up in 1905 with 'Une barque sur l'océan', which he then orchestrated. But not to his own satisfaction. With his few pupils he would always insist on the difference between 'orchestration' and 'instrumentation': the first captured the overall 'glow' of the piece, the second merely dished out elements of the score mechanically – this to the first violins, that to the clarinets – leaving the work lifeless. Over a century later, we may feel that Ravel, always his own harshest critic, was unduly unkind over 'Une barque'. But he could not ignore the fact that the same year of 1905 had seen the first performance of one of the prime masterpieces of Impressionist music which undoubtedly can boast of 'orchestration': Debussy's *La Mer*.

Not only does the work have what painters call a 'tonality' – nothing to do with the musical term, but meaning an overall colour and texture to which all details in some sense conform – but it employs painterly techniques of highlighting and *pointillisme*. For the first eight bars of the central movement, 'Jeux des vagues', string tremolos, tinkles from harps, glockenspiel and cymbals, and swoops and gurgles from flutes and clarinets combine to paint a picture of sea swell and spray; only after this do we hear anything like a tune. Before this, at a climax in the first movement (fig.8), a kind of *pointillisme* with multiple brush strokes operates in the texture where there are no fewer than seven separate lines sounding simultaneously. Not only is this aural overload immensely exciting, but no two versions of it will ever sound the same, in line with Chabrier's wonderful remark, already quoted, that 'The sea is a theatre that only gives first performances'.

But texture is only one of the many facets of *La Mer*. Debussy also employs at least four kinds of scales: the usual major and minor; pentatonic ones, as on the black notes of the piano; whole-tone ones which, having no natural resting point, can sound either murky and threatening, or unstable and so useful for transitions; and one sometimes called the 'harmonic' scale. This is a scale of C major but with F sharps and B flats, called 'harmonic' because it draws on the harmonic series that sounds naturally above every note. In the first movement its most magical appearance is in the theme near the start for four muted horns over strings and harp, these accompanying instruments being momentarily stilled into repetitions, as though they two are enchanted by the tune. Here we can find Debussy joining the Impressionist painters in their claim to be 'naturalistes'.

Water fascinated both Debussy and Ravel elsewhere: in the former's 'Reflets dans l'eau', 'Jardins sous la pluie' and 'Poissons d'or', and the latter's long struggles with an unfinished opera *La Cloche engloutie*, while both composed portraits of the water nymph Ondine. But, like Ravel, Debussy was also fascinated by bells: we may set his 'Cloches à travers les feuilles' and 'La Cathédrale engloutie' against Ravel's 'La Vallée des cloches', 'Le Gibet' and 'Laideronnette, impératrice des pagodes' and argue interminably about which of the composers is the more imaginative. If the two works containing the word 'cloches' might, just possibly, be subject to a variant of Cézanne's formulation ('Debussy/Ravel is nothing but an ear. But what an ear!'), there can be no mistaking the deeper feelings roused by both 'La cathédrale engloutie' and 'Le gibet' – of some kind of solemn ritual in the former, in the latter of naked terror. It is in works like these and Ravel's *Trois Poèmes de Stéphane Mallarmé* that Impressionism and Symbolism meet, rendering meaningless all attempts to separate them.

In 1918 Jean Cocteau, still on a high from the 1917 performances of Satie's *Parade*, wrote, 'Impressionism has fired its last rocket; it is for us to set the fireworks for a new fête.' Of course he was wrong. Musical Impressionism has gone on quite happily until the present day, even if the musical language has radically changed. In the USA Aaron Copland has cast a spell with his evocations of wide open spaces as, on a less natural, more manufactured front does John Adams with *A Short Ride in a Fast Machine* (perhaps marginally indebted to Honegger's locomotive *Pacific 231*?). Meanwhile in England Benjamin Britten has tapped into the North Sea for the 'Sea Interludes' in *Peter Grimes*, and in France Olivier Messiaen, 'naturaliste par excellence', has written a host of works depicting not only birds themselves, but their habitats and the times of day in which they were singing, as well as giving vivid descriptions of Nature's depths and heights in *Des Canyons aux étoiles*.

We can have no reason to expect that Musical Impressionism will die any time soon. But nor can we expect that it will ever again reach the depths and heights of that extraordinary period between 1880 and the First World War, when it gave birth to some of the most beautiful and evocative music ever written.

This article benefits from my conversations with two people who both knew Cocteau and Stravinsky well: Madeleine Milhaud, Darius's widow, and Doda Conrad, the bass in Nadia Boulanger's famous madrigal group.

37 JEAN COCTEAU AND IGOR STRAVINSKY

In 1959 Jean Cocteau was living in the little village of Milly-la-Forêt, not far from Fontainebleau. One day the mayor and two of his junior officials came to see him and asked whether he would design murals and stained glass windows for their abandoned 12th-century chapel, as he had done for the fishermen's chapel at Villefranche. He was happy to do so and, as the chapel had been a place where lepers came to be cured, took herbs as his guiding motif.

But, being Cocteau, he wasn't content just with herbs. To the left of the door is a cat – straddling Cocteau's signature – looking up in wonder at the giant gentians round the door. On the opposite wall, above the altar, Christ rises from the tomb, guarded by three Roman soldiers. Are *they* looking on in wonder? Not at all. One's yawning, one's snoring, and the third seems to be asleep: an all-too-real representation of blind and deaf humanity. In front of the altar Cocteau is now buried: on his tomb, the words: 'Je reste avec vous' – 'I am always with you'. But if Cocteau does remain with us, it has to be asked: 'What as?' Publicity monger? Opium addict? Or the man whom André Gide said was 'incapable of taking anything seriously?'

He was born in Paris in 1889 – the year, not inappropriately, of the fourth great Exhibition. His own exhibitionism revealed itself first in a love of the theatre: his first hero was the actor Edouard de Max, his first book of poetry was called *La Lampe d'Aladin*, and he was to remain a hero-worshipper and a practitioner of magic. In 1910 Diaghilev's production of Stravinsky's *The Firebird* offered him both heroes and magic, even if Stravinsky, whom he first met backstage at this ballet, was a decidedly reluctant hero. But for Cocteau, the artist as hero was a necessary figure. As he was to write a few years later, 'the artist travels by car, the public by bus; hardly surprising the latter are always behind.'

Remarks like this, together with the yawning soldier at Christ's tomb, do suggest that Cocteau might, just possibly, have been an 'élitist'. The singer Doda Conrad recalled:

> I was impressed that Cocteau, when he spoke to somebody like me, spoke a little in a sort of slang, as one would speak to a football player or a bicycle champion, using words I would be able to understand, and never one with three syllables, because that would be too difficult for me.

Cocteau remained a distant admirer of Stravinsky through the three years from *The Firebird* to *The Rite of Spring*, of whose opening night he has left a graphic description. But he had reservations about this work – a masterpiece, certainly, but for Cocteau it was tainted with a Wagnerian, overwhelming quality. As he wrote in *Le Coq et l'Arlequin*, the 1918 pamphlet of aphorisms proposing a new way forward for French music, 'The score doesn't leave us time to say "phew"'. Cocteau, for all his elitism, and despite Conrad's testimony, preferred to treat his audience as intelligent accomplices, and boasted that when producing his own plays he'd often had points clarified to him for the first time by someone like the chief electrician. Still, his immediate reaction after the *Sacre* was to try and engaage Stravinsky as a collaborator on a ballet called *David*, about the slayer of Goliath. Stravinsky didn't want to know. So, in 1915, Cocteau took the idea to Satie instead and, shorn of its biblical references, it turned into the ballet *Parade*. Sporting a revolver, a typewriter and sirens in the score, and Picasso's Cubist sets and costumes, *Parade* was notorious overnight, Cocteau calling it 'the greatest battle of the war' – not very tactfully since it coincided with French troops mutinying at the front.

In an ideal world, he once admitted, an artist would have no need of collaboration. As Madeleine Milhaud remembered:

> Of course Jean always had the impression that he did everything himself. Satie said, 'When Jean was painting the sets for *Parade* and composing the music, Picasso and I were watching him.' I think Jean had the impression that he was the father and founder of the Groupe des Six, and in fact every picture of the group – there are three of them – is always with Jean.

Certainly Cocteau was keener on Les Six being Les Six than they ever were. A composer like Milhaud, for example, had no intention of being confined by Cocteau's prescriptions for a new kind of French music, made up of circus tunes, street bands, jazz and so on. But he was quite happy to go along with Cocteau when it suited him; as in the ballet *Le Boeuf sur le toit*, based on Brazilian popular tunes and set in America during Prohibition. As his widow said:

> If you stop and analyse that phenomenon, it does look rather strange, but the logical link with Cocteau lay in the fact that it was performed by clowns, the Fratellini brothers who were sort of mimes, in slow motion, so absolutely in contradiction with the music, which was extremely rapid. That was Cocteau's idea, and it works.

In fact, the *lack* of such a counterpoint between music and dancing was one of the very things Cocteau had criticised in the production of the *Sacre*. Stravinsky had taken slight umbrage at Cocteau's criticism of him in *Le Coq et l'Arlequin* (though he was not quite as umbrageous as Cocteau liked to make out), and the two men didn't see each other much in the years immediately after 1918. But their paths, though distant, were surprisingly parallel. Both were attached to simplicity with an ironical edge: in Stravinsky's case, involving an ironical view of music history. He'd given up bulldozing audiences; but was he still as dominating in the musical world as he had been before the war? In Doda Conrad's view he was

> dominating completely, to the point that I contend that the composers who were born, say, in 1900 were handicapped because of his strong personality. Of the composers who could fight Stravinsky, the only one in France I could think of would be Poulenc, because Poulenc had his own little language which went its own way. But others born in those years suffered very much, and that's why they turned to Erik Satie, to be shielded from Stravinsky; because Satie was very independent of Stravinsky, as he was of Ravel and Debussy.

Both Stravinsky and Cocteau were quick to see the poetry in everyday things. In the ballet *Les Mariés de la Tour Eiffel*, to which five of Les Six contributed, Cocteau claimed he was 'rehabilitating the commonplace. It is my task to present it as though it was still in the first flush of manhood.' And here, Cocteau made his first explicit reference to

Petrushka: *Les Mariés*, he said, should have the same resonance for French audiences as *Petrushka* had for Russian ones.

Les Mariés de la Tour Eiffel is about the misadventures of a petit bourgeois wedding party, held on the lower platform restaurant of the Eiffel Tower on 14 July. Surrealism is rampant: every time the official photographer tries to take a picture of the wedding party – 'watch the birdie!' – out of the camera comes an ostrich pursued by a hunter, a bathing beauty from Trouville, a very large baby, and a lion who eats a general. The general is, to put it mildly, not accorded the respect due to his rank, yet there is no doubt that Cocteau was deeply patriotic – he entered the war, in Misia Sert's words, 'dressed by Poiret (the leading dress designer of the day) as a benevolent male nurse', and his election to the Académie française in the 1950s was not cause for any ironical comment, at least not on his part. In *Les Mariés*, he made fun of the old general precisely out of a patriotism that demanded things should be organized otherwise. As it is, the general is swallowed by the lion, who then disappears into the camera. Finally the camera speaks the line 'Je voudrais rendre le général' – a triple pun, 'rendre' meaning 'to take a snap of, to restore, or to vomit'. As if that wasn't shocking enough, the reply comes: 'Il saura bien se rendre lui-même' – yet a fourth pun, meaning 'he'll be quite capable of surrendering on his own', thus recalling some of France's less-than-heroic moments. Madeleine Milhaud, attending the premiere, noted the audience's sharp intakes of breath.

The first step towards a reconciliation between Stravinsky and Cocteau came with the performances of Sophocles's *Antigone* in 1922, in Cocteau's shortened version. He had, he said, 'removed the fat' from a masterpiece. Cocteau himself spoke the abbreviated choruses through a hole in the middle of Picasso's décor – and not only the choruses! He was having a row with the Surrealists at the time, and the startled audience received Sophocles's text interlarded with Cocteau's shouts of 'Push off, Monsieur Breton! Surrealists out!' But, as Madeleine Milhaud remembered, perhaps the most intriguing feature of all was the delivery of the actors:

> Jean had shortened *Antigone* because he had decided that as we were living in the time of aeroplanes, life went very fast, so we couldn't have a long play any more, and a few weeks later he put on a *Romeo and Juliet* lasting 20 minutes or so. I may possibly be exaggerating but not much. He didn't like the actress who was to

play the name part in *Antigone*, but then he happened to see a very beautiful girl and said 'That's my Antigone, that's exactly the girl I want to have.' But then it turned out she was Rumanian, had only just arrived in Paris and didn't speak a word of French. 'Oh, never mind', said Jean, and began to teach her the role, dividing the syllables so that each was se- pa- ra- ted from the next. It was, I have to say, very astonishing, but when she rehearsed with the other actors, who spoke in a normal manner, it was impossible. 'Oh, never mind', said Jean, 'everybody is going to speak the same way.' So that play was performed like a play of cannibals ... and it was extremely beautiful.

Stravinsky thought so too. And I presume with that curiously emphatic style of declamation in mind, he asked Cocteau to provide a text for a well-known myth. It would be in Latin, because Stravinsky saw the language as 'a medium, not dead, but turned to stone, and so monumentalised as to have become immune from all risk of vulgarisation'. The choice of the Oedipus story came soon afterwards. Doda Conrad was impressed because...

> ... Stravinsky had Monsieur Cocteau shouting the story through a megaphone. I'd already heard Cocteau do things of that kind in *Les Mariés de la Tour Eiffel*, which was one of the great works of Les Six. I think the idea of the megaphone amused Cocteau very much. I was greatly impressed by Stravinsky's really important historical idea of having the words spoken in the language which the audience understands – that is, in French in France, in English in England and so forth – but sung in Latin, which was completely logical because the Latin language is a language which belongs to the whole of Western civilisation.

Cocteau, then, was being consistent in his use of certain effects, and maybe if there'd been words in *Parade*, the Managers would have used megaphones too. This kind of distancing and Cocteau's insistence that the architecture of a theatre piece is more important than its characters, might together suggest a certain coldness, a bloodlessness. This is surely to miss the point. Stravinsky, for one thing, was quite clear about what he wanted from Cocteau: not a drama, but a 'still-life', and in performance all the characters except Tiresias 'should give the impression of living statues'. The economy and discipline of Cocteau's final text, after he had been made to rewrite his original, and its 'removal of fat' gave Stravinsky the opportunity to expand it again, though certainly not in the sense of making it fatter. But does Gide's accusation, that Cocteau was 'incapable of taking anything seriously', really hold up with regard to *Oedipus Rex*? Or at all?

Madeleine Milhaud's memories are of someone

> extremely elegant, very thin, he spoke very fast and I'm not quite sure he listened to you, but then I don't think he listened to himself either because he was already far away. He was extremely good-hearted and I know he helped many young people with extreme generosity. He was very human, but then, if one thought about Jean, one had the impression he was a sort of theatre character, rather artificial. But then you met him again, and all that vanished.

Doda Conrad gives another picture of Cocteau's complexity:

> You say that Gide thought Cocteau was joking all the time. Well, I'll read you a little excerpt from a letter Cocteau wrote to Marie-Blanche de Polignac after the death of her husband Jean, and I don't think André Gide, who had a heart that was as dry as a diamond, could have written something as moving. 'Since I saw Jean the day before he fell ill, I always see his charming face between earth and heaven as if he were floating on the surface of a final truth. Your solitude is not one, it is not a real solitude because he lives in a world that is not of today, one that is much less vague than the world of today in which death exists. He is in you and he is in all the rooms of your house and there's no beginning and no end. He leads you and he envelops you.' That is very moving and it's not at all in Cocteau's habitual tone.

The villagers of Milly-la Forêt also knew Cocteau's warm-heartedness at first hand. Yes, he was a serious artist – his films readily proclaim that – but he was not often solemn. Easily bored too: by the pompous, the stupid and, one has to admit, by routine repetition. 'See luck in miscalculations', he once wrote. The worst one could say, in this respect, is that he didn't always know how far he could unreasonably go.

This item is the script for a BBC Radio 3 documentary celebrating the 1992 centenary of Arthur Honegger's birth. The producer was Arthur Johnson. Contributions include excerpts from my interviews with the composer's pupil and biographer Harry Halbreich, his children Jean-Claude and Pascale, Madeleine Milhaud and the conductor Paul Sacher; also taped interviews from the BBC archives with Darius Milhaud, the conductor Boyd Neel and the composer himself. The title is taken from Honegger's own collection of 35 articles, *Incantation aux fossiles*, published in Lausanne in 1948. His 'Petit Prélude' to the book makes clear that the fossils are music critics, and not confined to those of his own time. The musical works mentioned were, of course, featured through excerpts.

38 INCANTATION TO THE FOSSILS – ARTHUR HONEGGER

Disc: Pacific 231

Harry Halbreich: Of course, it's very well known that when *Pacific* became such a popular piece, Honegger got very upset about it because it obliterated all his other music; it was all people wanted to hear about. So he even went as far as to say he had never thought of a steam engine when he wrote it, but of course that's not true. Certainly the piece outgrew the idea and became a piece of absolute music, because what *Pacific* is actually about is not the realistic description of a steam engine, it's simultaneously a rallentando in tempo and a crescendo in time values. The values get smaller, but the tempo gets slower, which partly compensates. And another aspect, it's a figured chorale, modelled on the great organ chorales of Bach. Bach and the steam engine – I think it's a very typical meeting of 1923!

RN: So *Pacific 231* isn't quite what it seems at first hearing. It's as well to get rid at once of any lingering notion that Honegger was some sort of colourist who dealt in broad, sloppy strokes. His son Jean-Claude remembers a more practical side to him:

Jean-Claude Honegger: His music is a marvellous architecture, very well built. He said always that music has to be well built, like a ship, and that a lot of music, if they put it on the sea, was going to float upside-down! When I was young, we talked about my electric train or my steam engines, and when I was in my twenties he asked me more about my motor-bike than about my feelings, religion or anything. My first memory of my father, when I was a very, very young boy, was when he came to the house where I was living with my mother and he had a new Bugatti – a beautiful red racing car – and he took me in this Bugatti, long before the war, to ride round Paris.

RN: This was in the late Twenties, the time of Fernand Léger and the glorification of the machine; the time too of Diaghilev, Les Six and the bright young things. So was Honegger essentially of this period? Was he indeed 'of France' or was he rather a citizen of the world?

Paul Sacher: He hated it, at the border, when someone asked him, 'Do you have something you would like to declare?' and he said, 'No', then the man said, 'Open the suitcase!' He would say, 'Why does he ask? He would do better to open the suitcase immediately, not ask me first if I have something. When I say I have nothing, I have nothing.'

RN: Honegger was in fact Swiss by birth, his parents coming from Zürich, but he was born in Le Havre and this Swiss/French dualism ran right through his life and music. Did it perhaps cause problems?

Harry Halbreich: No, I can see only advantages. I think it's good not to be shut in. In any case Honegger was a very open-minded man. This is clear when you look at a catalogue of his works: he wrote music of every possible kind. He had no prejudice, no snobbery about minor genres, he wrote wonderful operettas. He also wrote a large amount of film music, and in his films there are lots of *chansons*, many of which were hits in the 1930s. So he could have had a Kurt-Weill-like career.

RN: He had some lessons at the Zürich Conservatory, but his later musical training, from 1911 to 1913, was at the Paris Conservatoire.

Pascale Honegger: When he arrived in Paris in 1911, his parents were still living in Le Havre, so he used to travel between there and Paris every week to spend the weekend with them. Then in 1913 his parents returned to Switzerland and at that point there was talk of sending him to Germany. My father then sent a long, and astonishing, letter to them saying that, first of all, he was already in France, that he knew what the French musical education was like at the Conservatoire, and that it seemed to him far more advanced than that in Germany. He felt it was vital, in order to be at the forefront of progress, to remain in France.

RN: At the Conservatoire, Honegger made a lifelong friend, Darius Milhaud, although, even then, their musical tastes differed.

Darius Milhaud: Maybe, when we were young students, I would have the scores of *Pelléas* and *Boris Godunov* under my arm, and he would have some Strauss and some Reger.

RN: Their counterpoint teacher, André Gedalge, complained that Honegger wrote lovely tunes and then savaged them with barbaric harmonies. But he had no doubt that the young man was gifted.

Disc: String Quartet 1

Reger rubbing shoulders with Debussy at the start of Honegger's First String Quartet, finished in 1917. He was indeed a Romantic and made no bones about the fact. His membership of Les Six was also exactly what he said it was: an act of friendship involving no aesthetic ties whatever. The group provided useful publicity for an up-and-coming composer and in any case Honegger was never overly impressed by Satie or his music.

Madeleine Milhaud: When the Groupe des Six began, Satie made a distinction between Honegger and the others: I don't think Honegger's was exactly the type of music that he liked. Honegger couldn't take criticism, in fact. At that point he was very hurt – it was a little weakness.

RN: One of his strengths, though, was his astonishing technique which was to stand him in good stead all his life. For one thing, it enabled him to choose a style for a particular piece and be totally convincing in that style. So he didn't actually cast aside the frivolous gaiety enjoined on Les Six by Cocteau – for Honegger, it was just one option out of many.

Disc: Piano Concertino

No prizes for guessing that *Rhapsody in Blue* had hit Paris the year before ... By that stage, though, Honegger had no need to prove himself: three years earlier his oratorio *Le Roi David* had made the 29-year-old composer famous overnight.

Harry Halbreich: When it first came out, a French critic wrote, 'There's such an authenticity in evoking the atmosphere of Israel 3,000 years ago, only a born Jew could have written it' – and of course, Honegger wasn't Jewish. But when you listen to a song like

Mimaamaquim, his last song, which is a setting of the opening verse of the *De profundis*, Psalm 130, on the Hebrew words, he must have studied synagogal song (maybe Milhaud gave him some clues about that). But he always seems to feel genuine, whatever style he chooses, and yet he's always himself.

Disc: Le Roi David

Darius Milhaud: At this time, *Le Roi David* was played constantly, and always with this enormous success that marks only those works which have a sort of direct appeal to the public by their simplicity. Also, you know, at this time, the public, which is like a child, felt 'Oh! But we understand modern music!' because it was so simple and direct.

RN: In Honegger's defence it should be said the work was written for amateurs, and as incidental music in a long play. It may seem curious, in view of the influence of J S Bach on the work, that Prokofiev should have remarked to Honegger a few years later, 'You and I are the only two composers who aren't going *back* to something.' But perhaps this testifies to Prokofiev's realization of how well assimilated the Bachian influence was, so it is never felt as any kind of gimmick. From then on, though, through the 1920s, Honegger was very much going forward.

Harry Halbreich: He had had early successes with *Le Roi David* and *Pacific 231* and other works and he had become, in his late twenties and early thirties, the most widely performed composer of his generation, and a really popular one. Milhaud never reached that popularity, and in a way there was slight envy. But after that series of very successful pieces, he was maybe a little spoilt by success and he resented the fact that some later pieces were not as well received; because he evolved and wrote more difficult pieces.

Judith got a cooler reception than *Le Roi David*, because it's a more difficult piece, maybe a more interesting one. And then came his most radical masterpiece, *Antigone*, which is his only full-scale opera – and when I say 'full-scale', it's a 45-minute opera in fact; I call it an 'imploded' opera, like those very small stars called supernovae. If you read Cocteau's libretto aloud, it takes you 26 minutes, and 44 minutes to listen to the music. It's a most unusual proportion: usually a 26-minute libretto, read, produces a two-hour opera.

RN: It was typical of Honegger's realistic approach to life that he should stress the anguish and violence in the Antigone story, and his realism at this time extended to his own life as well. He knew that two women were passionately in love with him – the singer Claire Croiza and the pianist Andrée Vaurabourg, known as Vaura. Each of them was to bear him a child. But the fact that Croiza bore him a son, Jean-Claude, in 1926 did not prevent him from trusting his own feelings – and marrying Vaura a fortnight later. Both women played a large part in his artistic life, and Croiza no doubt influenced him in one of his most striking innovations.

Jean-Claude Honegger: My mother was very close to Valéry and to Claudel and to composers who had the sense of the word and who tried to make it clear, and I know that Camille Maurane, one of her favourite pupils, always said that my mother wanted to read the text, know the text and understand the text before singing. I know that my father, in *Antigone*, wanted to put his own mark on this text because he said the French didn't sing very well – they didn't sing like they spoke.

Pascale Honegger: He had the same taste as Claudel for putting the accent on the first syllable so that this syllable fixed the word in the audience's ear. To begin with, the singers of course protested violently. I remember, when *Antigone* was being rehearsed at the Opéra in 1943, all the singers were saying, 'No one's ever going to be able to sing that'. And my father said, 'Just work at it for a bit.' And after that they all turned round and said, 'We've come back to a style we'd forgotten! In fact that goes much better, it's impossible to do it any other way.'

RN: ... and it comes into its own when, in reply to the chorus leader's suggestion that Polynices's burial might be the work of the gods, Creon furiously retorts, 'Assez de sottises, vieillesse!'

Disc: Antigone

Even so, Honegger had no time for talk of revolution in music. He was a respecter of tradition, though not, as *Antigone* tells us, of routine. Still, anyone reading the score of the opera in the later Twenties could be forgiven for regarding it as revolutionary. The Opéra-Comique refused to put it on and it was first performed in Brussels in 1927. The reception was fairly unenthusiastic.

Pascale Honegger: He was sensitive to the criticism of his public, but not to that of the specialists, because he thought that he had not written well enough to be understood by the public, and it was terrible for him to think that his job was not well done.

RN: He was in fact always to be caught between his need for independence and his no less imperious need to communicate; and the price of his independence was paid, as usually happens with creative artists, by others as well as himself.

Pascale Honegger: For a start, when he married my mother, he said to her, 'We must agree, there can be no question of sharing a flat.' Each of them had their flat, very close to one another, and she agreed. I think she was intelligent enough to understand the reason.

RN: His concern for independence wasn't confined to his own case either: he believed liberty was the basic right of every human being. This belief came over in some surprising ways. Any conductor of Honegger's works notices at once how few dynamic markings he puts in his scores.

Paul Sacher: He was simply too lazy! And he had an excuse. He said, 'They are all good musicians, I think it offends to write everything down, they have ears, they can hear it.' It's true, I think musicians like the way he did it, because they are more involved, they have to listen, they have to collaborate. They know 'Now I am the soloist, now I am an accompanying voice.' That's very important. I remember once a musician in the orchestra asked, 'Maître, should that be an F or an F#?' And he said, 'Which would you prefer?' He knew perfectly well it was an F#, but he said he didn't want to be a dictator!

RN: In 1930, possibly in part as a result of the cool reception of *Antigone*, Honegger underwent a spiritual crisis amidst which he composed one of the key works of his career, *Cris du monde*.

Pascale Honegger: I think it came from everything he began to see happening all round him. My father was always noticing what happened round him and was always interested in the life of mankind in general. He used to work on his own in his studio, but he used to go out a lot and was very open to everything, so I think he was aware of all the problems that were building up. So when his friend René Bizet proposed this text, it corresponded to a torment he felt growing inside him as he saw what was happening in the world.

Harry Halbreich: I think the piece came too soon. It was a warning against dangers and problems which didn't yet seem to interest anybody – they weren't felt to be urgent, and now you have whole ministries to deal with them. I'm speaking of quality of life, pollution, noise, invasion of mass media. It's important to know it was written in 1930 because it was written in the wake of the great New York crash and of the crisis developing in Europe, everything that was leading up to the rise of Fascism, Hitlerism, Stalinisim and all the dictatorships. Honegger sensed it beforehand. No one likes Cassandras, so *Cris du monde* got a very cool reception. But he was never an ivory-tower composer; the very opposite, he always needed contact, he never wrote for his shelf. In 1932 he published an article 'Pour prendre congé', 'Saying farewell', which is a rather bitter article in which he just faces the fact that he has lost contact with the public.

Disc: Cris du monde

RN: By the mid-1930s the once popular Honegger was being written off as a shooting star – 'how sad, with all that promise' etc. Maybe Halbreich was right, and he had indeed been a little spoilt by success. His response to the public's rejection was not to face it, but to bypass it by turning to the cinema (though Milhaud and others did likewise for purely practical reasons, since the money available for concert commissions had been severely reduced by the financial crash). But Honegger also saw the necessity as an opportunity: here, he felt, was an opening for cinema to become the opera of the modern world.

Pascale Honegger: He used to say he would look at the rushes and then go off at once and write the music while he had all the rhythm and natural sounds of the film in his ears. His technique – and it was quite a technique! – allowed him to do that without any problems and he didn't feel called upon to rely on any profound inspiration, as he did for his symphonies and other major works.

RN: But film music could have its dangers ...

Darius Milhaud: Honegger wrote a lot of film music, which has one great drawback: because with film music you are obliged to write extremely fast, you don't have time to control yourself, and then the danger is that you can get a little bit in the habit of writing more rapidly – with less control, perhaps.

RN: Harry Halbreich disagrees ...

Harry Halbreich: Honegger always managed to keep a dividing line, and even when he wrote as many as eight or nine film scores a year, he still lavished two years' work to finish a quartet or a symphony. Of course the polyphonic fabric and the harmony are far more complex, intricate and elaborate in a concert piece. But I think, whatever he did, he had that absolute Swiss sense of craftsmanship. He wanted to be an artisan.

Disc: Mermoz

Harry Halbreich: He wrote music for 42 films – that's a lot, even Shostakovitch only wrote 35 and Milhaud 25. I think the film directors loved working with Honegger because he was modest and not pretentious. He was very simple and flexible, always ready to rewrite or adapt to the director's most minute requirements, and he also had that chameleonesque ability to compose in different styles.

RN: Even when his title music to Anthony Asquith's *Pygmalion* (his only British commission) was ditched in favour of Johann Strauss, he took it equably. Indeed his natural good humour and ability to come out with a funny story hid the inner torment of those years even from his close friends.

Madeleine Milhaud: We travelled a lot with him. He was the easiest person in the world. At that time we had a car with only what we call a 'spider', a buggy seat, in the back and we were going to Brussels where there was going to be a performance of *Antigone*. I was driving, it was raining and Arthur was sitting behind in his raincoat, sleeping, absolutely indifferent to the weather, the cold, the wind. Then it got dreadfully foggy when we were crossing the Ardennes forest and he walked in front of the car so that I would know where I was going. We finally arrived in Brussels and five minutes later he was in front of a large glass of beer, enjoying life, absolutely normal.

RN: Salvation from Honegger's spiritual crisis came in the form of one man whom Jean-Louis Barrault was later to call 'an idiot of genius': the poet and playwright Paul Claudel. Honegger had been asked by the dancer Ida Rubinstein to think of writing a 'mystery' on the subject of Joan of Arc. Claudel eventually agreed to write the libretto, and Honegger later said (too modestly) that all the necessary music was implicit in Claudel's words, and that all he had to do was notate it. At all events, in this work Honegger, in following Claudel's instructions, was able to return at least some way towards the more popular idiom of *Le Roi David*.

Disc: Jeanne d'Arc

The first performance of *Jeanne d'Arc*, in Basle in 1938, was a magnificent success for Honegger – one could truly say, it saved him. He and Claudel immediately began work on another oratorio, *La Danse des morts*, inspired by Holbein's painting. *King David*, *Joan of Arc*, *The Dance of the Dead* – was Honegger a religious man?

Pascale Honegger: It's possible he had been a believer when he was younger. My own memories are more strongly about the end of his life, and I think that for him the war had been such an enormous shock, leading to a loss of hope in human values. He always had the desire for a god and for a belief in a hereafter, which was all the stronger because at that period life on earth was terrible. I had the impression that he had been too disappointed to retain his belief.

Harry Halbreich: He never had straightforward, unproblematic faith like Messiaen. He was a tormented man in that respect – he would have liked to believe. 'If only it were true!' But there are other great agnostics amongst 20th-century artists and composers who have managed to convey real religious feeling without being believers themselves. I'm thinking of Vaughan Williams, for instance.

RN: And the comparisons with Vaughan Williams don't end there. Both he and Honegger remained throughout their lives impervious to the fashionable and trendy, both believed in the symphony, both believed in tonality, both believed in the humanistic tenets so powerfully argued in *La Danse des morts*. The work contains an important solo for a baritone.

Paul Sacher: I call it a *baryton martin*, it's a high baritone, and it's the heart of the piece, this aria, therefore it's important to have a great singer: not only a good voice, but a personality who is able to give the atmosphere of that text.

Disc: La Danse des Morts Charles Panzera/Charles Munch

RN: It's tempting to regard that work, premiered in 1938, as prophetic. The dance of death that gripped Europe for the next six years did not form the easiest background for composing. And for Honegger, as for so many others, friendships became more than ever important.

Arthur Honegger: I have a great friend at Basle, a conductor who for more than 20 years has played my works everywhere and for whom I have written some of them, Paul Sacher. In 1938 he asked me to write a symphony for the Kammerorchester (or the Collegium Musicum) of Zürich. For more than a year I made repeated efforts, but was not at all satisfied. At last, during the unhappy days of the Occupation, I plunged back into the quartets of Beethoven, and the influence of these magnificent works stimulated me to start working again. I was finally able to send a score to Paul Sacher, who gave the symphony its first performance in Zürich on 18 May 1942.

Paul Sacher: He made me wait a very long time, but it came. He used to be a fiddler himself and he liked very much his own pieces for string quartet. The symphony is written for strings, and I think it's a great piece.

Disc: Symphony No 2 Closing Bars of the Finale

Paul Sacher: He said, 'If you like, at the end you can also have an oboe or a clarinet', but it's not true, because the trumpet gives a special colour and a special character to the melody. You have to have a trumpet!

RN: The message of the trumpet was clear enough in 1942, and in due course it even made its way to England. The conductor Boyd Neel was working as an Army surgeon at Roehampton, when he had an urgent call to come up to the BBC.

Boyd Neel: I was ushered in to a secret chamber in the bowels of Broadcasting House and on the table was a little tiny packet. And they said, 'This was parachuted into England last night. Your name appears on the packet.' It was from Arthur Honegger, who asked that this work (which was microfilmed and put into the packet) should be, if possible, conducted by me and played back to the Occupied countries, and he hoped that it would give them strength and hope in those dark days. It was the Second Symphony. So we played it the following week (at the Wigmore Hall on 26 April 1944) and two weeks later another packet arrived by parachute, saying, 'It was heard and it was wonderful and everybody was overjoyed and felt great hope.'

RN: Honegger had only been able to get the score of the symphony to Paul Sacher in Switzerland by himself going to Vienna in 1941, for the celebrations to mark the 150th anniversary of the death of Mozart.

After the war, this journey was held against him by some people as the act of a collaborator — which only shows the spirit of those dreadful days of 'purification'. It would have been more to the point to ask why Honegger, as a Swiss national, should have chosen to stay in Paris at all.

Pascale Honegger: He wouldn't leave France because he thought it was not fair. You had to stay with the people who were suffering and you had to support them by music, by art; if your life is not in danger, you have no reason to get away. Of course for Darius Milhaud, his life was in danger, so he went to the States. But for my father, he was Swiss, he was not a Jew, and he could stay there and make music — and music and art are necessary when you are unhappy.

RN: There were also interesting ways for a lover of liberty like Honegger to assert his independence of the occupying forces.

Pascale Honegger: With the words for *Judith* and the *Danse des morts*, it was wonderful for French people to hear words like 'Israël revivra'. When you could see German soldiers in the audience and you could sing that in front of them, that was wonderful!

RN: But overall the effect of the war on Honegger was enormously oppressive. The Second Symphony, written in the early years of the war, speaks of hope. By the end of the war, the Third Symphony speaks of disillusionment that men's liberty should have been so grossly outraged — 'De profundis clamavi'.

Harry Halbreich: There are *De profundis*'s all over: in *Jeanne d'Arc*, in *La Danse des morts*, in *Mimaamaquim*. But if I had to single out one movement from the five symphonies of Honegger, maybe I would take the 'De profundis' movement of the *Symphonie liturgique* which is, I think, one of the great slow movements in the whole of the symphonic literature.

Disc: Symphony No 3, 'De profundis'

In 1946, Honegger began a new symphony, dedicated to Paul Sacher, to whom he wrote, 'After the Third Symphony, I want to do something absolutely clear and simple, like life in your house in Switzerland, but I'm afraid of being banal or facile.' He needn't have worried: the lighter tone of the Fourth Symphony, 'Deliciae basilienses', did not entail any abandonment of technique.

Harry Halbreich: If you look at the finale of the Fourth Symphony, the recapitulation starts, exceptionally for him, with theme 1, then comes theme 2, but theme 1 is still around, and then there are five themes all together; and at the end you have a fantastic piece of polyphonic clockwork, of five polyphonic layers going on for 80 bars. What Mozart did for some 20 bars in the finale of the Jupiter Symphony, Honegger does for 80 bars.

Disc: Symphony No 4, Finale

Paul Sacher: The carnival in Basle is a mystic institution, The city is without light, it's night, black, and you are in the centre of the city, and at 4am from everywhere they come: drums and piccolos, and they have large lanterns and that's really an outstanding moment. Honegger took a very famous march, the Morgenstreich, and put it at the end of the last movement. It's a good 'homage to Basle' because everybody knows it.

RN: To this composer at the height of his powers the Fates dealt a cruel blow. After the privations of the Occupation, Honegger was delighted to be able to indulge once again his prewar appetite: 'it all goes into my composing', he confided to friends who were worried by his expanding waistline. But it did not, and in 1947, on his second visit to the USA, he suffered a serious heart attack. For weeks he was on the danger list, before being allowed to come back home.

Pascale Honegger: He had lost 20 kilos and there was a new white stripe at the front of his hair. When I went to collect him at the station I was absolutely thrown by that, but he was all right. Sadly, though, he insisted on living the life he had previously, going on long tours, conducting orchestras. At that period, just after the war, postal services were still not functioning properly, so when he went on a tour of Italy he had two suitcases containing all the orchestral material for his music. He carried the whole lot on his train journeys, with changes of train. Obviously, his heart wasn't up to it.

RN: Psychologically, the heart attack increased his tendency to pessimism, traceable in some degree as far back as *Cris du monde* in 1930. It's far more evident in a book of articles called *Incantation aux fossiles* (the fossils, as already noted, being critics of every time and place), and particularly in the series of published conversations called *Je suis Compositeur*, where Honegger disabuses his public of any notion that a composer's life is glamorous or well rewarded.

Darius Milhaud: He wrote a book which troubled us a little bit. It's a conversation with a French critic in which he complains all the time, very pessimistic about music, and we felt that he shouldn't complain of the situation of the musician as he had always been followed by success, step by step. But anyway he thought that the professional musician's life was terrible, and tried to discourage young people. I felt he was wrong in this attitude. I know it's a difficult profession, I know you can starve. This was the only point on which we disagreed – very strongly even.

Jean-Claude Honegger: In the beginning he had the feeling of a revolution he could believe in, something new was coming, something that was good for the people, and I think he was very sincere in that. During the war, though, he was very sad because he hated what he saw, all the misery people can inflict on others, and after the war he was still pessimistic because he was ill, and he saw things were not going on any better than before. It was the 1950s, and at that time everyone had a fear of the atomic bomb, and he was certainly very distressed about that – he said so.

RN: Another effect of Honegger's illness was, of course, to set limits on his independence, in all kinds of ways.

Madeleine Milhaud: When he was very ill, he didn't want to depend on his wife, but she decided she was needed. Very shortly before he died, he told me that she was there, but I have the impression that for him it was something absolutely unbearable. He loved her – it didn't make any difference to their relationship – but he couldn't stand, I think, to have anybody around.

RN: His pessimism came to a head musically in the last of his five symphonies, which he wrote in 1950, five years before his death. In each of his previous symphonies, there is some kind of hope offered at the end. Here, a vision of hope seems to be approaching, only to be cut short in the final bars.

Disc: Symphony No 5, end

The scherzo of this symphony takes a highly chromatic theme and puts it through all the procedures dear to the 12-tone serialists, the whole thing carried through with superb technical assurance, as always; but with an unmistakable distancing of irony. Works such as *Antigone* and the First Symphony prove that Honegger could have his gritty side, and passages in his early orchestral piece *Horace victorieux* could almost have been written by Alban Berg, but for the grey, faceless diktats of serialism this lover of independence had no time whatever.

Harry Halbreich: I remember one of my fellow students had brought to Honegger's class a string quartet written in the then very fashionable, desiccated 12-tone idiom. Honegger said nothing, he just took the score, called two of us to sit down at the piano and sight-read the thing, but he just whispered to one of us, 'Transpose the viola part one tone down!' The poor composer never noticed a thing ...

RN: Honegger preferred to be self-reliant. No gimmicks, no short cuts. He recognised that to proclaim oneself an independent is one thing – it sounds all very grand and noble. But living the life is something else. Its hard, hard work. And Honegger was a worker.

Pascale Honegger: He said once that simply the idea that a child might turn up at his studio without warning would be enough to block off his inspiration. This inspiration did not come to him easily for important pieces like symphonies and he needed both absolute peace and the ability to count on it.

Jean-Claude Honegger: When he lived in Paris, it was a rather noisy place, being on the boulevard de Clichy. That didn't disturb him at all, but a little noise, of someone ringing the telephone or knocking on his door, that was an awful shock for him. When he went to stay in a hotel, he took a 'Do not disturb' notice. And he had such a collection! He put it all over his door – 'Non disturbare', 'Nicht stören' – in about 50 languages, to keep people away as far as possible. He was very nice to us, his family. But *after* work!

Madeleine Milhaud: Honegger was one of those people who never open a letter, and after a month he threw them all away. Once I found a letter from Darius, and on the back of the envelope he'd written, 'Arthur, open it! It's me!'

RN: Honegger never bothered to butter up whatever musical establishment there was in France. He won no prizes from the Conservatoire, and certainly none from the Nazis. But at the end of 1954 he did accept his promotion to grand officier de la Légion d'honneur.

Pascale Honegger: He was very honoured, of course. He told me that he knew it was because he was going to die soon. He had a terrible, black sense of humour.

RN: He was also, as usual, telling the truth. He died, in his wife's arms, on 27 November 1955.

What, then, is his legacy? Having taught only a little, he had no phalanx of adoring pupils to perpetuate his memory. His widow, as a fine musician herself, felt that only the best possible performances were tolerable. But above all there was the year 1955.

Harry Halbreich: He died in the darkest age of the Cold War, when everybody believed there would be a nuclear catastrophe the next day. Musically, it was the same thing. He died at the height of the dodecaphonic, serialist terror. In Britain the situation was slightly different because there was no Pierre Boulez acting as a ruthless dictator and deciding that anybody not aware of the historic necessity of writing serial music was just no good.

RN: 'Just no good'. To anyone who knows even a little of Honegger's music, this is hard to take. In a century largely devoted to the brightly coloured and the episodic, his lyricism stands out. True, there are times when his teacher Gedalge's criticism does seem valid – when you just wish he would leave things alone a bit more and not give us quite so many notes, but the lyricism is never far below the surface. Complementing this lyricism is his music's extraordinary propulsive energy, very often launched by dotted rhythms.

Harry Halbreich: I think the dotted rhythms have to do with the fact that he remained basically a tonal composer. Tonal harmony implies a certain rhythmic articulation and phrasing. The dotted anacrusis before the barline is always one part of a harmonic cadence. I was practically his last student – I attended his teaching for half a year in 1953 – and one of the first things he told me, which strikes me to this day and which is a clue to his whole musical language, was, 'To me, a single note is a dominant' – which implies first of all a dynamic conception of music. A dominant implies a resolution. Tension/relaxation.

RN: ... which brings us back to the basic tradition of music and its time-honoured place in the world. His work, for all its emphasis on craft, dealt with the eternal verities: life, death, religion, singing, dancing, human contact. He himself summed it up better than anyone, talking about *how* he composed.

Arthur Honegger: The question is difficult to answer, because quite apart from the technical side of music, which anyone can learn, there is still sometimes the miraculous thing that the composers cannot explain better than anyone else. Yes, I say it is something of a miracle: for a melodic line or a rhythm that has already been used hundreds of times can suddenly become a stroke of genius. How can we explain this? That's why, in my opinion, music is much more related to magic art than to painting, sculpture, poetry or even architecture, which is nothing more than music solidified in space. She is far above them, intangible.

Disc: Jeanne d'Arc, end

As mentioned above, Honegger was situated at what we might call the 'serious' end of the Groupe des Six, the 'light-hearted end' being taken by Francis Poulenc, Georges Auric and Darius Milhaud, especially in his jazz pieces. But this is, of course, an unduly reductive view...

39 FRENCH BALLET, FRANCIS POULENC AND THE PLEASURE PRINCIPLE

They are the epitome of self-assurance: there they stand, top hatted, cane in hand, luxuriant beard meticulously trimmed – and eye openly roving. The expensively dressed middle-aged gentlemen who haunt the backstage area of the Paris Opéra in Degas's pictures tell us more about the realities of life in that institution than many a learned monograph. As one modern ballerina has noted, 'they did not come bearing subsidies from the Arts Council'.

They were the 'abonnés des trois jours', subscribers to the complete Opéra run of Monday, Wednesday and Friday performances. In a return for a hefty sum (many thousands of pounds in today's money) they were granted access not only backstage but even on to the stage itself between items. Access to singers' and dancers' dressing-rooms was negotiable with the artists concerned. Even as recently as the late 1920s the director, Jacques Rouché, failed to put a stop to the practice which, together with the notorious independence (to use no stronger word) of the Opéra stage hands, made production an even more hazardous business than normal.

Not surprisingly, it was the female ballet dancers who were the centre of attention. It had long been the tradition that any opera produced in this house had to contain a ballet, whether it forwarded the action or not (usually not). Even the great Verdi, when *Otello* was mounted at the Opéra in 1894, had to compose a ballet as part of the ceremony of welcome for the Venetian ambassadors in Act III, the only concession to his status being that he was allowed to keep it short. The style of dancing was essentially decorative, concentrating almost entirely on the female dancers, with the males reduced to the rôle of 'porteurs'. A generous display of leg and décolletage was considered more important than extravagant acrobatics – and again Degas's paintings of feathery tutus, elegant arms and, possibly submissive, black chokers give much of the flavour.

This was the state of French ballet when Francis Poulenc was born in Paris on 7 January 1899. From his parents he received a dual inheritance. His mother, Jenny Royer, came from a long line of Parisian craftsmen and brought with her a strain of freethinking independence and a deep love of the arts. She had been brought up, like all those of her class, to take it for granted that Paris was the centre of the civilised world. His father Emile, on the other hand, was a provincial from the Aveyron district, between Toulouse and the Massif Central, and a devout Roman Catholic. This dichotomy, which their son recognised, can be seen in him on many levels and it was one he never perhaps completely reconciled.

His mother was a talented amateur pianist and musical soirées were a regular occurrence. The young Francis preferred listening to the music from under the grand piano – except when it came to the Fauré First Sonata for violin and piano, when he would take refuge in his bedroom. His mother was his first piano teacher and his involvement with music up to the age of 14 remained casual.

Two encounters, though, marked him for life. The first was the arrival of Diaghilev's Ballets russes in Paris in 1909, and even more so their production of the three Stravinsky ballets, *Firebird*, *Petrushka* and *The Rite of Spring* between 1910 and 1913. Stravinsky's music was to remain a crucial influence on him until the Second World War at least, in its shapeliness and the clarity of its textures. Like everyone else, he was no doubt also bowled over by the spectacle and raw energy of the Ballets russes, and especially of Nijinsky who could be said to be a 'porteur' only in the sense that he was able to 'carry' a whole production.

Poulenc's other decisive encounter was with a nickelodeon in a Paris arcade, from which emerged the sounds of the eminent pianist Edouard Risler playing the 'Idylle' from Chabrier's *Dix Pièces pittoresques*. From that moment the 14-year-old Poulenc knew he was going to become a composer. In their different ways, both Chabrier and the Stravinsky of the early ballets were to some extent engaged in fashioning rustic materials for urban consumption, just as Poulenc was to do in the 1920s – he was thrilled when told that Ravel had praised his ability 'to write his own folksongs'.

Poulenc was involved in five ballet projects between 1921 and 1942. Two of these, *Les Mariés de la tour Eiffel* and *L'Eventail de Jeanne*, were collaborations for which he wrote three short movements in all. But the other three had music entirely by him, two of them being among his most popular and characteristic works.

The first of them, *Les Biches,* a commission from Diaghilev, was first performed by the Ballets russes in Monte Carlo in 1924, to great acclaim: 'if I may say so, a triumph', reported Poulenc. 'They had to raise the curtain eight times, which is very rare in Monte-Carlo. There have been at least 72 rehearsals, some 250 hours of work. That way one can get results.' It's a gloriously light-hearted piece, one that captures to perfection the spirit of the 'années folles'. It revelled in what the ballet historian Lynn Garafola has termed 'lifestyle modernism', the dancers representing not other-worldly creatures but the smart set of those frenetic post-war years. This is the chic, urbanised Poulenc at play.

His second complete ballet, *Aubade*, written in 1929 to a commission from the Vicomte and Vicomtesse de Noailles, could hardly be more different. Suffering one of the earliest of the bouts of depression that were to blight his life, Poulenc channelled his misery through the person of the huntress Diana, who finally has to accept that she must renounce love. The result, for all the classical formality of its outward surface, is one of the most moving pieces of music he ever wrote.

Finally, *Les Animaux modèles*, performed at the Opéra in 1942, is a transposition into dance of fables by La Fontaine in which, in a contrary sense to that of the poet, the animals are given human form. In that darkest year of the Occupation, it is not surprising that Poulenc should have taken the opportunity to prove his patriotic credentials. Not only did he chose a 17th-century stage setting, as being the most self-consciously French century of all, but he even inserted into the score at one point a reference to the tune 'No, you shall not have Alsace –Lorraine'. The German soldiers in the audience were, according to Poulenc, nonplussed by the hilarity around them.

Poulenc does not seem to have considered writing another ballet between *Les Animaux modèles* and his death in 1963. And yet his musical style is peculiarly suited to the medium. Like Stravinsky, he moulds his music in distinct, easily grasped phrases which have clear relationships with each other; and like Stravinsky, he frequently implies gesture (he himself was an expansive talker, much given to arm waving when excited). Two other works that have been used for ballet performances, the Concerto for two pianos and orchestra and the Sonata for clarinet and piano, though different in many ways, share this plasticity, as well as providing evidence of the composer's supreme melodic gift.

Both are what one might call friendly works. He wrote the Concerto for two pianos in two and a half months in 1932 to play with his friend Jacques Février, and the work was a hit from the first performance in Venice that September. It is hard to know what in it to admire most: the extraordinary gamelan effect at the end of the first movement, inspired by what Poulenc had heard at the 1931 Colonial Exhibition; the pseudo-Mozart of the second, with its superbly understated little forays into true Poulenc – and back again; or the irresistible brio of the finale, with its percussive (and fiendishly tricky) repeated notes, and the mixture of memorable, soupy tunes and wilfully dissonant scrunches to remind us that the 'années folles' had only just come to an end.

The Sonata for clarinet and piano of 1962 was one of his last works, but the vocabulary is recognizably the same – Poulenc toyed briefly with modernist styles, but soon decided to stick with what he was best at. He was always particularly fond of wind instruments and he exploits with unfailing inventiveness two of the clarinet's major assets: its flexibility and its capacity to sing long lines (there are reminiscences both of his opera *Dialogues des Carmélites* and of his *Gloria*). The shape of the Sonata, too, follows established precedent, culminating in a perky finale. But, as often with Poulenc, within the traditional format there are plenty of surprises – melodic, harmonic and, of course, gestural. Beyond that, for all the deliberate and carefully crafted vulgarities, the overall tone and control of both works verge on the aristocratic. Top hat and cane are in evidence, even if carried with a slightly more extravert air than Degas's balletomanes might have thought quite proper.

40 **FRANCIS POULENC – THE ROAD TO LA VOIX HUMAINE**

Francis Poulenc was for many years the victim of his own charm: both of his outwardly optimistic, witty persona and of those works of his that displayed similar features. Even before the invention of the Groupe des Six by a Parisian journalist in 1920, Poulenc's *Mouvements perpétuels* were to be found on the piano in every fashionable drawing room – 'So charming, my dear'; and (though this was not perhaps often mentioned) so easy to play compared with most of Debussy and Ravel. Had these elegant ladies known that already the young Poulenc was harbouring an ambition to write serious operas, they would probably have put it down to that age-old urge of every clown to play Hamlet.

Apart from this early recognition as a purveyor of light listening, Poulenc bore two other burdens. Firstly he was well off. On his father's side he was heir to the chemical firm now known as Rhône-Poulenc, and the general assumption was that he had taken to composing merely as a way of staving off boredom rather than out of inner necessity. Secondly, he had never studied music at the Paris Conservatoire, or indeed any other institution, confining himself to 58 composition lessons from Charles Koechlin between 1921 and 1925. Despite whatever friendships he might make with men like Milhaud and Honegger, for the mass of conservative critics this *fils à papa*, Daddy's boy, was well outside the magic ring and, initially at least, they gave their approval grudgingly, if at all.

The truth was that Poulenc was not at heart the insouciant *blagueur* he might appear, but *un inquiet*. He cared passionately about his composing and was fiercely determined to make good any deficiencies through sheer hard work. He was also quite unusually intelligent in choosing, or accepting, subjects that he could use to stretch his musical technique and understanding.

Each of his three operas explores paths off the beaten French operatic track. *Les Mamelles de Tirésias*, first given at the Opéra-Comique in 1947, is a kind of surrealist operetta on Apollinaire's text, and a brilliant balancing act between farce and a discussion of serious moral issues, such as feminism and the future of France. With *Dialogues des Carmélites*, premiered at La Scala in 1957, Poulenc moved decisively towards serious opera, turning the story of nuns executed during the Terror into a harrowing enquiry into the nature of grace – harrowing for Poulenc too, who suffered with his nuns to an extent dangerous for his mental health. Against heavy odds, the work was an immediate success and it was with energy and confidence restored that he began work in February 1958 on his third and last opera, a setting of Cocteau's monologue *La Voix humaine*.

Cocteau's one-sided telephone conversation had been very well received in 1930, with Berthe Bovy playing the role of 'Elle' or 'The Woman'. For the first performance of Poulenc's opera, at the Opéra-Comique on 6 February 1959, Cocteau was both producer and designer, and before that had taken a keen interest in the composer's progress. Poulenc for his part, worked on the score with enormous enthusiasm, writing to a friend, 'I am decidedly a man of the theatre' – a point on which he had had his doubts in the past.

The task facing him was, in any case, one to tax the most experienced operatic hand. The nearest 19th-century equivalent to this monologue would perhaps be the 'letter aria', as found in *Eugene Onegin* or *Werther*. But letter arias do not go on for 40 minutes, and the reader of the letter can always be allowed to vary the tone by breaking in with comments on what is being read. Clearly the life of a musical setting of *La Voix humaine* resided in at least two main elements: the declamation of the text, and the relationship between singer and orchestra. In both cases, Poulenc referred to established models, even if his personal voice is everywhere to be heard.

He admitted that he needed to have written *Dialogues des Carmélites* in order to grasp and express the heartbreak of this woman abandoned by her lover. Cocteau's text proceeds largely by implication (the news of the man's impending marriage is given merely by the words 'Demain? ... Je ne savais pas que c'était si rapide ... ') and Poulenc had to find a style or word-setting that was at once close to spoken French and yet charged with an inner tension – one might even say 'with an electricity'. For this he seems to have turned to Debussy's *Pelléas et Mélisande*, and especially to the last act, where we are again presented with the emotional fall-out of a love affair. As in *Pelléas*, the melodic line is often close to plainsong intonation, with many repeated notes, and with phrases also often repeated once or twice over unaltered harmonies. Poulenc felt the need to apologise to his friend Pierre Bernac for this technique, which he saw as being 'against all the rules'; at the same time, he realised it was to be an important element in the work's success, underlining as it does the obsessive nature of the woman's anguish.

What she says, and how she says it, has to be weighed against what we judge of her character and circumstances, and in this painful exercise the orchestra is the carrier of truth. Here again, Poulenc goes back to an old model, to Gluck's Orestes who sings 'Le calme rentre dans mon cœur' while agitations in the violas tell us the precise opposite. One might say that Poulenc's work is concerned with the repression of true feeling, that it is the flickering shadow thrown by the light of the great romantic opera he might one day have written.

Nowhere is this felt more powerfully than in a place where words and orchestra combine to tell the same story, where the woman remembers a moment of past happiness ('Souviens-toi du dimanche de Versailles et du pneumatique ... '). Here Poulenc allows the music to flower as in one of the great song-cycles such as *Tel jour telle nuit*, and because this phrase comes quite early in the opera, we carry it in our memory, hoping, as the woman does, to experience it again, and using it as an ideal against which to set the tortured fragments that follow.

Little need be said of the work's musical language. Poulenc knew he was not an innovator in this area like Debussy or Stravinsky, but claimed there was a place in musical history for composers who used other men's chords in a new way. As the American scholar Keith Daniel points out, the chords in *La Voix humaine* 'produce a sense of ambiguity rather than harshness'. Through them, we perceive the woman's tottering mental balance, anchored only by a stock of nine music motifs (obsessions?) which seem to lack identifiable reference points; and we may note also how anxious the composer was for the 'Elle' of the premiere, Denise Duval, to articulate clearly her climactic '*je devenais folle*'. Both Poulenc and Duval knew only too well the torments of depression and he thanked her for the fact that together 'we have made this beautiful, sad child ... which I am now convinced is a masterpiece'.

Before moving on finally to the three big names in modern French music, a few words about a minor master, with my gratitude to Dennis Hunt, Nicholas Kaye, Christopher Saward and Andrew Thomson for their helpful information.

41 MAURICE DURUFLÉ

Asked to name the most moving, the most characterful, the most spiritually profound, in short the best Requiem of the last 75 years, I suspect many music lovers would choose either Britten's *War Requiem* of 1962 or Duruflé's *Requiem* of 1947. They are, of course, two very different works, and the differences, between two composers who must both be labelled 'conservatives' by comparison with most of their contemporaries, highlight what one might call the 'revolutionary conservatism' of the French master, as opposed to the 'evolutionary conservatism' of his English counterpart.

Britten, for example, did not turn his back on the twelve-tone system, as we can see from his highly ingenious and personal manipulation of it in *The Turn of the Screw*. While there may be twelve-note rows in Duruflé's music, I would wager that they were there by accident. I am therefore using the word 'revolutionary' in three senses. Firstly, Duruflé was revolutionary in that he turned history back to a time when the basis of Roman Catholic church music was plainsong. Secondly, his approach was 'revolutionary' in that he 'revolved' all his composing life within the same narrow circle of musical ideas and language. Thirdly, and in the more usually accepted meaning of the word, much of his effort within that circle was forward-looking in trying to reconcile two apparently incompatible languages. In understanding his attitude to composition, it is therefore even more relevant than with most composers to look at his own history and *formation*.

He was born on 11 January 1902 in Louviers, some 70km north west of Paris. He attended a choir school from the age of ten, and by 17 was the organist of Notre-Dame in his home town. His father, an architect, did some work on the local mansion belonging to Maurice Emmanuel, then professor of history at the Paris Conservatoire, and one day Emmanuel asked Maurice to play him the Bach A minor

Prelude and Fugue. As a result, Emmanuel suggested he should prepare for the entrance examination to the Conservatoire organ class in October 1920.

To this end Duruflé undertook twice-weekly lessons with Charles Tournemire at Saint-Clotilde. And 'undertook' would seem to be the *mot juste* – Tournemire was inspirational as an improviser, but not apparently much blessed with patience or with any organized approach to teaching. After a year or so, Tournemire declared that Duruflé was ready to sit the October exam. Duruflé thought otherwise – and took himself off to Louis Vierne instead. As Duruflé later wrote:

> To the same extent that Tournemire made one feel he was sitting upon a volcano about to erupt, Vierne gave one a sense of complete ease. He was always the same from one day to the next, which was something to be thankful for.

Needless to say, Duruflé did pass the exam and went into Eugène Gigout's class, from which he seems to have learnt very little. But, with hindsight, we may think Duruflé was lucky in benefiting from the two opposing styles and characters of Tournemire and Vierne. Certainly they clearly exemplified the antinomy of freedom and discipline which lies at the heart of all art worthy of the name: in fugal improvisation, for example, Vierne was much stricter than Tournemire over formal shaping (even though it was left to Dupré, when he took over Gigout's class in 1926, to demand that the countersubject be retained throughout).

Duruflé duly won his Premier Prix in 1922, one of the five first prizes he was to gain, and in 1926 he wrote his first published composition, the Scherzo for organ op. 2, dedicated to Tournemire. The fact that it begins and ends slowly indicates that already Duruflé was not bound by convention. Even if the sudden stops and starts are not entirely persuasive, on other fronts much of Duruflé's style is already in place: sequences moving by thirds, harmonic extensions of the dominant seventh, tritonal alternation, the pedal used as much for melodies and staccato decoration as for bass underpinning and, of course, a pervasive modality born of the plainsong that lay at the heart of his teacher Tournemire's inspiration as well.

The *Prélude, récitatif et variations* for flute, viola and piano of 1928 shows no real advance whether formally or in language, and the composer still seems to be searching for a way to integrate modality with post-Debussyan chromaticism, so that the mood shifts disconcertingly between blandness and a Franckian/Chaussonesque intensity. There is still some formal drift in the first two movements of the *Prélude, adagio et choral varié sur le thème du Veni Creator* for organ of 1929, which won a prize from the Amis de l'Orgue. But things come together in the variations, and the final escape from A major is very exciting. But it was in 1928 that he had his first composition lessons from the recently appointed professor Paul Dukas, whose apparent severity, in the words of Duruflé's biographer James E. Frazier, 'concealed a man, to tell the truth, who afterwards disclosed himself full of kindness and concern'. In particular, his teaching emphasised the importance of musical architecture.

In 1930 Duruflé was appointed organist of Saint-Etienne–du-Mont, a post he held until his death, although his wife Marie-Madeleine shared the duties towards the end of life. That year he also wrote his Suite for organ op. 5, and here the modal and chromatic languages come together far more successfully. Textures are more imaginative too, and he shows that he was one of the few composers to whom 5/4 metre comes naturally. In one of two brief passages we find him in a sense 'looking forward' to Messiaen's *La Nativité du Seigneur*, although the truth is that both he and Messiaen were developing from Tournemire along different lines. Duruflé came to dislike the final Toccata, claiming the first theme was weak and that this vitiated the whole piece, and in the 1970s he completely rewrote the last line of the last page, making the ending less predictable, and twice as thrilling.

Duruflé's lifelong devotion to plainsong in his music did not, understandably, leave much room for humour. That he had a sense of humour cannot be doubted by anyone who has read his memories of Tournemire and Vierne (I particularly relish his portrait of Tournemire closing his eyes in tandem with the Swell box). His less serious side also comes over in the two orchestral works of 1936 and 1940, the *Trois Danses* and the *Andante et Scherzo*. The end of the third dance, 'Tambourin', emphasizes the extraordinarily wide outreach of a brand of light French music going back through Delibes to Adolphe Adam and no doubt beyond.

In 1943 Duruflé was appointed a professor of harmony at the Conservatoire and he remained in the post until 1969. His *Prélude et fugue sur le nom d'Alain* of 1943 was written in memory of the organist and composer Jehan Alain, a fellow composition pupil of Paul Dukas, who had been killed in action in the summer of 1940. The memorial aspect is foremost in the Prélude through quotations from Alain's *Litanies*. The Fugue, though, even if based like the Prélude on a musical transcription of the letters ALAIN, can almost be heard as celebrating his new Conservatoire post. This is a Vierne fugue rather than a Tournemire one – tightly organized, not too long, and with an irresistible impetus towards the final chord.

After the war, Duruflé added recital work and recordings to his activities, touring all over the world and recording major works by Bach for Pathé-Marconi, as well as a splendid performance of the Poulenc Organ Concerto in 1961, conducted by Georges Prêtre. His postwar compositions were mainly vocal. The *Quatre Motets sur des thèmes grégoriens* are already classics, and nowadays few weddings with choral pretensions are complete without 'Ubi caritas', just as decades earlier none was complete without 'the Widor'. Duruflé's final work, the *Messe 'Cum Jubilo'* for solo baritone, baritone chorus, organ and orchestra, is a generally dignified, restrained work, again based on plainsong themes.

His claim to fame, though, rests squarely on his *Requiem*. To those who say it copies Fauré, I would give Brahms's reply to the kind person who pointed out the resemblance between the first theme of the last movement of his First Symphony and the 'Ode to Joy' in Beethoven's Ninth: 'Any fool can see that.' Duruflé's attitude seems to have been the same as Ravel's: that copying the best models, whether plainsong or Fauré, still allows your originality to show through – provided you have any, that is.

In this work the integration of modality with chromaticism, and indeed with various classical tonal procedures, reaches its apogee. In the 'Introit', as with Fauré, a single chromatic alteration is often enough to deflect the argument on to an unexpected path. Chausson again makes a brief appearance in the compulsive minor triads of the 'Pie Jesu'. But against these borrowings, the strength of the work lies in the masterly control of atmosphere. Within a relatively narrow textural range, there is not a dull moment in the *Requiem*'s 40 minutes or so. So many details, on the page, look obvious. And yet ... they take us, as Tennyson wrote in a different context, into 'that new world which is the old'.

Finally, 14 articles on the Big Three of modern French music, Messiaen, Dutilleux and Boulez, all of whom I had the pleasure and privilege of knowing. Interviews with Boulez were in English, those with Messiaen and Dutilleux are translated from the original French.

42 MESSIAEN AND THE JOURNEY TO A WORLD BEYOND

If Messiaen is known at all to some outside the music world, it is probably for his interest in birdsong. But looking back over his composing life, we can see that birds were but one in a continuously expanding ensemble of resources, many of which ran clean against the temper of the age and changed the face of 20th-century music.

He was born in Avignon on 10 December 1908, the elder son of Pierre Messiaen, an English teacher, and the poetess Cécile Sauvage. From there the family moved first to Ambert in the Auvergne and then, when Pierre enlisted in the Army in 1914, to Grenoble. The war years were formative for the young Olivier not least in that he spent many hours at the piano playing and singing operas by Mozart, Gluck, Berlioz and Wagner, and putting on Shakespeare plays in his toy theatre (favourites were *Macbeth*, 'because of the witches and Banquo's ghost', *The Tempest* and 'the greatness of the mad King Lear berating the storm and the lightning'). Even if such a taste for the extreme and the supernatural is not exactly surprising in a young boy, it was to last until his death in 1992.

Two areas in which he departed from the Parisian ethos of the 1920s and 30s were religion and time. While doubt must be cast on his later strong implications that 'being born a believer' must have been a particular act of God because neither of his parents was religious (his father certainly was), his determination to bring his faith into nearly everything he wrote did mark him out as different: music for the church and music for the concert hall were generally regarded as separate entities. As to time, his organ piece *Le Banquet céleste* may belong to the church, but its ecstatically slow tempo puts the very notion of pulse under threat – something he would soon take over into his music for the concert hall.

In the course of his studies at the Paris Conservatoire between 1922 and 1930 Messiaen won no fewer than 14 prizes, seven of them *premiers prix*. Not surprisingly, his teacher Paul Dukas was happy to recommend such a pupil to the publishers Durand, and in 1930 they brought out *Diptyque* for organ, the *Préludes* for piano and a set of *Trois Mélodies*. *Diptyque* is subtitled 'essay on earthly life and blessed eternity' and Messiaen indulges his taste for extremes in the contrast between the fast, tortured chromaticisms of the first section and the very slow, beatific calm of the second. The eight *Préludes*, which Messiaen always considered his true opus 1, contain similar contrasts, if not so sharply distinguished. A critic at the first performance of six of them in March 1930 praised the 'beautiful sonorities, light and lively rhythms, interesting counterpoint, much delicacy, and unexpected endings'. For all the echoes of Debussy and Ravel, and even of Dukas, there is no mistaking either the individual voice or the absolute self-confidence. Debussy is heard still more clearly in the *Trois Mélodies*, especially in the conversational style of the second, a setting of a poem by his mother, that reminds us of the impact the score of *Pelléas et Mélisande* had on the composer in 1919. This was the only time he set words other than his own.

His first notable public success came in February 1931 when the forward-looking conductor Walter Straram gave the first performance of his 'méditation symphonique', *Les Offrandes oubliées*. Here again we find extremes of language and of tempo, this time with two slow sections enclosing a fast one. The first section, representing The Cross, is marked 'full of misery, profoundly sad', and Messiaen described it as consisting of phrases 'of unequal length, interspersed with long groans in grey and mauve' – one of the earliest instances of him specifying orchestral colours. In the second section, Sin, we are 'driven by madness and the serpent's forked tongue'. Here Messiaen pays tribute to the 1920s 'machinist' style of Roussel and Honegger, as well as to *The Rite of Spring*. The final section, The Eucharist, for strings alone, returns to the calm of the first, with E minor now transformed into E major.

Another first performance in early 1931 was of *La Mort du nombre* for the unusual combination of soprano, tenor, violin and piano. Like some of Bach's cantatas, it is a dialogue between fear (tenor) and hope (soprano) and it can possibly be heard as the offshoot of Messiaen's unsuccessful attempts at the Prix de Rome. Certainly the ecstatic B major of the ending reflects his love of Wagner's *Tristan und Isolde*, which was to bear richer fruit later on.

That September he was appointed organist of the Trinité church in Paris and the first organ work he wrote after this was *Apparition de l'Eglise éternelle*. In applying for the post, he had assured the curé that 'it is important not to disturb the piety of the faithful by using chords that are too anarchic.' While not eschewing moments of dense chromaticism, the piece, consisting of a 'granite-like crescendo' and matching decrescendo, does at least offer the pious faithful open fifths and triads at the end of every phrase, underlining the eternal, primordial nature of these basic chords, and of the Church. More challenging for both performers and listeners is the *Thème et variations* he wrote for his new wife, the violinist Claire Delbos, but again the tone is overwhelmingly positive, the suave theme being put through its paces in the first four variations before emerging in the fifth into the sunlight, high on the E string.

Meanwhile Messiaen continued his practically lone efforts to bring religion into the concert hall (not that fellow workers in the cause were always welcome: after one of the early Paris performances of Stravinsky's *Symphony of Psalms*, Messiaen was heard shouting 'Stravinsky is dead!'). Following *Le Tombeau resplendissant* and *Hymne au Saint-Sacrement*, he began work on a set of four orchestral pieces entitled *L'Ascension* and then transcribed three of the movements for organ, replacing the orchestral 'Alleluia' movement with a toccata, 'Transports de joie'. The first movement is built up of regular ascents to the climax of a major chord, a pattern similar to that in *Apparition*. The second expresses the wish of the mass of believers to shuffle off this mortal coil. The unaccompanied lines are inspired by the general shape of plainsong alleluias without actually quoting any specific one. After the toccata, in the tradition of Widor and Dupré, the final slow movement, originally scored for strings alone, presents another example of extreme tempo contrast, while its ascent in pitch marks the culmination of a tendency held in check until this moment.

In the summer of 1935 Messiaen composed his next organ cycle, *La Nativité du Seigneur*, which he regarded as his 'most substantial work so far'. The reviews were laudatory, Henri Sauguet going as far as to say that here 'Olivier Messiaen has reached the highest level of religious expression that music can achieve.' The nine movements (nine being the number of maternity) are contemplations both of personages in the Nativity narrative (The Shepherds, The Angels, The Wise Men) and of inherent ideas ('Eternal Designs', 'God among us'). Some familiar features recur, such as the fast, loud/slow, soft contrast in the two sections of the fourth movement, 'The Word', and the toccata figuration in the final 'God among us'. This also contains an example of Messiaen's fascination with number: the quavers in the final peroration are grouped 2+2+2+3 (=9).

As a composer committed to elucidating the truths of the Catholic faith, he was not in general concerned to write music illustrating his private life. But the joy of his marriage, and then of becoming a father, did find expression in the 1930s in two song cycles, *Poèmes pour Mi* ('Mi' being his wife's familiar name) and *Chants de terre et de ciel*. In both, text and music grew symbiotically, the composer working at the piano and singing 'with my terrible composer's voice'. The first cycle (again, nine songs) moves from thanking God for the gift of his loved one, through a terrifying vision of Hell, and back through the march of the 'two sacramental warriors' to the open sensuality of his wife's arms around his neck as he awakes, and the final fulfilment of his prayers. The music of the second cycle, after the gentle opening song, is more dissonant and the reviews drove Messiaen to defend himself with some vigour, telling the critics they should wash their ears out! As in the previous cycle, the depths of anguish are reached, here in the fifth song, before consolation is finally granted.

For Messiaen, these two cycles were wholly religious works, since God is present in all things. This being so, he was uninterested in charges of eclecticism: he admired both Massenet and Schoenberg, so why not do homage to both? The two specifically religious works he wrote before the war display the 'soft' and 'hard' aspects of his style. *O sacrum convivium* is now one of his best-loved pieces, raptly contemplative, in his favourite F sharp major. But the organ cycle *Les Corps glorieux*, in fact not quite finished when Messiaen was called up, was destined to perplex more than just the pious faithful, especially in the second and last of its seven movements. On the page, 'The waters of grace' looks straightforward enough, but Messiaen's extraordinary registration conjures up sounds that surely no organ had ever produced before. In the last movement the main flute theme represents God the Son, the descending chromatic phrases in the pedal God the Father, and the free quasi-atonal rhapsodies of the right-hand part the Holy Spirit – the result, for all its theological orthodoxy, well representing the 'mystery' of the Holy Trinity.

Messiaen was called up into the army at the outbreak of war, was captured by the Germans and in July 1940 was transported to a camp in Silesia. In captivity he wrote his *Quatuor pour la fin du Temps*, definitively and appropriately turning his back on the Austro-German tradition of development and on all sense of striving or anxiety. The 'end' referred to was not that of captivity, rather it was the abolition of time itself, as proclaimed by the Angel of the Apocalypse. We feel this most powerfully in the wonderful cello and violin solos of the fifth and final movements (the latter being a transcription of the final section of *Diptyque*). The first performance, on 15 January 1941, was given to 400 prisoners in Hut 27B. Although some of the audience were puzzled by Messiaen's spoken introduction, of the performance itself he later wrote that 'I was never listened to with such attention and understanding.'

A few weeks later he was repatriated and took up a post at the Paris Conservatoire. *Visions de l'Amen* for two pianos was commissioned in 1943 and was the first work to profit from the scintillating pianistic technique of his young pupil Yvonne Loriod. Messiaen, as second pianist, gave himself the themes and, as it were, the warm body of the work, while Loriod was assigned the bells, birdsong and other virtuoso embellishments. As Nigel Simeone has pointed out, 'another consequence of the separation of musical material between the two pianos is that all the movements progress through accumulation.' The ultimate result in the last movement is the grand, overwhelming realization of the potential of the Creation theme in the first.

Messiaen continued in his next two works to bring the truths of Catholicism out into the wider world. His 20-year-old pupil Pierre Boulez was turning the pages for the vibraphone player at the first performance of *Trois petites Liturgies* in April 1945 and, although he had reservations about the musical vocabulary, he remembers that 'the impact of the sound itself was enormous.' Messiaen followed Varèse and Stravinsky (the links with *Les Noces* are unmistakable) in taking the emphasis away from the strings: he asks for them to be placed in the centre and their traditional position in front is taken by the percussion section, forming a kind of *gamelan*. The performance provoked another of the Parisian scandals, offending through the hermetic symbolism of

Messiaen's words, the old-fashioned pentatonic tunes and not least the overall lushness of the sound.

It was perhaps inevitable that, after *Visions*, he would write a solo piano work for Yvonne Loriod, and a month before the premiere of *Trois petites Liturgies* she played the *Vingt Regards sur l'Enfant-Jésus* to a mixed reception. Both his use of irregular rhythms and the music's complexity were criticised, but no one could doubt its passion and large-scale structural coherence, grounded in the key of F sharp major to which seven of the 20 movements are attached in varying degrees. Four cyclic themes also run through the work: a theme of chords, the theme of God (beginning of I), the theme of the Star and the Cross (near the beginning of II), and the theme of mystic love (near the end of VI). As in the *Visions*, the theme (of God) mysteriously adumbrated in the first movement rings out triumphantly in the last.

For his third and last song cycle, *Harawi*, Messiaen adopted the idea of a cyclic theme from the two previous piano works. This, initially composed as a 'thème d'amour' for incidental music to a play about Tristan and Isolde, is the basis of the three symmetrical pillars of the work, movements II, VII and XII (I being in the nature of an introduction). In 1945 Messiaen was becoming interested in Peruvian mythology and the word 'harawi' in Quechua means a love-song that ends in the death of the lovers. The text includes not only other Quechua words but many invented ones, designed to articulate and colour the vocal lines. It is at least possible that, like its two predecessors, this cycle refers to Messiaen's private life, and in particular to his wife Claire who was now suffering from mental illness; it has been suggested that the central 'Adieu' may be addressed to the beloved (the 'green dove' of the cycle) whom he saw gradually retreating from him.

He then pursued the love/death syndrome in his two following works, to make up what he called his 'Tristan trilogy'. Serge Koussevitsky had commissioned him to write a work for the Boston Symphony Orchestra with no constraints of length, size of forces, style or deadline. Messiaen responded with the *Turangalîla Symphony*, by far his largest work to date. The predominant mood throughout the ten movements is one of joy, but Messiaen later indicated that it was 'joy as it may be conceived by someone who has glimpsed it only in the midst of sadness' – perhaps a further reference to his personal predicament. The title is made up of two Sanskrit words: 'turanga' means 'time that flows'; 'lîla', 'play' or 'sport'. These refer to the rhythmic games that Messiaen plays, as always evading the regular and obvious. Easier to grasp for the listener are the three main cyclic themes: the 'statue theme' (loud thirds on trombones and tuba), recalling the brutality of old Mexican monuments; the 'flower theme' (gently curling clarinets); and the 'love theme', first heard complete in the sixth movement, where the 'garden of the sleep of love' clearly refers to Tristan and Isolde on their mossy bank in Act II of Wagner's opera.

This passage also lies behind the third panel of the Tristan triptych, the *Cinq Rechants* for mixed chorus, possibly not completed until early in 1949, in which Messiaen identified as sources both 'harawi' and the 'alba', a warning (like Brangaene's) to two lovers that dawn is approaching. Among other love myths, the work refers to those of Orpheus and Bluebeard. The composer's invented syllables here come to the fore, and once again the range from solo simplicity to ensemble complexity is enormous. Also there are fewer oases of tonality than in the two previous works: in the words of Christopher Dingle, 'Messiaen was about to attempt to escape his personal circumstances in a new way.'

'Today will be a big day in music,' said Koussevitzky on 2 December 1949, the day of the first performance under Leonard Bernstein of the *Turangalîla Symphony*. This was no doubt true, but Messiaen had already realized that for him it also marked the end of a road. The signpost towards the new direction was marked 'experiments'. These were rhythmic, melodic and timbral in nature. Gone were the grand gestures: all now was economy and concision. *Cantéyodjayâ* is a transitional piece, in that it uses themes from the Tristan trilogy. Most radical is *Mode de valeurs et d'intensités*, in which three twelve-note groups overlap, each one of the twelve having its own duration, intensity and mode of attack. This, together with *Neumes rythmiques* and the two pieces called *Ile de feu* (Papua New Guinea) provoked a whole group of young composers, including Stockhausen and Boulez, to investigate the possibilities of this revolutionary idea.

In retrospect, Messiaen had reservations about what he had started. His immediate response was to return to the familiarity of a specifically religious field, and to employ only those aspects of his 'new mathematics' that chimed with his overall message. As organist at the Trinité, he improvised constantly, and came to think that a lot of good ideas were being thus wasted. *Messe de la Pentecôte*, which he premiered during Low Mass at Pentecost 1951, brings together various features that were preoccupying him: rhythm, plainsong, birdsong, and religious symbolism, together with some motifs from *Turangalîla*. The five movements accompany the main silent actions of the Mass: the entry of the priest, the offertory, the consecration, the communion and the recessional. In the third movement, Messiaen takes the plainsong Alleluia for Pentecost, 'Veni sancte Spiritus', and extends and chromaticises its intervals, alternating it with two different refrains. In the final recessional, birdsong reaches its apogee in the 'chorus of larks', decorating the rhythmic games around it. If, in Messiaen's recording, the larks sing rather more slowly than the marking 'Vif' might suggest, this was, as he told me, because at the time of recording the organ wouldn't speak any faster!

In 1951 he combined writing for organ with some of his most abstruse mathematical experiments in *Livre d'orgue*. Its seven movements display a similar cross-symmetry to that in *Les Corps glorieux*. I and VII are concerned purely with compositional devices; II and VI share material, as do III and V; IV, 'Chants d'oiseaux' forms a uniquely melodious centre, though birdsong also appears in VII. Perhaps the most immediately impressive and striking movements are III, 'Les Mains de l'abîme', and VI, 'Les Yeux dans les roues', responding to the surrealistic visions of the Old Testament writers Habakkuk and Ezekiel. The 'abyss' also relates to the mountains of Messiaen's beloved Dauphiné, and to its extremes of height and depth. Messiaen gave the first French performance at the Trinité in March 1955, to an unexpectedly large audience of some 2,000 people. He himself lost two buttons off his overcoat in the crush.

Part of the regulation duties of teachers at the Conservatoire was to provide test pieces for the end-of-year exams, and for the flute one of 1952 he wrote *Le Merle noir*. This is in three sections, the second a slightly extended variation of the first, followed by a coda. Each of the main sections is divided into six subsections: piano atmosphere/bird cadenza/combined song/expanded octaves/chords + silent bar/ 'un peu vif' with trills. In the coda Messiaen uses 12-note rows, transposed up a semitone each time they occur, producing an effect of increasing excitement.

The 1950s were the decade of Messiaen's deepest explorations of birdsong, most extensively in the piano cycle *Catalogue d'oiseaux*. In his next orchestral work, *Chronochromie*, birdsong assumes a more equal role among other musical material. In commissioning it, the Head of Südwestfunk Heinrich Strobel insisted on 'no *ondes Martenot*, no piano!' and so the piano is absent for the first time in one of his orchestral pieces since *L'Ascension* nearly 30 years before. The title combines the words 'chronos' meaning 'time' with 'chroma' meaning 'colour', since according to the composer 'the combinations of sounds and timbres, which are very complex, remain at the service of the durations, which they must emphasize through colouring them.' The overall quality of the work is massive and hieratic, vividly decorated with the sounds of mountain waterfalls. Birdsong is the total material of the sixth movement, where 18 separate voices are heard – at the first performance, together with boos and whistles. Messiaen complained that this was in fact the work's most charming movement …

In 1963 Messiaen's position in the musical world was finally recognized by the French Establishment, when the Minister of Culture, André Malraux, commissioned a sacred work for the dead of the two world wars, to be performed in the Sainte-Chapelle. Originally envisaged as a choral work, *Et exspecto resurrectionem mortuorum* was finally composed for wind, brass and percussion. While writing it, Messiaen admitted he 'surrounded himself with simple, powerful pictures: the stepped pyramids of Mexico, temples and statues of Ancient Egypt, Romanesque and Gothic churches.' The musical material ranges from an Indian rhythm symbolising the strength of the lion in the second movement, to the song of the Uirapuru (according to Amazonian legend, a bird you hear on your deathbed) in the third, to the 'enormous, unanimous, simple fortissimo' of the last.

The 18 movements of the organ cycle *Livre du Saint Sacrement* are divided into three sections: I-IV are acts of adoration before Christ, invisible but truly present in the Holy Sacrament; V-XI depict events in the life of Christ in chronological order; and XII-XVIII are meditations on liturgical mysteries. As Christopher Dingle has said, 'the emphasis seems to be on the awe and power of the mysteries being contemplated.' The brutality of VII and the 'walls of water' as the Red Sea is parted in XIII recall the raging Lear that had impressed the composer in childhood. At the other extreme lie the moments of repose, such as the gently repeated A flat major chords in VIII, and the plainsong for Corpus Christi that ends XI, as the act of transubstantiation is completed. Finally Messiaen signs off from his unique and all-embracing contribution to 20th-century organ music with the instrument's bottom C, ffff.

He never heard his last orchestral work, *Eclairs sur l'au-delà*, performed by the New York Philharmonic Orchestra on 5 November 1992, six months after his death. The work is a set of meditations on the Beyond and the heavenly Jerusalem. Never had his palette of sounds been so rich and varied, from the combination of muted and unmuted strings in V to the seven flutes and eight clarinets playing the songs of 25 birds in IX. The underlying duality of so much of Messiaen's music, between extremes of dynamics, tempo, language and texture, is summed up in the last two movements. From the dramatic, desperately striving music of 'The Way to the Invisible', we pass to the final movement where, as in earlier works such as *Visions de l'Amen* and *Trois petites Liturgies*, the tonality of A major symbolises the celestial light of Paradise. The journey has been accomplished. All searching, all striving is at an end.

43 MESSIAEN – ORNITHEOLOGY AND ALL THAT

According to the French writer Joseph Delteil, genius can be defined as 'the explosion of Nature in culture' – a definition well in line with the thinking of other French intellectuals such as André Gide, for whom Classical works in whatever field were beautiful only by virtue of their suppressed Romanticism.

Of course, the thesis is applicable not only to French artists, but to any true composer who, for example, ever tried their hand at a fugue. But it applies, I think, with particular force to Messiaen. For one thing, he was remarkably open in acknowledging the 'Classical' constraints he set upon his music; and for another, you'd have to be practically at death's door not to feel the impact of his Romanticism (no quotation marks).

In the past, this impact, and the explosion of Nature that regularly fuels it, have on many occasions proved too strong for the critics: as Messiaen said to me in an interview, after the premiere of the *Trois petites Liturgies* in 1945 'they emptied their dustbins over my head'. So it was good to find that the UK premiere of *Eclairs sur l'au-delà*, given by the London Symphony Orchestra under Kent Nagano on 21 November 1993, was greeted by widespread approval and joy, as well as with a huge ovation in the hall itself – after a silence that we were all reluctant to invade. The work, it is true, contained nothing startlingly new on the technical front. Presumably the composer felt that by his early eighties he had amassed quite enough techniques to see him through a work lasting a mere 75 minutes or so. It was at least mildly amusing to hear him juxtaposing pure triads and the impurest of dissonances, as he'd been doing for at least 50 years, and to realise that by following his instincts he was now bang up to date as a 'postmodernist'!

Even a quarter of a century later, it is still perhaps too early to say how new it was on the spiritual front. His widow called the work 'a set of meditations on the beyond and the heavenly Jerusalem', and as such it has clear forbears going back to *L'Ascension* of 1932. My own belief is that a great creative artist like Messiaen, who remained an adherent to a single faith illumining his music, must inevitably have new things to say about the Beyond on which, it is fair to assume, he meditated every day of his life. We can recognise this at least on some instinctual level, as the audience obviously did. The performance indeed blew holes in Messiaen's practice of explaining the technical details of his works. It didn't matter, surely, whether the birdsong came from Mars or whether the rhythmic patterns were those of Maori fertility rites: here, unmistakably, was a great composer at the height of his powers, producing a *summa theologica et ornithologica* of surpassing beauty and conviction.

Eclairs might in fact be a good work to put before someone wanting a way into Messiaen's music, since it has a directness, a clarity and above all a Romantic glow which had, perhaps, been lacking to some extent in the works since the opera *Saint François d'Assise*. But it's always dangerous to think you've got a great composer buttoned up. In Messiaen's case, there remains much real thinking to be done, some of which will involve not taking all his remarks about his music, or indeed his life, at face value.

I have a theory that much of Messiaen's apparently compulsive explaining (which both Boulez and Poulenc found so curious and, in Poulenc's case, irritating) was designed as a kind of smokescreen. All the things he says about his music are true, as far as they go, but really that's not very far. Any reasonably literate musician can test this by writing eight bars or so according to the dictates of Messiaen's *Technique de mon langage musical*. The result may be accurate in terms of interval, rhythm and texture. But I would put good money on the chances that it will also lack that extra something which no technical handbook in the world could possibly provide, and which Messiaen himself had no intention of divulging, most probably because he himself didn't know what it was.

It would be a brave critic, then, who stepped masterfully into this particular breach; as I've suggested, in another 50 years we may be able to see things more clearly. For the moment I'll put forward, in the most tentative way, two possible contenders. The first is, simply, melody. Here, I feel, the smokescreen has been pretty successful. Nearly all Messiaen's explanations have been about rhythm, harmony and colour, and where melody has been an issue he has tended with his usual modesty to bow out and give the birds all the credit. But when I recall my favourite Messiaen moments, the melodic line is always extremely strong: the wonderful Hollywood tune of the last movement of *Turangalîla*, the chorales of *La Transfiguration*, the more lyrical moments in 'Dieu parmi nous', practically the whole of *Poèmes pour Mi* and *Trois petites Liturgies*, and now the hypnotic final movement of *Eclairs*. Why was he so cagey about melody? Was it just modesty?

To try and give a tentative answer to this, I move on to my second contender for that 'extra something'. By his own admission, Messiaen was a naïve composer [see also Boulez, article 47]. More than that, he spoke up for naivety as one of a composer's most valuable possessions, and one very hard to hold on to in the hullabaloo of the modern world. We might expect then that in Schiller's well-known distinction between 'naïve' and 'sentimental' artists, Messiaen would prove wholly unsentimental. This turns out to be not entirely the case. True, he does not conform wholly to any of the three subdivisions Schiller makes within the sentimental category: he is not elegiac, mourning the past (Ravel's *Le Tombeau de Couperin*), he is not satirical, attacking the present (Koechlin's anti-serial antics in *Les Bandar-Log*), and for the most part he is not idyllic, proposing an ideal as being the present in the knowledge that it is in fact a fiction (British post-World War I pastoral *passim*), even though in life he loathed cities and hankered after an existence on some desert island, no doubt with an inexhaustible supply of pens and manuscript paper. But he does fall firmly within Schiller's overall view of the sentimental artist as being reflective and critical. From the testimony of his Conservatoire pupils we know what a profound knowledge he had of the works of the past, being able, for instance, to play the whole of *Pelléas et Mélisande* by heart.

Even without this testimony, a look at the beginning of Chapter 8 of the *Technique de mon langage musical* shows us one of his fairly rare statements about melody, as well as the cast of his melodic thinking. The chapter begins with the words 'Melody has primacy. May melody, which is the noblest element of music, be the principal aim of our researches.' He goes on to say that his teacher Paul Dukas often spoke of intervals and of their choice, and quotes his own two favourites of the time (1944): the descending tritone and the descending major sixth, according to him a favourite of Mozart's. He then explains how he 'treats' the opening phrase of *Boris Godunov* by turning a descending fourth into a tritone. This is emphatically 'sentimental' behaviour.

And yet, as I say, it is neither elegiac, nor satirical, nor idyllic. This sentimental behaviour is, we might say, turned to naïve purposes. But then can the purposes remain naïve if they are subject to this kind of aesthetic engineering, just as *Boris* tritonalised no longer bears the same modal, peasant flavour? I have no ready answer to this. Suffice to say that some of Messiaen's melodies are sentimental in this sense, others are naive. I have reason to believe that he was the possessor of a naïve melodic strength long before his more sentimental self turned to the past to enrich its store. The French critic Gustave Samazeuilh, reviewing a performance of Messiaen's failed cantata for the 1931 Prix de Rome, *L'Ensorceleuse* (*Le Courrier musical,* 1 August 1931, p. 461), spoke of the work's 'poetical construction which gave proof of an inventive gift of rare quality, especially in the duet, the exquisite inflections of which would have delighted Emmanuel Chabrier.' And I feel it is typical of Germanic rigour that Schiller should talk of artists falling into either one of his categories or the other. Why not both?

That Messiaen's artistic life was not all plain sailing is clear from the extraordinary rift between the expansively colourful *Turangalîla* and the narrowly intellectual *Mode de valeurs*, completed within 12 months of each other in the late 1940s. Even though he came to have reservations about *Mode de valeurs*, this does not alter the fact that he felt the need to write it at the time. Delteil's 'explosion of Nature' is, after all, bound to give any artistic genius a headache from time to time. It's all too easy to label Messiaen, and then stop thinking about him – one can see the Reader's Digest heading : 'Unforgettable Olivier Messiaen, Birdman of the Dauphiné'. There's rather more to him than that. And if *Eclairs* is indeed a *summa*, as I've suggested, albeit not quite a final one, then it should serve to remind us what a quantity of materials there was calling for summation. There's the Messiaen sound too, and indeed the Messiaen silences ... Altogether, no one had written this sort of music before. It is to be doubted whether they will again.

This interview was recorded in a tiny, none too clean room in the bowels of Brent Town Hall. Messiaen was undaunted by his surroundings: like many great men, he carried his atmosphere with him.

44 MESSIAEN AT 70 – AN INTERVIEW

March 1978

Roger Nichols: Maître, a very general question first of all: if you look back over your career, can you distinguish any sort of curve or pattern? I'm thinking for instance of Beethoven and his so-called 'three periods'.

Olivier Messiaen: No, I don't think I have experienced this curve. There are a number of reasons for this: first, that I have never renounced my past. We are told that our past follows us and, as far as I'm concerned, that is absolutely true. I have held on to everything that I have done in the past, not only the works but the procedures, the attachments and the enthusiasms. Then again there is the fact that I have a class at the Conservatoire, and am surrounded by numbers of very young people. This has made me keep abreast of all techniques, languages and schools of thought, and I have been brought face to face with a quantity of schools and of different aesthetics. So there has been no curve. Instead, I possess a very rich, well-supplied ensemble of materials which is growing all the time, but without renouncing what has been in the past and without ignoring what will be in the future.

RN: A rather more specific question: the 1920s were the time of Les Six, and perhaps I'm right in thinking that the often frivolous nature of their music is not much to your taste, but at the time, when you were an adolescent, were you attracted by their work?

OM: I can't entirely agree with that description. Their music was *not* frivolous. I imagine you are thinking of the music of Poulenc, which was always attractive but not always frivolous. Milhaud and Honegger were also in the group, and they were *very* serious-minded, you could even say powerful composers. My first contact with the group was perhaps a little unusual. It came through the daughter of one of my father's friends who gave me Honegger's *King David*. This was a very important present. I loved this work a great deal, and spent a lot of time playing it and studying the score. Then there were several works by Milhaud that I was very fond of: for instance, I admired *The Choephori* very much.

RN: The vocal effects?

OM: Yes, but all that's a long time ago. I was very young! At that time they were the avant-garde. I was lucky enough when I first came to Paris – I was 12 – to be present at the premiere of Milhaud's *L'Homme et son désir* [6 June 1921]. This was at the Théâtre Pigalle, which no longer exists. The music was truly polytonal with four small orchestras and four simultaneous sets, and four different scenarios being acted out at the same time. It was something highly original for the period and, even though I was only a small boy, it made a great impression on me.

RN: Much the same sort of criticism has been levelled against Poulenc's religious music as against yours – charges of vulgarity.

OM: No, Poulenc has not suffered criticism, or only very little, but as for me! I have had to put up with the most terrible criticism! I was abused and slandered by music critics for 20 years, particularly from 1944-45 onwards. From then on, the critics became very hostile. For ten years they took their dustbins and emptied the contents on my head. It was terrible!

RN: The *Trois petites Liturgies*?

OM: And then *Turangalîla*. Everything.

RN: The *Cinq Rechants*?

OM: Not so much. It wasn't just the music and the musical aesthetics that made them angry with me. They were angry with me because I was a believer, because I was a Catholic, because I loved colour and because I was full of life. To see someone who was a believer, who had faith, who loved life and colour and who believed in the Resurrection – they couldn't stand it. Why, I don't know. I've never understood, but it infuriated them for a very long time. Then they calmed down, and even apologised to me – in public. It took ten years for their tempers to cool, but then they became very friendly.

RN: To appreciate fully the power and beauty of your music, should listeners be aware of its theological bases, even be sympathetic towards them?

OM: To understand my music, you must first of all be a musician! Of course there are listeners who are not musicians, and naturally, if you're going to understand the Mysteries of Christ, on which my music attempts to be a commentary, it will be easier if you're a believer. To understand the timbres, the harmonies and the sound-complexes of my music, you must love colour. You must be sensitive to colour and, if possible, you must understand the connection between sound and colour.

Then there is one other thing for which I have been greatly criticised: I am an ornithologist, and I have noted down birdsong all my life. Many people of course don't understand birds because they have never seen them and never heard them. Perhaps in England the situation is more fortunate, because there are little gardens everywhere, and at least you have the robin who sings and can be heard, but in France the French who live in cities have never seen anything except sparrows. They're not interested because they think a bird goes 'pi-pi-pi-pi' and that's all. In fact birdsong is *very loud*, its melodies are very loud and very powerful. A bird in the forest sounds very loud – like a clarinet or a trumpet!

All these things have led to my music being called 'incomprehensible', but I believe that even people who are not experts, who are not musicians, and are not interested in theology or ornithology, should be affected in some way if the music is sincere. When a piece of music is sincere, when it expresses an emotion faithfully, those who hear it get something from it. Maybe they don't do it consciously, but even so they receive a message that touches them. For me, that's the important thing. They're moved: that's what counts.

RN: And that goes for rhythm and ... ?

OM: Yes, for everything,

RN: We seem to have reached the birds already! Are you surprised that contemporary composers haven't made use of them?

OM: Ornithology is a relatively recent discipline. No one else has ever studied birdsong: other people have recorded it on disc and tape, but I am the only person who has really notated it. It's a very difficult job for a composer. Ornithologists are experts in their own field, but they're not trained in music and can't take down musical notation. It was pure chance that I became interested – I didn't do it on purpose – but in the end, when I'm dead and my music, my researches into rhythm, all that is completely forgotten, perhaps there will still be people to say I was of some use in developing the science of birdsong notation.

RN: You've said that you don't use a tape recorder. Is that true?

OM: Yes and no. I'm a man very much of the Middle Ages and at the same time very modern. I loathe my own time and I loathe cities. I would rather have been born in the Middle Ages or on a Pacific island, but all the same I have brought myself up to date. For example, when I made my first studies of birds, I used to cover the ground on foot, and it was very uncomfortable. If I wanted to work on the slope of a mountain, say, or down on the plain or round some pools, I would have to walk 10 or 15 kilometres, and when I got to the place where I wanted to work, it was too late, I was too tired and couldn't do anything. Now my wife takes me in the car, and obviously the whole business is quicker. I get there early, at 4am, without being tired. My wife follows me with a tape recorder. I make one notation on the spot with all the variations, and my wife makes a tape recording which is less varied than mine, but which captures everything exactly. Then I make a second notation from the tape recorder which is more exact but less artistic. In life generally, reality is something that changes and varies, but the tape recorder is very exact. So I always have my two notations, one exact and one more artistic, and I mix the two.

RN: You say that, when you listen to music, you 'see internally' certain colours. Does this connection between sound and colour guide you when writing your works?

OM: Yes, it's very important to me. After World War I, in 1918 my father and mother came to Paris, and they took my brother and myself all over the city – to the theatre, the Opéra, the Comédie-Française, the Louvre, and also to churches and especially to the Sainte Chapelle. The stained glass windows of the Sainte Chapelle were for me something amazing! I have never forgotten them. Much later, 50 years later, when André Malraux commissioned *Et exspecto resurrectionem mortuorum*, he said to me, 'Where do you want the first performance to be?' I replied, 'In the Sainte Chapelle.' The first performance took place at 11am one morning in May. The sun was shining through the windows on to the instruments, turning them red, blue, violet ... It was wonderful!

RN: And the next performance was at Chartres.

OM: Yes, but it was more beautiful in the Sainte Chapelle. Chartres was too large.

I think all living beings feel some sort of link between the senses. When you eat a good meal, you don't taste it only with the tongue. You taste it also with your nose. It's even truer for wine: for wine and liqueurs, the bouquet is just as important as the taste. If you have a cold, it's not so good. There are links too, I believe, between sight and hearing. There's certainly a link in my own case – I'm not ill, I'm in perfectly good health – but there is a link, and what is more, this link has an effect on the intellectual level.

Whenever I hear a sound or look at one in a score, I think of colours. Obviously, when I'm composing they come through very strongly, and I try and put these colours into my music. When I think of chords and sound-complexes, they carry with them combinations of colours. I have a theory: a sound-complex has *one* colour – a complicated colour or a simple colour, but it has one. If you transpose it a semitone, it's another colour; if you transpose it a tone, it's another colour again. So each sound-complex has twelve colours, but when the colours reach an octave from the original pitch, they repeat themselves. As you go up in octaves, the colours become brighter; as you go down in octaves, they become darker.

RN: So these colours are useful to you as a harmonic guide when you are composing?

OM: Yes, extremely useful, but of course I'm sure that in this feeling for colours and in the choice of them there's always something personal. On the most general level, there are obviously violent harmonies which are red and gentle harmonies which are blue, but the detail varies according to the person. I often asks these sorts of questions in my class. Some of my pupils laugh and think I'm mad, others say 'Yes' out of politeness and don't believe a word of it, but there are some who reply truthfully and in general they agree with regard to the principal colours. I think these connections are valid for all music by all composers. Certainly, classical tonal music is not so highly 'coloured' (apart from Scarlatti and Mozart who employed chromaticism). There are colours in Mozart's G minor Symphony and in the Commendatore's Supper Scene in *Don Giovanni*. Even in the first movement of Beethoven's Pastoral Symphony there are some coloured moments. You find colours in romantic music – Chopin, Wagner. As well as orchestral colours there are colours of harmony, of sound-complexes. Unfortunately, almost all contemporary music (Schoenberg's in particular) lacks colour. It is grey music. That's not a criticism: they may be masterpieces, they may be very beautiful, but they are grey music.

RN: But a lot if it is very chromatic ...

OM: Yes, too much so. Colour comes from a choice of chromaticism. If you play a cluster, you play all the notes at once and there are no colours. You get grey or black – colours are absent. To produce colours, you must suppress something. For example, that yellowy-orange sweater you're wearing, that colour absorbs certain rays and reflects others. It's the same with a chord: if you have 11 notes out of the 12 or 10 notes out of the 12, that produces a colour.

RN: And Debussy?...

OM: He is *very* highly coloured. His textures may be soft, light, hazy, but there are still colours. In the case of those composers who pile on the chromaticism, like Schoenberg, there are other qualities, but there is no colour. On the other hand, one very modern composer, Ligeti, produces colours, simply for the reason that his sound-complexes are not entirely chromatic and they move. You get moving colours, and in fact as coloration the result is very beautiful.

RN: And for you this movement is circular or ...

OM: In general, the shapes I see are spirals, like an S or like an 8. There are others – flower shapes, star shapes and shapes which don't exist in the outside world.

RN: You have always written the texts of your vocal music yourself, apart from the second of your *Trois mélodies* ...

OM: ... which is based on a poem by my mother. As you know, my mother was a very great poet, and she wrote something which was extraordinary, I would say almost unique in the annals of feminine literature. She wrote a poem of maternity, and not a poem of maternity for a child who had been born. No, for a child who was yet to be born. That too, I believe, has had an influence on my life, but it's an exclusively feminine emotion, so I have never dared to set it to music. I'm preparing a record at the moment on which this poem will be spoken by Gisèle Casadesus, one of the finest actresses in France, very sensitive, with a wonderful voice, and I'm accompanying her on the organ very quietly. [*L'Ame en bourgeon*, Erato STU 71104] I didn't intend to produce a finished 'work'. There's no question of that. The whole thing is very unobtrusive, but it is the best improvisation of my whole life, because it's a very beautiful poem, and I was deeply moved. On the record it comes before, during and after the poem.

RN: But apart from this improvisation and the second *Mélodie*, you have written all your own texts.

OM: Yes. I'm no poet, but I found it convenient. That way I could underline the rhythms of the music.

RN: In the *Poèmes pour Mi*, for instance, how did you set about it?

OM: I wrote the words at the same time as the music. I was at the piano, I sang the words, and if there was a syllable which was awkward for the voice, I changed it. Since I was the author, there was no problem.

RN: And the same for *Harawi* ...

OM: ... and for the *Cinq Rechants*. In that case, I made use of percussive phonemes and syllables which threw the rhythms into relief. And for the opera I'm working on at the moment [*Saint François d'Assise*] I've written the scenario, the text, designed the scenery, the costumes, everything myself. That way I'm entirely on my own.

RN: With your non-vocal works, does each one demand its own methods, or have you any set formula?

OM: I have no formula. I compose when I want to, and when I'm not in the mood, I don't compose.

RN: Do you make sketches?

OM: Yes, a large number. For the orchestral works, I generally make a first draft which contains just the music. Then I do a second draft with some of the orchestration, but considerably condensed on two, three or four staves, and then after that I write the full orchestral score. That means three versions at least. The opera is a more complicated business, as I'm in charge of the text, the décor, the costumes and the music. Everything fits in together. I believe Wagner worked the same way.

45 DEBUSSY AND MESSIAEN

There have been one or two composers in the 20th century who liked to think they were inventing music from scratch. Olivier Messiaen was never under such illusions. His relationship with a host of earlier composers was rich and complex, involving wholesale borrowing, stylistic imitation and especially amalgamation of the woof of one material with the weft of another to produce a texture that was pure Messiaen.

Together with Mozart, Debussy was the composer he loved and revered the most. In Messiaen's case, the two emotions were, I think, distinct. He loved Ravel's music too, but I cannot imagine him speaking of any Debussy work in the way he did of the slow opening solo of the slow movement of Ravel's G major Piano Concerto, as '*massenetising* a tune Fauré might have turned out on an off day'. It becomes clear from all that Messiaen said and wrote of Debussy that for him the older master could do no wrong.

We know of two crucial early contacts with Debussy's music, even if Messiaen spoke far more often of one than of the other. In his interviews with Claude Samuel, he remembers getting to know the piano *Estampes* as a boy before the end of the First World War. Although he doesn't develop the point, two features about the first piece in the set, 'Pagodes', must strike anyone who knows Messiaen's music even moderately well: Debussy's imitation of the gamelan orchestra he had heard at the Paris Exhibition in 1889, and the new use he makes of musical space – only at the end of the second piece, 'La soirée dans Grenade', does he break out from two on to three staves, but this expansion is already hinted at over and over again in 'Pagodes'. The *Estampes* as a whole, which set the seal on French so-called Impressionist piano writing after Ravel's isolated *Jeux d'eau*, were a wonderful lesson in keyboard spacing, which itself has always played a large part in what Messiaen calls 'colour'. For him, Debussy remained one of the great colourists in music and he was delighted to find that they shared a favourite colour: violet.

His other early contact with Debussy has been much discussed and analysed, not least because the composer himself defined it as a turning-point in his life. For Christmas 1918 his harmony teacher in Nantes, Jehan de Gibon, presented him with a score of *Pelléas et Mélisande*. It was, as Messiaen later admitted, an extraordinary gift for a provincial music teacher to have given, 'an unplayable work written by a semi-lunatic' (in an autograph draft of a letter that Christmas to his grandmother, the young Olivier mentions it first, before the halberdiers and mediaeval Breton peasants for his toy theatre!). He later described it as a 'bomb', the fallout from which was to be scattered over his entire career. In at least two cases, the influence of *Pelléas* is combined with that of Debussy's beloved *Boris Godunov*: in the first and subsequent pieces of *La Nativité du Seigneur*, the ubiquitous curling four-note phrase (up-down-up) with which the cycle opens is derived from the openings of both operas, while in Messiaen's late opera *Saint François d'Assise* the name role assimilates the 'vigour' of Golaud with the 'declamatory solemnity' of Boris.

On one occasion Messiaen defined himself as 'ornithologist' and 'rhythmician'. The first of these activities seems, on the surface, to owe absolutely nothing to Debussy's example, although much to the 18th-century clavecinistes and even to Ravel. Messiaen defended Debussy's apparent lack of interest in birds on the grounds that he had already done enough in the way of bringing Nature into his music. We should also bear in mind that Debussy died at 55 and who can say what he might have written had he lived for another ten or 20 years? At all events, Messiaen's description of birdsong as 'free, anonymous music, improvised for pleasure' and his admission that 'for me, the only music is that which has always existed in the sounds of Nature' bring us close to Debussy's letter over the early rehearsals of 'Ibéria' when, after a sticky start, conductor and orchestra 'have consented to be less earthbound and to take wing somewhat...It sounds as though it's improvised'. This joint search for 'la liberté' in music, much like Golaud's for 'la vérité', was probably doomed never to be wholly satisfied, but the search had to go on nonetheless.

Both composers were only too well aware of the paradox that freedom for a composer comes only through the acquisition of a technique. In this respect it is interesting to note that not only were they both very highly trained at the Paris Conservatoire, but at closely parallel ages: Debussy from ten to 21 (1872-1884), Messiaen from ten to 22 (1919-1931). It also seems likely that both men underwent a kind of compositional crisis in middle age, Debussy around 1911 after *Le Martyre de Saint Sébastien*, Messiaen around 1949 after the *Turangalîla Symphony*, provoked to some extent by an awareness of the immensity of their own techniques (what Debussy referred to as 'le coutumier métier', which could be relied upon to get you out of tight corners, but at what cost to the work as a whole?). Where Debussy turned for help to *Petrushka* (see the second book of *Préludes*, published in 1913), Messiaen chose to reinvent himself with the novel processes of the piano piece *Mode de valeurs et d'intensités*, as sparse and abstract as *Turangalîla* had been lush and subjective.

But for both men at all times, when routine aridity threatened, Nature was always on hand to offer help. The equation between Nature and nurture can be summed up in a very Debussyan antithesis that Messiaen gives in one of his books of conversations. Describing a tree, he claims that it possesses 'une logique fantaisiste, une fantaisie logique', a logic informed by fantasy, a fantasy governed by logic , (though the French typically leaves the participles unexpressed!). Neither for Debussy nor for Messiaen could there be any question of abandoning technique and, in that horrid phrase of some years ago, 'letting it all hang out'.

In this search for a freedom that nonetheless was subject to logic, both composers turned to rhythm. In calling himself a 'rythmicien', Messiaen meant, not someone who had 'got rhythm' in the jazzy sense and still less someone whose music was rhythmic in the manner of waltzes and marches, but someone who saw it as his job to explore the unknown possibilities of rhythm as a structural device – and in Messiaen's own case, even as a sensual one. Stravinsky famously referred to Debussy as having enlarged the boundaries of the permissible in the empire of sound, and for Messiaen some of Debussy's rhythmic discoveries were indeed keys to a whole new empire.

Two of these in particular are worth mentioning. It had been a general rule for hundreds of years until roughly the end of the 19th century that where two notes were tied, whether over a barline or within a single bar, a longer note would be followed by a shorter one. To reverse this relationship was to set up rhythmic insecurity to a greater or lesser extent. Debussy happily seized on this procedure to drown the insistence of a regular beat, possibly to render his music 'flou' (blurred or hazy) or at least to make it unpredictable. For Messiaen, too, the tyranny of the barline at times became oppressive, and his explorations of Indian rhythms show a parallel concern with rhythm in its own right, not tied down to a regular pulse. In his Conservatoire composition class, Messiaen also made much of Debussy's use of 'irrational' values – that's to say, groups of 5, 7, 11, 13 etc – and, rather unexpectedly, saw Debussy in this respect as a link between Chopin and Varèse. Messiaen's own use of irrational rhythms, while rarely approaching the complexity of a Brian Ferneyhough, is often quite taxing enough for the player, as in the very opening bars of the *Messe de la Pentecôte* where not only do we find a 3-against-2 but a group of 5 within it. To make matters worse, as Dame Gillian Weir once confided to me [see article 48], Messiaen used to insist that the passage had to be not only accurate but phrased musically as well! If this seems to take us some way from the relatively innocuous rhythms of Debussy's *Syrinx* for solo flute, we should observe the beautiful, and prophetic, group of 5 quavers in the penultimate bar of that piece …

The two composers did, of course, differ over a number of topics: Berlioz, for instance, admired by his fellow Dauphinois Messiaen for his command of colour and space, but provoking no more than grudging respect from Debussy. But there was more to unite them than to divide. In conclusion, I cannot do better than quote two little vignettes relayed by students of Messiaen's Conservatoire class, both concerning his playing of *Pelléas* on the piano – from the full score, naturally. First, of how wonderful the chords, especially the sevenths and ninths, sounded in his hands, even on the clapped-out pianos of the classroom. And secondly, of him suddenly stopping at one point in the opera and walking round and round the piano; 'I can't go on,' he said, 'it's too beautiful'. Both are, I think, a salutary reminder that Messiaen's own music, for all its complexity (but never complication), rests on his profound feeling for the beauty of God's creation in every possible domain. As for his organ works, despite the lack of any direct Debussyan model they are not the least nor the least beautiful of Messiaen's musical children.

46 RAVEL AND MESSIAEN – ACCORDS AND DISCORDS

In his article 'De la procession Debussy-Ravel', published in *La Syrinx* in February 1938, Messiaen wrote of the two composers:

> But then, there is *Pelléas*. There we come across a wall, a brutal, inexorable separation. The two men turn their backs on one another. *Pelléas* is truth through symbols, it is the unheard expression of the subconscious, it is the unhesitating decipherment of that exquisitely mysterious manuscript that is the human soul. Debussy – the shaper of the impalpable – possessed that powerful rhythm of love and fate that we find only in the prophets who sum up the times that precede and follow their creations.

'The unheard expression of the subconscious'; 'that exquisitely mysterious manuscript that is the human soul'; 'Debussy – the shaper of the impalpable'. If, as Messiaen claims, *Pelléas* represents a dividing line between Debussy and Ravel (even though this goes against Ravel's acknowledged passion for the opera), then it follows that the younger composer can in turn be defined as 'always aware (of himself, of what he does)', 'not overfond of mysteries and shadows' and 'a lover of the palpable'. We could even sum up this difference in the performing styles of the two on the piano: Debussy with his deep touch (Madeleine Milhaud who, as a young girl before the First World War played the first *Arabesque* to Debussy and heard him play, remarked, as did others, that his fingers seemed to melt into the keys so that you were unaware of hammers), Ravel with a touch that was dry, precise, not very attractive (his friend and pupil Manuel Rosenthal held his very low seat at the piano partly responsible). In this area, Messiaen's style as pianist was obviously far nearer to Debussy's than to Ravel's.

But the discords between Messiaen and Ravel are extremely various ... and combined with several accords, so that the situation is far from clear. A look at their musical backgrounds may be helpful.

Ravel's teacher Fauré used to give his pupils Massenet arias to copy, and so may be classed as following a certain 'French tradition', even if this, as evidenced between Rameau and Debussy, has been categorised by Pierre Boulez as a 'black hole'. Messiaen in his turn used, even if not often, to quote Fauré songs in his classes and was also known to sing bits of *Manon*. But here we find the first discord. In José Bruyr's second volume of *L'Ecran des musiciens,* published in 1933, he quotes Messiaen as saying, in an interview of October 1931, 'It seems to me inconceivable that Ravel has been able to take the Largo of his new [piano] Concerto seriously, this Largo that turns a passage of Fauré on an off day into Massenet.' Possibly Messiaen was expecting something more overtly impressive. If so, he was not alone: several reviewers thought 'Concertino' would have been a more accurate title for the work.

A second area of discord, albeit never openly expressed, was Messiaen's education at the hands of Paul Dukas. On the relations between Dukas and Ravel a great silence reigns – rather curiously, since both of them held in contempt the 'profane crowd' and exercised enormous care in writing their music, Dukas to the point of composing just one song and one piano piece between 1912 and his death in 1935. Ravel did go to Dukas's funeral, but this may just have been a case of 'good form'. No correspondence between them has been discovered. Mentions of Ravel's music in Dukas's letters are almost entirely critical, while the only one in the 700 pages of his collected writings comes in an article on Edouard Lalo: in parallel, the only mention of Dukas in Ravel's writings, in a letter of 26 March 1908 to his friend Cipa Godebski, occurs in a response to Pierre Lalo's review of the first performance of *Rapsodie espagnole* in which the critic 'flings a compliment my way : that my music doesn't resemble that of Paul Dukas. Heavens above, I do know that my virtues are not those of a Jew!' Not only does that make for uncomfortable reading today, it also flies in the face of Ravel's close attachments to many Jewish friends, not to mention his somewhat surprising espousal, in the 1930s, of the operas of Meyerbeer.

Such discord as existed, then, between Ravel and Dukas was more probably musical than personal. Some light may be shed by taking account of an outsider's view, namely Poulenc's. An attested admirer of Ravel's music (Ravel would give him hints about orchestration from time to time), Poulenc wrote to Armand Lunel in April 1937 on the visual aspects of opera, 'The vaults of [Dukas's opera] *Ariane et Barbe-Bleue* are deadly boring. And I don't mean the music. (I detest that of Dukas).' Again, writing to Pierre Bernac on 24 June 1944 about Messiaen, he says:

> When he invents his own form, as in *Visions* [*de l'Amen*], it's truly remarkable; in other passages that are more rigorously assembled, the influence of Dukas is baneful. I really don't think there's a worse one for everybody. Saint-Saëns's form, for instance, was able to act as a guide for Ravel. That of Dukas is a form based on forms.

It's not impossible therefore that Messiaen (even without reading these letters, he may well have picked up a general antipathy to Dukas's music that went beyond Poulenc), out of loyalty to Dukas responded sharply to a Ravel 'guided by Saint-Saëns' ... or by Massenet or Fauré.

Then there is the whole question of the 'return to classicism' : 'still the same old story', as Messiaen put it. He could accept *Le Tombeau de Couperin* and in any case he differentiated between Ravel and Ravelism which, as Dutilleux remembered all too well, was the accepted style at the Conservatoire in the 1930s. What he was against was the automatic, reach-me-down habits that stifled imagination. In his campaigning article 'Contre la paresse' (Against Laziness), published in *La Page musicale* on 17 March 1939 shortly before he began work on *Les Corps glorieux*, he wrote:

> Lazy, the artisans of sub-Fauré, sub-Ravel. Lazy, the pseudo-Couperin maniacs, the fabricators of rigaudons and pavanes. Lazy, the dreadful contrapuntists and their return to Bach who offer us, shamelessly, dry, gloomy melodic lines, poisoned by a semblance of atonality.

But, while distinguishing Ravel from Ravelism, Messiaen thought that, after *Daphnis*, Ravel moved away from his true gifts. Messiaen's pupil, the composer Alain Louvier, on discovering Ravel's Sonata for violin and cello, asked his teacher, 'What do you think about it?' To which Messiaen replied, 'I don't think anything ... As for Ravel, I forgive him because he wrote "Le Martin-pêcheur" with its chords.'

What Messiaen had no cause to forgive was Ravel's attachment to what the French call 'le merveilleux' – the land of legend and magic. *Ma Mère l'Oye* was in his kitbag during his time in the German prison camp, and George Benjamin also remembers him years later, playing it in class, the tears streaming down his face. As for *Gaspard de la nuit*, for Messiaen it was 'without doubt, together with the four books of Albéniz's *Iberia* and the Chopin *Etudes*, one of the summits of piano writing.' But to keep 'le merveilleux' from getting out of hand one needed a sense of structure, and here again Ravel and Messiaen were in accord. Ravel's formal concerns are well known and need little in the way of further exploration. But in the *Chansons madécasses* we find one formal procedure that was to bear fruit in Messiaen's music. In the second song, 'Aoua!', after a preliminary exhortation not to trust the white men, we hear of their promises to the natives; then, in the second bar of figure 2, the crucial 'et cependant ils faisaient des retranchements', 'and meanwhile they backtracked'. At this point, after 11 notes of the chromatic scale have been used, we suddenly hear, low in the left hand, octave C naturals – a note unheard until now. The effect is one of appalling menace.

There is no proof that Messiaen ever took this on board. But it is at least possible, in the light of what he told me in an interview [see article 44] about colour coming from the suppression of something. What he does not specifically mention is Ravel's technique of delaying the twelfth note in order to place it with formal, emphatic intention. But Messiaen himself does precisely this in 'Paysage', the second song of *Poèmes pour Mi*. The first three bars of the song, successively including two of the composer's 'modes of limited transposition' (3/1, then 2/2), give us all twelve notes except A natural: the text, 'The lake like a great blue jewel', is static. Then, in bar 4, this is contrasted with 'La route' (The path) – the poet's wife, Claire (Mi in the songs), can be heard as the way forward, and a plain, dynamic octave A points to their future together.

Although Messiaen never used the Fibonacci series to control rhythms or phrase lengths, in the way that, as Roy Howat has shown, Ravel did in 'Oiseaux tristes' and 'Alborada del gracioso' (I asked Messiaen directly, and he said, 'No. Instead I use the times of day', as he did in *Catalogue d'oiseaux* and elsewhere), his pupil Alexander Goehr records in his memoir 'The Messiaen Class', included in the volume *Finding the Key*, that:

> in analysing music, he implied that a sequence of absolute durations could be in its way as expressive as could be a melody of pitch

levels. So in 'Scarbo', from Ravel's *Gaspard de la nuit*, he drew our attention to the passage beginning in bar 121, which he analysed as a sequence of durations.

If, for simplicity's sake, we ignore the abrupt, staccato interruptions and count just the durations of the held notes in terms of quavers, we arrive at the sequence: 29/23/18/11/8/8/11/8/11/8. The apparent stability registered by the number 8 is somewhat undermined by the 3/8 time signature ... It goes without saying that at least part of Ravel's idea in writing these unequal durations was no doubt to paint the portrait of Scarbo the malevolent dwarf, the master of surprise. But Goehr continues:

> Such ideas are of great importance for the understanding of Messiaen's own work. When he selects a sequence of durations, as for example in the *Mode de valeurs et d'intensités*, or in *Livre d'orgue*, he composes them by arranging them in a specific order. The result is to be understood as a kind of melody of duration, coloured by chords and repeating figuration. In this way time is 'coloured', as is implied by the title of his – in my estimation – greatest orchestral composition, *Chronochromie* (1956-60).

At the other end of the musical scale, Messiaen had no liking for jazz and thought that 'the poetical, thoroughbred figure of Maurice Ravel was spoilt in his final years by those dealings with jazz that really had nothing in common with his personal affinities'. From the point of view of construction, there was also a question of consistency. Ravel knew perfectly well that the more traditional critics demanded a certain 'stylistic purity', which was exactly what was missing from *L'Enfant et les sortilèges*. As he wrote to Roland-Manuel on 30 August 1920:

> I can certainly confirm to you that this work, in two parts, will be distinguished by a mixture of styles that will be judged severely – something that will leave Colette indifferent, and about which I don't give a f...

But what were Messiaen's views about consistency? Boulez, for example, has said he much prefers Messiaen's pre-war works and those of the 1950s and beyond to those, like *Vingt regards*, *Harawi* and *Turangalîla*, that mix tonal and non-tonal elements [see article 47]. But obviously

Messiaen did not see this mixture as any kind of problem. And when it came to birds, he felt at liberty to put their songs in wherever he liked ...

Ravel, although he never had claims to be any sort of ornithologist, was very fond of birds and imitated their songs wonderfully, even when he was in a nursing home in 1936, the year before his death. Of course, birdsong in French music has a long history, from Janequin's *Le Chant du rossignol* and *Le Chant des oyseaux* in the 16th century to Couperin's *Les Fauvettes plaintives* and Massenet's 'La Charmeuse' in *Thaïs*. But Ravel was probably the first to introduce birdsong that lay outside the surrounding tonality; initially in the 'Prélude' to the ballet score of *Ma Mère l'Oye*, then in the miraculous move from house to garden in *L'Enfant et les sortilèges*. There is no proof that the 17-year-old Messiaen went to the first Paris run of *L'Enfant* in 1926 nor, after his return from Germany, to the run of *Ma Mère* in 1942 (seemingly the first performances in the capital of the whole ballet since 1915), each at the Opéra-Comique. But given his love of Ravel's music both seem at least probable; and in any case, the scores were published. And could the swanee whistle (flûte à coulisse) in *L'Enfant* have given him a taste for the ondes Martenot? It's possible to hear the whole of that scene as a model for the slow movement of *Turangalîla*.

Then there is the process of modelling. For Ravel, imitation was a fruitful source. As he explained:

> If you have nothing to say, you cannot do better, while waiting for your final silence, than to say again what has been well said. If you do have something to say, that something will never appear more clearly than in your involuntary infidelity to the model.

One rather strange example of Messiaen taking Ravel as a model occurs in the movement 'Amen du jugement' in *Visions de l'Amen*, where the strident opening bar is clearly borrowed from the closing bars of 'Oiseaux tristes', transposed up an octave. In general, though, Messiaen often followed Ravel's example, as in the five-note 'Boris motif' found in *La Nativité*, the first of what Messiaen called his 'beloved melodic contours', taken from the opening of Mussorgsky's opera. Boulez recalled Messiaen frequently saying, 'I found this in that composer, but I used it this way; I turned the chords around so that the relationships were not the same, but the basis is the same.' [see article 47]

It's clear from these various interactions that the Ravel/Messiaen relationship was at times confused, even contradictory. Ravel, talking about Messiaen to Manuel Rosenthal, said simply, 'Ça fait moderne!' – not necessarily, I think, an unqualified compliment. Messiaen for his part found annoying the way in which, as he heard it, Ravel's music 'grew, and grew ... ' and then didn't finish. Really? *Rapsodie espagnole*? *La Valse*? *Boléro*?

Even so, Ravel obviously recognized that Messiaen's music, despite its 'modernity', was worthy of encouragement. The *Société musicale indépendante*, which Ravel had helped found in 1909, followed tradition in possessing a committee; but in fact Ravel's own opinion was decisive, and it was surely due to him that the society programmed two of Messiaen's works: *La Mort du nombre* in 1931, and the *Fantaisie burlesque* in 1933, played by Robert Casadesus. As for Messiaen's opinion of Ravel's music, we can register his disappointment that the latter more or less abandoned the world of the 'merveilleux' – maybe his adoption of jazz in *L'Enfant* was enough to neutralise its magical elements. But I think one can sum up Messiaen's attitude to his senior by completing the quotation that began this article. Having described Debussy as someone who practised 'the unheard expression of the subconscious' and who was 'the shaper of the impalpable', he concluded by saying, 'despite all Ravel's genius – *I repeat, genius* – Debussy took the better part – that of the heart; it cannot be taken away from him.' So, it's a question of 'the heart'. But what is the 'heart' of a composer? Discuss ...

47 INTERVIEW – PIERRE BOULEZ ON MESSIAEN

March 1986

RN: You were in Messiaen's class in 1944. Can you put into a nutshell what his teaching was like?

PB: His teaching, compared especially with that of the other teachers, was absolutely marvellous because it introduced us to the music, to the core of the music. He was teaching harmony in these classes, not composition at all at this time. When I studied harmony with other teachers before, I always had the impression I was doing exercises completely detached from any kind of musical thinking, musical thought, musical style, and you observed rules without any relationship to composition. And I remember very vividly with Messiaen, he immediately made the relationship between the exercises (which you have to write, of course) and the compositions you were studying; and therefore he was making us very aware of the evolution of the harmonic style over almost 3 centuries, from the 17th century to the 20th, and when he wanted to write an exercise, he analysed or played, for instance, some pieces by Schumann. He wrote the exercises himself and he set them in the style of Schumann, or in the style of Mozart, or of Beethoven or of Debussy. We could therefore make a coherent thing of why the writing was this way and what sort of evolution there was from Mozart to Beethoven to Wagner, from Wagner to Debussy. As a teacher he was very much aware, and he made us aware, of the links between different composers and the evolution of the language. And for me that was really a big discovery.

RN: You've spoken of the history of music, as made by the great composers, being a history not of conservation but of destruction. Has Messiaen destroyed anything?

PB: I think so. You destroy because you want to find your own personality through these people. I can compare that to the Japanese Kabuki theatre. There is a symbol of people, when they are dying, going through a transparent paper screen, and when they have gone through the screen they have gone beyond death. That's exactly what happens to a young composer. He has to go through, otherwise he will never acquire his own personality. Destruction does not mean that you hate something; you have to destroy it to possess it. I think Messiaen made us quite aware of that, especially when he said, 'I found this in that composer, but I used it this way; I turned the chords around so that the relationships were not the same, but the basis is the same'.

RN: Eastern music has been important to Messiaen. Thinking of Ravel's remark that you should always be unfaithful to your models, I wonder whether Messiaen has been unfaithful to his Eastern models in any particularly fruitful way?

PB: I think he has been unfaithful for the very good reason that he did not know much about it! When Messiaen met the rhythms of India for the first time, he didn't know the music of India – he had read about it in books, but at that time there was no possibility of listening to it because there were no recordings, or very few. I remember very well that we heard together, in 1945, a recording from Bali. Somebody who was working in the Guimet museum, which is a museum in Paris devoted to the music of Asia, had a collection, very rare, of discs which were absolutely unknown, and Messiaen discovered the music of Bali with us, with his students. The influence was right and at the same time wrong. But I find the wrong influence is the best! The influence of Asia on Messiaen was one he absorbed completely but which has very little to do with the original music. The more you know of Asian music, the more you can see that Messiaen's music is different from it.

RN: Messiaen's piano piece *Mode de valeurs* had a tremendous impact in the early 1950s, but do you feel it was a dead end?

PB: I don't think it was a dead end. It was a road he did not go on himself, I don't know why exactly. He discovered these abstract categories, these 'Modes de valeurs', but they were rather fixed – the categories did not move: they were established at the beginning of the work and went through to the end without any change. I think that if he'd wanted to, he could have manipulated this technique with much more flexibility, with much more invention in a sense. But he used it very episodically after that; in the *Messe de la Pentecôte*, in organ works especially and also in orchestral works, but it was no longer the core of his expression. With him there is also something in his vocabulary which is strange to me. You have sometimes the music on the one hand and the technique on the other. He explains, you know, 'Here the music is this and the technique is that.' Which is strange for me, because for me the music *is* the technique and the technique *is* the music. That's like two mirrors which are parallel. That's one aspect of his thinking I could never really understand.

RN: Some years ago Messiaen said: 'I fear nothing, not even the common chord.' Does this return to major triads, to C major, strike you as a bit strange?

PB: From the stylistic point of view there are some things I don't understand deeply. I don't want the work to be so homogeneous that it reflects everything – for instance, in Berg's music you find this acceptance of other things, of other worlds. It is mostly justified by the theatre. But you have this complexity of languages, of vocabularies. In Messiaen, it's not the complexity of one language superimposed on another one, but there is a very strong academic tradition and he is very comfortable with that. As you say, that's the C major, although C major is not his favourite tonality; it's much more A major or F sharp major, and in this sense he is very near to Liszt. For me there is no problem in the two worlds coexisting – a very complicated world, very atonal and sometimes very aggressively so without any polarization of any kind; and then you find beside that the kind of relationship even Debussy would not have written any more. For me it remains something rather strange. I don't see the coincidence very much. I prefer much more the works in which his vocabulary is modal, as in *Poèmes pour Mi* of 1936, rather than the works in which he uses extremely non-tonal devices and extremely tonal devices. All these works, like the *Vingt Regards*, *Harawi*, *Turangalîla*, are for me rather puzzling. The works of Messiaen I prefer are those from before the war, like the *Poèmes pour Mi*, and the works which are after this period, like *Messe de la Pentecôte*, *Chronochromie*, which are much more tense and homogeneous, much more forward-looking, I must say.

RN: Some people have felt that Messiaen's preference for block forms is a kind of opting out...

PB: That's the French defect. Generally French composers have always composed by blocks. Take a comparison from the 18th century, between

Rameau and Bach – I'm not speaking now of the quality or any difference of level, I'm speaking simply of the way of putting together a piece of music. In Rameau, most of the time, you either have a recitative which is completely free, or you have these arias, or ballets especially, which are absolutely square, in the worst sense of the word. In Bach, even in the lesser pieces, you have the game of the polyphony which enriches the metrical aspect in many and various ways. In the beginning Debussy also composed in blocks: you have ABA or ABCAB. Ravel the same. Debussy gets rid of that in his late works, in the second movement of *La Mer* and *Jeux* and the Sonata for flute, viola and harp. I think those are the only examples you can find of French *durchkomponieren*. Composing by blocks, in a way, for me, that's dilettantism in music - sometimes on a very high level, but still a kind of dilettantism.

RN: The late works of Debussy, like *Jeux*, are they the ones Messiaen particularly likes?

PB: No, he prefers much more the earlier works. In this sense he is very French, although he certainly will not recognise it – he is a kind of erratic French. The French composer he is nearest to is Berlioz, and Berlioz also composed by blocks. Definitely!

RN: Is Messiaen intent on going against the accepted French tradition?

PB: Not at all. He is very much aware of his predecessors, of the influence that Berlioz had on him and Debussy also. There is the question of French tradition. *Is* there a French tradition? I don't think so, not in music. In painting, that's another matter. The tradition, for instance, Debussy refers to – let's go back to Rameau and so on – that was an abolutely absurd idea because it was during the war and there was a kind of anti-Germanism so strong that they *wanted* to have a French tradition. There was a French tradition until the 18th century: Ecole de Notre Dame and all through the 16th century. In the 17th century it was already becoming very questionable. Then in the 18th you find one or two people, but after that there's a hole, a black hole... Berlioz has nothing to do with that, not at all. The strongest influence on Berlioz was that of Beethoven and Weber, and a lesser influence was Mozart. After that you have this series of composers who were French but not especially interesting, all the Opéra-Comique tradition (very second-rate, one must say) and then again you have Debussy, who escaped this tradition completely. But Debussy is born from Wagner much more than from anybody else, so that is again German. You always find the best French composers have something to do with the German tradition. They are against it, they are sometimes violently against it, but they absorb it anyway.

RN: And here we have Messiaen writing an enormous opera to his own libretto...

PB: ...a typical Wagnerian gesture.

RN: If I may turn to another work, were you at the first performance of the *Trois petites Liturgies* in 1945?

PB: Yes, I was. Not only at the first performance, but at the rehearsals. It was the year I was in Messiaen's class and we were invited to come to the rehearsals. I was in fact turning the pages for the vibraphone player. I had not heard much in the way of modern music at that time. The winter of 1944-45 was the first winter after the liberation of Paris and the first season in which things were played that were really 20th-century. During the war we heard Honegger, mainly, and that was it for modern music. So when we discovered Stravinsky, Bartók and then Messiaen, it was a big discovery, and I remember very well the sonority of the strings, of the vibraphone and all the percussion, that was a completely new world for me. I had reservations already about the vocabulary, but the impact of the sound itself was enormous.

RN: And was the first performance really a scandal?

PB: Not at all. On the contrary, the audience was very enthusiastic. No, the scandal was in the press. People at this time were still very much under the spell of Stravinsky, and not the Russian Stravinsky but the neo-classical Stravinsky. And of course it was a crime of *lèse-majesté* to write music like the music of Messiaen! To have such 'vulgar' music was absolutely impossible. But that was in the press, the audience were enthusiastic. The première of the *Vingt Regards* was another matter; it was a much longer work and some of the pieces were much more abrupt.

RN: As a conductor, do you find Messiaen's tempi at all problematical?

PB: The question of tempi in Messiaen is a funny one for me. In *Chronochromie* we had difficulties with the orchestra, not really with playing but with sight-reading, because sometimes you have a very slow tempo in small values (hemidemisemiquavers, for instance) and then you have a quick tempo with, say, crotchets and quavers. And optically it is exactly the contrary of what you expect – I told him so as a matter of fact! If I had written *Chronochromie*, I would have done so in a way that the eye could follow the length of the durations.

RN: Messiaen didn't get very far with electronic music. Were you surprised by that?

PB: Not entirely. After a certain age you cannot get it any more. It's like home computers: you have children of seven or eight who are virtuosos and parents, who are perhaps more intelligent or better educated, who are completely disarmed by this technology. I think Messiaen was born too early. It was the same with Varèse. He was always dreaming of something, and when the beginning of the possibility was there, he was very uneasy with it. It can be disturbing, certainly, for a composer not to be able to master a new technique or a new way of expressing himself, but with Messiaen I don't see any tragedy in his music from this point of view. He wrote one piece of *musique concrète*, I remember very well, helped by Pierre Henry – that was in 1952, and he never went back to it, because certainly for him that was not a very gratifying experience.

RN: Finally, as a personality, would you say Messiaen was an obsessive?

PB: No, I would say that for me he is a mixture of mysticism and naivety; and with all the advantages of the naivety, because you don't have to deal with your own self-critical spirit, so you can dare to make some gesture that other people will never dare to do. And at the same time the kind of mysticism in which you are completely closed. That has advantages, it also has some difficulties. Self-criticism can sometimes be very helpful; if you have a kind of analytical self-judgment and not only a mystic, global judgment of yourself, that also can be very helpful. Myself, I am much more on the side of self-criticism. It's a question of faith. All his world is based on religion. That's a world that is closed to me and I cannot see how he can be happy, but certainly he is happy with it.

48 INTERVIEW – DAME GILLIAN WEIR ON MESSIAEN

Winter 1998, revised by Dame Gillian in 2019

RN: What was new about *Le Banquet céleste* in the 1920s, when he wrote that piece?

GW: He brought new sounds from the organ, making it imitate birds, water drops and other sounds of nature. In this piece the water-drops are the most obvious, and perhaps it is not too fanciful to imagine that they also suggest drops of blood, since the Celestial Banquet recalls Christ's words ('This is my Body … .my Blood') at the Last Supper and is at the centre of the Mass. Also he followed Tournemire in releasing the Pedal from its customary rôle as a bass line; and he used freely the mutations of the organ, combining them in new ways. This was a French baroque tradition, seen in the *jeux de combinaison* of Couperin and his school, but Messiaen's imagination created a host of new combinations. Later these were frequently used to imitate bird song; or a mixture of pitches were united so as to produce a ghostly suggestion of unison pitch in a melodic line (e.g. 'Les Eaux de la Grâce' in *Les Corps glorieux*). We know that his ear was extremely acute, and he trained his Conservatoire students by striking a note on the piano and having them concentrate on distinguishing its harmonics. So he would relish being able to make individual harmonics manifest on the organ through the mutation stops.

As for the music itself: its sense of timelessness is remarkable. The first chord lasts six seconds, during which nothing appears to happen. John Cage said of Messiaen's music that he didn't compose, merely juxtapose, implying that there was no sense of movement, no rhythm. But there is indeed movement; it comes from within the single chord in this instance as the dissonances in it seek to resolve. We hear one note aspiring to rise to its resolution, another wanting to fall, the throbbing harmonies creating a sense of motion even before they drift to the next chord like clouds shifting shape in the sky, until finally coming to rest on a concord. We simply have to change our sense of time and submit to his tempo, join with it. Debussy called this the experience of the 'sensory moment', a wonderful phrase quoted by Messiaen. This rhythm through harmony, present in Bach or Byrd, Beethoven or Busoni, becomes a whole philosophy in Messiaen.

RN: And what's difficult for the player about *Le Banquet celeste?*

GW: Despite its slowness it is actually one of the most difficult pieces; used to the motoric metre of, say, a Mozart sonata or 'The Arrival of the Queen of Sheba', where one is carried forward by the familiar shape of the figuration, the player has to learn to listen intensely to each chord and process it internally right from the beginning, or one can end up in effect still continuing in performance to *read* the notes. As in all music the shape of the line is of paramount importance, and when the pace is so slow this becomes harder to perceive and thus convey. All music is a curved line and one must hear – see – that arc in the air, that sigh, and avoid a mechanical plodding from note to note. As in the Hindu philosophy so much admired by Messiaen ('as above, so below') this curve is demonstrated in macrocosm in his 1969 work, the *Méditations sur le Mystère de la Sainte Trinité*. The 9 movements form a great inverted V or arc, the harmonies again providing the tension and release – the impetus – to move forward in a crescendo of intensity to the peak of the middle movement, coming finally to rest again at the end of the 9th. The listener needs to submit to this – to 'live in the moment' in the Buddhist phrase – and not be waiting subconsciously for the alternation of busy passages with more serene that is the norm in the repertoire we are more used to; those contrasting passages are of course there but the overall internal shape is nevertheless strong. It's important to recognise that for Messiaen rhythm was the *antithesis* of metre, and is not mathematical; it works through the alternation of tension and release, strong and weak, ebb and flow, arsis and thesis. Messiaen achieved this largely through his use of harmony and he knew that metre imprisons; rhythm brings life. This is often misunderstood by many schools of performance, particularly in the field of early music practice.

RN: What did he take over from the old French tradition?

GW: Chiefly the feeling for colour. The French organ school has always been colour-conscious. The organ in its modern form began in the Gothic era in the Brabant area and then broadly divided into two schools of organbuilding; one went down into Southern Germany and France, and the other into Northern Germany and the Netherlands. The latter developed the architectural logic that made its organs so perfect for the contrapuntal genius of such as Bach; its spatial characteristics (the physical lay-out) and its treble-to-bass balance (through scaling and voicing) supplied a transparent texture with perfect balance, the essentials for polyphony. The Southern organbuilders on the other hand developed their organs' rich range of colours, both those directly imitative (trumpets and clarions, flutes and strings) and also the mutations (stops not of unison pitch) that could be mixed to supply new ones. With such resources improvisation flourished in France and the tradition has continued to the present day. From the elegant baroque composers came those who added the sounds of drums and storms (the *Orage* in the Pedal division), up to Tournemire and the 20th-century experimenters.

Of these, Messiaen is the most remarkable, and indeed he was a synaesthete – he saw colours as well as hearing them, as Scriabin did, and was able to describe in detail the colours in all his harmonies. Colour affected him so deeply that when as a child he was taken to the Sainte-Chapelle in Paris he was so overcome by its famous windows that he fainted. For the rest of his life he said he considered stained glass man's most glorious invention. Clearly such dazzling magnificence fitted with his wish (as he told me once) 'to overwhelm'. Messiaen was not to be confined within the limitations of this world, and the longing for freedom – spiritual, artistic, technical – is paramount in everything he did. The complex rhythms he began developing in the 1950s are often seen as computer-like in their precision and to be reproduced with a mathematical exactitude, but in fact they are designed to *release* the music from the imprisonment of metre and set it as free as the birds he admired so much; or (as he wrote in *Les Corps glorieux*) to express the joy of the resurrected ones who are no longer hampered by a physical body or limited understanding, but now see all and know all.

RN: So the rhythms are not metronomically exact?

GW: This may sound contentious, as of course he wrote the rhythms as he wanted them played – a quintuplet is a quintuplet, a triplet a triplet. But they must still be played so that they have the *character* of a quintuplet or a triplet. A student once brought the 4th movement of the *Messe* to me and said triumphantly that she had worked out the complicated middle section (birdsong against water-drops) on her computer so it was exactly correct. I'm sure any computers listening would have loved it but it did not have life. A quintuplet (for example) is infinitely more than the division of a beat into five sections, it has an identity, a shape: it leaps from the first note as from a trampoline, soars through the air, and obeys gravity by falling gently to earth again. It's the performer's job to convey this, and to shape the figure by minute manipulations of timing and by subtleties of touch. This is what I mean by their being used, despite their apparent precision, to express freedom rather than succumbing to the deadening effect of simply thinking of them as pieces of time carved from a larger segment.

RN: Talking about the very beginning of *L'Après-midi d'un faune*, he said 'It falls too quickly and it rises too slowly'.

GW: That's very interesting. That's the kind of thing I mean here. It's vital for players of the organ in particular to realize that the organ is not a sterile, mechanical instrument as it is often called; it in fact has the power to transmit whatever one feels. It depends on the musician: if he can't imagine the meaning within a musical phrase it certainly won't be conveyed to the audience. We used to talk a great deal about the relationship between speech and music; that seems to have been forgotten lately. I use it constantly when teaching and it makes a big difference; the student sees at once that a phrase is someone speaking; so what words would they use? What kind of voice is employed here? Is it a question or an answer? Is it an emphatic statement? If it's a repetition is it in the form of an echo, gradually weakening and dying away, or one intended to increase the forcefulness of what one is asserting? Is the speaker eager to convince, with a consequent hurrying forward? Music is a language. I would like all music students to learn acting, and thus dramatic timing, because when we play we are taking on a rôle.

RN: Did Messiaen ever speak to you about his immediate predecessors, Dupré, Vierne, Tournemire?

GW: No; I wish I'd had the opportunity to speak with him on that basis. I never actually studied formally with Messiaen – perhaps I should have done that. But I do think that a work of art becomes an independent entity once it's left the pen of the creator, and I think Messiaen understood and appreciated that, because he showed his approval of many different interpretations of his music. Here again it sounds as if I'm saying 'Never mind what he wrote; do what you like', and that is absolutely *not* what I mean. What I do mean is that a fine interpreter makes a deep connection with the essence of the piece itself and becomes one with it, bringing something to it. Trying to copy what even the composer himself may do, or to follow instructions blindly, does not result in the same identification with the work, or the total conviction that in its turn convinces others. Now that we have many recordings of composers themselves playing their works there would otherwise be little point in anyone else doing so. I think of a work of art like a prism hanging in the air; as various parts of it catch the light, so it gives off various rays. (Fortunately Messiaen seemed very happy in my performances of his works so I guess I am doing something right!)

RN: What was distinctive about his own organ playing?

GW: For one thing, the slow pieces were *extremely* slow! A colleague tells of Messiaen's performing a *Tierce en taille* by Grigny, complete with (anachronistic) 32' stops, so slowly that the ornaments seemed endless; the listeners waited with bated breath and some amusement for the last note of the final trill to sink finally to rest. But his technique was stunning; his playing of his own virtuoso movements was breathtaking, and the musical intelligence that illuminated, for instance, the more abstruse movements such as the *Diptyque*, amazing. Naturally there is always great interest in a composer's performances of his own music. A characteristic of Messiaen's was its strength and passion, bringing an abandon that completely negated any sense of being locked in by the complexity of the notation. His creativity as a composer was reflected in his ability always to bring a work alive in performance. This constant renewal reinforces the belief that in a worthwhile work of art there is always more to discover; just as an Olivier or Gielgud can bring new revelations to a Shakespearean role, so we marvel at, say, Britten's playing and conducting of Mozart so brilliantly that new insights are brought even to Mozart. A performer must be more than one who reproduces, just as a translator is more than one who supplies dictionary definitions for his text, which is why I prefer the word *interpreter* and why our teaching should focus on so much more than merely reproducing the notes on a score and handing on miscellaneous information.

RN: Are the registrations that Messiaen puts at the head of his scores prescriptive?

GW: He did change them himself on occasions. There's a very interesting account of his registration practices by Almut Rössler, who worked with him a great deal on his organ music and gave the première of the *Livre du Saint Sacrement*. One needs to understand his organ at La Trinité, which was not a typical Cavaillé-Coll, despite the name on the nameplate, and to understand the effect that is desired. His registrations can't always be reproduced precisely. Sometimes even if one is using a stop of the same name it won't give the colour which was his original intention; or the dynamic level will be different on a German or English organ where the pungency of a French reed will often need help and where the mutation stops are thinner and do not combine in the same way. For example, he changed the registration in 'Alléluias sereins' once, when he was with me just before a recital. The RH part plays a delicate figure high on the keyboard and an 8' bourdon is asked for; to my surprise he changed that to a very big, loud *larigot* which happened to be available. However, that was useful in showing that he wanted his music to be clear, not to float about vaguely in a bathroom acoustic.

RN: What changes did he make to the Trinité organ over the years?

GW: He had various stops added to it, and he also added a combination action to make overall control easier. Near the end of his life he planned to update this, and also wanted some more exotic mutations: a *septième* and a *neuvième*. He'd played these two stops on a German organ and was thrilled by their possibilities: even more fascinating birdsong would be possible. But although preparations were being made to install them, these stopped when he died. Rather sadly, the organ was now no longer Messiaen's organ to be played, it was Messiaen's organ to be remembered – a national monument not to be changed. There is also a slight problem in that there is not a great deal of room left for more stops, but I think the chief reason was this one of 'freezing' something when the composer dies.

I'm both intrigued and occasionally exasperated by the fact that his music and its performance show signs of being frozen. Observing this process has given me an insight into musical history that I could not have had otherwise. It has made me read reports of events and people from the past with more scepticism. Through living with Messiaen's music for so many years and noting what he has said about it, how he played it to begin with, what he said about it at the end of his life and what was different from the beginning, I've seen just how much the performance of the music can change and how many ideas there can be about it. For example, at the end of his life he wanted extremely slow tempi in 'Les Bergers' *(La Nativité),* yet it's marked 'Vif et joyeux', and I believe he played it more quickly to begin with. It must give *some* idea of liveliness, of joy; these are the shepherds rejoicing, a joyous carol made from the plainsong *Puer natus*.

I think that when a composer plays, two things happen. First, he remembers the original incentive, the original inspiration. Second, as in Messiaen's case, he tries (unconsciously) to reproduce the quasi-meditative state in which he received it, and in which perhaps he wishes to listen to it. But this is not necessarily going to project it to an audience. That doesn't mean this particular piece should be very fast, but not *extraordinarily* slow as, at the end of his life, he was prone to ask people to play it. There is something different about a composer's playing and as I said earlier it's sometimes revelatory, but sometimes one thinks 'Well, this is a different thing from a performance'.

RN: Going back to the organ music of his immediate predecessors, are you aware, when you play Messiaen, of the feel of their music under your fingers?

GW: In the earlier works absolutely. The French make the distinction between the Symphonic tradition and the Romantic – Franck representing the Romantic, Widor and Vierne the Symphonic. Messiaen would have thoroughly studied and played these schools before embarking on his own stylistic experiments and their sense of the monumental is found right from the early *Apparition de l'Église éternelle* as well as the pianistic techniques. He was not fond of the classical organ, either historically or in its revived late-20th century form; he told me that he liked the power of the symphonic organ to overwhelm and that the classical organ did not serve this idea. I asked him whether the subtlety of a mechanical action was not an attraction, but clearly he felt that it was not compensation for the classical organ's lighter effect. The mark of the classical North German organ is its balance; no stop is very much louder than any other. There is a tonal difference of course between reeds and flues but not notably in the wind pressures, the dynamic levels. The Romantic organ developed along with the Romantic ideas of the struggle between opposing forces: God and Man, good and evil, love and hate ... reflected in the organs by much more extreme differences between loud and soft, and in performance between slow and fast. The organs grew bigger and the colours ranged from *ppp* to *ffff*, bringing to the organ the possibility of the Rossini crescendo, a wide-ranging increase in sound across the whole orchestra. The value of this range of power in Messiaen's extravagantly dramatic music, treating of apocalyptic subjects, is obvious. 'Les Mains de l'Abîme' *(Livre d'Orgue)*, for instance, engulfs the listener in sound as the hands cry out from the Abyss; 'Combat de la Mort et de la Vie' *(Les Corps glorieux)* shows Life and Death in 'stupefying' combat and then subsumed in a greater Life. However, colour consciousness was not as important to the symphonic composers as it was to Messiaen; for them form, line and an orchestral shape dominated (despite Vierne's scintillating *Pièces de Fantaisie* with its 'Gargouilles' and 'Naïades' and their like).

RN: I was surprised to find that, in the 1929 Conservatoire final organ exam, the Concours, which Messiaen won, of the four pieces three were improvisations and only one was a set piece, Bach's D major Fugue BWV 532. And I wondered whether this tension between improvisation and structure is something you feel when you play Messiaen's music?

GW: Structure was very important to him – for this reason he hated being called an Impressionist – but it is not a classical or even symphonic structure. We think of elements that are equal, of clear and logical relationships, as in a fugue or sonata form. But for him the structure was like an artist's collage; he composed a picture but with the colours made of sound. We think mostly of line and size, of measurements as in a building, but for Messiaen it was about impact and force. Just as in a collage there might be a piece of red fabric at the top of the right hand side, then a smaller piece of red at the bottom on the left, or some other balancing fragment forming a perfect relationship in terms of visual art, he made his own structures, and in the long French tradition of brilliant improvisers he was free to do that. The 'Offertoire' from the *Messe de la Pentecôte* is often considered fragmental: a bit of plainsong, some birdsong and drops of water – what a dog's breakfast it is! But it is not: he has 'composed' it, using that word in its literal sense of putting together the tone colours and fragments in such a way that they do form a structure which can be perceived and is satisfying. It is important for the performer to realize this. We are trapped in a linear sense of time;

to understand Messiaen we must escape this and instead develop a comprehension of the whole, with an instinctive understanding of the various colour, harmony and tonal relationships that go to make up the whole. Logical analysis alone will not suffice. Students often feel a kind of embarrassment when playing Messiaen: pushing along a torrent of semiquavers is easy, but discerning and conveying movement in a very slow line is much harder to handle. But when they understand that the music is saying 'Wait! Listen to me, look at me!', then it will work.

RN: It's curious that as the pace of modern life gets faster and faster, Messiaen's music seems to get slower and slower.

GW: Yes, it does, partly perhaps because he gets older and his perception of tempi changes but also because as life becomes more hectic we drift further from an ability to listen. We need to change our sense of time. It's interesting that theoretical physicists are now playing with the idea of time's not existing. First we had 'perhaps it can run backwards', as Messiaen postulated in the *Messe,* then 'perhaps there is no such thing as time'. That would be perfect for Messiaen, who sought to create a sense of timelessness in his music. I can't pretend to understand Einstein's theories in any detail but occasionally I do have a glimpse of the meaning of space and time being one, even perhaps in the second Choral of Franck, where for me a great bell tolls across a vast landscape while we stand by its tower and are one with the entire space rather than simply processing through it.

RN: And after the notes, the silences ....

GW: Well, Mozart said that the rests are more important than the notes. That's another reason for not urging the music forward as though it is in bouncy metrical patterns. The silences are full of music ... When I start to play a piece, I think of myself as drawing back a curtain and revealing the music that is already there; it already exists, and now we will hear it, see it. When we draw the curtain across again at the end, I'm certain it goes on playing, part of the music of the spheres. There's a superb quotation from the Bhagavad-Gita in a book about Messiaen concerning a lamp that burns in a windless place but does not flicker; one goes into a cave and there's a lamp burning, albeit no wind to stir it – it doesn't need to waver, its life is within it.

RN: Did Messiaen found a school of organ writing?

GW: He has had a lot of imitators. But the curious thing is that it always sounds like an imitation. I don't really think it's a style that can develop, especially as the harmonies he uses are instantly identifiable as his. I think Messiaen is a kind of shining, rainbow-coloured bubble that was thrown up from the sea of music and will probably just go back into it. I don't mean his music won't survive, only that I can't see the style developing.

RN: Does playing Messiaen's music make you hear other music differently – or play other music differently?

GW: I think it increases one's sensitivity to colour, and perhaps to shape. I think of motifs in a visual sense which increases one's appreciation of relationships. It's been wonderful to play plainsong in his music, both unadorned and re-shaped 'as though seen through a prism'. It needs the flexibility of a singer, and searching for the way to turn an apparently intractable keyboard into a singer's flowing line and infinite subtlety of timing is thrilling and can't help but have an effect on one's playing.

RN: Was he a patient teacher?

GW: I think so; one hears of his patience with his students at the Paris Conservatoire. He could sometimes be impatient with the organ, if it didn't have what he needed! On one occasion he changed the music rather considerably two or three hours before a recital of mine and I said 'But that *is* what you wrote!' He said 'I know, I know, it's my fault, but this is what I want now'. It was a recurring passage in the 'Offertoire' from the *Messe de la Pentecôte*. He wanted it played much more quickly each time it occurred – it's really quite a big difference - and I was thinking of people saying 'Heavens, she's getting it all wrong!' But he did change things quite often with people. It can be a great problem in competitions. I sit often on competition juries, and I can hear a competitor play something quite differently from what's in the score, and then numbers 2, 3 and 4 make the same alteration. I then find that they all have the same teacher, who claims to have been told by Messiaen to do it this way. What to do? Sometimes it's quite a big difference, as in 'Joie et clarté' from *Les Corps glorieux,* where Messiaen himself stopped after the first bar and closed the box. The registration here is always difficult to reproduce as it contains a 4' clarion. A French clarion is very telling and cuts through everything, so balancing the passage so that it does not obscure the trumpet solo is tricky. But myself, I think that to stop and close the box ruins the piece. Elsewhere he wrote of 'protons clashing' – very apt here – and pausing at that point arrests the outburst of energy that launches the piece into dazzling orbit. It also changes the rhythm. So why *do* that? But, who's to say ……!

RN: On this question of textual correctness, may I ask: at the end of 'Les Anges' in *La Nativité du Seigneur*, should the trill get slower?

GW: Some players do slow down, but no – I think that's a shame! For me the angels are simply gone; they've spread across the sky to deliver their wondrous message and now speed off into the distant heavens and vanish from our sight. Slowing down at the end of a piece is such a cliché, don't you think? In Messiaen, of all people, one wants to convey a dramatic image.

RN: For someone who never knew Messiaen and never saw a picture of him, how would you describe him?

GW: He was quite tall, but very stooped, like all organists! (I fight a perpetual battle with organ builders to get music desks in the right place and at the right angle.) He used always to wear open-necked shirts; no tie – he'd made a blow for freedom in that respect and wore brightly coloured and most attractive shirts. He was rather shy and quiet, serious, and not I think particularly ready to smile. He seemed almost naive, if one might use that word of such a great genius; he found the world a little alarming, I think, as well as disturbing. He had however great charm, and was very humble. In 1988 we were both in Sydney as Artists in Residence for the Australian Broadcasting Corporation, who mounted a festival of almost his entire output, bringing out Yvonne Loriod and other artists connected with him. I had the honour of playing all the organ music. He was besieged with fans and patiently stood signing autographs for scores of people, writing in full 'Olivier Messiaen, Sydney' and the date. He was presented with an Hon Doctorate by Sydney University, and accepting it he began by saying 'Thank you so much for this, I am not worthy of it'.

49 MUSIC IN PARIS IN THE 1940s

Even today, it's as well to be cautious in France talking about the Second World War – certainly to the French who lived through it. And even if you avoid the political minefields, there's still the question of France's pride …

But in the matter of musical composition and performance, here at least France's pride remained pretty well intact, as did her traditions, even if not everyone agrees about what makes a tradition, or about what makes it viable. Certainly the Nazis did not destroy the traditional French concept of the well-made piece, as we can see from a work such as Ibert's *Symphonie concertante* for oboe and orchestra, written right at the end of the 1940s. The composer and conductor Manuel Rosenthal remembers that the Germans weren't all bad:

> In May 1940 I was in the commandos on the border of a river overlooking the German army, which was on the other side. One night we heard through loudspeakers, coming from the German army, 'We know that in the regiment number xxxx, which is in front of us, there is a musician, and if he listens carefully, he will hear from our side one of his piano pieces.' And in fact I heard a little piece called *Bagatelle* which I had composed when I was 18 or 19, being played by a German pianist on the other side of the river. So you see, music never loses its superiority over even war and the army.*

It goes without saying that, under the Occupation, all kinds of music acquired a new slant, and often a new power. One of the finest of the wartime productions at the Opéra-Comique was of Debussy's *Pelléas et Mélisande*, mounted in September 1940 under Roger Désormière and recorded, with some of the same cast, the following spring. It's possible that the classic status this recording has acquired over the years

* The contributions of Manuel Rosenthal, Pierre Boulez and Madeleine Milhaud to this article are taken from conversations with the author.

had something to do with what the opera meant for its performers and audience at that particular time – certainly Irène Joachim, the Mélisande of the set, thought so. Surely Golaud's interrogation of Yniold in Act III spoke clearly enough of what Paris was suffering and would continue to suffer. 'I'm not a spy', retorts Golaud. No, of course not. Getting someone else to do your spying for you, that's not spying …

We can see with hindsight that the German occupiers were in something of a quandary over matters of culture. As avowed music-lovers, could they ban all public music-making? The musical German in fact became a cliché in French novels of the time. The 18-year-old Pierre Boulez arrived in Paris from Lyon in 1943:

> Of course the music of the Jews was not allowed – Schoenberg was not allowed, nor was Milhaud – but otherwise, in France at least, they did not bother about music at all. Hindemith was not performed, because he was a German and he was an enemy of the Germans. You did not hear very much of Stravinsky, even though Stravinsky was not forbidden – I heard some Stravinsky works during the Occupation. The big hero at this time was Honegger, and he was no more or less avant-garde than Hindemith, for instance. The big success at this time, I remember, in 1943 when I arrived in Paris, was his Symphony no 2 for strings. So it was a very ambiguous situation at this time. But there was no direct German indication that they wanted to dominate the French situation.

… otherwise they would hardly have allowed Honegger's opera *Antigone* – with its message of moral and political disobedience – to be given its Opéra premiere in January 1943, nor indeed a performance of his oratorio *Judith*, in which, as already mentioned, German officers had to sit in silence while the chorus intoned the words 'Israël revivra'.

Sometimes the Nazi-baiting was even more deliberate. In 1942 the Opéra-Comique put on Poulenc's ballet *Les Animaux modèles*, and the Germans in the audience couldn't understand the laughter at various points where Poulenc (this too already mentioned) had inserted references to the chanson 'Non, non, vous n'aurez pas l'Alsace et la Lorraine'.

The facts tell us that war can bring some unexpected benefits, even if they can never make up for the suffering it brings. The music of Georges Auric is a case in point. In the 1920s he had been the bright boy of French music: Cocteau dedicated the pamphlet *Cock and Harlequin* to him, Diaghilev commissioned him to write three ballets, *Les Fâcheux*, *Les Matelots* and *La Pastorale*, and he was married to one of the most beautiful models of the day. Then in 1931 he wrote a Piano Sonata which was panned by the critic Boris de Schloezer, who told Auric he should stick to film music (referring to his score for Cocteau's *Le Sang d'un poète*) and not hanker after the musical big time. Auric believed him. And it was only in 1943, driven by the calamitous state of his country, that he launched out again and composed his powerful settings of Aragon, *Quatre chants de la France malheureuse,* in the last of which, 'La rose et le réséda', he took a leaf out of Poulenc's book, quoting the 'Marseillaise'.

The unwillingness of the Germans to impose themselves on French musicmaking (why stir up the native population unnecessarily?) meant that they left the institutions pretty well alone. Jacques Rouché went on running the Opéra, as he had since 1914, while in 1941 the Conservatoire passed into the hands of Claude Delvincourt. Although Delvincourt's record has caused considerable controversy in recent years, Manuel Rosenthal had no doubts about his behaviour:

> The attitude of Delvincourt was very courageous, because he kept the Germans from taking the young students and sending them to Germany. To do that, he created what was called the 'orchestre des cadets', and this was how he could say no to the Germans: 'I need this orchestra to teach them how to play in an orchestra. You can't take them to Germany.' And he succeeded. He was also very close to a German called Heinrich Strobel, who wrote a life of Debussy. Although Strobel was serving in the German propaganda office, he was very sympathetic to the French.

Delvincourt was also determined that his students should be aware of the best of contemporary French music, and so he commissioned test pieces for the end-of-year exams, not from safe old has-beens (as had happened so often in the past), but from up-and-coming talents like Henri Dutilleux, who composed *Sarabande et Cortège* for bassoon and piano (1942), Sonatine for flute and piano (1943), the first two movements of the Sonata for oboe and piano (1947) and the *Choral, Cadence et fugato* for trombone and piano (1950).

As already remarked, it was in the September of 1943 that Boulez joined a preparatory class at the Paris Conservatoire:

> During the course of the year I heard, in the Conservatoire itself, of a very funny class, an exceptional class, given by a teacher quite unknown at this time – it was Messiaen. His students were considered like outsiders really. And I was interested and attracted by that.

A year later, just weeks after the liberation of Paris, Manuel Rosenthal was taking his first steps towards refashioning the French National Radio Orchestra:

> The orchestra was in a very bad state because of the Occupation, so for some weeks we just worked, without any programme, just to make the orchestra play well – you know, with a full bow, the style of the flute or the trumpet etc. And finally, when we gave our first concert, it was fantastic, very, very beautiful, so brilliant, full of joy and enthusiasm.

After the opening concert, which contained music by the allies (including Walton's overture *Portsmouth Point*), Rosenthal made it his aim to reintroduce Paris audiences to the music they'd been largely deprived of during the Occupation. First on his list came a series of seven concerts – Stravinsky *opera omnia*:

> The night I was conducting the *Four Norwegian Moods*, somebody made a noise in the audience, so much that the police came to take him away. After the concert, Messiaen came to me and said, 'Manuel, I want to apologise, because the person who made those disturbing noises is a pupil of mine.' I said, 'What is his name?' He said, 'Oh, no importance, you don't know his name, he's 20 years old and he's just a student.' I said, 'No, anyway tell me.' He said, 'His name's Pierre Boulez'.

Boulez later defended himself:

> Immediately after the war people were always speaking in terms of 'before the war'. People in Paris wanted the Stravinsky 'before the war'. We did not want at all that musical life would go back exactly as it was before the war. Because, firstly, we were young;

and secondly, Messiaen was in between. He was very careful, he was not a man for polemics, he was always very careful to be on his own and not to be participating in any kind of battle. So we were the ones who demonstrated, each time it was necessary, our disagreement with a kind of Establishment life. And I find that's very good. If I were 20 again, I would do exactly the same.

But demonstrations were not always called for:

> Bartók was not performed at all during the war. I remember, the first time I heard the *Music for strings, percussion and celesta* was in the winter of 1944/5. We discovered quite a lot of music, badly performed most of the time, because people were not acquainted with this music, and the people who were performing were also not very good – I mean, they were very devoted, very well intentioned, but not terribly good. I remember a performance of *Pierrot lunaire* under René Leibowitz which was terribly boring – which is difficult to imagine with *Pierrot lunaire*!

There was certainly nothing boring about the concert given in Paris on 21 April 1945, when Messiaen's *Trois petites Liturgies de la Présence Divine* rocked the critics back on their heels. Messiaen's very personal attempt to bring Roman Catholicism into the concert hall, and the equally personal nature of his own text – 'model in blue for angels, blue trumpet which prolongs the daylight' – did not find favour with intellectuals busy cutting their teeth on Existentialism. Neither did the opulent sounds of the *Liturgies* match the deprivation and unease of post-war Paris, where a takeover by the Communists seemed entirely possible. On the purely material front, Boulez found that getting to know modern music was one of many problems:

> The scores were not easy to find and some were impossible. Therefore for the works that were interesting to me, especially all the Webern pieces, I copied by hand. There was one printed score, for instance, in the hands of Leibowitz or someone like that, and then you took it for a couple of days, you copied it and then kept the copy. I also copied the Lieder op 22 by Schoenberg, because that score too was impossible to buy.

Did Boulez feel now that his works of the mid-1940s bear the stamp of their time?

That takes in my Flute Sonatina, for instance, and the *Notations*, those were really my spontaneous response to all that I heard: the *Sacre du printemps*, *Les Noces* and then the Viennese school and then the Messiaen pieces. And at that time, in late 1945, I reacted very quickly. I think that teaching is a very quick process. That's a kind of shock in your life, and if you don't have this shock, years of studying will not really make up for it.

It's as well to remind ourselves that, as always, this avant-garde touched only a tiny proportion of the great French musical public. For them, the end of the war meant trying to get back to a normal life, and seeing Paris again, free of tanks and grey-green uniforms – as Charles Trenet put it, 'Revoir Paris'. On the classical music front, one can point to three of Les Six who, a quarter of a century after the founding of the group, were pursuing their individual courses, though still in touch with each other. Milhaud had gone with his wife and son to America in 1940 – attending the Opéra premiere of Milhaud's *Médée* on 8 May, they could hear distant cannon fire, headed south and caught the last boat out of Lisbon for the USA. In June 1947, still in America, Milhaud received a letter from Poulenc in Paris, filling him in on the musical scene:

> Auric is still having a huge success with his films [notably Cocteau's *La Belle et la Bête*]. I see very little of Arthur, who's rather the isolated, gloomy great master these days. The young frequently find themselves disorientated between Messiaen and belated twelve-tonery – they're really looking forward to being taught by you.

Milhaud had done a deal with the Conservatoire by which he came over to Paris to teach every other year. His first big post-war commission in France came in 1947, as his wife Madeleine explained:

> The French state wanted to have some celebration of the revolution which took place in 1848 as it was the centenary in 1948. Jules Romains, the writer, happened to be on the committee, trying to organise the festivities, and he had the idea of asking Darius for a work. I think Darius had a tendency towards a sort of epic quality in his music: funeral marches, fanfares etc. So he wrote his Fourth Symphony '1848', published by Salabert. His other 11 symphonies

were published by Heugel, now Leduc, but Mister Heugel didn't like the idea of the revolution of 1848, so he didn't want to publish this one.

It's rather heartening to find the French returning to their old quarrels, as though the recent war had never been.

Poulenc stayed in France all through the war, composing and doing what little he could to help the French Resistance. One of the things he missed most were the recitals with his friend, the baritone Pierre Bernac, and after the war he returned to this partnership with a renewed appetite. And, as Rosenthal reminds us, Poulenc was not just a composer:

> The three best pianists in France after the war were not the virtuosos – so-called virtuosos – but Jean Wiéner, Francis Poulenc and Jacques Février. At one concert, I conducted Février and Poulenc playing the Poulenc Concerto for two pianos. I have very seldom heard such beautiful playing. We hear very brilliant pianists with fantastic techniques, but only these three were really attached to the quality of the piano sound. I would describe it as 'moelleux' – with a strong centre to the sound.

The decade of the 1940s could well be given the overall title 'War and Peace', and perhaps no French musical work sums this up so well as one already mentioned by Pierre Boulez, Honegger's Second Symphony for strings and trumpet. During the war the final trumpet chorale was heard as a message of hope; after the war as a celebration of triumph. At all times the symphony can be heard as a marvellous work, written by a Swiss citizen who, of his own free will, stayed in France during the Occupation, out of gratitude for all she had given him: technique, opportunities, friends.

Appendix: Opera and ballet premieres during the decade at the Opéra and Opéra-Comique

Opéra

1940	Milhaud: *Médée*
1942	Poulenc: *Les Animaux modèles* (ballet)
1943	Honegger: *Antigone*
1945	Honegger: *L'Appel de la montagne* (ballet)
1947	Sauguet: *Les Mirages* (ballet)
1948	Françaix: *Les Malheurs de Sophie* (ballet)
	Ibert: *Escales* (ballet)
	Delvincourt: *Lucifer* (ballet)
1949	Busser: *Les Noces corinthiennes* (prem at Opéra-Comique in 1922)
	Honegger: *La Naissance des couleurs* (ballet)

Opéra-Comique

1941	Chabrier: *L'Etoile*
1942	Delannoy: *Ginevra*
1943	R Strauss: *Ariane à Naxos*
1944	Sauguet: *La Gageure imprévue*
1947	Poulenc: *Les Mamelles de Tirésias*
1948	Koechlin: *L'Ame heureuse* (ballet)
	Milhaud: *Jeux de printemps* (ballet)
1949	Hahn: *Le Oui des jeunes filles*
	Tailleferre: *Paris-Magie*

These conversations with Henri Dutilleux took place in his Paris apartment on the Ile St Louis on 19 April 1991, belatedly after his 75th birthday on 22 January.

50 DUTILLEUX AT 75 – CONVERSATIONS

RN: You've spoken about a Slavic influence on your music ...

HD: I don't know whether there's a Slavic influence on my music, but there certainly is one in my make-up – I had forbears who were Slavs on the side of my maternal grandfather. His father was Polish, so sometimes I have followed my affection, my attraction if you like, towards the music of central Europe; maybe not necessarily Slav, but from central Europe in general, starting with Russian music.

RN: So you don't feel there's been a Slavic influence on your music?

HD: No, I think it's important that an art, whether it's music or literature, should keep its fundamentally national properties, whatever that nationality may be. It's good that artists of a particular country should also steep themselves in foreign characteristics – André Gide spoke of 'fermentation' (he even used the word 'yeast') the tiny grains of foreign leavening which keep a national art alive. On the other hand, at certain moments in history it's necessary to concentrate on purely national qualities. Debussy, for example, went to an extreme of nationalism in his tastes during the First World War, at the end of his life. Even in peacetime he held an analogous position, but on the strictly aesthetic front – it was a kind of detachment from the music of Wagner, which was perfectly understandable because it was necessary at that particular moment. Wagner's music was truly invading the music of France, especially through French intermediaries who were too much under his influence, particularly in the field of opera. But the language had a sort of grandiloquence that didn't match the French spirit at all, and in that respect Debussy was right, I think.

It's a question of historical context. We might mention France in the 1950s and 60s and beyond when we were invaded by music that depended, to a really exaggerated extent, on the serial system. I think that was dangerous too – people have used the word 'terrorism'. What could one do? Only defend oneself, not by words or manifestos, but by writing music. There are important moments of transition in the history of music like that, and serial music was a moment of transition. I should say though that, even for composers like me who are very far away from the Second Viennese School, serial music has contributed something. It's a matter I've thought about a lot, and I've studied in detail works written according to this technique, and that has forced me to consider my position, and perhaps I should have been rather different if this school, this music hadn't left its mark on me. You can find traces of this technique in my music, but obviously I've used it in a quite different way, not at all rigorously. I'm not totally opposed to its principles; what I'm against is the dogma, the authoritarianism that manifested themselves at that period.

RN: How did you learn about serial music?

HD: At the time I was completing my studies at the Paris Conservatoire in 1938, our professors never mentioned it to us. We knew the name Schoenberg, but not his works. It was only after the war that we got to know his music and that of his pupils. It's really strange that there should have been this eclipse, this total lack of interest that went on for years, from 1925 to 1950! I should add, since I was speaking just now of the music of central Europe, that I wasn't thinking specifically of Schoenberg's, but of composers like Bartók, whom we also got to know rather too late.

RN: After the war?

HD: Yes, and to a small extent during it as well. We heard the quartets, for example, but not often. There was a concert right in the middle of the Occupation at the Palais de Chaillot which included the *Music for strings, percussion and celesta*. I don't know that Bartók would have been very happy about that, as he'd declared his violent opposition against everything that came under the Nazi influence. He was one of those composers who were put to one side not, like Schoenberg, Milhaud or Paul Dukas, because he was Jewish, but because of his solidarity with those composers whom he admired.

RN: You've spoken of the advantages of studying harmony and counterpoint simultaneously ...

HD: Yes, because before coming to the Paris Conservatoire I was taught by an excellent musician, and a very good teacher, and he liked students to work at these two disciplines *almost* simultaneously, not absolutely. He said that I very soon developed enough of a harmonic sense to be able to go on to counterpoint. He taught counterpoint in a very rigorous manner (which is how it must be taught, or not at all), so that when I arrived in Paris I was already well enough prepared to be able to join both the harmony class and the fugue class. That wasn't what normally happened in French teaching at that time: you generally did perhaps three years' harmony, then counterpoint on its own, then fugue on its own. It's all quite different nowadays and people understand how necessary it is to bring the two techniques together as quickly as possible. I think it's necessary because it's to some extent a reflection on musical history, isn't it? Traditionally, French composers are more harmonically than contrapuntally orientated: they have a taste for the beautiful chord, and for many Frenchmen this harmonic richness and refinement have been the primary aim – and I may say I too have followed this path to some small extent all through my composing life. But I also needed to develop my contrapuntal technique as an antidote to it. In fact, when I was young I was very fond of fugue, which was perhaps another legacy from my Flanders ancestors.

RN: You've said that in the 1930s you had to combat the influence of Ravel ...

HD: Yes, because in France Ravel's reputation was at its height and he was played a lot. At the end of his life I went to several concerts of his music at the Théâtre du Chatelet and the Salle Pleyel, including one of the last concerts at which he was present in the year of his death, when Jacques Février played the Left-Hand Concerto with Charles Münch. Ravel then made a great impression on us, and for me I have to say that this influence was slightly overwhelming for a certain time. It was rather to the detriment of other influences that were also very important, Berlioz for example. At that time I didn't really know his music – that's to say, I adored *La Damnation de Faust* but I didn't know all Berlioz's output. Now I accept it in its entirety, even with its faults and mistakes; I think he was really the great French composer of the 19th century.

So then I had to liberate myself from certain influences. There are pieces of mine that are better known than others, for example some examination pieces I wrote after leaving the Conservatoire, such as a little Sonatine for flute. It's often been recorded in the United States, but I didn't want it recorded in France. There too you find traces of

Ravel's influence. It's a well-made piece, maybe even attractive, but not yet really my music. And then there's sometimes an influence of Fauré in my earliest pieces; Fauré left quite a mark on me when I was young – he was a fellow pupil of my grandfather, Julien Koszul, at the Ecole Niedermeyer.

RN: When you were a student, there was no analysis class at the Conservatoire. Was that a serious lack for a composer?

HD: Very serious, I feel, because after that you had to discover everything for yourself. I finished my studies in 1938 and then, during the Occupation, I was demobilised and returned to Paris. I was determined to read scores I didn't know, and even composition treatises like Vincent d'Indy's. I immersed myself in scores out of a desire to analyse them. At the Conservatoire we had passed abruptly from an excellent grounding in harmony, fugue and counterpoint to composition, for which we had no real basis. The basis has to be the study of scores, classical, romantic and modern.

I have to say that my dear teacher Henri Busser was not himself equipped to provide us with this sort of analysis. With Paul Dukas it was different. I never had the opportunity of being taught by him since he died in 1935, but his critical sense was very highly developed – as we know, perhaps too much so with regard to his own music. I've been told that when, at the first class he gave, he found that his composition students didn't know the Beethoven quartets, he became positively tyrannical. It was true for his students, it was true for us. We knew *some* quartets *slightly*. We were writing pieces for string quartet, but without knowing Haydn or Mozart or Beethoven.

RN: Can composition really be taught?

HD: I think it's possible to teach everything of a concrete nature: harmony, fugue, counterpoint, analysis, orchestration and how to listen to music. But as for composition, I don't think so. What I do think is that, quite apart from these transmissible techniques, some teachers are surrounded by a kind of aura. I don't think Fauré, in his profession as teacher of composition, had any startling gifts as an analyst; but he had an aura. Paul Dukas had one too, which was felt very strongly by his pupils, as did Darius Milhaud. Ultimately it's this that matters, though one can't cite a large number of instances. Both Schoenberg and Messiaen have this aura and technical knowledge as well.

RN: If we may turn to your own works, where should we begin? Is your Piano Sonata your opus 1?

HD: It was with the Piano Sonata that I took a step forward. It was a turning point, a work of transition, and from here onwards I had a clearer, more precise vision of my aesthetic orientation. That's to say, until then I hadn't been so far removed from what you might call those middle-of-the-road French composers who are rather too firmly attached to ideas of elegance, charm, with, even humour – of course, there's nothing wrong with humour in music, but not everyone is a Chabrier or a Satie. But from the Piano Sonata onwards I found I was much more interested by large forms, and even by the prospect of changing and renewing them. You can see in this Sonata the admiration I had for a composer like Dukas, who wrote a large Sonata, certain passages of which I like very much – the scherzo, for example, containing a fugue. I wanted to write a piano work with brilliant moments, but at the same time fairly profound in other ways. I wrote it for my wife, so I wanted her to be able to show what she was capable of. There are pages in the Sonata that I still like, others in which I don't really find my true self. But in general it has a character, I was going to say 'plethoric', which went somewhat against the music we in France were beginning to get to know: the piano writing of Webern, for example, in which he moves towards a total rarefaction ––although I didn't know his *Variations* at that time. I have to say, I prefer piano writing that is 'sensual', not too dry. From this point of view Shostakovitch's piano pieces don't move me at all because I miss the sensuality – even if there are pieces that contain humour and others that are very well made, like the Preludes and Fugues.

RN: Poulenc used to say, 'You must use the pedal like a good sauce'!

HD: Yes. But there needs to be an intellectual side too. I like Bartók's piano writing. But among French composers I'm particularly fond of Debussy's writing and Ravel, who was influenced by Liszt, and more recently Messiaen. Messiaen's piano music is rich in the domain of form and also of sensuality. One has to love Messiaen's music, no question! The interesting thing is that there's a logic to it. Even for those musicians who detest it, there is a sort of logic, or rather a coherence; you can't alter the notes or the harmonies. In my own music I follow somewhat the same principle, but in quite a different universe. When it comes to it, I need this coherence. It's in this sense that my String Quartet is coherent, because everything in it can be explained.

RN: Can we look forward to a second sonata from you?

HD: No, not a second sonata, but some shorter pieces.

RN: ... like the ones you've already written?

HD: Yes. For instance, the pieces that are slightly experimental, called *Figures de résonance* : there it's a question of capturing the resonance in different ways according to the layout. Then there's *Le Jeu des contraires*, and this Prelude will join two others that aren't published but which are finished, and then two more that I'll write next year, to be ready around November 1992. Together they'll all make a cycle, some of them being quite sizeable – one lasts seven minutes.

It's very hard to write for the piano today. Is there anything left to be discovered on the piano as it is? That's why some composers nowadays have moved toward the electro-acoustic field and synthesizers, because they think everything has been said that can be, using the piano in its pure state. It's possible. But I think the medium still offers opportunities to express oneself. It's the same with the string quartet: you could say there's no point in writing for that medium either, but that's really rather a narrow point of view.

RN: And after the Piano Sonata we come to the First Symphony ...

HD: This symphony follows rather the same path, this orientation toward producing something different from my earliest pieces. It wasn't a commission: I was keen to write a symphony, but a symphony that made a break with classical structures, if you like. The symphony begins with a Passacaglia, which is not regular practice; then, following this slow movement, comes an ultra-rapid Scherzo – and I'm pleased that Daniel Barenboim, in his recording, takes it at the right speed, because it's really a virtuoso piece and must be played as such, otherwise it's a bit heavy. Then comes a slow movement, the Intermezzo (again, a title that's not exactly symphonic) and then the Finale with variations. The Intermezzo, like the other movements, presents a single theme – or rather not so much a theme as a line. There is a thematic profile, a sort of insistence on returning to certain specific notes, but each movement ultimately treats the same idea. So, you see, the form is rather more subtle than in my Piano Sonata, and also there's something not found in my music until then: themes that subscribe to what one might call 'progressive growth'. There's a tendency – it's almost entirely intuitive – never to present the theme in its definitive state at the beginning. I'm not talking about cyclic form; that's different, because there it's a question of a theme which is laid down at the start, as in Debussy's String Quartet. In my case, instead of that there are small cells which develop bit by bit. This may perhaps show the influence of literature, of Proust and his notions about memory. It's a difficult thing to explain, but it's important because it's central to my preoccupations from this symphony onwards – in my String Quartet, for example, where the 'parentheses' act as reservoirs of sound events in which you find either commentaries on what has gone or prefigurations of what is still to come.

When I began to use this 'procedure', if we can call it that, it wasn't wholly conscious. That came later, and gradually I began to exploit it deliberately. That's not to say my First Symphony, for example, is easy to analyse, because many of its aims are disguised; but what are not disguised are the obsessional chords, pivot chords. You find these all through the work, especially in the second and third movements. It's a work I've altered at one point. When Charles Münch was rehearsing the piece with the Boston Symphony Orchestra in 1954, he said to me: 'I'm sorry, I don't like to tell you, but I've made a cut in the Finale. I think it improves the balance. See what you think.' I looked through my score again and realized he was right. Something needed to be done, but not a straight cut. I have to say that he'd found the best place to cut, not interfering with the harmonic flow or with the balance – Münch had an extraordinary intuition and sense of proportion. But I wasn't satisfied, so I rewrote a whole paragraph, shortening and transforming it.

RN: To come back for a moment to the idea of 'progressive growth', very easy to hear in your Second Symphony, had you studied the symphonies of Sibelius?

HD: No, I still don't know Sibelius that well. I have to say that for a long time he didn't really appeal to me. But I know his symphonic poems better, especially since I was in Finland three years ago. He's an underestimated composer, certainly. A French musicologist has even claimed that he was the worst composer of all time!

RN: I believe you changed the last chord of your Second Symphony?

HD: Yes. I thought the character of the work was marked by a feel of questioning, especially at the ends of the second and third movement, and that the [C sharp] major chord I'd chosen to finish the work was too affirmative, too positive. Now it finishes in a quite different way, in an interrogative sense – a little like Gauguin's famous painting *D'où venons-nous, que sommes-nous, où allons-nous?* When I was in Boston for the first performance under Münch, one of my friends took me to the Museum of Fine Arts and in front of this painting she said: 'That's the impression I had yesterday, listening to your symphony!' I hadn't thought of Gauguin when I was writing the work, but I think she was right about the interrogatory feeling.

RN: Are there other things you might like to change in a new edition of the score?

HD: Maybe the harpsichord, which I've taken out of certain passages because you can't hear it. It's a question of acoustics – it's an error in my orchestration, perhaps.

RN: Your next orchestral work was *Métaboles*, which you completed in 1964. You've spoken about the two interpretations by Szell and Münch ...

HD: Yes, they were very different in the sense that Szell's approach was more analytical than that of Münch who was above all intuitive. Szell studied the work more, 'at the table' if you like, just him and the score, before working with the orchestra. In working with the Cleveland players his preoccupation, I would say, was strictly acoustic: he was thinking above all about timbres and sonorities, and it's true that it's a work in which the sound/colours have to be brought out, with a differentiation between each section. The first movement, 'Incantatoire', focuses on wind instruments, particularly woodwind. The second, 'Linéaire', gives an important role to the strings, but much divided over a wide spectrum. In the third, 'Obsessionnel', the woodwind and brass combine. For the fourth, 'Torpide', it's the percussion and the brass, but very quiet, very distant, and for the last, 'Flamboyant', I used the whole orchestra. So it's necessary to take great care of the actual sounds, and there Szell did an astounding job.

Münch too, for his recording, worked tremendously. For example, in 'Torpide', which provides a moment of stillness in contrast with what preceeds and follows it, Münch understood that perfectly and didn't speed up, which is very tempting, especially if the audience get impatient and start to cough. It's a very difficult movement to bring off: one has to impose this vision on the audience. It's like one of those summer days when you are in a kind of torpor, a somnolence brought on by the heat.

RN: I'm interested in the title, *Métaboles*. You could have chosen *Métamorphoses* ...

HD: Yes, but I didn't want to use a title that had already been used by Richard Strauss and Hindemith and maybe others as well. But that wasn't the only factor. There was also the question of finding a title that corresponded as closely as possible with the form of the work, and over that I hesitated for a long time, hunting in a dictionary for words starting with 'méta' to indicate the idea of change, and I lighted on ... 'métaboles'! I already had an idea, a vision of the overall form when I began the work. And in each of the five movements there's an element destined to undergo the process of 'progressive growth', and an element which will recur and develop in the movement that follows. At the end of the first movement you find the opening of the second – or rather, the other way round – you could compare it with the way tiles overlap on a roof. This element undergoes a succession of changes, of metamorphoses until, after a certain number of them, as with insects, you find that there's an essential change in its nature: the original idea is almost unrecognisable. At the end of the most rhythmical movement, for example, you find a rhythm that will grow progressively as the basis of the following movement, and so on almost to the end of the work. But at the very end the metabolic process is halted by a return to the main element of the first movement. The circle is closed in a way that corresponds with the notion of time as circular, as in the seasons of the year. It's a rather personal kind of form, and I have to say I'm happy with the term 'métaboles', even though some people have been surprised and said to me: 'Yes, but it's too closely linked with biology or even medicine.'

RN: In the central movement you briefly introduce serialism. Was this part of your initial vision?

HD: Oh no! When I talk of 'vision', it was simply of the form in the shape of an arch. In any case, there are always moments when surprises in the way a piece is developing force you to modify your plan a little. At the start of the third movement there's a melodic line E-D#-A-G#-D-C#-G-F#-C-Bb-F-B on a solo double bass, built symmetrically. I then took the line apart and changed the intervals by inverting them. Various composers who had not been very interested in what I was doing until then – Boulez's entourage and Boulez himself – did take an interest in this score. Perhaps it was because I involved myself to a small extent in serial matters. But there's only one point – at the end of the third movement, where the series is presented vertically in four successive three-part chords – at which the work is really serial, and it's less than four bars long. Otherwise the work is far from being serial.

RN: Given that you mentioned a moment ago the 'terrorism' imposed by the serialists, I wondered what the force was of the title 'Obsessionnel' ...

HD: I didn't choose it as a tease, although I could have done! One of the things about the serialist doctrine that I can't accept is the abolition of the idea of supremacy. In my opinion, one can't consider all the notes of the chromatic scale as being equal, because we are all still (and I think it's a good thing) the inheritors of a tradition. Personally I'm not at heart an atonal composer.

RN: You also follow tradition in that some of your music is inspired by literature – I'm thinking of your cello concerto *Tout un Monde lointain*, and its Baudelairean associations. I see too that the first of its two slow movements was originally called 'Vertige', but that you later changed this ...

HD: ... because I found that the title belonged to one of the large French perfume houses, Coty in fact. But I preferred 'Regard' because of the reference in the Baudelaire poem to the green of his mistress's eyes and I also thought it was closer to the spirit of the music. Rostropovich on the other hand thought it was a pity because, when he played this movement, he was so high up in the cello's range that he had a feeling of vertigo! He was very surprised by this alteration – but now he's accepted it.

The second slow movement is very different. It's called 'Miroirs' and for several reasons, firstly because of the reference to Baudelaire, to the poem 'La mort des amants':' ... leurs doubles lumières ... ces miroirs jumeaux.' This was an opportunity for me to write several pages using a mirror technique in retrograde movement. But not only that – the mirroring occurs in every direction, not only the vertical and horizontal. I must explain too that the lines by Baudelaire which appear as an epigraph at the beginning of each movement were added afterwards. I didn't have any lines of Baudelaire in mind when I started composing, although it's true I was already immersed in Baudelaire's world. Then I said to myself, 'I'm full of this atmosphere, so be it!'. And later on, when I was nearly at the end, I sought out these correspondences. I may have thought about them a little as I composed, but at all events I was determined to avoid illustration.

There's a lot I could say about this score ... Also about the influence of the soloist on the composer, in the sense that I'd been struck by the beauty of Rostropovich's tone, not only in the normal range of the cello, but also high on the A string, which is rare. I worked on the piece between 1967 and 1970 and each time Rostropovich travelled to the West I would show him the new pages, and I had the impression that he was going back home and working on them. But no, he didn't have the time! We met ten days before the premiere at the Aix-en-Provence festival and I realised he didn't know the piece. We had to work very intensely – rehearse, rehearse, rehearse every day. We even rented a studio so we could do so at night without disturbing anyone. After ten days, he knew the work wonderfully well and there were passages he could play by heart; and he felt the music the same way I did. His is an astonishing brain.

RN: Reading the poems you've quoted from, I was particularly struck by the last one, 'La voix', in which the poet says, 'Two voices spoke to me. One, insidious and strong, was saying "The Earth is a cake full of sweetness", ... and the other "Come! Oh come and journey in dreams ..."' Does an artist have to make this choice?

HD: Certainly. It connects with the very notion of work. Baudelaire says somewhere that 'work makes you stronger.' It's a very moral notion. Asceticism comes into it: the artist has to renounce so many things, so many pleasures. Also he's not happy unless he can find the opportunity to realise his true self. Personally, I spend some of my time getting rid of obligations which use up your week and I only find my equilibrium when I'm deep in my work and thinking of nothing but that. There's a spiritual side which one must safeguard at all costs. I've always felt it, but more and more because the material things of life absorb you to such an extent, and especially these days. It's tempting to behave like some people who think only of making appearances on television or on the radio, but in the final analysis that's not how you create a body of work. You do that by this constant searching, and through a spirit of renunciation.

RN: You have a house in the country?

HD: Yes, where I can forget Paris and its claims on me. It's a vital refuge.

RN: As to your working methods, I know that for your string quartet *Ainsi la Nuit* you made some preparatory sketches. Do all your works pass through this stage?

HD: No. In that case there was a particular reason, namely that I hadn't written for string quartet except during my youth, and I absolutely needed to work on making *studies* – often highly technical studies on the instrumental front, concentrating on a particular element: sonorities, harmonics, pizzicatos, sounds made near the bridge, everything you can think of in the way of making sounds. I wanted first of all to think only of these, without bothering too much about form. I made these studies and sent them to the Juilliard Quartet who had time to work on them over the summer. Next I wanted to give all this a consistency, and that's what leads to the fact that this work, which begins with rather short movements sounding a bit like engravings, gradually takes on more consistency. If you go on to the end of the work, you can see that the language has taken on more density, more consistency, and that finally, in writing this work, I made some slight progress in self-discovery.

The work now can stand up to extremely strict analysis: which is strange, because when I began it I wasn't thinking precisely in terms of form. I knew I'd be looking for a form that was different from the classical ones, but it was primarily the material that interested me. And then the titles themselves were added. Some of them have a slightly cosmic, even sacred air, like 'Miroir d'espace' or 'Litanies', which has religious connotations. As for the title *Ainsi la Nuit*, that was my invention.

RN: Before you began, did you study the quartets of the past: Beethoven, Bartók?

HD: Mostly the classics, especially Beethoven, and in particular opp 95 and 127; other composers too, but mostly Beethoven who has always provided me with sustenance in plenty. I also learnt a lot from the Bartók quartets, which owe so much to Beethoven, but I didn't want to study them too much at that moment; also those of Schoenberg slightly and Berg too, although I was rather nervous of immersing myself too deeply in the *Lyric Suite*. It's prodigious music – and prodigiously realized too – but maybe I was afraid of being too influenced. On the other hand I did study Webern over the matter of timbre, in the little pieces called *Bagatelles*. But I didn't spend much time on the French quartets written after Debussy and Ravel, such as those of Honegger and Milhaud, although I did study the two Milhaud quartets (nos 14 and 15) that can be combined to make an octet. Another quartet I did look at was the one by Florent Schmitt – very difficult string writing and very little known; but it's a fine work and ought to be played.

RN: The title *Timbres, espace, mouvement*, was that entirely your own invention?

HD: Yes. If you like, I took two of the three dimensions, keeping 'espace' and 'mouvement', but substituting 'timbres' for 'temps'. It's not absolutely pure music. It's a great problem, I admit. It's true, when I was younger I said that I refused to write programme music. But you can see that for both *Tout un Monde lointain* and for *Timbres* there are references, either to the world of poetry or to that of painting – in the latter case to Van Gogh's *La Nuit étoilée*, an enormously powerful and disturbing masterpiece. 'Movement' and 'space' are both there. The action of the picture is nearly all in the sky, between the monstrous, outsize stars, and to a smaller extent on the ground, with the little church and then the immense cypress tree, which follows the line of the church spire, giving the impression of aspiring towards the infinite – a mystical, vertiginous sensation, such as you feel when you're alone in the countryside or by the sea.

I'd often seen the picture in reproduction and I'd never thought of it in terms of music. That happened following an emotional shock when I saw the painting itself in the Museum of Modern Art in New York. When Rostropovich commissioned me to compose a work for his first season conducting the Washington National Symphony Orchestra, I immediately had the idea of writing a piece inspired by this painting; though, again, without wanting to illustrate it exactly. But I had the painting in my head all the time I was composing, it's true.

It's a diptych and, at the moment, I'm thinking of adding something in the middle. The scoring is not conventional: there are no first or second violins or violas, only 12 cellos and 10 double basses, together with woodwind, brass and percussion. I chose this formation especially to try and get across this impression of emptiness and space in the centre of a musical work. It's more a psychological than an acoustical space, though it is acoustical as well. Now I'm inserting a movement before the second part of the diptych just for the 12 cellos, who will find themselves somewhat exposed. It's not long, about six minutes altogether, but maybe it gives a better balance to the whole. It's an experiment, and perhaps when I hear it I'll be disappointed ...

RN: When we were discussing *Métaboles*, you spoke of the contrast between static and dynamic, and I wonder whether in this painting too ...

HD: Yes, there are static moments. The sections are highly contrasted. There's one at the start which is fairly static, then one that is very dynamic, and the music returns to the static section from time to time. It may sound improvised, but it's not, it's very rigorously structured. Formally, it gives the impression of great mobility. As for the sonority, it's not the same as in other scores of mine, and also there's great violence – the painting, that is extremely violent.

RN: And then *L'Arbre des songes*. I'm intrigued by the title ...

HD: It's the unchanging idea of the tree: in a tree you find everything, from the roots up to the outermost leaves. There's a symbolism in a tree that has always impressed me deeply. I've often stood for a long time in front of a fine oak or a fine cedar, and in fact the music unfolds rather in that way. The title came after the piece was written. I could equally well have called it *L'Arbre sonore*, for instance. The 'songes' is something else; it gives a more poetic resonance – for me now, rather too poetic. It could have been called simply *L'Arbre*. Why not?

I wanted to write a concerto but not one that was too virtuosic. It does contain some virtuosity, but I wanted the soloist and orchestra to mingle frequently, so that it wouldn't be just a violin part with orchestral accompaniment. Even so I did spend quite some time with Paganini's *Caprices* and a number of other pieces for solo violin, remembering what Ravel did so successfully in *Tzigane*, for example. I don't think I would have been able to manage a grand concerto. In *Tzigane* Ravel achieved exactly what he wanted, it's a *tour de force*, but this wasn't what I had in mind. I wanted a work with more depth, and for the orchestral surroundings to be rich too.

RN: We come back, too, to the ideas of the 'mirror' and of a duality, because at the start the second phrase is the mirror of the first.

HD: It's a palindrome, in fact. There are a lot of them in my scores, as there are in those of classical composers. Sometimes the palindrome is a perfect one, sometimes not. In my quartet *Ainsi la Nuit*, in the movement called 'Miroir d'espace', it's perfect, not only from the point of view of pitch but of durations too. But elsewhere in the work the palindromes are not perfect, and deliberately so.

RN: At the opening of the Concerto there's the interval of the perfect fourth which is heard melodically on the violin and harmonically in the orchestra ...

HD: That's deliberate, yes ...

RN: I assumed so! It's a kind of diagonal writing ...

HD: Yes, that's it. It's a score you can analyse in depth and very strictly, because you also have the interludes and in those, for orchestra alone, you find elements that recur in other movements. The pitched percussion, with their ringing, crystalline sounds, play an organic role in the work. They play almost always between the different movements and if you take their melodic line, you can find it again in the central movement, the main slow movement; and there the intervals are inverted. This chiming element extends more and more in the final section, to the point that you feel it invading the whole sound world. I wanted that to grow little by little.

In my Cello Concerto you also find a transitional passage between the movements which plays an organic role, but there it's different. It's a kind of 'theme of chords' which gradually spreads out like a fan. It's a parallel procedure, because it serves as a link between the different sections. But each is organic, each has links with the rest of the score.

RN: And finally, *Mystère de l'instant* ...

HD: This shows a rather different approach from the organisational and formal point of view, as though I perhaps wanted to renew myself. There isn't this constant reference to the concept of memory, and yet

I hope it's formally quite strong, and well balanced. Why *Mystère de l'instant*? There are these two words: 'mystère' for one, with its slightly spiritual feel; and 'l'instant' because I tried to fix certain moments like 'instantanés' – like snapshots. I even thought of calling it *Instantanés*: a succession of moods, but not necessarily linked one to the other. The idea came to me from a chance occurrence. Our country property looks out over the confluence of the Loire and the Vienne, and one summer evening, around 11 o'clock, when there was still a little daylight left, I went for a short walk just beyond our village and I was very intrigued by a succession of birdcalls. They weren't nocturnal birds and each one was singing a distinct song – there were perhaps hundreds of them and they were coming closer and closer. Each one had its own timbre, and also a rhythm that was totally unorganised. This was what made it so captivating, and this lack of organisation attracted me. I said to myself, 'Yes, I'd like to record that.' So the next day I went back at the same time with a tape recorder ... but nothing happened! And since then I've never heard the phenomenon again. So the opening of *Mystère de l'instant* goes back to that idea – it's a kind of impressionism, which I know does exist in my music – but without trying to imitate the birdcalls exactly. Even so, the first movement is called 'Appels'. The strings are very much divided and this happens still more as the piece progresses; and irrational rhythms make a brief appearance too.

RN: I was struck by a paradox: that despite this organisation 'by snapshots', there's a tremendous surge of energy driving on to the end.

HD: Yes, there's an ascensional movement and an increasing density in the texture. In fact, the work now exists in two versions. The first is the one for 24 strings, plus cimbalom and percussion, as premiered by Paul Sacher in Zurich. And then it's been performed with a larger string band: not by doubling all the instruments in parallel, but by doubling the violins, tripling the violas and cellos, and quadrupling the double basses.

RN: I'd like finally to ask you a few more general questions. Have you ever been tempted to try electronic music?

HD: I wouldn't say I've been greatly tempted, but if I hadn't had a job at Radio France which kept me very busy at the time of the first experiments with *musique concrète* in France, I might perhaps have followed these events more closely. The fact was, when I closed my office door in Radio France and got back home, I was thinking only of my own music. So it was a question of time, but also the beginnings of *musique concrète* and of electronic music generally took place very slowly. The search was on for sonorities, for *objets sonores*, and to produce any kind of original sound took hours on end. I took part in these experiments to begin with, but then no more.

Also I have to say that, when I went to concerts to hear pieces in this new medium, I was often disappointed, because I found the timbres so frequently vulgar. But on the other hand, there were other times when I said to myself, 'Ah! If one had the time, one could make something out of that.' In certain cases, that may have given me ideas for works written for traditional orchestras. Now, of course, all that has developed enormously and there are composers who write very expressively for the medium. But for me, I think it's too late, because what I want is to express myself using the means to hand. I hope that's not just an excuse ... certainly it's not from a lack of curiosity. But I don't see how, if I spent time at IRCAM, or if I had spent months at the Groupe de Recherches at Radio France, that would have helped me develop or find my own voice more easily.

One regret of mine is that I haven't written for the voice more than in the few songs I composed when I was 20 or 25 and some that are unpublished. That's what I have in mind now: to write something at any rate for the voice, even perhaps with orchestra – it could be a work that would fit with a staged presentation. I'm thinking seriously along these lines.

RN: And do you think there's a place in music for chance procedures?

HD: A very small one, yes – homoeopathic, maybe! Personally, I've used it to give sections suppleness from the rhythmical point of view, so I've written passages in free rhythm. I know other composers are more ambitious in this area. One has to take account of doctrines and writings – writings especially, because it's very interesting to read John Cage, but I have to say that he interests me more when I read him than when I actually listen to his music. But his writings, inspired by Far Eastern philosophy and Zen in particular, they're very attractive. All that can suggest ways forward.

RN: Do you work at the piano?

HD: A great deal. I go between this table and the piano – an engraver's table, because it's not flat but sloping, which makes writing easier. I use the piano a lot because I like the control it gives and the contact with the sound. At the same time, I know one shouldn't spend all one's time at the piano: it's not good for thought. But certain composers have worked entirely at the piano: Stravinsky, for example, and Ravel. Roussel much less – he wasn't much of a pianist – and you can sense it in his writing. Berlioz too didn't play the piano but the guitar, and that too had its points.

RN: When we were talking about Roussel, you mentioned what you called his 'motoric' side. Is that something you have to guard against in your own music?

HD: Yes, I think so. But with Roussel, that was part of his language, his trade mark. Sometimes I've found that a little irritating in his music, although in general I admire it greatly.

RN: And Berlioz? What are qualities that particularly strike you?

HD: The sense of modernity. He was one of the only composers of the 19th century who was already using the modes, whether in *L'Enfance du Christ* or *Roméo et Juliette*. One's tempted to say 'it's the extraordinary modernity of his orchestration', but it's not only that, it's precisely this well-grounded language: in 'Le songe d'Hérode', for example, in *L'Enfance du Christ*, which I think is one of his finest pages. The mixture of tonal and modal writing is superb. He's always inventing something.

It's very hard to put my finger on what it is exactly that affects me the most in his music. Maybe it's also connected with what we know of his life, his disappointments and adventures. I always find the *Symphonie fantastique* extraordinarily original, even if there are borrowings from Beethoven, and there especially I manage to forget the autobiographical side; one could almost speak of 'pure music' because that's what it's now become.

RN: As you say, you've written rather little for the voice. Do you think opera is a valid form for the 20th century, or indeed for the 21st?

HD: You know, I was listening to Messiaen one day, at a meeting in the Ministry when we were talking about music and France, and the future of opera in particular, and he said: 'Ah! opera contains within itself the seeds of its own demise.' But he himself has written an opera! He's the one you need to ask ... He's written a work which, even if it's not an 'operatic' opera, is one with some marvellous passages of lyricism, of incantation. As for what I think, it's that Liebermann, when he was director of the Paris Opéra, had reason to ask me several times to think about an opera. But you need first of all to have written music for the voice and to feel at ease in that field. And then there are some problems I haven't resolved, even though I've made various attempts. When I won the Prix de Rome, it involved a hybrid subject. The Prix de Rome cantata was a précis of an opera, the situations followed each other at speed and you had to demonstrate your theatrical gifts. The thinking, in giving the prize to people like me, was that we were necessarily going to write for the theatre, which was untrue in my case. I love the theatre, I love the atmosphere but, when you write for the theatre, you have to abide by a certain convention, and I have to admit that I have great difficulty observing the convention of sung conversation and of finding a way of composing such conversation that sounds like me. So I intend to concentrate on the voice before thinking about opera. We shall see.

RN: One last question: although I know that you're not in favour of dogmatism in any sense, is there any advice you would like to give the young composers of today?

HD: Learning to be a composer involves a great deal of self-teaching, even with the best professors. You must always rely on yourself, have a taste for adventure and be extremely curious about everything that's being created all round you. Go and listen to music, but start off by trying to get to know the great works of our own time and, naturally, of the past. But while remaining extremely curious about what's going on round you, allow yourself the possibility of refusal, to know when to refuse, not to be a composer who accepts everything. One sees clearly enough with a certain hindsight (as I can, being the age I am) that not everything is valid. Nadia Boulanger passed on to us this saying of Paul Valéry, which I think is very true: 'Artists are judged by the quality of what they refuse.'

51 **DUTILLEUX AT NEARLY 90**

July 2005

The slightly stooping figure makes its way down the steps somewhat gingerly. The knee operation may have been a success, but at 89 one doesn't take risks. The only surprising thing is that the whirlwind of shouts and applause doesn't lift Henri Dutilleux up to the dome of the Royal Albert Hall, posing unexpected angles for the Proms cameraman.

Stravinsky was given in later years to asking of any new work by another composer, 'Who needs it?' The Proms audience on 27 July 2005 were greeting the London premiere of Dutilleux's *Correspondances* with a resounding 'We do!' But not only that. The response was not merely one of musical enthusiasm, though that it certainly was; it was also a show of genuine affection and gratitude towards a man who has remained true to himself throughout his long life, and in doing so has graced us with some of the most moving and beautiful music of the 20th century – and, happily, beyond.

He has also remained extraordinarily young in spirit. He had travelled from Paris the day before, and the organisers not surprisingly thought he might opt for an early night before the premiere. But when the hotel closed the bar at 11pm, Dutilleux mused, 'I wondered whether there might be a night club … ' In the event there wasn't, but the morning after the premiere he appeared to harbour no ill will. Indeed, he was particularly happy about how things had gone on every front: 'I was touched by Mr [Nicholas] Kenyon's invitation, all the more so as everything in London is always so well organised and the musicians everywhere are on my side (*favorables*).'

He did go on to mention one or two other places where the organisation, and rehearsals especially, had not been up to scratch (I forbear to name names), and in any case 'I don't make a habit of travelling to every premiere'. Indeed not, or he would be in constant movement round the globe. I should also say that there is a gentle subtext to his remark, in that in another interview some years ago [see previous article] Dutilleux stated firmly that a composer's job is not to become a media personality but to stay in his studio composing.

Whether we take this to refer to Pierre Boulez or not, is of course up to us.

He was generous in his praise for Barbara Hannigan's singing of the solo part, 'and from memory', and agreed that the CBSO's playing of the work had settled still further since the British premiere in Birmingham earlier in the year. As he justly remarked, 'Ma musique est difficile, mais jouable.' And 'chantable' too. I wondered why he was now, at this late period in his career, concentrating on the medium of voice and orchestra. He pointed out that there had been earlier attempts, most notably his settings of poems by the Resistance writer Jean Cassou, where he prefers the orchestral versions to the piano ones. But he has always been a lover of what he calls '*les grandes voix féminines*'. Now that he has renounced the idea of ever writing an opera (he says he still can't find a satisfactory way of writing recitative that goes beyond *Pelléas*) the song cycle remains an obvious vehicle through which to express this desire.

Correspondances was written for Dawn Upshaw, who sang in the premiere with Rattle and the Berlin Philharmonic in September 2003. The cycle he is now planning will be for Renée Fleming. Both will be organised around a 'central idea'. In *Correspondances*, this idea is space and the cosmos, realised most memorably in the last of the five songs, 'De Vincent à Théo ...', in which van Gogh tells his brother 'I go outside at night to paint the stars', leading to a quotation from Dutilleux's earlier orchestral work *Timbres, Espace, Mouvement ou La Nuit étoilée*. By contrast the cycle for Fleming will be based on the idea of time. This too has been one of Dutilleux's continuing interests, most notably through the notion of memory with all its Proustian associations, as we can hear in two of his own favourite works, the string quartet *Ainsi la nuit* and the Cello Concerto *Tout un Monde lointain*. At the moment he is reading the poetry of the late Jean Tardieu; once the texts are decided, only then will he start composing.

He has never been happy with the label '*indépendant*', suggesting as it does someone who tries to deny their past. At the same time he is irritated when dictionary entries insist on how much his music has been influenced by Debussy, Ravel and Roussel. Of course, if you're brought up in that domain, some of their music gets in one's bones. But (and this was certainly a new idea for me) he feels late Fauré also deserves a mention. And even the Second Viennese School: '*le sérialisme provoque des questions.*' Not that he ever wished to join some of his friends in protesting openly against serialism. In his view, the best answer to the 'serial terror', as he has called it, was to write good music.

Then there are his Polish roots. These entered the discussion when I touched on the point that so many of the stories told in his songs are stories of human tragedy – the poems of Cassou, the Jewish children chanting 'Pourquoi nous?' in *The Shadows of Time*, the memories of Solzhenitsin (albeit tempered with gratitude) in *Correspondances*. 'It's what is called the duty of remembrance (*le devoir de mémoire*). It's something of an obsession. It's hard. I was born during the 1914 war and my father fought at Verdun. I spent my childhood in a devastated city.' Then he paused and said, 'The Poles went through much worse times.' This reference may be explained by the fact that his maternal grandfather, Julien Koszul, a musician and a friend of Fauré, was Polish, and Dutilleux reckons that this may be the source of the '*fond de mélancolie*' he feels within himself.

Reluctant he may be to set himself up as a media guru, but this certainly doesn't mean he's a total recluse. He continues to keep his finger on the pulse of Parisian musicmaking, so I asked whether he thought contemporary French music was in good shape. 'That's difficult to answer, because it's in the middle of a process of evolution.' But if we agree that variety is a healthy sign, then, yes, the signs are promising. He mentions Betsy Jolas, and Edith Canat de Chizy who, although more or less unknown in Britain, is already a member of the Institut. I volunteer Jean-Louis Florentz, whose untimely death last year has been lamented in many quarters (though, again, his music does not figure in the UK record catalogues). Dutilleux recalls an early cantata, *Requiem de la Vierge*, even if at that time Florentz was still unduly under the Debussy/Ravel influence, and says, rather feelingly, that he was 'a victim of serialism; he couldn't accept it.' Then there are better-known names such as Eric Tanguy, Pascal Dusapin ('a very free spirit') and Philippe Manoury, who intrigues Dutilleux by his masterly integration of traditional and electronic means.

He has considerable interest too in the British composing scene. Apart from George Benjamin, Julian Anderson and Oliver Knussen, he was very impressed by two composers he taught at Tanglewood in 1995, Kenneth Hesketh and Andrew McBirnie, and continues to follow their output.

Finally, I returned to a point he'd made in an earlier conversation, that when he was a student at the Conservatoire there was no course in analysis, and that to a large extent he learnt analytical techniques on his own by studying scores of music that interested him. As a pendant to his admission that he had taken the occasional look at d'Indy's composition treatise, he now told me the story of the 19-year-old Marcel Mihalovici being asked by Ravel, 'Who are you studying with?' Mihalovici replied, 'Vincent d'Indy'. 'What a shame!' said Ravel, 'you're a goner, (*vous êtes perdu!*). He bases all his teaching on the Beethoven sonatas.'

In any case, Dutilleux is not convinced that analytical dexterity has much to do with composing. For every work the form has to be rethought. The crucial element, and this very much goes for his own works, is 'l'idée centrale'. No more convincing evidence could be provided for this than his Violin Concerto, whose title, *L'Arbre des songes*, combines the mysterious, meditative aspect of the dream with the logical structure of the tree, growing entirely from a single seed. Similarly, for a piece of music you find a central idea, then you construct a system from it. If I had to give one piece of advice to listeners to his music, it would be to concentrate particularly on the fragments heard in its quiet openings, since this is where the seed is often planted (in the Violin Concerto, in the soloist's rising fourths).

One of his remarks might be cause for surprise: that his catalogue of works is 'pas important'. Until you realise that he is talking quantity, not quality. But who decides how many works a composer should write? Dutilleux's œuvre talks quality – witness the requests for works from performers the world over.

52 HENRI DUTILLEUX – OBITUARY
22 January 1916 – 22 May 2013

Henri Dutilleux, who has died aged 97, was the outstanding French composer between Messiaen and Boulez and, like both of them, achieved a wholly individual synthesis of ear-catching colours and harmonies with formal rigour. In a musical world where many loudly proclaim their independence, he was a true but discreet 'indépendant'.

Artistic talent came to him from both sides of his family. His paternal great-grandfather, Constant Dutilleux, was a friend of Delacroix and Corot: a Corot landscape, handed down through the family, hung above the fireplace in the composer's Paris apartment. His maternal grandfather, Julien Koszul, of Polish descent, had been a fellow-pupil of Fauré at the Ecole Niedermeyer and later, as director of the Roubaix Conservatoire, had encouraged Roussel to leave the navy and concentrate on music.

Born in Angers, Dutilleux moved to Douai after the first world war with his family. He studied at the local conservatoire with Victor Gallois who, unusually for the time, made him work at harmony and counterpoint almost simultaneously, instead of regarding the first as a preparation for the second. Gallois also had the distinction (unenviable, in Dutilleux's view) of having won the Prix de Rome in 1905, the year Ravel was disqualified in the preliminary round; 'my own reservations', wrote Dutilleux later, 'with regard to the Institut and officialdom in general stem in part from that'. But he always spoke highly of Gallois' teaching, and when he entered the classes of the Gallon brothers Noël and Jean at the Paris Conservatoire in 1932, he was 'déjà armé'. He flourished too in the composition class of Henri Busser, but in retrospect wished that he had been able to profit more from Maurice Emmanuel's history classes, and even that he had pursued his early organ studies with Marcel Dupré – even though he never regarded Dupré highly, either as player or composer. 'Tournemire was a different matter.'

This ambivalent relationship with virtuosity lasted throughout his life. On the one hand, unlike most students, he actually enjoyed writing fugues as an abstract discipline. On the other, he enjoyed, by his own admission, not only 'a taste for a beautiful chord' but also the visceral excitement of fine performers doing difficult things well: he liked Barenboim's recording of his First Symphony because he took the scherzo at the correct, headlong tempo. Setting one aspect off against the other produced many of the most exciting and rewarding moments in his music.

In 1938 he crowned his Conservatoire career by winning the Prix de Rome, although, in line with his cool attitude to official honours, he thought his 1937 entry, when he came second, was a better piece. But perhaps the most perceptive comment on Dutilleux's Prix de Rome offerings had been made in 1936 by Maurice Emmanuel, who wrote to Busser that 'at no point was Dutilleux banal: perhaps he interpreted the subject in too gloomy a light, but several happy ideas on the melodic front justified his [third] prize'. Dutilleux's fight against banality was indeed to be chronic, and one of the things that made him a slow composer, to his own chagrin. An attraction to melancholy was also innate, if counter-balanced by his increasing admiration for Berlioz.

The outbreak of war cut short his stay in Rome, and he returned to Paris. During the Occupation he was accompanist for a singing class at the Conservatoire and was appointed 'chef de chant' at the Opéra (preparing Pfitzner's *Palestrina* in 1942 was 'one of the most miserable experiences of my life'). In the meantime, in 1941 he met the pianist Geneviève Joy, who was to become his wife five years later and, following a performance of his *Sarabande pour orchestre*, his abilities as an orchestrator were widely remarked upon.

But the mature Dutilleux had little time for any of the music he wrote before the Piano Sonata, which Joy premiered at the Société nationale de musique in April 1948. It is a large work, taking us away from the Ravelian influence which bedevilled much of French music in the 1930s and early 1940s, and celebrating a pianism that is 'sensual, not too dry'. It was a turning point in his career, and from here on he was 'increasingly interested in large forms, with a desire to change and renew them'. But he never returned to the piano for this purpose, preferring to limit himself to shorter pieces in what he confessed was a difficult medium for the 20th-century composer.

Nor did he experiment with electronic music, although his post as Head of Musical Illustration at French Radio for 18 years from 1945 gave him access to the wherewithal. Instead, ever the 'indépendant', he preferred to see what could still be made with traditional resources.

The answer, as provided by his First Symphony, was 'a great deal'. Its broadcast, on 7 June 1951 under the baton of Roger Désormière, led to many performances over the next few years and to the spread of Dutilleux's reputation outside France. His independence of traditional models shows both in his adoption of a passacaglia as the opening movement and in the smaller instrumental groups (for instance, piano, timpani and clarinets) which often oppose the orchestral mass.

This success was repeated by his music for Roland Petit's ballet *Le Loup* (1953). Later he would accept only the second of its three scenes as worthy of performance, but the whole score, transmuting various Stravinskyan rhythmic and melodic procedures and with more than a nod in the direction of *La Valse*, is among the most sheerly beautiful scores he ever wrote, with a bittersweet tone that was to become one of his hallmarks. It was also one of his wife's favourites out of all his works. The Second Symphony, premiered by Charles Münch in Boston in 1959, continued the antagonistic preoccupations of the First, with a constant smaller orchestral group formally acknowledged in the score. But again Dutilleux was not merely copying the procedures of the 18th-century concerto grosso: the interplay is highly nuanced, with the smaller group prompting, interrupting, even contradicting the larger one, and the brass writing, as the composer admitted, owes something to Count Basie and Duke Ellington. Its subtitle, 'Le double', also bears on Dutilleux's interest in flux and, nourished by his love of Proust, in the actions of memory. These preoccupations informed each of the four major orchestral works Dutilleux worked on between 1959 and 1985.

Métaboles was commissioned by George Szell for the Cleveland Orchestra, and it was premiered by them in 1965. Dutilleux referred to it as 'a Concerto for orchestra' and he had in his mind's ear 'the purity and timbral éclat' of the Cleveland players, 'their luminosity, especially in the woodwind'. The 'méta' of the title indicates what Dutilleux called the 'progressive growth' of one idea into another, this growth being coloured by the privileging of the different orchestral families in the course of the work's five movements, culminating in a more expansive version of the opening 'Incantation'. This allusion to the magic of music was not haphazard. Dutilleux believed in composition as a quasi-sacred occupation and permitted himself to utter (for him) harsh words about composers who spent more time in front of television cameras than in front of their manuscript paper.

The three orchestral works that followed touched again on virtuosity and its relationship with structure. The two concertos – *Tout un Monde lointain* (1967-70) and *L'Arbre des songes* (1979-85) – written respectively for cellist Mstislav Rostropovich and violinist Isaac Stern – are grounded respectively in the world of Baudelaire and in the idea of arboreal ramification, and both conjunctions brought with them a high degree of virtuosity, focussed, in the case of *Tout un Monde*, on Rostropovich's especially beautiful tone high on the A string. But, as usual, these virtuosic and colouristic aspects are set against formal ones, such as the retrogrades in the Cello Concerto's fourth movement, 'Miroirs'. Between these two concertos came *Timbres, espace, mouvement* (1976-78), inspired by van Gogh's painting *La Nuit étoilée*. Like Debussy over *L'Après-midi d'un faune*, Dutilleux was quick to resist the notion of any too schematic correspondence between the music and its referend, but he did admit that his omission of violins and violas was suggested by 'the vertiginous impression of space, of emptiness' between the church and the cypress on the ground and 'the celestial vault'. Although Dutilleux never used overtly religious words or symbols in his music, he recognised the 'mystic, cosmic' element in this piece, quoting van Gogh's letter to his brother: 'I have a terrible need for religion. So I go outside at night to paint the stars'.

One of the works of which Dutilleux was proudest was his string quartet *Ainsi la Nuit* (1973-76). Before writing it, he studied the literature intensely (Beethoven, particularly op. 95 and op. 127, Bartók, Webern's *Bagatelles*, but not Berg's *Lyric Suite* – 'I didn't want to get too close to it!') and even after that went through the stage of writing sketches, called *Nuits*, exploring individual string textures. Only then did he set about constructing what he later felt was one of his most coherent works, coherence for him standing higher in the hierarchy of aims than any melodic, harmonic or colouristic features. The work immediately became a classic of the genre.

That Dutilleux was no ivory tower composer but one alive to the darker side of the 20th century became clear in his chamber work *Les Citations* (1985-90), originally written for Aldeburgh but revised for the 50th anniversary in 1990 of Jehan Alain's death on active service, and in *The Shadows of Time* (1995-97) in which three boy soloists, representing concentration camp victims, sing the heartbreaking refrain 'Pourquoi nous?' Between these two he broke new ground for him in *Mystère de l'instant*, one of the last of Paul Sacher's commissions for the Basle Chamber Orchestra: instead of the Proustian density of interrelated thoughts, the work consists of 'ten sequences of varying proportions, each conveying a particular aspect of the sound world, recorded spontaneously without a prepared outline as a basis'. But on repeated listening the hand of Dutilleux, the master of structure, remains audible, even if less conspicuous.

In 2002 he wrote *Sur le même accord* for Anne-Sophie Mutter and this was followed by two orchestral song cycles, *Correspondances* and *Le Temps l'horloge*. As often, he had particular performers in mind: for *Correspondances*, completed in 2003, Dawn Upshaw and what he heard as the 'instrumental quality' of her voice. The texts are letters from Prithwindra Mukherjee, Alexandr Solzhenitsin, Rainer Maria Rilke and Vincent van Gogh, the latter quoting the words cited above, followed by an extract from *Timbres, Espace, Mouvement*. In writing the four songs of *Le Temps l'horloge* he had in his ear the rich, dramatic voice of Renée Fleming. He also valued the long, enthusiastic letters she wrote him as the composition proceeded, and not least her professionalism at the premiere of the whole cycle in Paris in 2009, when she was unhappy with her performance and insisted immediately on singing it again. For the first two songs he turned to poems by Jean Tardieu, for the third to Robert Desnos's 'Le dernier poème', already set by Poulenc, and for the last song he returned to Baudelaire and to his injunction to 'get drunk! On wine, poetry, virtue, or whatever!' Although Dutilleux's longevity may partly be ascribed to regular consumption of the best Bordeaux could provide, his compositional control is, needless to say, as complete as ever. As in *Correspondances*, the accordion is brought in off the boulevards to make a respectable contribution.

His wife died of cancer at the end of 2009, and without the support of her cheerful, vigorous common sense he lived through some dark months. But in 2010 he began to think about writing some children's pieces for piano. Then, going backstage at the end of that year to congratulate Myung Whun Chung after one of the best performances he had ever heard of *Métaboles*, he was asked by the conductor to compose these for orchestra ... Sadly, his response to *Ma mère l'Oye* was never to be written.

In the last decades of his life, Dutilleux was invited all over the world to performances of his music. His generosity in accepting was counterbalanced by his unwillingness to leave his studio on the

Ile Saint-Louis, which was the heart of his existence – he liked to quote Baudelaire to the effect that 'le travail fortifie'. If never exactly clubbable, Dutilleux was one of the gentlest and most charming of men, with a delightful sense of humour. He was also inexhaustibly kind: what other composer of international stature would offer to find out for an English visitor the Bibliothèque nationale's dates of opening? He had a strong line in self-deprecation (on learning that a young English composer was notably slow in delivering, he commented, 'Il n'est pas le seul') and this, together with his refusal to pontificate, perhaps contributed to the slow growth of his fame. But it was indeed a 'croissance progressive', and by the time of his death it had reached a climax comparable with that of *Métaboles*. Its 'résonance', and that of his highly wrought, intellectually tough and deeply passionate music, will undoubtedly ring on through the 21st century and beyond.

53 ANDRÉ SCHAEFFNER AND PIERRE BOULEZ

A review for the TLS of the following two books:
André Schaeffner: *Variations sur la musique* (Fayard, 1998)
Pierre Boulez, André Schaeffner: *Correspondance 1954-1970* ed. Rosângela Pereira de Tugny (Fayard, 1998)

In his late seventies, André Schaeffner confessed to what he felt was his bad habit of jumping from one subject to another. Bad habit or not, it led to a career as critic, historian and ethnomusicologist with no parallels in the French-speaking world. As Pierre Boulez says in his introduction to their correspondence:

> His erudition was certainly impressive but equally, and perhaps more so, the perspicacity of his viewpoint, the sharpness of his attention and the individuality of his relationship with the object that was being observed and studied.

Born in 1895, Schaeffner studied at the Schola Cantorum and through his friendship with Wanda Landowska came to write a well-received article on the harpsichord. At the same time he was working as a music journalist and collaborating on a book on jazz. In insisting that no history of the subject could be written without understanding the musics of Africa, Schaeffner upset both those who preferred to regard jazz as entirely American in origin and those who, though they might be wowed by Josephine Baker, thought this outpost of barbarism to be no fit subject for serious scholarship.

In 1931, after a visit to Africa to study indigenous music in its native habitat, he returned to Paris to found the department of musical ethnology in the Musée d'ethnographie du Trocadéro, later the Musée de l'homme. He remained its director until 1965, collecting non-Western instruments and writing a classic text on their origin.

But Schaeffner's bad habit prevented him from immuring himself totally in tam-tams and marimbas. For more than sixty years he was in the swim of Parisian musical activity and in an article on, say, Stravinsky the reader is liable to be brought up short by an attestation that Schaeffner has in front of him a handwritten letter from the composer which says, about *The Rite*, that 'Satie once told me that Debussy was critical of the orchestration'. It has to be admitted that he is rather quick to claim priority in spotting this or that – the text of *Variations sur la musique* is peppered with references to facts that have been overlooked and to influences that have never been catalogued (such as that of *L'Histoire du soldat* on sections of Schoenberg's *Serenade* or of Rimsky-Korsakov's *The Maid of Pskov* on Debussy's habit of repeating phrases). This can make him sometimes a tough adversary, sometimes a touch obsessive, as over his distinction between Valéry's Monsieur Teste and Debussy's abbreviated M. Croche, where he's not even wholly consistent. In general though, he's a good-humoured writer, both of articles and letters, and his wide-ranging mind comes up with some fascinating comparisons.

I cannot, I think, do better in giving the flavour of that mind and of the writing that emerged from it than by indulging in his own bad habit and taking a few disparate subjects more or less at random. Already in 1946, Schaeffner was taking an ethnologist's view of atonality and putting it over with characteristic wit:

> I know too many ways of putting together musical scales differently or giving them different temperaments, of including or excluding privileged or forbidden notes, of fashioning intervals other than ours to allow myself to be persuaded that atonality is the *only* remedy for an exhaustion of major and minor, which in any case I don't believe in…Erik Satie was pleased to remind us of one of Alphonse Allais's characters, an imaginary inventor who patented a procedure for removing elasticity from rubber. It could be that someone one day may discover a method of removing from music that ultimate evil, namely sound.

Then there are his puncturings of long cherished ignorances and suppositions. The Musée du Conservatoire was given an almost complete Javanese gamelan in February 1887, so Debussy and others did not need to wait until the 1889 Exhibition to hear these sounds, although of course they may well have done so. Airy speculation about what works of Schoenberg Debussy might or might not have known can be held in check by indubitable facts. In the article 'Variations Schoenberg', written in 1951 in response to Boulez's 'Trajectoires' (both are printed as appendices to their *Correspondance*), Schaeffner verifies that in 1912 Parisians could have heard *Verklärte Nacht* and read the third movement of the op. 10 Quartet in a magazine to which Debussy was a contributor; in 1913 they could have heard the 'Song of the Wood Dove' and the op. 11 piano pieces played by Robert Schmitz, and read an extract from those pieces in a book on modern harmony; and in 1914 they could have heard the op. 19 piano pieces played by Alfredo Casella and read in another magazine a song from *Das Buch der hängenden Gärten*. So when, in 1915, Debussy warns that Stravinsky *'incline dangereusement du côté de Schoenberg'* (leans dangerously in the direction of Schoenberg), the chances are that he knew what he was talking about, as usual.

Boulez's first contact with Schaeffner came through their articles on *Pierrot lunaire* mentioned above. Schaeffner corrected some of Boulez's errors (duly acted upon when the latter's article was reprinted in *Relevés d'apprenti*), but with a mixture of authority and sympathy which made clear to the apprentice composer that here was no *vieux de la vieille*. It was a true meeting of minds and, as the excellent editor of the correspondence says, a lucky one in that the gap left by the death of neoclassicism was ready to be filled by ethnic elements. She also argues, persuasively for me, that Boulez's works tend towards a ceremonial gravity which may well be traceable to the knowledge passed on by Schaeffner. Certainly, thanks to him, there was never any danger of Boulez treating non-Western music as a quick exotic fix – a charge which Boulez himself has implicitly levelled against Messiaen, who remained relatively ignorant of this music's ritual bases and used it to a large extent simply because he liked the noise it made.

The correspondence between Schaeffner and Boulez gravitates round Debussy, Stravinsky and Schoenberg. As we know from Boulez's 1948 article 'Propositions', he had read Artaud before meeting or corresponding with Schaeffner, but it was Schaeffner who made the specific link between Artaud and Debussy's *Pelléas*, prompting the 'cruel' interpretation of the opera which Boulez conducted at Covent Garden in 1969 and put on disc the following year. In letters to Schaeffner Boulez lets go with splendid verbal virtuosity against the caricature of Debussy as a *'voluptueux lymphatique'* (a flabby voluptuary) and as a *'débile mollasson qu'on présente comme le fin du fin de la musique française entre les marrons glacés et Chanel no 4 (ou 5 ou 10?)'* (a spineless sponge representing the ultimate goal of French music, somewhere between the *marrons glacés* and Chanel no 4, or 5, or 10).

On Stravinsky, Schaeffner develops points of view already aired in his 1931 monograph. In the appended article 'Renard et l'époque russe de Strawinsky', commissioned by Boulez in 1954, he notes that the composer's Russian music is quite different from any Russian music that had gone before, and that his returns to earlier preoccupations are always given a different emphasis, that *'aucune expérience n'a été définitivement close'* (no experience has been definitely closed off), a judgment surely not lost on a younger composer just embarked on a lifetime of works-in-progress. And though Schaeffner concurs when Boulez finally, after anguished ratiocination, plumps for the 'verdeur' of *The Rite* over the more studied atmosphere of *Les Noces*, they agree to differ about the nature of the flute/clarinet passage in *Symphonies of wind instruments*. Schaeffner hears it as pastoral, Boulez (with his Roman Catholic upbringing) rather as the continuation of the liturgy; but as for the high-pitched lament at the beginning, it's the sudden entry of a Low Mass, and 'I should always want to play this passage like, for example, the low, muttered dialogue between the priest and his choirboy at a Low Mass'.

He goes on to suggest further comparisons with the murmuring that precedes trance and with the violin in traditional Chinese theatre – whereupon a punctilious editorial note informs us that the indication 'Violon chinois' is indeed to be found in the autograph sketches for the second version of *Figures-Doubles-Prismes* in the Paul Sacher Foundation in Basle.

Much of the volume is concerned with *Pierrot lunaire*, both the problems of performance and the awfulness of the poems – though Schaeffner produces strong evidence that Laforgue had read them in 1885 and used them for his own, superior ends. Harnessed to *Pierrot* comes *Le Marteau sans maître*, and here Schaeffner the ethnomusicologist was doubly valuable, not only introducing Boulez to non-Western instruments but physically abetting him in smuggling gongs and tam-tams through the cellars of the Palais de Chaillot, no doubt to avoid the time, paper and expense involved in any French bureaucratic exercise.

Inevitably, there are repetitions both within and between these two volumes. But they are a small price to pay for the continuously high level of stimulation, the *Correspondance* whetting the appetite for the complete Boulez letters that will no doubt appear one day – though let us hope, not for many years. My sharpest visual memory from either volume comes from a Boulez letter of 1966:

> The public, by and large, always give me the impression of being, for the most part, like the pigeons in the square. When a male wants to attack them, they scatter in terror, but guided too by reason, so as not to lose sight of the conqueror! Novelty is like that: people fear it, and demand it…

54 THIRTY YEARS OF IRCAM 1977–2007

History

In the field of music the French Revolution was a mixed blessing. True, it gave rise to the Conservatoire de Paris, but court patronage was no more. Napoleon approved of Spontini, but understandably he had more important things on his mind than subsidising composers, and so things continued through the 19th and early 20th centuries – the Establishment view being, if the bourgeoisie wanted their musical cake, they could bake it themselves.

The turning point came with the 1937 Exposition Internationale des Arts et Techniques, when the French state, having once commissioned Berlioz to write his *Requiem* and *Grande Symphonie funèbre et triomphale*, now broke nearly a century's ensuing inactivity by commissioning a number of French composers, including Auric, Milhaud, Honegger, Messiaen and Poulenc, to write works for the Exposition. The advent of World War II and the Occupation prevented any immediate follow-up to this, as did France's slow post-war recovery. But the seed had been sown.

That Paris in the 1920s had been the musical centre of the world is generally acknowledged. But its pre-eminence depended to a considerable extent on powerful individuals: Diaghilev most prominently. And so it was to be after World War II when Pierre Boulez emerged as the leader of the young Turks of French music.

He had come from St Etienne to Paris to study with Messiaen, but was horrified at the city's slaphappy way of organising its music, and no less at the low standard of performing anything later than Ravel. Typically, he was not prepared to wait for ever for someone else to inject some purpose into Paris's musical life, and in 1954 he set up modern music concerts at the Petit-Marigny theatre. But a plea to the Minister of Education for funds was met with the objection that 'your programmes are far too revolutionary; France, gentlemen, is the country of the balanced way (*le pays de la mesure*)'. It would be another 15 years before Boulez really got his hands on the levers of French musical power.

The founding of IRCAM

The motor behind Boulez's vision was the crudeness and unresponsiveness, as perceived by him, of the electronic tools of the time, which were unable to fulfil his own compositional ideals, especially in combining electronics with live performers. But if IRCAM could never have come about without Boulez's drive and vision, nor could it without the support of President Georges Pompidou. It was he who in 1969 pushed through the creation of the Centre named after him, designed by Renzo Piano and Richard Rogers, and incorporating the Institut de Recherche et Coordination Acoustique/Musique with Boulez as its director. The bulldozers moved in next to the Place Igor Stravinsky in 1973 and the following year Boulez was ready to announce the fourfold aims of IRCAM: research, compositions and their promotion, teaching and publishing.

As things turned out, not all these aims were to be easily compatible. In particular the demands of research and of composition were often to pull the resources of the institution in different directions. By 'research' Boulez meant research into the new and exciting world of electro-acoustics, which he himself had already dipped into in a 1972 version of ... *explosante-fixe* ... for flute, clarinet, trumpet, harp, vibraphone, violin, viola, cello and electro-acoustic equipment, and which he felt offered unlimited opportunities for producing the sounds of the future. IRCAM's first music computer, named 4A, was installed in 1976. The following year the Centre Georges-Pompidou and IRCAM opened their doors, even if the plaster of the underground building was not yet dry. 70 concerts spread through the year presented Boulez's version of which composers were of value in the immediate past, and currently (Ligeti, Carter, Berio, Nono, Takemitsu, Ferneyhough, but not Reich or Glass or Dutilleux). The message was 'We go on from here.'

The early years

This was easier said than done. One of the basic problems was that if you engage first-rate practical musicians you should not be surprised if, rather than explore electro-acoustics, they go their own way and stick to modifying the traditional instruments they grew up with. By the end of 1980, the five departmental heads, including Berio, had all left and it became obvious that some reorganisation was needed.

Boulez responded by splitting IRCAM into two groups: musicians and scientists. But what was to be their relative standing? And how were they fully to comprehend each others' concerns and language? These internal problems were compounded by impatience and resentment among musicians outside IRCAM, who saw large amounts of money going into it and not much coming out.

This was understandable – and Boulez's trenchant pronouncements that, for example, 'At my age and in my position I refuse to be dependent on the kind of nonentities who join committees' didn't help. But it was not all bleak. In 1983 a disc was produced called 'A portrait of IRCAM', containing sound examples of the research being undertaken: synthesis and sound simulation, psycho-acoustics, composition with real sounds and word synthesis, and it sold well. It also contained an extract from *Répons*, Boulez's first work using IRCAM's electronic resources together with conventional instruments. A first version of this piece (with the 4A now developed into the 4X capable of 200 million operations per second) had been heard in 1981 and greeted, with relief in many quarters, as a masterpiece. At the same time there were complaints from technical staff, as recorded by Georgina Born (a cello-playing ethnographer who studied the institution at first hand in 1984) that three of the best pieces to come out of IRCAM – *Répons*, Jonathan Harvey's *Mortuos plango, vivos voco*, and York Höller's *Arcus* – 'could just as well have been made without all the technological resources of IRCAM, with existing music software or even simple analog devices, and did not really utilize the unique computer music possibilities of IRCAM'.

Perhaps all these negative responses were only to be expected, since no such ambitious musical enterprise had ever been started from scratch before. At least one could say that the reign of 'la mesure' was over. And certainly, for all the tensions within IRCAM, there was no let-up in energy. The Ensemble intercontemporain, a small performing body specialising in contemporary music and conceived by Boulez as a necessary adjunct to IRCAM's research and compositional activities, went from strength to strength, while IRCAM's tenth anniversary in Spring 1987 was celebrated with commissions from six composers, including Philippe Manoury, Kaija Saariaho and George Benjamin. In 1988 a doctorate in 20th-century music was instigated in tandem with three other Paris institutions and in 1990 the first session was held of a year-long course in computer theory and practice for young composers.

IRCAM and the outside world

In 1992 Boulez decided to stand down as director, perhaps recognising that his own high profile was influencing IRCAM too strongly, however he might try to mitigate this. It is significant certainly that from this same year, under the new director Laurent Bayle, dated the production of the magazine *Résonance,* containing 'user-friendly' articles, and the opening-up of the institution to the general public (*première opération portes ouvertes*). This was followed in 1993 by setting up the Forum Ircam 'aimed at reinforcing the links with the musical community'. These moves were undoubtedly politically motivated to some extent, since the grumbles over IRCAM's generous funding had not gone away, but they also marked a new confidence in now possessing techniques that could be taught, and there were conversely always things to be learnt: the *Agora* festivals, initiated in 1998, take contemporary music out for a fortnight each June into theatres, cinemas and open spaces in Paris, from which feedback can be stimulating. This led in 1999 to the founding of a new department of 'choreographic invention'. IRCAM also began to expand its activities beyond France, for example through the *Ecrins* programme (*Environnement de classification et de recherche intelligente de sons*), a sound sample database, available online or via the internet, which users can enrich with their own samples. The open-door policy is emphasised by the provision of courses in composition and in the use of information technology, and in 2003 an Internet programme was set up to teach music to 1700 schools throughout France. It is also possible for the public to visit IRCAM (tel: 01 44 78 48 16) and taste the delights, among other things, of the anechoid chamber in which the resonance is nil. This forms part of another of IRCAM's projects, the regulation of acoustics for concert halls.

Past and future

It is still too soon perhaps to pontificate on the success or otherwise of IRCAM. It has to be said that, despite IRCAM, composition involving electronics remains the preserve of a minority of 'serious' composers, and for obvious practical reasons. At the same time an institution that has attracted Berio, Murail, Grisey, Lindberg, Birtwistle, Benjamin, Harvey and Saariaho, with Messiaen, Ligeti and Stockhausen coming to give lectures, can in no way be written off as irrelevant. The general consensus might be that in those years around ten really good works have emerged – as examples beyond the three mentioned above I have been offered Murail's *Désintégrations*, Lindberg's *Joy* and Birtwistle's *Mask of Orpheus*, among others. Whether you think that is enough for the time and money spent will depend on your point of view, especially if you are a conventional French composer working outside the system – or, in the case of Xenakis, a composer whose already existing technological institute was totally by-passed. But the pedagogical aspect must remain important. George Benjamin says he has learnt a lot about organization and timbre simply from working in such a highly structured environment: 'rational thinking can strengthen your dreams'. Jonathan Harvey, who visited IRCAM regularly, spoke highly of the technical help he received, reckoning that the ivory-tower mentality was a thing of the past. Certainly an engagement with the outside world is proclaimed in the numerous CDs, books and periodicals about new music that IRCAM has been putting out. Above all, it has been a powerhouse for new ideas and a meeting place for composers from all over the world.

If there is a threat to IRCAM, other than a reduction in funding due to world financial instability, then it comes from the proliferation of small computers possessing extraordinary capabilities – and getting smaller and more capable all the time. If pop musicians can top the charts with discs produced in their bedrooms, then IRCAM needs to keep working to stay ahead of the game. To this extent political and technical realities combine to keep it travelling along this road to greater openness. For the time being though, and over 20 years after Boulez left the helm, IRCAM, both organisationally and musically, seems to be in excellent shape.

55 ADIEU, PIERRE BOULEZ – OBITUARY

26 March 1925 – 5 January 2016

Roger Nichols: So what are your chief memories of the time around 1945?

Pierre Boulez (testily): People continually asking 'Do you remember the quality of the meat before the war?'.

Nostalgia was never an item in Boulez's repertoire, his thoughts turned always to the present and especially to the future, whether his own or that of music in general. His reply also demonstrates an impatience with the commonplace which marked his dealings with the French establishment, both musical and political, giving rise to the notion of him as one of the awkward squad, very full of his own ideas and unwilling ever to compromise. To some extent, this is true. But it's far from being the whole picture. Unquestionably, without his compositions, his legacy of recordings as a conductor, his writings on music and his administrative skill and drive, the musical scene today would be of a quite different order. This dominance was partly achieved by the application of remorseless logic to both organisational and interpersonal problems. But at the same time he was a man of great warmth and charm.

He was born on 26 March 1925 in Montbrison, a little town 35km north west of Saint-Etienne, into a stable middle-class family. His father, Léon, was an engineer, the technical director of a steel works, and both he and his wife, Marcelle, were educated as Catholics. Before coming to Paris in the autumn of 1943, Boulez's most extended period of education was in the seminary in his home town between 1932 and 1940. While he felt distaste for what he saw as the priests' 'mechanical attitude that had nothing to do with profound conviction', the habits of hard work, discipline, order and early rising remained with him. Little in his lifestyle, opinions or music would ever lead one to realize that he was a Southerner, his birthplace a mere 30km away from Chabrier's.

Young Pierre's high marks in chemistry and physics at the local seminary led Papa to hope his son might follow in his footsteps – a hope not impeded by the fact that in Montbrison there was no musical activity whatever outside piano lessons. But these were enough for Pierre to sense that music was to be his métier and, via Saint-Etienne and Lyons, in 1943 he decamped to Paris and the Conservatoire. In the autumn of 1944 he entered the class of Olivier Messiaen, 'without whom I would never have become what I have'. Even so he embarrassed his teacher by being at the forefront of those booing Stravinsky's *Norwegian Moods* in a festival of that composer's music. Despite his admiration for the man, he always had reservations about some elements of Messiaen's musical language. Turning the pages for the vibraphone player at the first performance of *Trois petities Liturgies* in 1945, he appreciated what he later called 'the side-order' – the gamelan-inspired sounds – as well as Désormière's sober and efficient conducting, which would be a model for his own. But the swooping of the ondes martenot and the sugary added sixths prompted talk of 'bordello' music, leading to a temporary cooling of relations between the two composers.

As Boulez later said, you learn quickly when you're primed to do so. He studied in Messiaen's class for no more than a year, although he attended his extramural analysis classes for rather longer, studying, among other things, Berg's *Lyric Suite*, *Pierrot Lunaire* and *The Rite of Spring*. He also took weekly counterpoint lessons from 1944 to 1946 with Honegger's wife Andrée Vaurabourg, who remembered that 'he never missed a lesson and was never late'. His short piano pieces *Notations* from 1945 show him following the 12-note path of Webern, who was to remain one of his favourite composers. Like Les Six after the First World War, though in very different terms, he was set on striking out along new paths, and it was no accident that his key Stravinsky pieces were *The Rite of Spring* and *Les Noces*.

A combination of their violence with his own impatience can be heard in his Sonatine for flute and piano and in his first two Piano Sonatas of 1946 and 1948. Already he was using the 12-note series in a personal way, refusing to be bound by Schoenbergian rules. In the Sonatine, the writing for piano, 'the archetypal instrument of delirium', set the explosive pattern for later keyboard works, especially the Second Piano Sonata (1948), which nearly 70 years later is still a stiff test for the virtuoso: Messiaen claimed that Boulez 'totally transformed the sonority of the piano'. The First Sonata, as the writer and producer Dominique Jameux pointed out, is built on binary oppositions which would later feature in Boulez's 'open-form' works (choose either this or that), while in the Second Sonata, lasting some 30 minutes, there are no fewer than 69 indications of 'subito' and 'subitement'. But also from 1948 dates the sensuous work for soprano, chorus and orchestra *Le Soleil des eaux*, in which we hear not only his attraction to the female voice, but his delicate, exact orchestral writing, proving that the calculating mathematician also has a warm heart. The piece is also one of many that he later reworked (in this case, four times over the next 17 years). He never felt the need to apologise for these 'works in progress', claiming that it was merely professional to try and improve one's technique and that hearing performances of one's music was 'the best way of learning what you have done wrong!'

His run-ins with the French musical establishment did not get under way immediately, perhaps because between 1946 and 1956 he found congenial employment with the Jean-Louis Barrault theatre company as musical director, which involved some writing of incidental music, but also conducting of other composers' scores with players of variable ability. This provided invaluable experience in tempering his natural impatience with anything that was not perfect. The composers never had anything but praise for his professionalism even though, as with Milhaud's music for Claudel's *Christophe Colomb*, they could not help but realize the gulf fixed between their musical idiom and his. But he was still far from happy with the general standard of Paris musicmaking, and looking back in later years would castigate all his Conservatoire teachers except Messiaen as incompetent, as he did the performances of music by the Second Viennese School, which in his view did nothing but damage to the composers' reputations. The repertoire in Paris too was restricted, and it was not until 1958 that Boulez heard Mahler for the first time, in Germany. Meanwhile he was in contact with other enquiring minds such as Cage and Stockhausen, who arrived in Paris in 1949 and 1951 respectively, but essentially he trod a lonely path, with no readymade outlet for his music. The initial versions of *Le Soleil des eaux* (1947) and especially of *Le Visage nuptial* (1946), both for vocal forces and orchestra, consolidated his reputation for writing music that was difficult, even impossible, to perform.

With Barrault's company Boulez had no more than 10 to 15 players at his disposal, but he reckoned it helped his conducting to start with such small forces. Encouraged by Barrault, in 1953 he inaugurated the concerts of the Domaine musical, dedicated to older music, including Dufay, Gesualdo and Bach as well as Beethoven's *Grosse Fuge*, and to contemporary works by Stravinsky, Varèse and the Second Viennese School – not least to show how the latter *should* be conducted! At the same time, he was attending the modern music summer schools in Darmstadt, allied with concert series in Donaueschingen and Baden-Baden. The first piece of his really to hit the headlines, *Le Marteau sans maître* for alto and six instruments, was first performed in 1955 at the ISCM Festival in Baden-Baden. The French committee, which had refused to sponsor the work, walked out, but Stravinsky later found it the most impressive piece he knew from the younger generation. The generous percussion section owes much to the one in Messiaen's *Trois petites Liturgies* and this sparkling, pseudo-Asiatic sound world would be Boulez's preferred one from now on.

Boulez later stated that the work's reference to *Pierrot Lunaire* was 'intentional and direct'. This may well have surprised those who had been outraged by Boulez's 1951 article 'Schoenberg est mort', in which he castigated the older composer for not having pursued the serial system to what Boulez felt were its necessary conclusions, particularly in the realms of rhythm and form – Webern was much more to his taste in these respects. But in that article Boulez had singled out for praise three remarkable phenomena in *Pierrot*: non-repetition, 'anarchic' (that is, anti-tonal) intervals, and contrapuntal construction. The last two of these were to remain hallmarks of his own style. Meanwhile in the first book of *Structures* (1951–52), for two pianos, he had drawn what he felt were necessary conclusions from the serial idea.

His activities in the early 1950s also included writing a number of articles, some, as above, sharply polemical, or at least taken as such. His wish to see all the opera houses in the world blown up was clearly a deliberate exaggeration, aimed not at the buildings *per se* but at the cult of socializing and diva worship that opera encouraged, not to mention the accommodation the music had to make with the exigencies of staging; and his claim that any composer who had not felt the imperative need of the 12-note technique was inadequate to his times (thereby dumping some 95% of his composing colleagues) was again an intentional overstatement.

With the Third Piano Sonata, begun in 1956 but still unfinished at his death, Boulez turned to the concept of the 'open work' or 'work in progress', inspired by Mallarmé's *Livre*, his unrealised 'total book', and also by the novels of James Joyce, in which an end is permanently kept in view without being achieved, and in which the work (the labyrinth) is explored by a variety of routes, like the city of Venice. This process undoubtedly constituted a wide extension of the performer's freedom as found in the continuo keyboard part of baroque music; at the same time Boulez set his face against total improvisation as being a breeding-ground for cliché.

By 1959 he had progressed to conducting full-scale orchestras, but without making any kind of splash. Then, at the Donaueschingen Festival that year, the conductor Hans Rosbaud was taken ill and hospitalized only a few days before the opening concert, and in desperation the director Heinrich Strobel asked Boulez to take over. The first half of the progamme contained premieres of works by Boulez's contemporaries, therefore unknown to the general public. But the second half consisted of Bartók's *The Miraculous Mandarin* of 1918-19; Boulez had never heard it nor even seen a score ... The performance was a triumph. Among those applauding were committee members of the Concertgebouw who came round afterwards and asked Boulez, would he come and conduct their orchestra in Amsterdam? And would he please include *The Miraculous Mandarin?* This was where Boulez's international conducting career began.

In that same year of 1959, he left a Paris whose 'organisational stupidity' was more than he could stomach for Baden-Baden, where he signed a contract with the Südwestfunk radio station to conduct concerts of 20th-century music. He taught at Darmstadt and Basle, his pupils including Cornelius Cardew, Gilbert Amy, Jean-Claude Eloy, Heinz Holliger and Paul Méfano, and continued work on another masterpiece, *Pli selon pli,* for soprano and orchestra, which had begun in 1957 as two *Improvisations sur Mallarmé*. Further movements were performed in Baden-Baden, Donaueschingen and Cologne before the premiere of the complete work in Donaueschingen in 1962. Boulez's large-scale control (the five movements together last over an hour) is as impressive as his ever-inventive imagination in the matter of pure sound. Altogether, in the words of Paul Griffiths, 'because Boulez so wholly takes possession of his texts instead of merely setting them, the work is a portrait also of himself'.

Boulez made a high-profile return to Paris in 1963, conducting both a 50th-anniversary performance of *The Rite of Spring* in the Théâtre des Champs-Elysées and Berg's *Wozzeck* at the Opéra, where all ten evenings were sold out. No less remarkable was his successful insistence for the latter on the unprecedented number of 35 rehearsals, and on the same orchestral players being present for all rehearsals and performances, putting an end to a long house tradition of tolerating substitutes. The triumph of these performances was matched by that of his version of Berg's *Lulu* 16 years later (with 40 rehearsals).

Not everything in Paris, though, went his way. Successes such as his seductive *Éclat*, for 15 instruments (1965), and semi-theatrical *Domaines* (1968) and his collaboration with Wieland Wagner on the Bayreuth *Parsifal* of 1966 (repeated in 1967, 1968 and 1970) had to be set against his failures to persuade André Malraux to accept his recommendations for reorganising French musical life, and the collapse of plans made with Jean Vilar for a refashioning of the Opéra. Boulez's indignant ripostes, 'Why I say NO to Malraux' and the notorious 1967 interview in *Der Spiegel* in which he advocated blowing up the world's opera houses, did little to further his cause inside France, entertaining though they might have been for outsiders.

From 1959 he made his home in Baden-Baden. How deeply he minded his separation from his native country it is hard to say. The evidence suggests that he was prepared to wait, like De Gaulle, until the state of disarray became self-evident enough to lead to his recall. In the meantime he had been appointed principal guest conductor of the Cleveland Orchestra in 1967 and was invited by William Glock in 1968 to become chief conductor of the BBC Symphony Orchestra, a task he took up at the beginning of 1971 and fulfilled to great acclaim. It was his mission to introduce the British public to the masterpieces of the first half of the 20th century, without a knowledge of which, he felt, they were bound to find the music of their own time incomprehensible. In this, he was relating to his own experience, since Mahler had been joined by composers such as Schoenberg and Varèse in finding little or no place in French musical life before the war. His concerts at the Round House, in particular, marked a turning point in London's musical life. Also in 1971 he was appointed to succeed Leonard Bernstein as music director of the New York Philharmonic. Even if there were tensions between Boulez's goals and the more conservative attitudes of the orchestra's patrons, the recordings he made with the orchestra (including an utterly miraculous *Miraculous Mandarin* and a lithe reading of *Valses nobles et sentimentales*, completely purged of false sentiment) testify to the quality of his direction.

The bristly, antagonistic side of Boulez's character needs to be set against the fact that throughout his career he was outstandingly successful in his relationships with performers. Stravinsky, after meeting Boulez in Hollywood, wrote to Nadia Boulanger that he 'made an excellent impression on us all: an absolutely top-class musician, highly intelligent, he has fine manners and is probably a generous man'. Boulez's biographer Dominique Jameux noted two main points at rehearsals with the BBC Symphony Orchestra: firstly, the total dedication to the work in hand; and secondly, Boulez's jokes. He seemed to have an unerring ability to judge when the tension needed relaxing. The combined result was often an early end to the rehearsal, always a winning ploy with orchestras.

If some critics have lamented the time Boulez's conducting took from his composing, the man himself had no such doubts. Although he never listened to his own recordings (again, no nostalgia), the rest of us cannot but be grateful for his versions of his favourite composers: the three of the Second Viennese School, Debussy, Ravel, some Stravinsky and some Bartók. His detestation of the opera cult did not in the least affect his love for particular operas, not only Berg's *Wozzeck* and *Lulu* but *Pelléas et Mélisande*, the *Ring* and *Parsifal*. For *Pelléas* at Covent Garden he vowed to 'burn the mist' off the work and duly did so – not everyone was happy, but the opera took on new significance, its close links with *Parsifal* intensified, while the blaze of brass at the end of Act IV, accompanying Pelléas's murder, marked the opera as belonging unmistakably to 'the theatre of cruelty'. As for the *Ring*, the choice of Boulez to conduct the centenary performances at Bayreuth in 1976 was highly contentious (the first Frenchman ever, and the first non-German except Toscanini), but again justified by results, even if some traditional patrons wanted their leitmotifs more prominently displayed; instead, Boulez chose to integrate them into the texture, reducing their role as what Debussy unkindly dubbed 'calling cards' and emphasising Wagner's unparalleled control of long stretches of music. He also held out against what he called the 'barking' style of some of the singers, believing with Nietzsche that Wagner was 'a master of the miniature', and that forcing the tone turned the whole into an undifferentiated mush. For Boulez it was a bruising encounter, to the extent that he was left wondering whether he could in fact conduct. Happily, it was a short convalescence.

Although he did not feel any regrets, this workload did lead to a slight slowing-up in his compositional output throughout the 1970s, down to five works: *Cummings ist der Dichter* (1970), for voices and instruments; *...explosante-fixe...* (1971, and ultimately revised and incorporated into *Mémoriale, 1985*); *Rituel in Memoriam Bruno Maderna* (1975); *Messagesquisse*, for solo cello and six other cellos (1976), and the four *Notations* (1978) – about an hour's music in all. Boulez's enemies, whom his intransigence had created in some numbers, especially in Paris, put it about that he spent his time going round the world conducting only because he was written out as a composer. This charge, to be repeated by the unthinking at various times over the following decades, can now fairly be classed as ludicrous, given the quality of the five works mentioned above. *Rituel*, deriving from a single sound-block and in this sense obeying the 'necessity' that Boulez had found lacking in the serial Schoenberg, has a ritualistic structure surely proclaiming the composer's debt to his upbringing. This work, and the five *Notations*, orchestral reworkings of short piano pieces of 1945, have regularly been greeted by non-specialist audiences with the greatest enthusiasm.

It should be clear by this point that Boulez can only be termed a phenomenon. My own view is that it took him, being a naturally modest man, some time to realize what an exceptional musician he was. But his impatience with mediocrity was duly tempered by time and experience, and even some tonal composers were allowed to have their good points. In parallel with this, his own music began to soften its edges and even perhaps adapt its forms in some degree to the understanding of the average listener. If *Pli selon pli* (1957, finally revised 1989) is still bewildering for some, there was a wider acceptance of *Domaines* (1968) for clarinet and six instrumental groups, partly because of its clear structure and partly because of the extreme, exciting virtuosity demanded of the clarinettist, exceeded only by that in *Dialogues de l'ombre double* (1985) for clarinet and electronics, where even lighting plays a crucial role.

Boulez's move to Baden-Baden and his abandonment of France prompted disobliging references in the press to 'Herr Boulez'. Then one day in 1970, at his country pad in Southern France, the phone rang: 'we have the Élysée Palace on the line: will you take the call?' Boulez, thinking it was a prank, replied that he really was rather busy and could they call back in a couple of hours. Two hours later the phone rang again and a voice said, 'Ici Georges Pompidou'. Would Boulez come back to Paris? Yes, said, Boulez, but not to conduct: 'what I want is a centre for musical research'. And so was founded the Institut de Recherche et Coordination Acoustique/Musique (IRCAM), which found a home in the bowels of the Centre Pompidou.

Among the Institut's aims, as defined by Boulez, was research into acoustics, into instrumental design ('instruments have scarcely changed over the past two or three centuries'), and into the problems of composition itself. Since nothing of the sort had ever been attempted before on this scale, inevitably there were difficulties; musicians and scientists did not always see eye to eye, even where their roles were clearly defined, and the enemies were eager to pounce on perceived failings. As the musician and anthropologist Georgina Born says in her study of IRCAM's beginnings, 'Throughout the early period and until the mid-1980s, Ircam remained heavily dependent on American computer music expertise and also on the technologies that these researchers brought with them'. This put an extra stick into the hands of those French critics who, not without reason, felt that IRCAM was swallowing up large amounts of state money with little to show for it – the capital cost of the building was already quoted as $12m in 1973, even though Boulez insisted on IRCAM being independent of the Ministry of Cultural Affairs so that it would be able to accept outside money for running costs. Boulez also instigated the building of the complementary Cité de la Musique on the northern outskirts of Paris, incorporating the new Conservatoire and then the Philharmonie de Paris concert hall, opened in 2015.

Much of the criticism was directed at Boulez personally, one critic accusing him of being 'the new Lully'. Boulez's definitive reply was a 45-minute work, aptly named *Répons*, which depended heavily on IRCAM's electronic resources. The premiere of its third version, given in October 1984 before an audience including Madame Pompidou and Jacques Chirac, more or less silenced criticism (though there were no doubt some who thought that Boulez's outstanding gifts as a composer made this less than a fair trial of IRCAM's validity, which needed to be seen to succeed with a wider sample of composers). The long trills, already heard in embryo in *…explosante-fixe…*, now become a salient feature of the music and, with passages of almost jazzy ostinatos, mark a change from the non-repetitive, continuing variation that had in general characterised his music up to this point. But if the articulation of the discourse is now a little easier to follow, the language itself is as challenging as ever.

As for Boulez's ear for sound (one orchestral player claimed he could tell in what key a pin dropped), *Répons* proved it to be undimmed; the listener indeed, continuously seduced by the sheer beauty of the textures, has cause to be grateful for the greater clarity of the structure in that it prevents the work from being merely a warm-bath experience. *Répons* reached its present length in 1988.

One of Boulez's major works of the 1990s, *Sur Incises*, is another example of his many open-ended 'works in progress', growing gradually from a tiny piano piece, *Incises*, written for a competition in 1994, to one more than 40 minutes long for three pianos, harps and percussion, completed in 1999. It also took the delirious piano to new heights, and depths – one of the most sheerly exciting works of the century, with a further emphasis on repeated notes that at times make it sound like a later model of Honegger's *Pacific 231*. In 1992 he conducted the Peter Stein production of *Pelléas et Mélisande* for Welsh National Opera, awarded the International Classical Music award for opera production of the year, and brought out the inherent strength and cohesiveness of Debussy's score even more strikingly than in his 1969 performances at Covent Garden.

In his 70th birthday year in 1995 he conducted the London Symphony Orchestra in a series of concerts around the world, including London, Paris, Vienna, New York and Tokyo. His 75th birthday year was the focus of similar activity, but before then, in 1997, he announced that he would be devoting most of his time from here on to composing – a commitment he repeated more forcefully in 2000. Eight of the original twelve *Notations* remained to be developed (in fact only one, no. VII, would be added to the original four), as well as a number of new projects including, to use Paul Griffiths's apt phrase, a further 'settling of old scores'. An idea for an opera, once mooted in collaboration with Jean Genet, was not revived after the author's death. Boulez also continued to record through the decade for Deutsche Grammophon, including mesmeric performances of Messiaen's *Chronochromie* (Cleveland Orchestra, 1993), of the Ravel Piano Concertos (in G, Zimerman/Cleveland, 1994; in D, Zimerman/LSO, 1996) and, in the following decade, a complete cycle of the Mahler symphonies.

However, despite his declared intent, from 2000 onwards his travelling and conducting continued practically unabated. On the compositional front most of his time was spent revising and rearranging earlier works: the only completely new piece, for piano, is tellingly entitled *Une Page d'éphéméride* (2005). London and Paris were among the centres to mark his 90th birthday with concerts, and various box sets of recordings were released. But in 2010-11 Boulez's health deteriorated and by the early months of 2012 his eyesight was seriously affected. For some time he had been planning a violin concerto for Anne-Sophie Mutter, a reworking of *Anthèmes 2*, a delightful, magical 20-minute work for violin and live electronics (1997), but sadly this never materialised.

One friend who worked with Boulez in America reckoned that, for all his intellectual rigour, he was essentially a doer rather than a thinker. Composing is a lonely business, and as he grew older he increasingly relished the company of other musicians, with a special fondness for the young, towards whom he was firm and uncondescending. He continued to make good jokes, and rehearsals with his own Ensemble Intercontemporain were conducted in a happy atmosphere in which the highest standards of attention and execution were simply taken for granted.

His personal life remained hidden – clearly not by accident, since he was reported as saying he would be the first composer to lack a biography. He was devotedly served from the early 1970s by his manservant, Hans Messmer, and by his highly efficient assistant Astrid Schirmer, and was close to his elder sister Jeanne and his younger brother Roger, who both survive him, as well as their children and grandchildren.

To some extent the relaxed Boulez was the result of having finally got his own way in the things that mattered to him, something perhaps only a certain brutality, allied to genius, could have achieved: he explained in a television interview that, to begin with, he was the dog barking outside the tent – now he was inside the tent he had no need to bark. The caustic, peremptory tone of much of his writing is intended to wake us up. As he said in 2000, echoing words of Désormière, 'you mustn't be discouraged: be aware of the inertia of others, and be more stubborn than they are' – a notably more diplomatic pronouncement than those of 20 years earlier, when he snapped at an interviewer who accused him of being 'somewhat sectarian': 'I am not somewhat sectarian, I am completely sectarian'; or when he stormed that 'at my age and in my position I refuse to be dependent on the kind of nonentities who join committees!' Professor Born's accounts of committees set up within IRCAM testify to Boulez's unwavering impatience with such things.

Age brought a softening of his stance on other topics too. A group of British critics, talking with him about British composers and knowing his general lack of enthusiasm in this area, were surprised when the name of Vaughan Williams came up and Boulez retorted, 'Vaughan Williams ... now *he* is interesting'. At the Edinburgh Festival he also admitted that he himself and like-minded colleagues in the 1950s and 60s had underestimated the public's need to have musical ideas repeated.

If Boulez was intelligent enough to know his own value, he was also kind and without self-importance. He would happily stand in a corridor for 20 minutes between two three-hour rehearsals to record an interview, with technicians jostling his elbow, and then deliver himself of a 15-minute disquisition on Messiaen which could easily have been broadcast unedited [see article 47 above]. Dominique Jameux ended his biography of Boulez with the words: 'outwardly he gives an impression of resolution, mental alacrity, perseverance and self-justification – inwardly, one of evaluation, amendment, realism and self-criticism'. If Boulez's utter conviction of the value of his mission, to write music worthy of his time and to fight cynicism and indifference wherever he found them, made him a formidable enemy, it was also the driving force behind his uniquely valuable contribution to the musical world of his time. Perhaps the final words should belong to Désormière, quoted by Boulez in his deeply moving memoir of that conductor: 'Precision, a mark of aristocracy'.

INDEX

Adam, Adolphe, 36, 268
   Giselle 35, 37
   Toréador, Le, 209
Adams, John: *A Short Ride in a Fast Machine,* 181, 236
Aeschylus, 173
Alain, Jehan, 268–9, 353
   Litanies, 269
Albéniz, Isaac, 58, 184
   Iberia, 206, 298
Album des Six, 175
Alexandra of Denmark (wife of Edward VII), 179, 180
Alfonso XIII, 184
Allais, Alphonse, 219, 357
Amette, Léon-Adolphe, Archbishop of Paris, 109
Amy, Gilbert, 370
Andersen, Hans Christian, 157
Anderson, Julian, 199, 200, 348
Ansermet, Ernest, 74, 185
Antheil, George: *Ballet mécanique,* 173
Apollinaire, Guillaume, 56, 88, 92, 152, 172, 176, 204, 263
Aragon, Louis, 231
Armingaud, Jules, 27
Armingaud String Quartet, 26
Artaud, Antonin, 358
Artusi, Giovanni, 119
Asquith, Anthony, 250
Astruc, Gabriel, 222
Auber, Daniel-François-Esprit, 11, 54
   Haydée, 47
Audran, Edmond: *La Mascotte,* 168
Auric, Georges, 154, 165, 174, 175, 177, 259, 320, 324, 361
   Belle et la Bête, La, 324
   Fâcheux, Les, 321
   Matelots, Les, 321

   Moulin Rouge, 177
   Pastorale, 321
   Piano Sonata, 177, 321
   Quatre Chants de la France malheureux, 321
Axsom, Richard, 153

Bach, Johann Sebastian, 17, 21, 31, 44, 199, 243, 246, 269, 271, 305, 309, 368
   Fugue in D major BWV 532, 315
   Prelude and Fugue in A minor, 266–7
   St Matthew Passion, 108
Baillie, Isobel, 76
Baillot, Pierre, 25
Baker, Janet, 76
Baker, Josephine, 356
Bakst, Léon, 109, 228
Balakirev, Mily: *Islamey,* 197
Barbier, Jules, 121
Bardac, Raoul, 93
Barenboim, Daniel, 332, 351
Barrault, Jean-Louis, 250, 368
Bartók, Béla, 89, 199, 306, 323, 328, 338
   Miraculous Mandarin, The, 370, 371
   Music for Strings, percussion and celesta, 323, 328
   String Quartets, 338, 339, 353
Barzun, Jacques, 1
Basie, Count, 352
Bathori, Jane, 227
Baudelaire, Charles, 18, 199, 200, 211, 336, 337, 353, 354, 355
Bavouzet, Jean-Efflam, 143
Bayle, Laurent, 364
Bax, Arnold, 79, 80
Beckett, Samuel, 133
Beethoven, Ludwig van, 8, 9, 11, 12,

17, 47, 121, 156, 190, 200, 218, 269, 284, 302, 330, 338, 339, 344
  Grosse Fuge, 368
  'Kreutzer' Sonata, 191
  String quartets, 330, 338, 353
  Symphony no. 6 ('Pastoral'), 12, 288
Bellini, Vincenzo, 15, 18
Benjamin, George, 189, 190, 192, 193, 196, 298, 348, 363, 364, 365
Berg, Alban, 140, 256, 304, 339
  Lulu, 371, 372
  Lyric Suite, 339, 353, 367
  Wozzeck, 140, 370, 372
Berio, Luciano, 362, 364
Berkeley, Lennox, 198
Berkeley, Michael, 199
Berlin, Irving: *That Mysterious Rag,* 173
Berlioz, Hector, 1–14, 15, 26, 30, 31, 46, 144, 170, 183, 203, 232, 270, 294, 305, 329, 344
  Béatrice et Bénédict, 232
  Benvenuto Cellini, 13, 14
  Damnation de Faust, La, 13, 26, 30, 46, 329
  L'Enfance du Christ, 1, 13, 46, 344
  Francs-juges, Les, 7
  Herminie, 5
  Huit Scènes de Faust, 2, 3
  Neuf Mélodies, 7
  Nuits d'été, 13
  Requiem, 13, 28, 31, 361
  Roméo et Juliette, 46, 344
  Sardanapale, 6, 7
  Symphonie fantastique, 1, 3–9, 11–14, 344
  Symphonie funèbre et triomphale, 13, 361
  Traité d'instrumentation, 14
  Troyens, Les, 14, 85, 132, 143, 232

Bernac, Pierre, 265, 297
Bernhardt, Sarah, 67
Bernier, Julie (later Julie Lalo), 26
Bernstein, Leonard, 276, 371
Birtwistle, Harrison, 364, 365
Bismarck, Otto von, 37, 85
Bizet, Georges, 22, 24, 42
  Carmen, 114, 140, 209, 210, 212, 232
Bizet, René, 248
Blakeman, Edward, 154
Blanche, Jacques-Emile, 77
Blau, Afred, 46
Bliss, Arthur, 198
Blondin, C., 129
Bodin, Thierry, 50
Boieldieu, François-Adrien:
  Le Bouquet de l'Infante, 209
Born, Georgina, 363, 374, 377
Boughton, Rutland, 80
Boulanger, Nadia, 237, 345, 372
Boulez, Jeanne, 376
Boulez, Léon, 366
Boulez, Marcelle, 366
Boulez, Pierre, 89, 104, 191, 192, 196, 197, 257, 274, 276, 281, 282, 296, 300, 302–7, 320, 322, 323, 324, 325, 336, 347, 350, 356–60, 361, 362, 363, 364, 365, 366–77
  Anthèmes, 2, 376
  Cummings ist der Dichter, 373
  Dialogues de l'ombre double, 373
  Domaines, 371, 373
  Eclat, 371
  …explosante-fixe…, 362, 373, 374
  Figures-Doubles-Prismes, 359
  Improvisations sur Mallarmé, 370
  Marteau sans maître, Le, 196, 359, 369
  Mémoriale, 373
  Messagesquisse, 373

Notations, 324, 367, 373, 375
Page d'éphémiride, Une, 376
Piano Sonata no. 1, 367
Piano Sonata no. 2, 367, 368
Piano Sonata no. 3, 369–70
Pli selon pli, 370, 373
Répons, 363, 374, 375
Rituel in memoriam Bruno Maderna, 373
Soleil des eaux, Le, 368
Sonatina for flute and piano, 324, 367
Structures, 360
Sur Incises, 375
Visage nuptial, Le, 368
Boulez, Roger, 376
Bovy, Berthe, 264
Bozzacchi, Giuseppina, 38
Brahms, Johannes, 28, 190, 269
Breitkopf und Härtel, 31
Bréville, Pierre de, 54, 70
Britten, Benjamin, 198, 236, 312
    Peter Grimes, 236
    Quatre Chansons françaises, 198
    Turn of the Screw, The
    War Requiem, 266
Bruneau, Alfred, 45, 46, 109
Bruyr, José: *L'Ecran des musiciens*, 296
Bull, John, 227
Bülow, Hans von, 28
Burne-Jones, Edward, 62, 65
Busser, Henri, 70, 330, 350, 351
    Noces corinthiennes, Les, 326
Byrd, William, 227, 309

Caccini, Giulio, 118
Cadou, André, 67
Cage, John, 153, 154, 160, 168, 308, 343, 368
Cairns, David, 8
Calvocoressi, Michel-Dimitri, 73, 217

Campanini, Cleofonte, 80
Campbell, Mrs Patrick (Beatrice Stella Cornwallis-West), 61, 62, 63–4, 65, 66, 67
Canat de Chizy, Edith, 348
Caplet, André, 67, 108, 109
Cardew, Cornelius, 370
Carraud, Gaston, 218, 220
Caron, Rose, 100–1
Carré, Albert, 66, 120, 124, 137, 144
Carter, Elliott, 362
Carter, Philip, 160
Carvalho, Léon, 23
Carvalho, Marie Caroline, 24
Casadesus, Gisèle, 289
Casadesus, Robert, 301
Casals, Pablo, 226
Casella, Alfredo, 226, 227, 358
Casken, John, 199
Cassou, Jean, 347, 348
Cézanne, Paul, 93, 99, 234, 236
Chabrier, Emmanuel, 27, 45–59, 85, 103, 148, 174, 209, 235, 260, 283, 331, 366
    À la Musique, 58
    Briséis, 49
    Dix Pièces pittoresques, 233, 260
    'Mélancolie', 233
    'Sous bois', 233
    L'Étoile, 57, 326
    España, 28, 50, 51, 58, 209, 210, 232
    Gwendoline, 47, 52, 53, 58
    Impromptu, 233
    Roi malgré lui, Le, 51, 55, 58
    Souvenirs de Munich, 58
    Vollaieries (Farmyard songs), 58
Chabrier, Marcel, 49
Chaigneau, Thérèse, 183
Chalupt, René, 154, 157
Champeaux, Guillaume de, 116

Charles X, 6, 10
Charpentier, Gustave: *Louise*, 120
Chausson, Ernest, 43, 44, 54, 57, 71, 72, 85, 86, 102, 174, 269
Chausson, Jeanne (née Escudier), 145
Cherubini, Luigi, 8, 11, 15
Chevillard, Camille, 70
Chirac, Jacques, 374
Chopin, Fryderyk, 15–20, 89, 148, 186, 223, 289, 294
   Allegro de concert, 16
   Etudes, 298
   Mazurkas, 16
   Nocturnes, 17, 19
   Piano Concerto in F minor, 20
   Polonaise op. 44, 16
   Polonaise-Fantaisie, 16
   Préludes, 17, 19
   Sonata in B flat minor, 19
Chung, Myung-Whun, 354
Citron, Pierre, 14
Clampin, Fiona, 198
Clark, Edward, 71
Claudel, Paul, 177, 247, 250, 251, 368
Clementi, Muzio, 18, 19, 87, 153
Clustine, Ivan, 222–3
Cobban, Alfred, 10
Cocteau, Jean, 137, 152, 165, 168, 171, 172, 173, 174, 178, 219, 236, 237–42, 246, 264
   Coq et l'Arlequin, Le, 175, 238, 239, 321, 324
   David (planned ballet with Stravinsky), 171, 238
   Dieu bleu, Le, 171
   Lampe d'Aladin, La, 237
   Midsummer Night's Dream, A (planned ballet with Ravel, Satie and Varèse), 171
   Sang d'un poète, Le, 321
Colette, Sidonie-Gabrielle, 299

Collet, Henri, 175, 176
Colonne, Edouard, 64
Conrad, Doda, 237, 238, 239, 241, 242
Constable, John, 232
Cooper, Douglas, 97
Cooper, James Fenimore, 11
Cooper, Martin, 38
Coppola, Piero, 74
Copland, Aaron, 236
Corder, Frederick, 79
Cornejo, Manuel, 183
Corot, Camille, 350
Cortot, Alfred, 148, 226
Costallat (publisher), 45
Coty (perfume house), 336
Couperin, François, 219, 300, 308
Crane, Walter, 61
Crawford, Francis Marion, 125
Croiza, Claire, 247

Dale, Benjamin, 79
Daly, William H., 77, 82
Daniel, Keith, 265
d'Annunzio, Gabriele, 106–9
Dante (Dante Alighieri): *Francesca da Rimini*, 125
Darré, Jeanne-Marie, 32
Davioud, Gabriel, 222
Davis, Colin, 13
Debussy, Claude, 14, 17, 18, 28, 32, 44, 54, 57, 58, 61, 62, 69–141, 151, 155, 156, 161, 170, 173, 174, 180, 181, 182, 189, 190, 192, 193, 197, 199, 205, 217, 218, 219, 220, 227, 232, 233, 234, 235, 236, 239, 245, 263, 265, 271, 289, 291–4, 295, 301, 302, 305, 309, 327, 331, 339, 347, 353, 357, 358, 372
   Arabesque no. 1, 295
   Chansons de Bilitis, 77, 126
   Children's Corner, 82, 87, 95, 227

Cinq Poèmes de Baudelaire, 85
Damoiselle élue, La, 75, 76, 77, 118
En blanc et noir, 32, 89
L'Enfant prodigue, 77, 100, 102
Epigraphes antiques, 193
Estampes, 78, 87, 291
   'Jardins sous la pluie', 235
   'Pagodes', 291
   'Soirée dans Grenade, La', 211, 291
Etudes, 89, 95, 99
Fantaisie, 104
Gladiateur, Le, 92
Images for orchestra, 104, 233
   'Gigues', 81
   'Ibéria', 88, 95, 292
   'Rondes de printemps', 81
Images for piano, 87
   'Cloches à travers les feuilles', 236
   'Poissons d'or', 78, 236
   'Reflets dans l'eau', 236
L'Isle joyeuse, 78
Jeux, 74, 88, 104, 105, 228, 229, 305
'Mandoline', 78
Martyre de Saint Sébastien, Le, 91, 106–9, 293
Masques et Bergamasques (planned ballet), 228
Mer, La, 73, 74–5, 87, 103, 105, 107, 235, 305
Nocturnes, 69, 73, 78, 102–3, 118
Pelléas et Mélisande, 1, 23, 32, 61, 69, 77, 80–1, 82, 86, 87, 96–7, 98, 102–3, 105, 107, 110, 111, 112, 113, 114–41, 144, 170, 196, 219, 222, 245, 264, 271, 282, 292, 294, 295, 319, 358, 372, 375
Prélude à l'après-midi d'un faune, 32, 70–1, 73, 78, 81, 86, 102, 105, 126, 217, 230, 234, 311, 353
Préludes, 87, 293

'Cathédrale engloutie, La', 236
'Ce qu'a vu le vent d'ouest', 107
'Général Lavine excentric', 87
'Minstrels', 87
'Voiles', 87
Printemps, 32, 233
Proses lyriques, 126
Sonata for flute, viola and harp, 305
Sonatas, 89, 99
String Quartet, 71, 72, 78, 86, 102, 333
Syrinx, 294
Debussy, Claude-Emma ('Chouchou'), 87, 107
Degas, Edgar, 90–101, 259, 262
   Coiffure, La, 97–8
   Falaise escarpée ('Steep coast'), 99
   Mélancolie, La ('Melancholy'), 97, 98
   Viol, Le ('The Rape'), 98
Degas, Hilaire, 90
Delacroix, Eugène, 350
Delafosse, Léon, 63
Delage, Maurice, 215
Delage, Nelly, 215
Delage, Roger, 50, 55
Delannoy, Marcel: *Ginevra*, 326
Delbos, Claire, 272, 275, 298
Delibes, Léo, 35–9, 53, 268
   Alger, 36–7
   Belle Fille de Cadix, La, 232
   Coppélia, 37–8, 170
   Deux Sous de charbon, 36
   Lakmé, 37
   Roi l'a dit, Le, 37
   Source, La, 37
   Sylvia, 37, 170
Delius, Frederick, 76
Delouart, Marie (later Marie Ravel), 210
Delteil, Jacques, 280, 283

Delvincourt, Claude, 321
  Lucifer, 326
Demuth, Norman, 198
Dent, Edward J., 81, 112, 131
Desaymard, Joseph, 45
Desnos, Robert: 'Le dernier poème', 354
Désormière, Roger, 136, 137, 141, 319, 352, 367, 376, 377
Dessay, Natalie, 87
Destinn, Emmy, 222
Diaghilev, Serge, 38, 88, 152, 170, 171, 172, 177, 206, 222, 228, 229, 230, 237, 244, 260, 321, 361
Diamond, David, 215
Dingle, Christopher, 276, 278
Dodgson, Charles Lutwige, 157
  (as Lewis Carroll): *Through the Looking-Glass*, 157
Dolmetsch, Arnold, 227
Dreyfus, Alfred, 135, 144, 213, 214
Dubois, Théodore, 87, 127, 143, 146
Duchamp, Marcel, 152
Dufay, Guillaume, 368
Dufranne, Hector, 124, 129
Dukas, Paul, 23, 43, 44, 120, 138, 140, 228–9, 230, 268, 271, 282, 296, 328, 330, 331
  Ariane et Barbe-bleue, 138, 297
  Péri, La, 223, 224, 228, 229, 230, 231
Dumas, Alexandre, the Elder, 63
Duncan, Isadora, 229
Duparc, Henri, 27, 29, 57, 71, 209
Dupré, Marcel, 226, 267, 272, 311, 350
Durand, Jacques, 27, 94, 107, 108, 143, 215, 233
Durey, Louis, 174, 177, 178
Durif, Frans, 51, 55
Duruflé, Marie-Madeleine, 268

Duruflé, Maurice, 266–9
  Andante et Scherzo, 268
  Messe 'Cum jubilo', 269
  Prélude, adagio et choral varié sur le thème du Veni Creator, 268
  Prélude et fugue sur le nom d'Alain, 268
  Prélude, récitatif et variations, 267
  Quatre Motets sur des thèmes grégoriens, 269
    'Ubi caritas', 269
  Requiem, 266, 269
  Sonatine for flute, 329
  Suite, op. 5, 268
  Trois Danses, 268
Dusapin, Pascal, 348
Duse, Eleonora, 106
Dutilleux, Constant, 350
Dutilleux, Henri, 1, 52, 197, 199, 297, 321, 327–55, 362
  Ainsi la nuit, 332, 333, 338, 341, 347, 353
  L'Arbre des songes, 340, 341, 349, 353
  Au Gré des ondes, 197
  Choral, cadence et fugato, 321
  Citations, 353
  Correspondances, 346, 348, 354
  Figures de résonance, 332
  Jeu des contraires, Le, 332
  Loup, Le, 352
  Métaboles, 334–6, 340, 352, 354, 355
  Mystère de l'instant, 341–2, 353
  'Nuits' (original title for *Ainsi la nuit*), 353
  Oboe Sonata, 321
  Piano Sonata, 331, 332, 351
  Sarabande et cortège, 321, 351
  Shadows of Time, The, 348, 353
  Sonatina for flute and piano, 197, 321

String Quartet, see *Ainsi la nuit*
Sur le même accord, 354
Symphony no. 1, 332, 333, 352
Symphony no. 2, 333–4, 352
Temps l'horloge, Le, 354
Timbres, espace, mouvement, 339, 347, 354
Tout un Monde lointain, 336–7, 339, 347, 353
'Vertige' (original title for *Tout un Monde lointain*), 336
Duval, Denise, 265
Dyck, Ernest van, 48

Edward VII, 179
Einstein, Albert, 316
Elgar, Edward, 63
   Dream of Gerontius, The, 69
Ellington, Duke, 352
Elman, Mischa, 226
Eloy, Jean-Claude, 370
Elsner, Józef, 19
Emmanuel, Maurice, 266–7, 350, 351
Enescu, George, 194
Enoch (publisher), 52
Erlanger, Camille, 70
Evans, Edwin, 79
L'Eventail de Jeanne, 261

Fabre, Gabriel, 61
Falla, Manuel de, 58
Fauré, Gabriel, 1, 23, 27, 33, 60–8, 71, 72, 164, 181, 182, 203, 211, 212, 217, 223, 225, 227, 269, 296, 297, 330, 347, 348, 350
   Barcarolle no. 6, 63
   Caligula, 63, 64
   Dolly, 63
   Naissance de Vénus, La, 227
   Pavane, 203
   Pelléas et Mélisande, 60, 62–8

Piano Quartet no. 1, 63
Piano Quartet no. 2, 63
Poème d'un jour, 227
Requiem, 63
Shylock, 63, 64
Thème et variations, 63
Valses-caprices, 63
Violin Sonata no. 1, 63, 260
Ferneyhough, Brian, 294, 362
Ferté, Armand, 67
Feuillard, Louis, 72
Février, Henri, 106
Février, Jacques, 262, 325, 329
Field, John, 18
Flaubert, Gustave, 96, 149
Fleming, Renée, 347, 354
Florentz, Jean-Louis, 348
   Requiem de la Vierge, 348
Florian, Jean-Pierre Cloris de
   Estelle et Némorin, 5
Fokine, Michel, 109, 205, 228
Forbes-Robertson, Johnston, 62
Fornier, Estelle, 5
Fouquier, Henri, 61
Franc-Nohain (pseud. for Maurice Etienne Legrand), 212
Françaix, Jean: *Les Malheurs de Sophie*, 326
Franck, César, 31, 43, 44, 45, 81, 86, 102, 103, 147, 151, 181, 314
   Chasseur maudit, Le, 81
   Choral no. 2, 316
   Piano Quintet, 147
   Symphony, 226
Fratellini brothers, 239
Frazier, James E., 268
Freitas-Branco, Pedro de, 208
Frogley, Alain, 198
Fugère, Lucien, 23
Fuller, Loïe, 149, 225

Gabor, Zsa-Zsa, 177
Gagliano, Marco da, 118
Gallois, Victor, 350
Gallon, Jean, 350
Gallon, Noël, 350
Garafola, Lynn, 261
Garden, Mary, 69, 124, 129, 137–8, 139
Gauguin, Paul: *D'où venons-nous, que sommes-nous, où allons nous?*, 334
Gaulle, Charles de, 170, 371
Gauthier-Villars, Henry ('Willy'), 125, 217
Gedalge, André, 191, 245, 257
Genet, Jean, 375
Gershwin, George, 200
  Rhapsody in Blue, 245
Gerville-Réache, Jeanne, 124, 128
Gesualdo, Carlo, 368
Gibon, Jean de, 292
Gibson, Alexander, 74
Gide, André, 16, 18, 19, 242, 280, 327
Gielgud, John, 312
Gigli, Beniamino, 25
Gigout, Eugène, 267
Glass, Philip, 192, 362
Glinka, Mikhail, 184
Glock, William, 371
Gluck, Christoph Willibald, 88, 100, 115, 117, 121, 170, 265, 270
  Armide, 114
  Iphigénie en Aulide, 100
Godebski, Cipa, 296
Goehr, Alexander, 174, 192, 199, 298
  Finding the Key, 298
Goethe, Johann Wolfgang von, 8
  Faust, 1, 2, 11
  Leiden des jungen Werthers, Die, 131
Goubault, Christian, 219
Gounod, Charles, 21–24, 42, 91, 131, 205

  Ave Maria (after Bach), 21
  Colombe, La, 23
  Faust, 21, 22, 23, 36, 178
  Fernand, 22
  Médecin malgré lui, 22
  Mireille, 23
  Mors et vita, 24
  Petite Symphonie, 21
  Philémon et Baucis, 23
  Rédemption, 24
  Reine de Saba, La, 23
  Roméo et Juliette, 23, 24
  St Cecilia Mass, 22
  Sapho, 22
Gowers, Patrick, 154, 155, 156, 160, 161, 162, 163, 169
Grieg, Edvard
  Peer Gynt, 223
  Piano Concerto, 25
Griffiths, Paul, 154, 155, 158, 162, 167, 168, 370, 375
Grigny, Nicolas de, 312
Grisey, Gérard, 364
Groupe des Six, Le, 174–8, 219, 238, 244, 245, 263, 284
Guérin, Jacques, 154, 158, 163, 164, 168
Guéritte, T.J., 71
Gutmann, Adolf, 18
Guzman, Blanco, 179

Habeneck, François, 25
Hahn, Carlos, 179
Hahn, Reynaldo, 106, 179–82, 185, 212, 218, 227
  Bal de Béatrice d'Este, Le, 179
  Ciboulette, 181
  'Ciel est pardessus le toit, Le', 182
  Dieu bleu, Le, 171
  'Fêtes galantes', 182
  Marchand de Venise, Le, 181

Mozart, 181
'*Offrande*', 181
Oui des jeunes filles, Le, 326
Piano Quintet, 180–1
Si mes Vers avaient des ailes, 180
Sonatine, 180
Violin Sonata, 180–1
Halbreich, Harry, 194, 243, 244, 245, 246, 248, 249, 250, 251, 253, 254, 256, 257
Halévy, Fromental, 21, 142
Juive, La, 23, 47
Hambourg, Mark, 226
Handel, George Frideric, 19, 156
'Arrival of the Queen of Sheba, The', 309
Hannigan, Barbara, 347
Haraucourt, Edmond, 63
Harvey, Jonathan, 363, 364, 365
Harvey, Martin, 62
Haydn, Joseph, 53, 225, 330
Hervé (pseud. for Louis-Auguste-Florimond Ronger): *Le petit Faust*, 23
Hesketh, Kenneth, 348
Heugel (publisher), 325
Higson, Arthur, 76
Hiller, Ferdinand, 8
Hindemith, Paul, 320, 335
Hoffmann, E.T.A., 37, 212
Höller, York: *Arcus*, 363
Holliger, Heinz, 370
Holloway, Robin, 199
Holst, Gustav, 81–2
Planets, The, 82
Homer, 72
Honegger, Arthur, 174, 175, 176, 194, 195, 243–58, 259, 263, 271, 284, 306, 320, 339, 361
Antigone, 246, 247, 256, 320, 326
L'Appel de la montagne, 326

Chant de Nigamon, Le, 176
Cri du monde, 248, 249, 254
Danse des morts, La, 251, 253
Dit des Jeux du Monde, Le, 176–7
Hommage à Ravel, 194
Horace victorieux, 256
Incantation aux fossiles, 254
Je suis compositeur, 255
Jeanne d'Arc au bûcher, 250, 251, 258
Judith, 246, 253, 320
King David, 175, 246, 250, 285
Mermoz, 250
Mimaamaquim, 246, 253
Naissance des couleurs, La, 326
Pacific, 231, 173, 236, 243, 246
Piano Concertino, 245
Pygmalion, 250
Sonatina for violin and cello, 195
String Quartet no. 1, 195, 245
Symphony no. 1, 256
Symphony no. 2, 252, 325
Symphony no. 3 (*Symphonie liturgique*), 253
Symphony no. 4 (*Deliciae basiliensis*), 254
Symphony no. 5 (*Di tre re*), 255
Honegger, Jean-Claude, 243, 247, 255, 256
Honegger, Pascale, 243, 244, 247, 248, 249, 251, 253, 254, 256, 257
Howat, Roy, 196, 298
Howells, Herbert: *In Gloucestershire* (String Quartet no. 3), 198
Hudson, William Henry, 67
Hughes, Herbert, 79
Hugo, Jean, 154, 158, 159
Hugo, Valentine, 137
Hugo, Victor, 8, 10, 11, 60
Hernani, 10
d'Humières, Robert, 226

INDEX

Hummel, Johann Nepomuk, 18, 19
Huneker, James, 19
Hunt, Dennis, 266
Huysmans, Joris Karl: *A rebours*, 107

Ibert, Jacques, 319; *Escales*, 326;
    Symphonie concertante, 319
Ibsen, Henrik, 61, 110
d'Indy, Vincent, 27, 31, 49, 57, 71, 72,
    108, 112, 114, 143, 145, 151, 219,
    224–5, 330, 349
    Istar, 223, 224
Inghelbrecht, Désiré-Emile, 139,
    213–4
Ingres, Jean-Auguste-Dominique, 22,
    91, 93
IRCAM (Institut de Recherche et
    Coordination Acoustique/
    Musique), 361–5, 374
Ireland, John: Sonatina, 198
Ivry, Benjamin, 215

Jameux, Dominique, 372, 377
Janequin, Clément;
    Le Chant des oyseaux, 300;
    Le Chant du rossingol, 300
Jean-Aubry, Georges, 194
Joachim, Irène, 87, 136–41, 320
Jolas, Betsy, 348
Jourdan-Morhange, Hélène, 215
Joy, Geneviève, 351
Joyce, Eileen, 25
Joyce, James, 369
Juilliard Quartet, 338
Jullien, Louis Antoine, 70
Jusseaume, Lucien, 124, 129, 137

Kalisch, Alfred, 79
Kaminsky, Peter, 200
Karsavina, Tamara, 149, 225
Kaye, Nicholas, 266

Keats, John: *Ode on a Grecian Urn*, 4
Kenyon, Nicholas, 346
Kerman, Joseph, 51
Knussen, Oliver, 348
Kodály, Zoltán, 230
Koechlin, Charles, 64, 65, 217, 263
    L'Ame heureuse, 326
    Bandar-Log, Les, 282
    Promenade galante, 64
Koszul, Julien, 330, 348, 350
Koussevitzky, Serge, 275, 276

Lacôme, Paul, 55
Lacordaire, Jean-Baptiste, 22
Ladies' String Quartet of Edinburgh,
    71
Lalo, Edouard, 24, 25–9, 42, 45, 296
    Ballade à la lune, 27
    Chant breton, 27
    Fiesque, 26
    Namouna, 24, 27, 28, 126
    Piano Trios, 27
    Roi d'Ys, Le, 25, 26, 27, 28–9
    Symphonie espagnole, 27–8, 209
    Zuecca, La, 27
Lalo, Pierre, 218, 220, 231, 296
Laloy, Louis, 190, 219
Lamartine, Alphonse de, 22
Lamaze, David, 215
Landowska, Wanda, 356
Lassus, Orlande de, 91
Lawson, Peter, 154, 155, 164, 166, 168
Leblanc, Georgette, 66, 67
Lecocq, Charles, 54, 55
Leduc (publisher), 325
Léger, Fernand, 244
Le Marc'hadour, Yvon, 208
Leeds Choral Society, 227
Leibowitz, René, 323
Lerberghe, Charles Van, 65
Lerolle, Christine, 96

Lerolle, Henry, 90, 96
Lerolle, Marie Escudier, 96
Lerolle, Yvonne, 96
Lesueur, Jean-François, 21
Liebermann, Rolf, 345
Liebich, Louise, 77–8
Ligeti, György, 200, 289, 362, 364
Lindberg, Magnus, 364, 365
Liszt, Franz, 8, 9, 12, 15, 18, 19, 31, 33, 105, 304, 331
   Totentanz, 105
Lockspeiser, Edward, 192, 232
Loriod, Yvonne, 274, 275, 280, 287, 318
Louis XIV, 110, 204
Louis XVIII, 10
Louvier, Alain, 297
Louÿs, Pierre, 61, 89, 90
Luart, Emma, 76
Lugné-Poe (pseud. for Aurélien François Marie Lugné), 60–1, 62, 66
Lully, Jean-Baptiste, 110, 374
Lunel, Armand, 296

Macdonald, Hugh, 23, 33
MacGregor, Neil, 97
Mackail, John William, 61–2, 65
Maddison, Adela, 63
Maddison, Frederick, 63
Maeterlinck, Maurice, 60, 61, 66, 121, 122, 123, 124, 126, 132, 133–5
   Pelléas et Mélisande, 60–7, 110, 125, 130–1, 132–5, see also Debussy, Claude and Fauré, Gabriel
Maeterlinck, Renée, 67
Magnard, Albéric, 142–5
   Bérénice, 145
   Chant funèbre, 144
   Guercoeur, 142, 145
   Hymne à la justice, 144

Piano Trio, 145
Quintet for flute, oboe, clarinet, bassoon and piano, 143
String Quartet, 145
Symphony no. 3, 144, 145
Symphony no. 4, 145
Violin Sonata, 144, 145
Yolande, 143
Magnard, René, 145
Maguenat, Alfred, 82
Mahler, Gustav, 368, 371, 375
   Symphony no. 4, 227
   Symphony no. 8 ('Choral symphony'), 80
Mallarmé, Stéphane, 61, 192, 369
Malraux, André, 278, 287, 371
Manchester, Duchess of, 179
Manet, Edouard, 233
Manoury, Philippe, 348, 363
Mariés de la Tour Eiffel, Les, 177–8, 239, 240, 241, 261
Marnold, Jean (pseud. for Jean Morland), 219
Martin, Charles, 152
Marty, Georges, 45
Mascagni, Pietro: *Cavalleria rusticana*, 54
Massenet, Jules, 40–4, 54, 63, 64, 111, 143, 146, 179, 180, 205, 225, 273, 296, 297
   Cid, Le, 54
   Don César de Bazan, 209
   La Grand'Tante, 41
   Hérodiade, 41
   Manon, 44, 296
   Roi de Lahore, Le, 42
   Roma, 228
   Thaïs, 300
   Werther, 41, 44, 131, 132, 180, 264
Massine, Léonide, 172
Matisse, Henri, 97
Mauclair, Camille, 220

Maurane, Camille, 247
Max, Edouard de, 237
Mayerl, Billy, 25
McBirnie, Andrew, 348
Meck, Nadezhda von, 38
Médrano Circus, 172
Méfano, Paul, 370
Memling, Hans, 61
Mendelssohn, Felix, 2, 11, 19, 22, 26, 180, 206
Menuhin, Yehudi, 27
Mérode, Cléo de, 181
Meshcherskaya, Princess, 60
Messager, André, 27, 52, 125, 129
    Basoche, La, 131, 132
    Isoline, 52
Messiaen, Olivier, 193, 194, 195, 196, 197, 203, 204, 236, 268, 270–318, 322, 323, 324, 330, 331, 344–5, 350, 358, 361, 364, 367–8, 369, 375, 377
    L'Ame en bourgeon (organ improvisations), 289–90
    Apparition de l'Eglise éternelle, 272, 314
    L'Ascension, 272, 277, 280
        'Alléluias sereins', 313
    Banquet céleste, Le, 270–1, 308, 309
    Cantéyodjayâ, 276
    Catalogue d'oiseaux, 277, 298
    Chants de terre et de ciel, 273
    Chronochromie, 277, 298, 304, 306–7, 375
    Cinq Rechants, 285, 290
    'Contre la paresse', 297
    Corps glorieux, Les, 273–4, 277, 297, 308, 310
        'Combat de la Mort et de la Vie', 315
        'Eaux de la Grâce, Les', 308
        'Joie et clarté des corps glorieux', 317

Des Canyons aux étoiles, 236
Diptyque, 271, 274, 312
Eclairs sur l'au-delà, 278–9, 280–1, 283
L'Ensorceleuse, 283
Et exspecto resurrectionem mortuorum, 278, 287
Fantaisie burlesque, 301
Harawi, 275, 290, 299, 304
Hymne au Saint-Sacrement, 272
Ile de feu (I and II), 276
Livre d'orgue, 277, 298
    'Les Mains de l'abîme', 315
Livre du Saint Sacrement, 278, 313
Meditations sur le Mystère de la Sainte Trinité, 309
Merle noir, Le, 277
Messe de la Pentcôte, 276–7, 294, 303, 304, 310, 316
    'Offertoire', 315, 317
Mode de valeurs et d'intensités, 276, 283, 293, 299, 303
Mort du nombre, La, 271, 301
Nativité du Seigneur, La, 268, 272–3, 292, 300
    'Anges, Les', 318
    'Bergers, Les', 314
    'Dieu parmi nous', 282
Neumes rythmiques, 276
Offrandes oubliées, Les, 271
Poèmes pour Mi, 196, 273, 282, 290, 304
    'Paysage', 298
Préludes, 271
Quatuor pour la fin du Temps, 274
Saint François d'Assise, 281, 290, 292
Technique de mon langage musical, 281, 282
Thème et variations, 272
Tombeau resplendissant, Le, 272
Transfiguration de Notre Seigneur

Jésus-Christ, La, 282
Trois Mélodies, 271, 289, 290
Trois petites Liturgies de la Présence Divine, 196, 274, 275, 279, 280, 282, 285, 306, 323, 367, 369
Turangalîla Symphony, 196, 275, 276, 277, 82, 283, 285, 293, 299, 300, 304
Visions de l'Amen, 196, 274, 275, 279, 297
  Amen du jugement, 300
Vingt Regards sur l'Enfant-Jésus, 197, 275, 299, 304, 306
Messiaen, Pierre, 270
Messmer, Hans, 376
Metzler (publisher), 63
Meyerbeer, Giacomo, 8, 32, 45, 296
  Huguenots, Les, 23
  Prophète, Le, 36
Mihalovici, Marcel, 349
Milhaud, Darius, 31, 87, 148, 154, 162, 163, 165, 168, 174, 175, 177, 194, 238, 239, 245, 246, 249, 250, 255, 259, 263, 284, 285, 320, 324, 328, 330, 339, 361, 368
  Boeuf sur le toit, Le, 177, 239
  Choéphores, Les, 177, 285
  Christophe Colomb, 368
  Création du monde, La, 177
  L'Homme et son désir, 177, 285
  Jeux de printemps, 326
  Maximilien, 147–8
  Médée, 324, 326
  Saudades do Brasil, 177
  String Quartets nos. 14 and 15, 339
  Symphony no. 4 ('1848'), 324
Milhaud, Madeleine, 154, 158, 161, 163, 164, 165, 166, 168, 169, 175, 237, 238, 239, 240, 242, 243, 245, 250, 255, 256, 295, 324
Mirbeau, Octave, 60

Moke, Camille, 5, 6, 8
Molière, 22
Monet, Claude, 93, 180, 233, 234
Monteux, Pierre, 223
Monteverdi, Claudio, 112, 118, 119
  Ariana, 118
  L'Incoronazione di Poppea, 118
  Orfeo, 118
Morillot Deschamps, Mme, 214
Morisot, Berthe, 99
Morley, Thomas, 227
Mossolov, Alexander
  Iron Foundry, 173
Mottl, Felix, 47, 143
Mozart, Wolfgang Amadeus, 156, 180, 218, 282, 291, 302, 305, 309, 312, 316, 330
  Don Giovanni, 22, 227, 288
  Requiem, 15
  Symphony no. 40, 288
  Symphony no. 41, 254
  Zauberflöte, Die, 53
Mukherjee, Prithwindra, 354
Munch, Charles, 251, 329, 333, 334, 352
Murail, Tristan, 364, 365
Musset, Alfred de, 206
Mussorgsky, Modest, 128
  Boris Godunov, 245, 282, 283, 292, 300
  Khovanshchina, 184
  Nursery, The, 128
Mutter, Anne-Sophie, 354, 376

Nagano, Kent, 280
Napoleon I, 10, 170, 361
Napoleon III, 38
Neel, Boyd, 233, 252
Nerval, Gerard de, 1
Newman, Ernest, 21
Nichols, Sarah, 154, 157, 165, 167

Niedermeyer, Louis, 150
Nietzsche, Friedrich, 191, 372
   Origins of Tragedy, The, 219
Nijinsky, Vaslav, 171, 230, 234, 260
Noailles, Comtesse de, 19
Noialles, Vicomte de, 261
Noialles, Vicomtesse de, 261
Nono, Luigi, 362
Nuitter, Charles (pseud. for Charles Truinet), 37

Offenbach, Jacques, 37, 42, 85, 179
   Grande-Duchesse de Gérolstein, La, 85
Ohana, Maurice, 52
Olivier, Laurence, 312
Orledge, Robert, 108, 152, 154, 156, 158, 161, 164, 166, 167, 168

Paderewski, Ignacy Jan, 32–3
Paganini, Niccolò: *Caprices*, 240
Palestrina, Giovanni Pierluigi da, 91, 108, 191
   Missa Papae Marcelli, 108
Parisian Quartet, 72
Pergolesi, Giovanni Battista, 153
Périer, Jean, 125, 129
Perrin, Emile, 36
Petit, Roland, 352
Peyser, Joan, 198
Pfitzner, Hans: *Palestrina*, 351
Piano, Renzo, 362
Picabia, Francis, 152
Picasso, Pablo, 152, 171, 172, 238, 240
Pickford, Mary, 172
Pierné, Gabriel, 43, 81
Pinter, Harold, 133
Poe, Edgar Allan, 147
Poiret, Paul, 240
Poise, Ferdinand: *Le Roi Don Pèdre*, 209
Polacco, Giorgio, 82

Polignac, Marie-Blanche, 242
Polignac, Princesse de, 56
Pompidou, Claude, 374
Pompidou, Georges, 362, 374
Poulenc, Emile, 260
Poulenc, Francis, 56, 58, 148, 154, 161, 174, 175, 176, 185, 195, 239, 259–65, 281, 284, 285, 296, 297, 321, 324, 325, 331, 354, 361
   Animaux modèles, Les, 261, 320, 326
   Aubade, 261
   Biches, Les, 261
   Concerto for two pianos and orchestra, 262, 325
   Dialogues des Carmélites, 262, 264
   Gloria, 262
   Mamelles de Tirésias, Les, 195, 212, 263, 326
   Mouvements perpétuels, 263
   Organ Concerto, 269
   Rapsodie nègre, 176
   Sonata for clarinet and piano, 262
   Sonata for piano duet, 176
   Sonata for two clarinets, 176
   Tel Jour telle nuit, 265
   Voix humaine, La, 264–5
Prêtre, Georges, 44, 111, 269
Prix de Rome, 2, 6, 7, 11, 22, 27, 36, 40, 41, 43, 50, 85, 91, 92, 102, 112, 146, 219, 272, 283, 345, 350, 351
Prokofiev, Sergei, 142, 246
Proust, Marcel, 17, 18, 109, 180, 181, 191, 333, 352
Prunières, Henry, 217
Puccini, Giacomo, 141
   Tosca, 228
Purcell, Henry, 227
Puvis de Chavannes, Pierre, 97, 100

Quincey, Thomas de: *Confessions of an Opium Eater*, 8

Rachmaninov, Serge, 12
Rameau, Jean-Philippe, 115, 143, 227, 296, 305
   Les Indes galantes, 209
Rattle, Simon, 347
Ravel, Joseph, 210
Ravel, Maurice, 14, 58, 64, 71, 72, 81, 82, 92, 102–5, 111, 112, 113, 147, 151, 152, 153, 155, 161, 171, 173, 174, 177, 179, 183–221, 228, 230, 234, 235, 236, 239, 263, 271, 292, 295–301, 303, 329, 331, 339, 344, 347, 349, 350, 372
   Adélaïde, ou le langage des fleurs, 204–5, 206, 224, 230
   Boléro, 104, 105, 191, 192, 206–7, 208, 210, 213, 301
   Chansons madécasses, 214, 298
      Aoua!, 298
   Cloche engloutie, La (abandoned opera), 236
   Daphnis et Chloé, 196, 205–6, 217, 218, 228, 230, 297
   Don Quichotte à Dulcinée, 28, 192, 207, 208, 211
   L'Enfant et les sortilèges, 111, 112, 113, 188, 195, 206, 218, 299, 300, 301
   Gaspard de la nuit, 185, 186, 191, 196, 298
      'Gibet, Le', 193, 194, 196, 236
      'Scarbo', 299
   Habanera (for two pianos), 211
   L'Heure espagnole, 195, 196, 205, 211–2, 217, 218
   Histoires naturelles, 58, 112, 170, 212, 217, 219
      'Le Martin-pêcheur', 297
   Introduction et Allegro, 198
   Jeux d'eau, 87, 185, 186, 192, 193, 234, 291
   Ma Mère l'Oye, 151, 155, 191, 195, 196, 205, 223, 230, 297, 300
      'Laideronnette', 236
   Miroirs, 186, 191, 196, 198, 219
      'Alborada del gracioso', 204, 211, 217, 232, 298
      'Barque sur l'océan, Une', 218, 235
      'Oiseaux tristes', 196, 298, 300
      'Vallée des Cloches, La', 236
   Paméla, ou les deux roses (abandoned title for *Adélaïde*), 231
   Parade, La, 204
   Pavane pour une Infante défunte, 75, 185–6, 191, 198, 204
   Piano Concerto in G major, 105, 189, 195, 204, 291, 375
   Piano Concerto for the Left Hand in D major, 105, 189, 195, 207, 233, 329, 375
   Piano Trio, 191, 219
   Rapsodie espagnole, 198, 211, 296, 301
      Habanera, 218
   Shéhérazade (overture), 215, 218
   Shéhérazade (song cycle), 191
   Sonata for violin and cello, 297
   Sonatine, 186, 191, 198
   String Quartet, 198, 219
   Tombeau de Couperin, Le, 186–7, 191, 196, 206, 282, 297
   Trois Poèmes de Stéphane Mallarmé, 236
   Tzigane, 206, 220, 240–1
   Valse, La, 104, 105, 193, 204, 206, 301, 352
   Valses nobles et sentimentales, 82, 104, 186, 192, 196, 198, 205, 219, 223, 230, 231, 371
   Violin Sonata, 194, 195
   Vocalise-Etude en forme de Habanera, 211

Wien (original title for *La Valse*), 204, 206
Reber, Henri: *Traité d'harmonie*, 127
Reger, Max, 245
Régnier, Henri de, 60, 61
Reich, Steve, 362
Renard, Jules, 219
Reveleau, Marie, 187
Reyer, Ernest: *Sigurd*, 100
Rhône-Poulenc, 263
Richter, Hans, 24, 81
Rilke, Rainer Maria, 354
Rimbaud, Arthur, 182
Rimsky-Korsakov, Nikolai, 106, 193
   Capriccio espagnole, 223
   Maid of Pskov, The, 357
Risler, Edouard, 227, 260
Robinson, William Ellsworth ('Chung Ling Soo'), 172
Roger-Ducasse, Jean, 106
Rogers, Richard, 362
Roland-Manuel, Alexis, 175, 191, 218, 220, 299
Rolland, Romain, 112
Ronald, Landon, 65
Rosbaud, Hans, 370
Ronsin, Eugène, 124
Rosenthal, Manuel, 187–8, 295, 301, 319, 321, 322, 325
   Bagatelle, 319
Rossetti, Dante Gabriel, 69, 75, 76
Rossini, Gioachino, 11, 30, 315
Rössler, Almut, 313
Rostropovich, Mstislav, 336, 337, 339, 353
Rouart, Henri, 93
Rouart-Lerolle (publisher), 152
Rouché, Jacques, 136, 223, 225, 259, 321
Rousseau, Henri ('Le Douanier'), 94
Roussseau, Jean-Jacques, 209, 210

Roussel, Albert, 71, 108, 151, 175, 271, 344, 347, 350
Royer, Jenny (Poulenc's mother), 260
Rubinstein, Anton, 19
Rubinstein, Ida, 106, 108, 109, 149, 225, 250
Rubinstein, Nicolas, 32
Russ, Michael, 189

Saariaho, Kaija, 363, 364
Sacher, Paul, 243, 244, 248, 251, 252, 254, 342, 353, 359
Saint-Saëns, Camille, 13, 14, 18, 27, 30–4, 42, 43, 44, 72, 180, 203, 227, 297
   Ascanio, 203
   Danse macabre, 32
   Etienne Marcel, 203
   Henri VIII, 32
   Javotte, 33
   Portraits et souvenirs, 31
   Princesse Jaune, 31
   Samson et Dalila, 33
   Septet, 33
   Symphony no. 3, 226
   Tarantelle, 30
   Timbre d'argent, Le, 31
Salabert (pubisher), 324
Samazeuilh, Gustave, 283
Samson, Jim, 189
Samuel, Claude, 291
Sarasate, Pablo de, 27, 209
Sargent, John Singer, 65
Satie, Alfred, 150
   Souvenir d'Honfleur, 166
Satie, Conrad, 165
Satie, Erik, 52, 81, 92, 150–173, 174, 175, 180, 194, 219, 230, 239, 245, 331, 357
   Aperçus désagréables, 151
   Belle excentrique, La, 158

Cinq Grimaces, 152
Diva de l'Empire, La, 151
Embryons desséchés, 152, 168
En Habit de cheval, 152
Fils des étoiles, Le, 151
Gnossiennes, 151
Gymonpédies, 150, 151, 155, 156, 157
Je te veux, 151
Médecin malgré lui, Le (additions to Gounod's opéra-comique), 155
Mercure, 153
Messe des pauvres, 151
Nocturnes, 153, 164
Ogives, 150
Parade, 152–3, 164, 169–73, 236, 238, 241
Pièces froides, 151
Prélude en tapisserie, 166
Préludes flasques (pour un chien), 152
Premier Menuet, 153
Relâche, 153, 164, 166
Sarabandes, 150, 152
Socrate, 153, 161, 162, 164
Sonatine bureaucratique, 153
Sonneries de la Rose + Croix, 151
Sports et divertissements, 152, 166
Tendrement, 151
Trois Enfantines, 158
Trois Mélodies, 150
Trois Morceaux en forme de poire, 151, 152, 163
Vexations, 160
Satie, Jane, 150
Sauer, Emil, 226
Sauguet, Henri, 219, 272
Gageure imprévue, La, 326
Mirages, Les, 326
Sauvage, Cécile (Messiaen's mother), 270, 289
L'Ame en bourgeon, 289–90

Savigny, Charles de, 142
Saward, Christopher, 266
Schaeffner, André, 356–60
Schiller, Friedrich, 282, 283
Schirmer, Astrid, 376
Schloezer, Boris de, 231
Schmitt, Florent, 71, 106, 146–9, 175, 225
Antoine et Cléopâtre, 149, 224
Mass, 147
Musiques intimes, 148
Palais hanté, Le, 147
Psalm 47, 147
Salammbô, 149
Sémiramis, 146
String Quartet, 339
Suite en rocaille, 148
Three Rhapsodies, 148
Tragédie de Salomé, 149, 223, 224, 225–6, 229
Schmitz, Robert, 358
Schneider, Louis, 228
Schneitzhoeffer, Jean
Sylphide, La, 35, 37
Schoenberg, Arnold, 71, 197, 198, 273, 289, 320, 328, 330, 339, 358
Buch der hängenden Garten, Das, 358
Drei Klavierstücke, op. 11, 358
Gurrelieder: 'Song of the Wood Dove', 358
Lieder op. 22, 232
Pierrot lunaire, 323, 358, 359, 367, 369
Serenade, 357
String Quartet no. 2, op. 10, 358
Verklärte Nacht, 358
Scholes, Percy, 198
Schumann Robert, 8–9, 19, 26, 89, 156, 186, 302
Carnaval, 226
Fantasie, 226

Kreisleriana, 219
Schuster, Frank, 63, 65
Schwob, Marcel, 125
Scott, Walter, 11
Scriabin, Alexander, 310
Segalen, Victor, 74
Sert, Misia, 215, 240
Seurat, Georges, 171
Séverac, Déodat de, 71, 72
Shakespeare, William, 11, 121, 130, 270, 312
  Hamlet, 2
  King Lear, 270
  Macbeth, 270
  Merchant of Venice, The, 63
  Romeo and Juliet, 240
  Tempest, The, 46–7, 55, 270
Shaw, Bernard, 21
Shostakovich, Dmitri, 250, 331
Sibelius, Jean, 333
Simeone, Nigel, 274
Singher, Martial, 208
Six, Les, see Groupe des Six
Smith, Richard Langham, 210
Smithson, Harriet, 2, 5, 6, 13
Smyth, Ethel, 227
Solzhenitsyn, Alexandr, 354
Sophocles, 173
  Antigone, 240, 241
Speyer, Edgar, 73
Speyer, Leonora, 82
Spontini, Gaspare, 8, 361
Stalin, Joseph, 230
Stamaty, Camille-Marie, 18
Stanford, Charles Villiers, 80
Stein, Peter, 375
Steinway (piano maker), 37
Stern, Isaac, 353
Steuermann, Eduard, 197
Stockhausen, Karlheinz, 276, 364, 368
Straram, Walter, 271

Strauss, Johann II, 148, 250
Strauss, Richard, 70, 79, 94, 112, 245, 335
  Ariadne auf Naxos, 326
  Elektra, 80, 193
  Feuersnot, 219
  Salome, 222
  Sinfonia domestica, 80
Stravinsky, Igor, 38–9, 152, 153, 174, 184–5, 193, 194, 199, 200, 203, 226, 237–42, 260, 261, 265, 274, 293, 306, 320, 322, 344, 346, 358, 359, 369, 372
  Apollon musagète, 38
  Capriccio, 185
  Concerto for piano and wind instruments, 185
  Firebird, The, 106, 193, 222, 237, 238, 260
  Four Norwegian Moods, 367
  Grand sommeil noir, Un, 193
  L'Histoire du soldat, 357
  Jeu de cartes, 193
  Mavra, 185, 195
  Nightingale, The, 193
  Noces, Les, 185, 274, 324, 359, 367
  Oedipus Rex, 185, 241–2
  Petrushka, 88, 193, 222, 240, 260, 293
  Pulcinella, 153
  Renard, 359
  Rite of Spring, The, 99, 146, 171, 172, 193, 194, 196, 226, 233, 238, 239, 260, 271, 324, 357, 359, 367, 370
  Sonata for Two Pianos, 161
  Symphonies of wind instruments, 185, 359
  Symphony of Psalms, 185, 272
Strobel, Heinrich, 277, 370
Stuckenschmidt, Hans Heinz, 214

Suddaby, Elsie, 76
Swift, Clive, 154
Swinton, Mrs George Campbell, 66
Sylvester, Victor, 25
Symons, Arthur, 71–2
Szell, George, 334, 352

Taffanel, Paul, 143
Tailleferre, Germaine, 174, 177
   Paris-Magie, 326
Takemitsu, Tōru, 362
Tanguy, Eric, 348
Tardieu, Jean, 347, 354
Tariot, Antoine-Jules, 36
Taruskin, Richard, 193, 194
Taudou, Antoine, 64
Tchaikovsky, Pyotr Ilyich, 32, 38, 60
   Eugene Onegin, 264
Tennyson, Alfred, Lord, 269
Teyte, Maggie, 80, 81, 227
Thomas, Ambroise, 27, 47, 63, 131, 167
   Mignon, 23
Thomson, Andrew, 266
Thomson, Virgil, 110, 113, 167, 200
Tinan, Madame Gaston de ('Dolly'), 69, 134
Toscanini, Arturo, 372
Tournemire, Charles, 267, 268, 269, 308, 310, 311, 350
Trentini, Emma, 80
Trouhanova, Natalia (Natasha), 149, 223, 225, 228, 229, 230
Turner, Joseph Mallord William, 93, 232

Upshaw, Dawn, 347, 354
Utrillo, Maurice, 195

Valéry, Paul, 247, 345, 357
Vallin, Ninon, 76
van Gogh, Théo, 347
Van Gogh, Vincent, 347, 353, 354
   La Nuit étoilée, 339, 353
Varèse, Edgar, 143, 171, 274, 294, 307, 369
   Amériques, 173
Vaughan Williams, Ralph, 81, 131, 198, 214–5, 251, 377
   London Symphony, A, 81–2
Vaurabourg, Andrée, 247, 367
Velázquez, Diego, 185, 186
Verdi, Giuseppe, 33, 259
   Don Carlos, 132
   Otello, 259
Verlaine, Paul, 57, 182
   'Green', 181
Verley, Albert, 156
Viardot, Pauline, 15, 22
Vidal, Paul, 176
Vielles Poules, Les, 180
Vierne, Louis, 267, 268, 269, 311, 314
   Organ Symphony no. 3, 226
   Pièces de fantaisie, 315
Vieuille, Félix, 124, 129
Villiers de l'Isle Adam, Auguste, 60
   Axël, 60
Villon, François, 72
Viñes, Ricardo, 71, 78, 81, 152, 210, 214, 227
Vinot, Gustave, 150
Virgil, 11
   Aeneid, 62
Viseur, Georges, 136
Vollard, Ambroise, 94
Voltaire, 93

Vogler, Paul, 61
Vuillemin, Louis, 217
Vuillermoz, Emile, 217, 219

Wagner, Richard, 17, 21, 28, 37, 45, 47, 48, 54, 57, 58, 85, 88, 92, 117, 121, 123, 127, 128, 142, 144, 170, 174, 180, 183, 190, 203, 205, 217, 232, 270, 289, 290, 302, 305, 327
   Fliegende Holländer, Der, 47
   Lohengrin, 92, 100
   Meistersinger von Nürnberg, Die, 48, 53, 85, 143, 180
   Parsifal, 31, 44, 53, 85, 88, 142, 371, 372
   Ring des Nibelungen, Der, 47, 69, 218, 372
   Tannhäuser, 36, 85, 114, 126
   Tristan und Isolde, 47, 48, 53, 57, 85, 87, 142, 144, 180, 276
Wagner, Wieland, 371
Walker, Alan, 19
Walsh, Stephen, 193
Walter, Bruno, 203
Walton, William: *Portsmouth Point*, 322
Weber, Carl Maria, 305
   Oberon, 45

Webern, Anton, 104, 197, 198, 199, 323, 331, 339, 367, 369
   Bagatelles, 339, 353
   Variations, 331
Weill, Kurt, 244
Weir, Gillian, 294, 309–18
Wharton, Lord, 65
Whistler, James McNeill, 61
White, Eric Walter, 193
White, Pearl, 172
Whittaker, W. Gillies, 71
Widor, Charles-Marie, 272, 314
   Toccata (from Symphony no. 5), 269
Wiéner, Jean, 325
Wilson-Huard, Frances, 183
Wolff, Albert, 67, 137
Wood, Henry, 69, 70, 72, 73, 74, 75, 77, 82, 198
Wood, James, 97

Xenakis, Iannis, 365

Ysaÿe, Eugène, 12, 32, 144

Zelter, Carl Friedrich, 2
Zimerman, Krystian, 375
Zola, Emile, 93, 144, 180, 204, 234